FROM THE MARGINS TO THE CENTRE

A History of *The Irish Times*

FROM THE MARGINS TO THE CENTRE

A History of *The Irish Times*

DERMOT JAMES

THE WOODFIELD PRESS

This book was designed and typeset in 12pt on 15pt Garamond
by Carrigboy Typesetting Services for
THE WOODFIELD PRESS
17 Jamestown Square, Dublin 8
www.woodfield-press.com
e-mail: terri.mcdonnell@ireland.com

Publisher
Terri McDonnell

Publishing Editor
Helen Harnett

House Editor
Suzanna Henry

A catalogue record for this title is
available from the British Library

ISBN 978-1-905094-04-2

Printed in England
by MPG Books, Bodmin, Cornwall.

TO GLADYS

We first met in *The Irish Times*, and remember with affection all those with whom we shared experiences working for what Richard Crossman of the *New Statesman* once described as 'the best *Times* this side of the Atlantic'.

Contents

Preface

———✦———

Others might have written this story differently;
there is more than one book in a newspaper.[1]

THIS IS AN ATTEMPT TO TELL the story of *The Irish Times* from its foundation in 1859 to the present day, and how it was established by its first proprietor, the twenty-three-year-old Lawrence E. Knox, a supporter of Isaac Butt's Home Rule policy. After Knox's death fourteen years later, the newspaper was purchased by John Arnott, a successful Scots-born entrepreneur with business interests in Cork, Dublin and Belfast. Holding the view that it would be in his own and Ireland's interest to maintain the union with Britain, Arnott changed the paper's political stance, dropping its support for Home Rule and adopting the unionist cause. This, of course, would cause problems later when the events between 1916 and 1922 effectively left *The Irish Times* politically stranded, and the ensuing years found the paper's successive editors struggling to find a new identity – a process that continued until Douglas Gageby's editorship more than four decades later.

Among a number of biographies written or edited by the paper's journalists, several have included descriptions of various aspects of *The Irish Times* at the time, including those by Patrick Campbell, Lionel Fleming, Brian Inglis, Donal O'Donovan and, more recently, by Conor Brady and Andrew Whittaker. During the eighties, Tony Gray, who was then freelancing in London, suggested the production of a history of the newspaper and he began to research the idea after terms had been agreed. While still far from complete, a decision was made to put the project 'on ice' due to the company's financial situation. A decade later, Gray used much of the material already collected for his book about Smyllie, but died (in 2004) before work could be resumed on the original project. While each of the other volumes mentioned had been concerned principally with the lives of individual editors or staff journalists, the present work is the first attempt to cover the

---

[1]   Hugh Cudlipp, writing about the *Daily Mirror*.

Lawrence Knox founded *The Irish Times* at the age of twenty-three, at a time when four other morning newspapers and one evening title were already being published in Dublin.

story of the newspaper itself from its origins to the present day. I suspect that one of the reasons why such a history has not already been published is that, while copies of every issue were filed (and continue to be available on microfilm, and are now available using the recently introduced online archive), virtually no records were kept. *The Irish Times* may have been the newspaper of record but it certainly didn't keep them. In this connection I have some sympathy for the late Lord Burnham who, when he embarked upon writing a history of his own paper, found it necessary to include the following explanatory note:

> I have found my task very difficult. The *Daily Telegraph* may have broken records, it certainly kept none and I have to do my best with casual references in books by members of the staff, a few scrappy memoranda and letters, a fairly reliable memory, and the files of the newspaper itself …

Over the years I collected memorabilia and personally kept as much data and records of salient events in the paper's history as I could find. 'With the assistance of John Vincent of the library staff, I was the first to successfully list the names of all the paper's editors to date. This fact alone points to the extraordinary situation whereby one of the finest newspapers in the world, one that had such an interesting history, did not keep a record of the names of its editors, much less a record of anything else. It has been a matter of ongoing regret to me that, because most newspapers focus almost all of their attention on the next day, there seemed to be no time to ensure that history was not forgotten.

As I had already embarked on a second career in writing a few books, some of my former colleagues who were aware of my interest, encouraged me to undertake this volume, thinking that I was especially well placed to undertake the task.

One of my best friends at school was Jack Young, whose father, Dick, worked in the advertising agency business. In fact, he ran his own agency, Wilson Young, which Jack subsequently inherited and from where, for many years, he directed the advertising campaigns of *The Irish Times*. My best subject, by far, at school was English, and I was quite good at drawing, a combination that made me consider getting into the advertising agency business too. When, fortuitously, the High School of Commerce at Rathmines announced the commencement of a new two-year diploma course in advertising, I enrolled, learning about layout, copy writing, psychology and typography. This last involved learning about beards, kerns, serifs and descenders – an entire vocabulary that has since become almost as obsolete as Cornish and Manx. Shortly before the course

---

The Advertising Business

If I were starting over again, I am inclined to think that I would go into the advertising business in preference to almost any other. This is because advertising has come to cover the whole range of human needs, and also because it combines real imagination with a deep study of human psychology.

Franklin D. Roosevelt.

---

ended, I began applying for jobs, starting with the larger agencies at the time: Arks, McConnells, and O'Kennedy-Brindley, but to no avail. Likewise with the smaller ones, Domas, Wilson Hartnell and even Padburys (which was owned by Frank Padbury, one of the lecturers at Rathmines) but they all regretted that business was so poor that no new staff were being taken on. This was 1946, one of the depressed years after the Second World War when work was very difficult to find in any sphere and when newspapers were running four- and six-page editions.

My father knew somebody-who-knew-somebody in Helys, one of the biggest printing companies in Dublin which was also involved in occasional publishing, so I tried my luck there. George Hetherington, the managing director, listened sympathetically, before explaining that he had no vacancies either, but promised he would write to me. His letter came a few weeks later, advising me to go to *The Irish Times* because, as he explained, it had an advertising department.[2] He had arranged that the managing director, Mr Tynan O'Mahony, would see me. O'Mahony, who was, incidentally, one of three Catholics in senior management there at this time, told me to start on the following Tuesday (Whit bank holiday fell on the previous day). Michael Clarke, the advertising manager, introduced me to the front counter staff and I commenced my career at 'Number Two' counter, in the public office, accepting pre-paid classified advertisements – everything from Articles for Sale to Death Notices.

It did not take long for me to appreciate that the paper's advertising department did not design advertisements but simply accepted them. However, it was a job, even though my starting salary was a mere £1 per week. To put this in context, I should point out that Douglas Gageby's first job, when he joined the army in 1943, paid him two shillings a day, while Brian Inglis was initially not paid at all when he joined the editorial staff of the paper. In London, James Cameron, 'who entered the back door of journalism with the daily function of filling paste pots and impaling other newspapers on the files', started

---

[2] Co-incidentally, Hetherington joined the Board of *The Irish Times* seven years later.

work with the *Manchester Weekly News* at fifteen shillings a week. Louis Heron, a future editor of *The Times*, commenced his journalistic career at seventeen shillings and sixpence, while Harry Bartholemew, who went on to become chairman of the Mirror Group, got a head-start at thirty shillings a week. As for me, I enjoyed the buzz of working in a famous newspaper and, for the next fifteen years or so, worked in every section of the advertising department. I quickly came to appreciate its vital importance in the workings of the company, realising for the first time that newspapers rely on advertising rather than the sale of the product for the bulk of their revenue.

From this it can be seen that I joined the company in the mistaken belief that this was the commencement of a career in advertising rather than, as it turned out, in newspapers. Because the paper's editorials were at the time bespattered with French and Latin tags, perhaps I may be permitted to use one here: my new-found situation was a case of *faute de mieux*.[3] Another young man, Aubrey Fogarty, after joining the staff alongside me at the same time, took a different route. As soon as the advertising business recovered about five years later, he left the newspaper business to embark upon a career in advertising. He joined O'Kennedy-Brindley and, two agencies later, he set up his own, Fogarty Advertising Agency, and soon began sending display advertisements to 'Number Five' counter where he had worked some years before. He died in 2002, but his agency, now AFA O'Meara Advertising, survives him, and his son Stuart is a director and a major shareholder.

During those early years, I regularly saw a number of the famous characters associated with the paper, resulting in my being a member of the ever-decreasing number of people who can still remember some of the paper's great worthies. These included R.M. Smyllie, Brian O'Nolan, Patrick Campbell, Brian Inglis and Lionel Fleming on the paper's editorial side, as well as Sir Lauriston Arnott, J.J. Simington, 'Pussy' O'Mahony, J.J. McCann, T.D. Atkinson and Jack Webb on the administration and production side of the house.

For part of this earlier period, I had to check every advertisement that appeared each day and, to do this, I needed space to spread the day's copy. For this I was allocated the subeditor's room upstairs, situated off a dingy corridor – a room unused until evening time by the night staff subeditors. The room's appearance cannot have been greatly dissimilar from the one Charles Dickens worked in when, as a young man, he was a newspaper reporter. In fact it was almost, but not quite as bad as the one in the *Northampton Chronicle* described by Michael Green[4] while working there after service during the Second World War:

---

3   For want of better.
4   *Nobody Hurt in Small Earthquake.* Please note that where subsequent references to persons quoted in the text are made, the actual source of the quotation will invariably be found in the Bibliography.

The reporters' room was filthy. Half-filled cups of cold tea littered the oilcloth–covered table where junior members of the editorial staff worked. Some cups had green bubbles floating in them. Stale cheese sandwiches, curled at the edges, jostled with screwed-up scraps of paper.

After working in every section of the advertising department, I then began to find myself acting as a kind of emergency dog's-body, covering for members of staff who were unfortunate enough to fall ill. My first assignment in this fashion was to act as assistant to Ernest Branston, who was both manager and editor of *The Irish Field*. This two-man operation managed the company's racing and horse-breeding newspaper, so it mirrored the entire management of the daily paper, albeit in miniature, thus providing me with a fair appreciation of how the wider company worked. Branston was a chain-smoker, lighting each cigarette from the previous one, and he stored his very considerable supplies in the office safe that, almost unbelievably, contained absolutely nothing else. While on this assignment, I developed a minor sideline, designing display advertisements for the *Field*; it was the only time I was ever to make good use of my course at Rathmines.

Shortly after this, I had to stand in for the cashier, handling incredibly large sums of money, most of which I carried to the Hibernian Bank each day, where I was treated not only with genuine kindness but – as representing one of the larger accounts there – with some respect. Later, when Albert O'Keeffe took ill, I was sent to act as assistant to Paddy Campbell, the works manager who, while unfailingly kind to me, could deal very harshly with any of his staff who required disciplining. I heard words used there that I had never come across before. Later still, I did a six-month stint as an advertising representative and, having been allocated the run-down area of Dublin's north inner city, I began to wonder if someone was really doing more than just testing my stamina.

There were a few other postings, but by far my most interesting assignment was to cover for Tony Lennon, the paper's librarian, when he became ill. This was the nearest I ever got to working in the editorial department, but initially I found the situation embarrassing because I was expected to *head* a department with a staff of four, without any prior experience of its workings. To this day I have never understood why I had not been asked to simply help out, but to their eternal credit, John Gibson, Margaret Lightfoot and the others managed to overcome any resentment they may have initially harboured. I quickly came to enjoy this proximity to the newsroom, as well as meeting and working with the journalists there. Matt Chambers, then news editor, having learned that I had some ability at drawing, asked me to produce maps for the paper, a move which, however inadvertently, was to lead to the subsequent setting up of the paper's fine Studio which, even yet, is without equal in Ireland. It was also at this time that I was given my first opportunity to review a book for the paper, but a more difficult assignment would have been hard for me to imagine. Marshall McLuhan's *Understanding Media* created something of a stir at the time, being considered a brilliant exposition on communications, but I found it a difficult read, with his definitions on information theory and his pandects about hot and cold media (newspapers are hot). He claimed that more thought goes into the production of advertisements than into that of either news (in newspapers) or in programmes (television), but his book is probably now best remembered for the phrase: 'the medium is the message'.[5] Around this time I began contributing occasional articles for the paper, at first for *An Irishman's Diary*, and later, more general items, often about Germany, including a description of the still largely ruined Dresden less than a year after the fall of Communism; an article about Erich Honecker, the former East German head of state; and (in *Rite and Reason*) one about Martin Luther's little-known wife, Katherina von Bora, 'the first woman of the Reformation'.

A return to the advertisement department led to my appointment as assistant to the advertising manager, Jack Briggs who, like Matt Chambers, was a gentleman in every sense of the word. When, at this time, the paper decided to become involved with 'First Day Covers' in connection with new postage stamps, I designed a number of covers but the idea was dropped when An Post (the Irish postal service), recognised the potential and got in on the act. One day during the early sixties, the chairman, Major McDowell, arrived to discuss some matter with Jack and, as he passed my desk, his eagle eye saw some bar and pie charts illustrating advertising and circulation trends and how the three morning newspapers were sharing the market. He asked where they had come from and seemed surprised that they were my own handiwork. Shortly afterwards I was summoned to his office in the old boardroom where he appointed me to be his personal assistant.

Suddenly, I found myself at the very hub of the company's decision-making during the years when the idea of forming a trust was not yet even a glint in the chairman's eye. This had to wait until 1973 when a massive increase in profits – certainly compared with anything before that – led him to actively pursue what then became an urgent goal. It took McDowell more than a year to put all the pieces together relating to the trust, which should surprise no one who has read the Articles of Association. Just two months after the formation of The Irish Times Trust was announced, the news was published that I had been appointed company secretary of The Irish Times Limited. My appointment as company secretary of the Irish Times Trust Limited followed four years later and, in typical McDowell belt-and-braces style, I additionally became deputy secretary of the operating company, while Arthur Houston was appointed both secretary of the operating company and deputy of the trust.

---

[5]   More than forty years later Tom Koch, while agreeing that there was some truth in the cliché, argued that new technologies have created a radical change in the way information is transmitted so that his dictum should now be reversed to read: 'the message is the medium'.

Most of the real secretarial work, i.e. company returns etc., was handled by Stokes Kennedy Crowley, a firm of accountants founded in the late nineteenth century by Mr Robert Stokes. The firm, with several name changes, has continued an association with *The Irish Times* ever since the newspaper became a limited company back in 1900. My duties were all the more interesting by virtue of their being multifarious, and even included skimming through all three Dublin morning broadsheets and the four main London heavyweights for the chairman, so that he was aware of what the competition was up to. I was also responsible for ensuring that libel threats were dealt with expeditiously and, as one of the cheque signatories, I regularly found enormous batches of them on my desk. Most of the office correspondence was also my responsibility and, of course, as secretary, I also attended and recorded the minutes of the board meetings.

I took early retirement just two decades later, but continued to act as a consultant to the chairman, and I found the resulting freedom from stress while still 'having a finger in the pie' very agreeable. All my working life has thus been spent in the service of The Irish Times Limited, during which time I gained a very wide set of experiences in various departments.

My thanks are due to my former colleagues who have helped in various ways, especially to those who have read sections of the text. I also wish to acknowledge the assistance so readily provided by the Manuscripts Department of Trinity College, Dublin; the Archive Department of University College Dublin; George Wheeler, whose grandfather was the paper's second editor; and by the ever helpful and patient Esther Murnane and Irene Stevenson in the Library of *The Irish Times*.

As will be seen, footnotes have been kept to a minimum. Where quotations from the writings of named persons are made in the text, the source concerned will be found in the Bibliography. And finally, references to this newspaper by name are almost invariably printed throughout this volume as *The Irish Times* even where, in the original, the title appeared simply as '*Irish Times*'.

George Shaw
&
George Wheeler

1859–1877

'In the Beginning ...'

LAWRENCE EDWARD KNOX, a twenty-three-year-old army major, founded a new thrice-weekly newspaper in 1859 and named it *The Irish Times and Daily Advertiser*. He may not have been aware that, thirty-six years earlier, there had already been a newspaper of the same title which, however, like many of the papers launched during this period, had a very brief life. Fifty years later, his newspaper was to comment on the founder's choice of title:

> In fixing his choice on *The Irish Times* as the title of his new enterprise, Major Knox was reaching a decision at the expense of originality. It was unquestionably an effective name for a newspaper whose aim was to interpret the sentiment and desires of those elements of Irish life that were not given to think mercurially, but had been made to do duty before.

Knox, whose parents were Arthur Knox of Trotton, Sussex and Lady Jane Knox, daughter of the Earl of Rosse, had a brief army career serving in the Crimean War and attaining the rank of Major. He then became Member of Parliament for Carlow and a supporter of Isaac Butt's fledgling Home Rule movement, so it was hardly a coincidence that his newspaper appeared on the streets around the same time that a petition (said to have been signed by half a million Irishmen) was presented to Queen Victoria praying for the right of self-determination. Isaac Butt, a prominent barrister, did not agree with the recent

George Shaw, the first editor of *The Irish Times*, resigned after fourteen weeks, returning to his other position as a prominent academic at Trinity College, Dublin. As this move coincided with the decision to change the paper from a tri-weekly to a daily newspaper, it appears that Shaw anticipated that he would be unable to continue 'double-jobbing', although his successor was to manage to do so with considerable success. *(Photo: Courtesy of the Board of Trinity College, Dublin).*

Fenian outbreaks but he did recognise the extent to which misgovernment had resulted in their actions. As he was famously to state: 'I have long since had the conviction forced upon me that it is equally essential to the safety of England, and to the happiness and tranquillity of Ireland, that the right of self-government should be restored to this country'. The timing of Knox's launch seems to support the supposition that he wished to use his newspaper to further Butt's cause, yet he described his *Irish Times* simply as 'a new Conservative newspaper'. A year later, the paper described itself as 'the Protestant and Conservative daily paper' and, in 1882, as 'Moderate conservative'. During 1887 it was calling itself 'Independent (i.e. Liberal Conservative)', and it was not until 1895 that it finally declared itself 'Unionist'.

The 1850s saw a flurry of newspaper launchings, at least partly the result of a combination of the tax reforms. The Government reduced the tax on advertisements in 1833 and abolished it in 1853, while stamp duty was reduced in 1836 and abolished in 1855 –

just four years before Knox launched his *Irish Times*. The removal of these taxes almost coincided with the introduction of steam-powered printing, resulting in a huge expansion in the newspaper industry, with sales in Britain and Ireland rising by some 600 per cent between 1856 and 1882.

Launched at this auspicious time, the first issue consisted of four pages, each having six columns, the first two pages being devoted entirely to small advertisements. The editorial content was, therefore, relegated to the third page, and the fourth page contained yet more advertisements. In all of this, his publication appeared little different from almost every other newspaper of that time and, in particular, suffered from the limitations imposed by the relatively primitive printing machines available at this period.

At the outset, his newspaper's main rival was the *Dublin Daily Express* which had been steadily increasing its sales over the previous four or five years, and in doing so had become the largest-selling paper in the metropolis. The *Freeman's Journal,* established in 1763, was also performing well but Dublin's oldest surviving newspaper, the *Saunder's Newsletter,* was experiencing financial problems. The *Journal* had been greatly strengthened following a take over by Sir John Gray, described as a Catholic establishment figure and commemorated with a statue erected in Sackville Street in 1879. Gray's newspaper's fortunes were greatly enhanced when he supported Daniel O'Connell's programme of constitutional nationalism. Another existing title, the *Morning News,* had just then – as *The Irish Times* was to do later – made the decision to become a daily newspaper. During that same year, W.H. Smith, the founder of the wholesale news agency business that bore his name, was entertaining the idea of purchasing the then ailing *Dublin Evening Mail* in order to turn it into a morning paper. However, he came to the conclusion that the market was already overcrowded and changed his mind. Not surprisingly, when the new *Irish Times* was launched, he was 'doubtful of its prospects'.

The Original Irish Times

A precursor of *The Irish Times*, bearing the same title, was printed for its proprietor, James Duggan, at 15 Trinity street, Dublin and issued intermittently from 1823 to 1825. It was priced at five pence. A copy dated March 10 1824 reported the sentence of death passed upon two prisoners for robbery at Ennis, and the transportation of another for manslaughter. The result of the latter case 'gave great satisfaction to the crowded court.' After the paper 'folded', another 34 years were to elapse before the first issue of the present title appeared.

Competition between the five morning papers – and indeed, with the two evening titles – was intense. Even at this period the London newspapers – notably the newly founded *Daily Telegraph* – were being aggressively promoted in Ireland. However, the invention of a new means of rapid communication, the telegraph, began to work to the advantage of the Irish papers competing with the London titles. Armed with this latest invention, the local press was enabled to receive all the foreign news at the same time and, therefore, make it available to Irish readers before the English papers arrived.

The first issue of the new *Irish Times* went on sale on Tuesday, 29 March 1859, bearing the imprint 'Printed and published at the Office of the Irish Times, No. 4 Lower Abbey Street for the Proprietor, by David Towson'. It would seem from this announcement that Knox saved himself considerable expense at the outset by having his newspaper printed by an established printer, and it is known that he was renting office space at the same address. Eleven years later, *The Irish Times* announced that a new printing press had just been installed but did not specify whether or not Lawrence Knox had purchased the machine, though the fact that the new press had been installed at Abbey Street suggests that his printer had made this purchase. This latter conjecture seems all the more likely to be correct because only twelve years after this, a brand new press was being used – this time installed in new premises at Westmoreland Street where the paper was to be printed for more than one hundred and thirty years.

Lawrence Knox's ambition had been to be the proprietor of a daily newspaper but, initially, he settled for publishing thrice weekly. As noted in an *Irish Times* article published in 1909, the paper's golden jubilee year, 'the same shrewd sagacity which enabled the founder to fix the constituency to which he was firmly convinced he could appeal with success in Ireland, warned him that it was wise to hasten slowly. He therefore started with a tri-weekly paper, published every Tuesday, Thursday and Saturday', and when he was satisfied with the public reaction, he announced fourteen weeks later that

> in consequence of the great success that has already attended *The Irish Times,* the Proprietor has been induced to establish it as a daily paper to enable the Conservative members of the community to enjoy a first-class daily paper at a far cheaper rate than was ever yet published in Ireland.

While he had been searching for an editor, it seems he had in mind the old adage, 'If you want something done quickly, ask a busy person'. Knox chose as his first editor Dr George Shaw, a senior academic at Trinity College, Dublin, where he had become a scholar in 1841. Four years after taking his degree in 1844, Shaw became a Fellow, later a Senior Fellow and Senior Dean. The entry for George Ferdinand Shaw in *Who Was Who, 1897–1915* stated that he was born on 26 June 1821, and was married to Ellen, daughter of

John Shinkwin. His 'recreations' were stated to be 'Novels, plays, operas'. According to the *Modern English Biography* (1921), Shaw was 'joint editor of the *Irish Times* about 1861; edited *Saunders' Newsletter*, [and was] principal leader writer on the *Evening Mail*, 1870'. It is also known that Shaw was writing leading articles for *The Nation*.

The reference to Shaw being 'joint-editor about 1861' is, however, incorrect. It seems likely that, from the outset, Shaw realised that being in sole charge of the new paper was taking up too much time in his otherwise busy life. We know for a fact, thanks to family papers, that George Wheeler, his brother-in-law, had been writing the paper's leading articles from the fourth issue onwards, that is, exactly one week after the paper's foundation. When Shaw resigned after only fourteen weeks – well before 1861 – Knox appointed Wheeler to the position, and the fact that this coincided with the decision to publish daily rather than on three days per week, was very probably a factor in Shaw's decision to quit. Shaw's continued involvement in several other newspapers seems to have prompted McDowell and Webb to write that his energies were 'mainly devoted to journalism'. Indeed, they went further, observing that he was 'something of a maverick among the Trinity Fellows [and] used the college more as a base of operations than as the centre of his life'. All of this appears to repudiate the picture of the man throwing up the editorship of *The Irish Times* in order to devote himself to an academic life. Indeed, it probably prompted Cruickshank and the same professor Webb to comment that, although Shaw 'contributed little to the scholarship of Dublin, he contributed much to its entertainment and was very popular'.

In the meantime, it is quite impossible to identify anything of Shaw's influence on the paper that he had edited, or part-edited, for less than a few dozen issues. As proprietor, Knox had identified a gap in the market for his newspaper and this, more than anything else – including Shaw's editorship – may have contributed crucially to its very successful launch. Dr Shaw, who was not averse to the use of Latin tags in his writings, then returned to academia, no doubt taking the advice of Horace: *Atque inter silvas Academi quaere verum.*[1] When he died in 1899, *The Irish Times* devoted considerable space to his widely attended funeral and to his achievements but, curiously, without any specific reference to his having been the paper's first editor.

> The citizens of Dublin and, indeed, the Irish people of every party and class, will deeply regret the decease of the distinguished scholar who was an ornament to Trinity College, and throughout his long life laboured earnestly to maintain its great reputation and influence, and who also, in his connection with Irish journalism, of which he was always proud, chivalrously contributed by his pen to the success of all sound and charitable causes. … He

---

[1] (To) 'seek the truth in the groves of Academe'.

was heard with profit and pleasure on City platforms, and last week presided at a public meeting when he seemed perfectly fresh in mind and vigorous. ... As a writer, Dr Shaw was brilliant and versatile, and his views on topics were always uttered with manliness. With Pressmen in all positions he was friendly, and had a high idea of their responsibilities.

The attendance at his funeral included Sir William Kaye, C.B., representing the Lord Lieutenant, Sir David Harrel, K.C.B., Undersecretary, Sir Andrew Reed, Inspector General, R.I.C., and a number of high-ranking judges. George Salmon, the Provost, led a large contingent from Trinity College; also present were the Church of Ireland Bishop of Ossory and the Deans of St Patrick's, Christ Church and the Chapel Royal. As *The Irish Times* reported: 'Seldom, indeed, have the evidences of esteem and respect for the memory of a Dublin citizen been more marked. The remains were brought from the late Dr Shaw's rooms in the College to the College Chapel where a Memorial Service was commenced. ... The funeral then proceeded to Mount Jerome Cemetery where the burial service was concluded'. (All of this was to happen in forty years time, but is recorded here at this point in order to provide a more complete picture of the man who had been chosen to be the first editor of Knox's paper).

With issue number 32, published on 8 June 1859, *The Irish Times* became a daily newspaper, indicating that its founder was satisfied that his venture was proving successful, even if his paper looked little different from almost any other newspaper of the period. With no illustrations, the overall effect was very grey indeed. A modest-sized advertisement carried the following information:

> NEW CONSERVATIVE DAILY PAPER
> The Irish Times, with two editions, is
> Now published every day, for
> ONE PENNY.
> The First Edition is published at Half-
> Past Two o'Clock, and the Second Edition
> At Half-past Four o'Clock.
> The Conservative members of the Com
> mittee can now, therefore, enjoy the
> Advantages of a first-class daily paper for
> ONE PENNY
> IRISH TIMES OFFICE
> 4 LOWER ABBEY-STREET, DUBLIN

The emphasis on the price at one penny – stated twice – was important as the paper claimed to be the first in Ireland to be published at that price. Three of the other existing titles dropped their prices immediately and the fourth followed later. Among the classified advertisements in that same issue was one inserted by the paper itself seeking an advertisement canvasser, 'a respectable and active person', as well as two 'turn-over apprentices', and specifying that 'any that have been employed on a newspaper will be preferred'. The main editorial article on that date commented upon Queen Victoria's speech to the Westminster parliament:

> Her Majesty's Speech will give a deep satisfaction to almost every class of her subjects. 'A strict and imperial neutrality' is announced to be the policy of England; and the preservation of peace with both belligerents [a reference to France and Prussia], her Majesty's hope. Perhaps the best way to appreciate the merits of this speech is to consider the parties whom it will excessively disoblige. The smaller German states [Germany had not yet been united] will receive it with much disgust. It is a wet blanket to their martial order, and it compels them to recognise the disagreeable fact that, if they indulge in a war with France, they must do it at their own expense. England approves of the expulsion of the Austrians from Italy, and does not apprehend danger from Louis Napoleon.

Having thus dealt with the political situation in Europe, the editorial article turned its attention to the situation as it saw it in Ireland:

> Here we have little reason for a change of rulers, for the present government has proved itself a truer friend to Ireland than any of its predecessors. The concession of a Packet Station to Galway, in the teeth of violent English prejudice and opposition, will be greatly remembered as a practical proof of a genuine inclination to do justice to Ireland.

The interesting point here concerns the paper's critical words about 'violent English prejudice', but the experiment of introducing transatlantic liners to the port of Galway was not a long-time success. A substantial amount of the news being reported in this first daily edition was devoted to the debates in parliament at Westminster. On this particular day, the only reference to Ireland concerned 'the Earl of Carlisle's[2] objection to the Lord Lieutenant's alliance with the Roman Catholics'. With most of the Young Irelanders in exile and Fenianism not yet effectively organised, there was little Irish news to report anyway, excepting, as mentioned above, the inauguration of the port of Galway as a terminus for transatlantic traffic. The consequent arrival there of a ship from New York was duly reported along with the information that the voyage had taken six days and thirteen hours, and that 494 passengers had disembarked.

---

[2]   Carlisle was to become Lord Lieutenant for the second time three months later.

In charge of this first daily issue of the paper was George Bomford Wheeler[3] whom Knox had appointed as the paper's second editor following Shaw's early departure, and while it is recorded that Major Knox had made Wheeler 'a very handsome offer', the actual details are not now known. The fact that he was Shaw's brother-in-law and had been assisting him almost from the outset must have facilitated a smooth changeover. This family connection – and because the two men shared a common academic background – may well have been an important factor resulting in there being no evidence of any change in the paper's style or outlook. Another factor, of course, must have been Knox's own views concerning his paper's policy, no doubt ensuring that his editor continued to lend the paper's support to the growing Home Rule movement.

Wheeler was born in Dublin in 1802, son of James Wheeler, a Dublin merchant. He had entered Trinity College, Dublin in 1829, gaining his B.A. and M.A. degrees, and went on to become a distinguished Latin scholar (very useful when writing leading articles!), translating the works of Homer, Socrates and Virgil. During his time in college, he was highly regarded as a tutor. One of his pupils was Hugh McCalmont Cairns who had matriculated in 1834 at the age of 14. An article in the *Northern Ireland Law Quarterly* (Winter 1975) mentioned that Cairns never ceased to remember and acknowledge his debt to Wheeler who had an extraordinary number of future judges among his pupils. Cairns went on to become the first Irishman to head the English Bar, the first and only Irishman to be head of the English judiciary, 'and the first graduate of Dublin University ever to sit in a British Cabinet'.

An article published in the *Belfast News Letter* stated that Doctor Wheeler's first connection with the press 'was as a writer for the [Dublin] *Daily Express*'. He had been contributing articles to a wide range of publications including *Chamber's Edinburgh Journal* and *All The Year Round,* the latter publication founded by Charles Dickens with whom Wheeler was friendly. After describing Wheeler's industry as 'immense and untiring', the *News Letter* continued: 'What was more remarkable than his industry was his truly retentive memory. He hardly forgot anything that he read, or any publication that fell within the compass of his experience. In everything he wrote there was the grace and style of a classical scholar'.

He was well advanced in years when he decided to take Holy Orders; today, he would be described as a 'late vocationer' in the Church of Ireland. His first clerical appointment was as chaplain to the Dublin Smithfield Reformatory Prison, after which he was curate at St Mary's Church in the city, before becoming Rector of the parish of St Paul, Ballysax (The Curragh), in 1865, a position he held until his death. From this, it will be seen that,

---

[3]   The author is most grateful to his grandson – who also bears the name George Wheeler – for providing most of the personal details about his grandfather, appearing in this chapter.

as an editor and a clergyman, he represented an early example of double-jobbing. In doing this, he was an editor from Sunday evening until Friday night, and a Rector from Saturday morning until Sunday afternoon. One of Wheeler's four sons, also named George, briefly recalled the family's first arrival at Ballysax:

My father was presented to the Rectory of Ballysax, near the Curragh Camp which was in the parish, and … he brought his large and happy family to the Rectory which my mother at once proceeded to christen 'Liberty Hall'. A delightful existence we had, studying, walking on the farm, and carrying out the mild recreations of those times, the chief of which was croquet.

George Senior continued to write extensively, and in an article penned for a religious publication, the *Sunday Magazine*, he described his home:

The parlour in the Glebe House of Ballysax is a fine large room, nearly square. At the front end there is a very broad window … from which we look down into a richly cultivated valley, then over a succession of low hills and onto the [Curragh] Camp built on the long hill, 460 feet above sea level. … We see the extended lines of the camp, in which today there are 9,500 men. The clock tower stands in the centre, but we regulate our clocks by the mid-day and evening guns. … From that parlour window you can stretch your view away to the 'Chair of Kildare' where the kings of Leinster, in old days, were crowned. …
    While I write this, a thunderstorm is raging, and the lightning flashes over the vast scene. It is awe-inspiring and terrible. We are used to the roar of heavy guns here, and to the rattling fusillade of musketry, yet how poor their sound seems compared with the voices of Heaven's artillery!

Ballysax was a small parish so his parochial duties were not onerous, though at times he had a 'bonus' congregation from the nearby military installation. After Wheeler's death, the *Belfast News Letter* described how:

He used to retire [to Ballysax] with delight every Saturday morning and the occupations of which were a healthful and mentally most beneficial relief after his week's drudgery at the press. He was a great favourite at the [Curragh] Camp. … In compliment to him, the bandsmen of various regiments often got up musical services which would have done credit to a cathedral choir.

Writing about the British army establishment at the Curragh, Con Costello mentioned Ballysax a number of times, once in connection with Dr Wheeler and his relationship with the soldiers at the Camp:

The Curragh Camp itself is in the parish of Ballysax, and during the ministry of Rev. Dr. George Wheeler (1865–1877) it is known that soldiers from the camp regularly attended the church. He was a great favourite of both officers and men, and on Sunday evenings St. Paul's presented a truly brilliant spectacle from the crowd of redcoats who came to worship there and hear Mr. Wheeler's simple and telling discourses.

Having completed his Sunday duties, Wheeler used to drive to Newbridge, where he caught a train to Dublin to serve his office as editor of *The Irish Times*. It might be thought that at this time a newspaper having a largely Protestant readership and edited by a member of the Established Church of Ireland, would pay little attention to news of Catholic interest. A minor example occurred when a Catholic priest died suddenly while celebrating Mass at Whitefriar Street Church, Dublin. Father Spratt[4] was described as a

> truly good and amiable man, called from the scene of his beneficent and pious labours, leaving a void which cannot be readily filled. There was no path of Christian duty, no application of Christian charity that was stranger to Doctor Spratt's heart or to his daily life. The orphan found in him a father and the homeless wanderer of the streets a refuge.

Staff numbers at this time stood at just over fifty, and nine years after the paper had been established, Knox's wage was £4.10 weekly. Wheeler, the editor, was being paid £5 weekly and, although he had ceased to act as editor, Dr Shaw was receiving £3.3. – possibly because he continued to write for the paper. Only four other persons were being paid £3 or more; approximately 20 were being paid between £2.10 and £1.10 and the wages of the remaining 26 employees ranged between £1 and five shillings weekly.

At the beginning of each new year for the first decade or so, the paper printed its thanks to all who were supporting it. In January 1867, it added that 'its position is now too well known and acknowledged by all to render it necessary that we should do more than return our warmest thanks for the brilliant success it has achieved. … Hitherto the attainment of an Irish journal of a circulation of three or four thousand a day was regarded as an extraordinary success which few could ever reach'. Knox and Wheeler, proprietor and editor, were between them managing a well-run newspaper which was able to claim on its first anniversary that 'its circulation during the six months of 1860 had been increased by about twenty-five per cent'. The curious reference to 'the six months of 1860' may have been the result of a typographical error; perhaps the intention had been to refer to the *first* six months of the year. It seems strange that references to the paper's sales in the Board Minutes Books during the first 100 years were almost always expressed in vague terms such as 'sales for the past quarter were slightly up', or even that sales 'were now greater than at

---

[4]   Father Spratt was born in 1798, giving rise to a joke that he had been 'in arms himself during that troubled time'.

any time since the Boer War'. Of course, records of precise figures were indeed kept, but almost all of these records have been lost.

By early 1860, average daily sales had reached a very creditable 8,700 and by September of the same year this figure had reached 10,000. In achieving this total, the paper had not only surpassed the long-established *Freeman's Journal* (at 8,000) but enabled it to claim that its sales already exceeded 'by several thousand that of any other Irish newspaper, and [somewhat surprisingly] also that of any conservative newspaper in the United Kingdom'. A year later, annoyance was expressed because 'one morning paper [probably the Dublin *Daily Express*], amongst the many attempts to check our progress, gave for a while a free supplement'.[5]

An unusual compliment was paid to Knox and his newspaper during its sixth year in the form of a piece of music entitled *The Irish Times Galop*. This lively dance composition was described as 'original, pleasing and spirited, and the melody goes tripping along in well-marked time, which must ensure it a prominent place in the ballroom programme'. The *Drogheda Argus* commented: 'The galop is dedicated to Captain L.E. Knox, the spirited and enterprising proprietor of *The Irish Times*. Not even a 2–4 galop measure can, however, keep time, we fancy, with our able and flourishing contemporary's rate of progression, which goes ahead with an ever-accelerating movement'.

For some time after its launch, *The Irish Times* inserted birth, marriage and death notices free of charge, treating them as news rather than as advertisements. These notices were sometimes seen as a kind of barometer of a newspaper's readership, so it was with some further annoyance that *The Irish Times* noted that several of its competitors were not only 'lifting' these notices from its columns, but also taking death notices from some of the London papers. However, as it also observed, the latter were often up to a week late and were of no interest to Irish readers.

Classified advertisements – 'small ads' – were a strong feature from the outset. The paper's news coverage was better than that of any other local paper, helped by the decision to be the first in Dublin to avail of the new telegraph system and also by the decision to appoint its own local correspondents throughout the country. Distribution posed great problems for all the early newspapers, but the rapidly expanding railway network proved a great boon, enabling *The Irish Times* to announce that it 'could be purchased in any point of the country where transport permitted' as it was available, in most cases, by noon.

However, by far the most serious constraint facing all newspaper proprietors throughout this period was that imposed by the existing printing presses, because these early machines could only print a single sheet of paper at a time. The use of large sheets enabled two pages to be printed simultaneously, after which two further pages were completed when these

[5]   *The Irish Times*, 12 December 1861.

R. HOE & CO., of LONDON,
Are the
ESTABLISHED

They manufacture and supply everything the Printer needs, from the smallest requisite of the Composing Room to the Mammoth Machines used by the large Daily Newspaper Offices with the greatest circulations, the latest of which turns out 96,000 perfect papers per hour, folded to half-page size. Their New York Works alone cover a floor space of over twelve acres, employing some thousands of workmen, and their London Works cover a floor space of over four acres, employing nearly a thousand workmen.

1800 and before.

FRANKLIN'S
OLD WOODEN
HAND-PRESS.

Constructed in
1833.

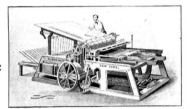

R. HOE & CO.'S

FIRST SMALL CYLINDER
NEWSPAPER PRESS.

1851.

R. HOE & CO.'S

TEN-FEEDER
TYPE REVOLVING
NEWSPAPER PRESS.

R. HOE & CO.'S

FIRST STEREOTYPE
WEB PERFECTING
NEWSPAPER PRESS,
WITH FLY.

1872.

From the 1830s onwards, the firm of R. Hoe & Co. was one of the most important manufacturers of printing presses and the first machine used by *The Irish Times* was almost certainly very similar to the 1833 machine shown above left. The replacement press purchased in 1873 may well have been the model introduced in 1872 and illustrated above right. The firm later changed its name to Hoe & Crabtree, from whom the company purchased two further presses, one in the early 1920s, and the second in 1952. Subsequently, German-built MAN-Roland web-offset machines were utilised, a move that resulted in *The Irish Times* becoming the first Irish metropolitan-based newspaper to print regularly in colour.

sheets were turned over. Effectively, newspapers were thus restricted to four pages per issue, and this slow printing method made it difficult for the successful papers to increase their sales. A most important breakthrough came about when rotary presses became available, permitting much faster speeds and allowing for larger pagination. *The Irish Times* commented on this technological advancement during the paper's fiftieth anniversary:[6]

> It has been the fate of many newspapers to find their infancy beset by commercial and financial difficulties. The only difficulties of *The Irish Times* were mechanical, not monetary. The needs of an expanding newspaper were held in check by the limitations of the printing press.

The Irish Times was the first in Dublin to install a rotary press, followed by the *Freeman's Journal* in 1872, and then by *Saunder's Newsletter* and *Daily Express* in 1875 and 1877 respectively. During the paper's first seven years, it charged the same advertising rates as the *Journal* and the *Express*, but when the strength of its readership became more widely recognised for its value to advertisers, charges were raised and it became the most expensive medium then available in Ireland. The paper's particular readership was later to become ever more important when, by the 1880s, although sales of the *Freeman's Journal* had already begun to overtake those of *The Irish Times*, the latter continued to be the stronger advertising medium.[7]

After it was overtaken by the *Journal* and, later, when sales of the *Irish Independent* surged ahead, the paper adopted the idea of publicly referring to its sales figures in very general rather than in specific terms. This policy was continued into the late 1940s, even though most of the important advertisers and their agents knew that its sales were far smaller than its main competitors. When Professor Cullen adverted to what he termed 'this elusive question of newspaper circulation', he found that the problem could only be overcome by 'some fleeting estimate'. Writing about newspaper sales in 1857, two years before the appearance of *The Irish Times*, he was forced to calculate the figures for the existing Dublin dailies, surmising the details as follows: *Dublin Daily Express*, 2,000; *Saunder's Newsletter*, 1,200; and the *Freeman's Journal*, 600.

From 1949 onwards, the circulation sales figures for *The Irish Times* have been externally audited by the Audit Bureau of Circulations (ABC), so that the subsequent details are readily available to anyone interested, but prior to that date it has been possible to trace very little information, and the few details now known may be summed up as follows:

---

[6]   *The Irish Times*, 8 June 1909.
[7]   The *Freeman's Journal* claimed sales of 39, 872 in its issue of 21 February 1881.

1873	15,888
1879	18,689
1889	30,542[8]
1890–1938	Between 22,000 and 30,000
1939	25,748
1940	22,000 approx.
1948	36,095

Information about the newspaper's revenue during its early years is equally scanty, but the following figures give some idea of how it progressed during its first seventy years:

1863	£700 approx.
1869	£1,200
1879	£2,200
1889	£2,900
1899	£4,800
1909	£4,900
1919	n. a.
1929	£8,600

By 1864, the paper's sixth year, it had settled into a recognisable format with a strong emphasis on international news, often concerning little-known, far-off wars and disputes, which were often couched in detail which seemed to assume that readers were already fully informed about the background to these incidents. The business of the Irish courts and parliamentary debates at Westminster were also covered in considerable detail. In an editorial, *The Irish Times* commented on recent parliamentary proceedings and, in doing so, nailed its colours firmly to the mast:[9]

> Mr. Bright, who knows absolutely nothing of Ireland, and never expressed one word of sympathy for her suffering, had the hardihood to say on Friday night that, 'by the consent of every man, Catholic and Protestant Ireland is disloyal and disaffected to this house and to the English Government, probably more than it has been in any period in its history'. A statement more opposed to facts never was made in the House of Commons, or out of it. Ireland is thoroughly loyal, and well affected to the Queen and to the Royal line in which the inheritance of the Imperial Crown is vested. In no part of her Majesty's dominions is her character more respected, or her happiness more desired, than in her realm of Ireland. Though we rarely, and but fitfully, enjoy the sunshine of the presence of Majesty, we know and feel it is a miserable and selfish clique which interposes its shadow between the Sovereign and a faithful people. Irish men are ready now, to contend to the death for the honour of her Majesty and the dignity of her Crown, and for the integrity of the constitution.

8   The figures for 1873, 1879 and 1889 were for June in each case.
9   *The Irish Times*, 14 March 1864

This photograph of the actress, Joanna Lumley addressing the Philosophical Society in Trinity College, appeared in the paper during April 2007. Because the picture, as published, extended to the far right hand corner of the room, a small bronze plaque was also featured. The latter, as it happens, commemorates a prominent nineteenth-century Trinity academic who, in addition to his college duties, was the first editor of *The Irish Times,* although he resigned this post after just fourteen weeks. The bronze low relief, commissioned by the college, was executed by Oliver Sheppard, RHA (1865–1941), whose best-known work, *Cuchulain,* is in the GPO.

On the same page, there was a report headlined 'The Church'. If such a heading appeared today it would be above an item concerning the Roman Catholic Church, but in 1864 – certainly in *The Irish Times* – this referred to the Established Church. In fact it specifically referred to a charity sermon given by the Church of Ireland Archbishop of Dublin in aid of the City of Dublin Hospital, in which he made the point that 'it received no parliamentary support, being entirely dependent upon voluntary subscriptions'. He then added that 'there were only two paid officials connected with the institution, the apothecary and the matron, whose united salaries only amounted to £100 a year'.

A year earlier, during October 1863, the *Drogheda Reporter* carried a short news item about Knox, 'the very spirited proprietor of *The Irish Times*', who, it continued has in many matters set an example to the other proprietors well worthy of imitation. Last Saturday evening he entertained the entire staff of his paper, numbering some 110 individuals at a magnificent banquet in the Antient Concert Rooms, Dublin. Several gentlemen of the city were also invited to the banquet, besides representatives from the provincial press. The entertainment was given in no niggardly style, but was entirely first-class. Employer and employed were thus brought into more intimate and more friendly and social relationships with each other, assembled at the same well-stocked board. The friendly feelings created by this means must have a better effect than all the rules of any trade society.

In 1865 the paper trumpeted the news that it had 'by many thousand copies per day, the largest circulation of any newspaper in Ireland'. It also reported the details of the inquest on an accident which occurred when a Dublin horse-drawn omnibus fell into a Grand Canal lock at Portobello. The inquest concerning the six persons 'who were so suddenly hurried into Eternity on Saturday night' heard that there had been sufficient time to let out the passengers before it toppled in, and the incident was made worse when the lock-keeper closed the sluice-gates thinking that the vehicle would float. Instead, as the paper recorded, 'the waters rose above the roof and not a sound seems to have been uttered by those inside'. In that same year, one of the paper's leading articles described the assassination of President Lincoln while he attended a theatre performance in Washington:

> A pause had taken place in the performance when the shot was heard. A great cry arose, succeeded by the silence of horror, for the President had been mortally wounded in the hour of his greatest triumph by the hand of an assassin. Insensible now to praise or glory he was carried to the White House, and expired at an early hour of the following morning.

Another death during that same year also prompted comment in the paper. It occurred shortly before the special day that Austria had set aside in order to celebrate the inauguration of the Dual Monarchy with Hungary:

> Death in a terrible form has visited the Imperial family since the day for the coronation had been fixed. The Archduchess of Austria, daughter of Duke Albert, only ten days since beamed in the freshness of youth and beauty, full of health and life. Attracted by some spectacle in the streets, she stepped rapidly to a window of the Ducal Palace and stood upon a match dropped by some careless hand. In a moment the flames enveloped her, and Archduchess as she was – only in her eighteenth year, preparing for her nuptials with the heir to the Crown of Italy – she was borne scorched and scared, to the chamber she never was to leave. They hoped against hope for days … but on Thursday morning she breathed no more, and the Austrian Court was bereft of its most charming ornament.

The Great Dublin Exhibition – the third in eleven years – was opened in May 1865 by the Prince of Wales, following a procession from the Mansion House through parts of the city to the exhibition site at Earlsfort Terrace:

I Never Read Them …

'The newspapers, Sir, they are most villainous – licentious – abominable – infernal, not that I ever read them – no – I make it a rule never to look into a newspaper'.

Richard Brinsley Sheridan, 1751–1816

Arches of flags were extended in three places across Dame Street, in which thoroughfare a very fine view of the procession could be obtained. At this time the procession was considerably more than a mile in length. … The roof of the Bank of Ireland was furnished with its quota of spectators while inside the [Trinity] College railings, adventurous gownmen placed themselves upon the pedestal intended for the statue of Edmund Burke, whose genius we can all admire, and which few students of the present day can ever hope to equal. Other gownmen plucked up courage enough to soar as high as Oliver Goldsmith – we mean to say that they perched themselves on the statue of the poet, and from this position they uttered their cordial welcome to England's future king.

The newspaper's very small typefaces and the lack of illustrations continued to give it a very sombre appearance, not least on the front page which continued to carry nothing except small advertisements. In one issue, in June 1867, the Dublin, Wicklow and Wexford Railway was offering cheap fare excursions to Powerscourt and the Seven Churches, notwithstanding the fact that no railway line served either Enniskerry or Glendalough. The firm of Cartright and Davis (By Her Majesty's Letters Patent) was advertising 'painless teeth and stump extraction by congelitation (without Chloroform)'. The Society of Saint Vincent de Paul announced its Annual Bazaar in the Rotunda Rooms for the poor of Dublin, with music provided by several bands including that of the 25th Regiment. The Colony of Natal offered free grants of 200 acres of land and other privileges to emigrants possessing a capital sufficient to stock same, stressing that 'the climate is one of the finest in the world. The soil is most productive, the rearing of cattle, horses, sheep and Angora goats is a profitable occupation. Pastoral runs of one thousand five hundred acres can be granted for a term of eight years at a rent of two pence per acre'.

Meanwhile, Fenianism had begun to feature in the news, along with many rumours of recruiting and training. A report which described the military pursuing fugitive Fenians in the mountains of Kerry ended with the news that 'Bishop Moriarty preached in the Catholic Cathedral today on the subject of the outbreak, which he greatly deplored, and denounced the miscreants who had attempted to incite insurrection. He rejoiced that the people had not joined them'.

Early newspapers carried no illustrations at all. This example was the first to appear in *The Irish Times,* and continued to be utilised for many years by other newspapers as well. Lord Burnett referred to the same illustration when writing about the *Daily Telegraph*: 'These small drawings of ships then used in the shipping advertisements represent the very beginnings of display advertising'.

One of the editor's sons, Arthur William Wheeler, wrote a brief but incomplete account about Fenian activity in the neighbourhood of Ballysax during this period. James Fitzgerald, a local man who worked for the family as a 'steward, ploughman, milker and general factotum', had just returned from America. Although the Wheelers did not know it, his return had been arranged so that he could drill local young men for the planned Fenian uprising. Part of the younger Wheeler's account reads:

James Fitzgerald, or as he was more popularly known, 'Jim,' joined the little nest at Ballysax. … He was his Reverence's man, and well liked by everybody. By us boys, he was considered a hero. He had been a Confederate soldier, had been at the battle of Gettysburg, and had been promoted captain for some deed of bravery of which he would never tell us, and curious to say, during the four years of his campaigning had never once been wounded. Many tales of escapes – and escapades – he told us over the harness-room fire and enrapturised us all with his descriptions of battles and sieges. … He was every inch a soldier and yet to us as gentle as our mother.

This account then went on to relate how the police had arrested many local men and charged them with treason and felony. 'During all this feverish business, Jim continued to act as if he was not interested at all. Occasionally he was out late, but no suspicion attached to him in our minds, nor indeed in the minds of the constabulary'. At this point, disappointingly, the narrative abruptly ended.

One especially long leading article during the newspaper's ninth year – just two decades after the Great Famine – provides an interesting insight into what might be presumed to have been the thinking of both Wheeler and Knox on the subject of landlords and tenants, and seems to lend weight to the view that most of the landlords were reading the English newspapers rather than *The Irish Times*. Those who, today, would dismiss *The Irish Times* of that period as either 'a Protestant newspaper' or as 'a Unionist newspaper' (even though it was both), might be surprised at the tenor of some of its early opinion pieces. The following was prompted by a court case taken by the Law Life Assurance Company, which had recently purchased 'at an insignificant price' the vast Martin estate in Connamara, against a tenant:

> How the London Company ... have acquitted themselves of the duties attaching to their position as landlords has hitherto been a matter of painful rumour and judicial reproof. A liberal treatment of the tenantry might have been fairly expected from a wealthy London proprietary, who had purchased the territory when Irish land was at its lowest point of depreciation and who, by the mere fact of their being a company of absentees, were exempted from all those undefined but, in the aggregate, heavy claims which residence imposes on a landlord. ...
>
> But the public opinion, impalpable and unsettled as it was, which was gradually gathering around the name of the Law Life Assurance Company as landlords, has now acquired a body and substance from the deliberate verdict of one of the most distinguished Irish judges. That verdict may be summed up as follows: The company have law on their side, and justice, reason, and public policy against them. They refused to do for their Irish tenants what every English landlord does for his English tenant. They would neither effect themselves the necessary improvements, or, rather, the operations absolutely necessary to the business of farming, nor would they put the farmer in a position to expend his own money in doing so. They raised the rent more than twenty per cent after a few year's occupancy, then gave a three year's lease and – a few years after its expiry, evicted him – not for non-payment, because he had always paid his rent punctually, not because he was an unimproving tenant, seeing that he desired nothing better than to improve his farm, not because he was an unintelligent, worthless Celt, for the judge concluded the contrary to be the case from the documentary evidence before the court; but because he sought security from that form of oppression and plunder which consists in giving a tenant land which cannot be cultivated without effecting certain improvements [and then], a few years after the expiry of the three years lease, evict him.

A further example of how the paper viewed landlords – again, as absentees – appeared two years later, when a deputation from several railway companies sought government support to obtain loans at reduced rates:

> The British Government have supported by their credit the railway enterprises of India, and there are equally strong reasons for their supporting the railway enterprises of Ireland ... There seems to be no reason why a satisfactory arrangement should not come to the Government and the Railway Companies, as there is no serious risk to be incurred by the former, and no sacrifice to be demanded of the latter which they are unwilling to accord.

Mr. Robinson, Chairman of the Limerick and Waterford Railway, made a remarkable statement concerning the line which he represented. He said that not one of the absentee landlords through whose lands that railway ran, has taken a share in or contributed any money to the construction of the line. Yet the railway had enhanced the value of these absentees' property by at least 30 per cent. ... Now, here is a specimen of what absenteeism does for Ireland. The absentees derive all the profit that results from resident industry and enterprise, and they contribute nothing thereto.

It might also seem surprising that, in 1868, *The Irish Times* expressed support for plans to erect a statue to William Smith O'Brien, who had been tried for treason two decades earlier. His was just one of four further names of disparate worthies that included Prince Albert. The paper was critical of the fact that, although a fund had been established some years earlier to erect a 'Prince Consort Memorial', nothing further had happened. It went on to advocate that 'the grounds of the Dublin Society [Leinster Lawn] be adorned with the appropriate memorial of a Prince who promoted every useful civilising art'. As well as calling for memorials to Edmund Burke and Henry Grattan, the article questioned the reasons for the delay in proceeding with the O'Connell monument in Sackville Street. The foundation stone had been laid four years earlier but it was to take another eighteen years before completion. In 1875, the paper was looking forward to the city being 'graced by another work of art conceived by the genius of the late lamented Foley'. The famous Irish sculptor had died a year earlier, but the paper had learned that the bronze statue had just been successfully cast:

> We need scarcely say that the approaching completion of the Grattan Monument is a matter on which the citizens of Dublin have every reason to congratulate themselves. Apart altogether from his political character, Grattan will always be counted among the most eminent of Irishmen. ... There never lived a man who loved his country with a purer love, or who toiled more sedulously and zealously to promote its happiness. At this day Irishmen of all political opinions can afford to view Grattan with an impartial eye.

In a leading article published in 1868, the paper contrasted the fact that while no great public work had been accomplished in Dublin during the previous year, 'our merchants and traders had done much to beautify the city', and then added:

> The Liffey still remains unpurified, and twice every twenty-four hours exposes a black mass of mud ... a positive source of malaria and disease. ... For years, too, the public has been calling for the erection of a wide, spacious and level bridge in place of Carlisle-bridge. A vast proportion of the whole traffic of the city passes over that bridge, with what danger to person and property the numerous accidents which have occurred there sufficiently prove. We should be laughed at, and have been laughed at, on requesting that one year's revenue

returned into the British treasury from the Irish woods and forests should be devoted to the erection of a work so necessary for the convenience, safety and adornment of the city.

A private citizen of Dublin [Sir Benjamin Lee Guinness] expended nearly £200,000 in raising in all its pristine beauty the sacred pile of St. Patrick's Cathedral. … But round the fane [temple], almost contaminating its architecture, a ring of ruinous tenements, leaning against each other for mutual support, is still permitted to exist.

While 1869 saw the tenth anniversary of the paper's establishment, there was no mention in its columns of this significant milestone; it was continuing to flourish but was just about to be overtaken in circulation terms by a rejuvenated *Freeman's Journal*. There was little news of importance on the day, though a short account about a railway accident near Clonmel included the curiously worded sentence: 'No lives were lost but several persons are more or less injured'. The first item in the paper's 'Fashionable Intelligence' column, which often told of the comings and goings of royalty and the aristocracy, concerned a Catholic service in Paris. It related how 'a religious service for Good Friday, including the Adoration of the Cross, was celebrated yesterday at noon in the chapel of the Tuileries, and was attended by their Majesties the Prince Imperial and members of the Court'. More typical, perhaps were the frequent piquant inclusions of news about the British aristocracy. For example (and it would be difficult to invent a better one):

The Prince of Wales has gone on a short visit to the Duke of Grafton, having been the guest for the last few days of Mr. Henry Chaplin at Newmarket, where his Royal Highness calculated on a big coup in backing the Marquis of Hartington's *Belophoebe* for the Cambridgeshire, but found himself outwitted to the extent of a couple of thousand pounds by *Jongleur* who, at 40 to 1, carried the French colours to easy victory.

This column, which was subsequently renamed the 'Court and Personal' column, continued to carry the royal coat of arms in its headline until the title was eventually changed to 'Social and Personal', the title for the current advertising feature. Until the sixties, advertisements for this column continued to be referred to as 'Fash', shorthand for the original title, 'Fashionable Intelligence'.

Knox suffered a personal setback during the 1870 elections when, having stood as a candidate for Mallow, he failed by a narrow margin to gain the seat. He remained a supporter of Isaac Butt, though the latter was finding that Home Rule – by itself – was not attracting sufficient voters. The candidates who had won their seats had added denominational education and other causes in their programmes, marking a change in the movement's strategy that neither Butt nor supporters like Knox found to their liking.

In a speech made in Aberdeen, Gladstone had shown some unexpected ignorance concerning the aims of the Home Rule movement – had he not been listening to the Irish

MPs pleading the cause at Westminster? Perhaps he was confused because the other agendas – including the land problem and the university question – were complicating the issue, and Home Rule itself seemed to be gradually becoming a movement for complete independence. Attitudes towards it began to divide on sectarian lines, and the change in its character caused it to lose much of its earlier strong Protestant support, especially in Ulster. Not surprisingly, *The Irish Times* began to abjure too, turning instead to what it saw as the safer option of Unionism. Coincidence or not, this was happening around the same time that the proprietorship of the paper was about to change from Lawrence Knox, a supporter of Butt, to Sir John Arnott, a very successful businessman who figured that Ireland's growing prosperity was conditional upon the union with Britain. Added to this, Butt's leadership was weakening and six years later he was dead, thus opening the way for Parnell.

When the paper's founder, Lawrence Knox, died unexpectedly in January 1873 at the age of thirty-six years, every column in his newspaper published on the following day – including the advertisement columns – was lined with thick, black rules to signify mourning. The heavily ruled main leader column announced:

> Yesterday, at twenty minutes past four in the afternoon, at his residence, Fitzwilliam Square, Major Lawrence E. Knox, founder and proprietor of the *Irish Times*, was unexpectedly taken away in the midst of a career of usefulness, and when he was most hopeful for the future of his country. For some days he had been suffering from an attack of Scarlatina, which he seemed to have surmounted, but yesterday his pulse became more feeble at the time we have stated, clasping the hand of a near relative, he gave one short sigh and died.

Five days later, the paper described his funeral as one 'which embraced all classes of the public, and showed the universal esteem in which the late Major Knox was held. Upwards of 150 carriages attended. The Lord Mayor was present in his state coach draped with mourning emblems'. Others attending included the Lord Mayor of Belfast, the Mayor of Sligo, and both of the paper's first two editors, Dr Shaw and Dr Wheeler. 'At Mount Jerome cemetery, the coffin was flanked by the *Irish Times* literary and printing staff on one side, and the commercial staff on the other, followed by the *Irish Times* Band.' During its centenary year, the paper published a letter from a G.R. Mahon giving a few details about the founder's life, adding the following verse from a 'lament' on his death:

> He would have made each Irishman his brother
> Who firmly in his cause believes;
> Have party hues all blended with each other –
> The Northern lilies twined in South green leaves.

After an interval of several months, Knox's widow sold the newspaper to Sir John Arnott, who went on to personally direct it almost into the twentieth century, and whose family

The first Sir John Arnott, a very successful businessman, purchased *The Irish Times* in 1873 from the founder's widow for the sum of £35,000 and immediately set about investing in new equipment and increasing staff numbers. Although he had many other interests, he continued to personally direct the paper's fortunes until his death in 1898.

continued to control the company for almost fifty more years. Edward Dwyer Gray, interviewed by the *Freeman's Journal* about newspapers 'coming on the market', commented that this seldom happened except when a proprietor died. When this did occur, sums paid for the goodwill of a going newspaper seldom averaged more than four or five years' purchase of the net profits'.[10]

Arnott had arrived in Ireland from Scotland in 1834 at the age of 20 'to seek his fortune'. That he succeeded in his ambition there can be no doubt; during his very successful business career he contributed large sums to charity and when he died he left over one million pounds in his will. The announcement of his newspaper acquisition was published in the paper on 23 May 1873 where it was stated that the purchase price was £35,000 and that Sir John had afterwards visited the premises, and for the first time inspected the typographical, telegraphic and other departments of the establishment. It may seem curious that this shrewd and very successful businessman had expended a very considerable sum before satisfying himself about the state of the paper's staff and equipment. He must have been sufficiently impressed by the paper's progress to date and the quality of what would be termed today as 'the product'. Following this inspection, he

[10]   *Freeman's Journal,* 26 March 1887.

Dr. Shaw, the paper's first editor, is seen (second row, wearing top hat) in this photograph of a family group thought to have been taken following the funeral of the paper's second editor, George Wheeler, in 1877. Most of the others present seem to have been members of Wheeler's family (to whom Shaw was related), and George Wheeler's three sons have been identified in the picture as follows: Arthur, first left in second row, Richard, far right same row, and George junior, first left, back row. The photograph was taken at Ballysax. *(Photo. courtesy of the Wheeler family).*

decided to make additions to the editorial and other staffs and 'especial care was to be taken with commercial and industrial topics hitherto somewhat neglected'. He then arranged to insert a further special announcement in the paper stating that 'its columns shall continue to be devoted to the interests of the country, to the promotion of harmony and good feeling amongst all classes; in fine, to whatever is truly useful, loyal and patriotic.'

He paid tribute to Major Knox, 'the late, generous and high-minded proprietor', and personally hoped 'to heal unhappy differences, and allay those angry and bitter feelings engendered by the past'. He promised that no expense was to be spared to secure the earliest intelligence for the paper's readers, 'especially for those of our Irish metropolis – at one time allowed to be the most refined and polished city in Europe'. Thirty-six years later, during the paper's jubilee year (and after remarking that 'no man can celebrate his fiftieth birthday without some reviewing of the past'), the anonymous writer commented that one great advantage had come with the change of ownership:

From the very outset, every department began to feel the stimulating effects of the ripe and keen commercial judgement which Sir John had acquired in the course of his long mercantile career. In every direction the paper steadily grew, until the day came when its old home was no longer big enough for its needs.

The unexpectedly early end of the Knox era had seen *The Irish Times* firmly established as Ireland's leading daily newspaper. It continued to report the affairs of the Protestant churches, but was also frequently covering news concerning the Roman Catholic Church. On several occasions during the 1870s, the Catholic Institute for the Deaf and Dumb at Cabra had inserted half-page advertisements listing donations and subscriptions in aid of the work of the charity. The manner of the paper's reporting of Catholic events, often in great detail, seems to place some assumptions about its religious outlook during this period in a different perspective from the view more often stressed, as the following (1875) may help to demonstrate:

> Yesterday being the first Sunday of the New Year, the Lord Mayor, as is usual when a Catholic fills the civic chair, heard Mass at Marlborough-Street Cathedral. The Lord Mayor, vested in his robes of office, was accompanied by the Lady Mayoress … and by several members of the Corporation, who were also in civic robes, and was attended by Mr. Hayes, Secretary, and by the Mace and Sword Bearers and Officer of Commons. His Lordship, who drove in his State carriage, escorted by mounted police, was received at the principal entrance by the Rev. Mr. M'Swiggan who conducted him to St. Kevin's chapel, where his Eminence, Cardinal Cullen, the Most Rev. Dr. Crane, Bishop of Sandhurst, the Most Rev. Dr. Quinn, Bishop of Maitland and other clergy had assembled. A procession was then formed, the Lord Mayor walking beside the Cardinal up to his appointed place in the sanctuary, where the other members of the Corporation had already taken their seats.

The full report continued for twice the above length. Later in that same year, just to make the point that even when a Cardinal sneezed, it was not unusual for *The Irish Times* to report the details:

> The Press Association is authorised to contradict the alarming rumours circulated respecting Cardinal Manning's health. [He had become a Cardinal ten years after his appointment as Archbishop of Westminster in 1865.] Though suffering from a severe cold, no danger can be apprehended, and he was able to meet the members of the Acadamy yesterday afternoon.

Seven years later, after Archbishop McCabe was made Cardinal, the paper reported on the visit to Rome by a delegation to express the thanks of Irish Catholics to the Pope. The Pope's response was reported as follows:

> In creating the Archbishop a Cardinal, I have wished not only to reward his numerous great services, but also to give to Ireland a fresh token of the traditional love of the Papacy towards her. Ireland deserved this affection by her unshaken constancy in the Catholic faith, and her devotion and attachment to the Holy See. She is at this moment in the throes of a great

danger [a reference to Fenianism]. … I feel confident she will show herself animated with the spirit of sagacity and moderation, and thus render herself more and more worthy of my affection. … I wish Cardinal McCabe a happy return to Ireland, and beg him to assure my Irish children of my sentiments of affection towards them. His Holiness then blessed all Catholic Ireland.

James Carlyle, the manager, signed an agreement during 1874 to pay the sum of £25 per annum to a Mr J. McSheehy to continue the rental of the premises at Abbey Street. The terms provided 'that *The Irish Times* be given a lease of 15 years or such as may be agreed …', but the company decided to move to new premises at Westmoreland Street just eight years later.

Before this happened – just four years after the paper's founder died – its second editor was killed in an accident that occurred as he was driving to Newbridge on his way to his office in Dublin. George Wheeler's carriage overturned, as a result of which he suffered a fractured hip. He was carried to the hotel at Newbridge where he died later. *The Irish Times* reported his death next day:

> It is with the deepest and most profound regret that we announce the death of Rev. Dr. G.B. Wheeler, for many years editor of this paper and the Rector of Ballysax, whose long, active and almost blameless life came to a painless end at five o'clock yesterday morning. The recollection of his venerable and most kindly presence, and the intimation of his most unexpected death, are so fresh upon us who knew and loved and worked with him so long, that we have not the heart to do more than register his death. [After the accident], with characteristic fortitude, he bore the pain with equability of spirit and good humour that never deserted him, and even after being carried into the Crown Hotel and having had the fracture set, he kept up his spirits, and showed little sign of the torture he was enduring. On the Monday, two gentlemen from this office visited him at the hotel and found him in excellent spirits … looking so well that they little anticipated so fatal a result.

Another article described Dr Wheeler as a modest, retiring man. Despite the very private life which he led, few Irishmen 'will be mourned by a larger circle of friends and whose memory will be honoured by so many deep and sincere admirers':

> By virtue of his position in connection with Trinity College, the Church, this paper, and his own abilities and social virtues, he might have commanded the welcome *entree* into any society; but from all the mingling with the busy world, outside the *Irish Times* and his own parishioners at Ballysax, the Doctor held aloof.
>
> For this reason, among many reasons we might mention, it is that – in spite of his great and multiform attainments, his fifty-odd editions of classical books, his well earned reputation as a scholar, his long connection with this journal as Editor, and his popularity as

a preacher – Dr. Wheeler was comparatively speaking, unknown to the outside world. …
Search the files of this paper from its inception and not a single line, not one unfair word,
not one disingenuous argument will be found in anything written by Dr. Wheeler. …

What we have said indicates but faintly and most imperfectly the claims Dr. Wheeler had,
and ever will have on an Irish public. To the conductor of what is surely not presumption on
our part to call one of the great leading dailies, the temptation to indulge in the strong and
bitter language is oft times very great.

Somewhat strangely, the article concluded with an appeal for subscriptions to a memorial
fund set up to support his widow and children who had been 'very slenderly provided for'.
The article continued: 'Had he been less unselfish; if he had considered his own interests
more, and those of the public less; he might have died a comparatively wealthy man'.
Although the fund was established under the auspices of an impressive committee, there
was no further reference to it in subsequent editions.

For Sir John Arnott, the most pressing step was to find a new editor for his newspaper.
Information about this person or where he had been working previously no longer seems
to exist. Of his name, we only knew him by his initials, J. A. Scott until – in an old wages
book that very recently came to light – he was named as *James* Scott. This small detail
represents almost the only firm piece of information now known about the paper's third
editor who went on to serve in that capacity for twenty-two years.

James Scott

1877–1899

⸺➤●◀⸺

Making 'no secret of its preference for Imperial rule'

S IR JOHN ARNOTT APPOINTED James Scott as Dr. Wheeler's successor and the paper's third editor, about whom, as already mentioned – despite his subsequent twenty-two years service – almost nothing is now known. However, a newspaper handbook (*British Newspapers in the Nineteenth Century*), was to credit him with the fact that under his control *The Irish Times* had been 'steered through the difficulties and dangers of the Home Rule crisis in 1886'. Scott inherited the post as the editor of a newspaper that had recently, under Arnott's proprietorship, transferred its support to the cause of Unionism, a political adjustment which, however, did no harm to its continuing success. Isaac Butt died in May 1879, only two years after Scott had become editor. Although under the Arnott proprietorship the paper had already abandoned its support for Butt's Home Rule policy, Scott generously recorded some of the late leader's achievements:[1]

> All Ireland will hear with regret that Isaac Butt is no more. The powerful brain and strong-built frame that carried their owner through so much trying toil, mental and physical, have succumbed at last … The Stroke that stayed his life-long activity fell crushingly on mind and body. From the first day he was confined to his couch he was intellectually dead. And now the physical end has come too, and friends and foes … must feel that a great void has been made.
>
> To his party the loss is irretrievable. Vast experience, consummate tact, a suppleness of resource and a facility of expression unsurpassed in his generation, made Isaac Butt the life and soul of a movement which but for him would never have assumed the dimensions it attained in its palmy days. For thirteen years he was the leading figure in the Irish political world, wielding an influence unparalleled since the death of his great forerunner in the chiefship of the masses. …

---

[1] *The Irish Times*, 6 May 1879.

Under Butt, the call for Home Rule did not seek a total break with England, though this was changing and one consequence was that the paper distanced itself from the movement. As Fintan O'Toole was to write, *The Irish Times* perceived Ireland as 'part of the greatest empire the world had ever seen, and the paper was happy that this should be so'. The paper viewed the stirrings of militant nationalism as 'no more than a foolish distraction', and was happy to see a growing Catholic professional class beginning to find the paper more to its liking than its competitors. One of Scott's earliest leading articles, justifying the paper's outlook, maintained that:

> As all sensible and unprejudiced people here always knew, the real difficulties of Ireland are economic and agrarian rather than political. For nearly twenty years, much of the energy which could have been profitably applied to the country's material interests has been expended in a vain and unpractical pursuit of the *ignis fatuus*[2] of Home Rule.

Although the *Freeman's Journal* now had a greater circulation, *The Irish Times* continued to be a successful commercial venture because, even in the late-nineteenth century, the size of a paper's circulation was less important than the quality of its readership. To date, some of the worst difficulties facing the paper had been mechanical, because printing machines still ran at very slow speeds, thus limiting the requirements of a paper with an expanding readership. During 1861, *The Irish Times* increased its width to eight columns, each of which was extended to 23 inches in depth. In 1867 this already rather clumsy size was further enlarged in order to add an extra (ninth) column[3], but two years later, a new press, with the capacity to print an eight-page paper made it possible to revert to a more easily handled six-column page. Further developments soon allowed for another increase in pagination, resulting in the following announcement being made on 22 November 1873:

> This morning, *The Irish Times* consists of TWELVE PAGES. Owing to the importance of the closing proceedings of the Home Rule Conference yesterday, *The Irish Times* of today, with 72 columns, *is the largest daily paper ever published in Ireland.*

Another difficulty facing all newspapers when *The Irish Times* began publishing resulted from the fact that much of the news was being transmitted by postal delivery. The telegraph system was still in its infancy and such services as were available were in the hands of companies 'in dealing with whom, editors and newspaper managers were, as a consequence, subject to many annoying limitations'. In 1869, an Act of Parliament was passed enabling the Postmaster General to buy out the existing telegraph companies. *The Irish Times* then announced: 'We shall henceforward be able to place before our readers in

---

[2]   Foolish torch.
[3]   The New York *Morning Courier* was printed during the 1850s with no less than eleven columns.

the most complete form, all the important events in England and Scotland, and reports of Parliamentary and other proceedings in London contemporaneously with their appearance in the leading English and Scotch journals'.

The paper continued to comment on international, national and local events. An example of the last occurred when, in 1879, the local Grand Jury – the forerunners of the county council system – opposed an attempt to run a steam tramway from Dublin to Baltinglass. The decision angered *The Irish Times*:

> The Tramways Bill for opening up communication between Dublin and Baltinglass had the approval of the Government Engineer, of the local county surveyor, who is an engineer of capacity and experience; of the ratepayers generally, and of the landed proprietors along the highroad over which the line would pass. No one who had a right to speak seemed to be against it. Certainly no one at all appeared against it or urged any reason why it should be rejected; but the Grand Jury were above reasons – we are almost inclined to say above reason – and in a very unreasoning and arbitrary fashion threw the proposed measure aside as unworthy of consideration. Yesterday they adhered to their resolve of last week.
>
> Of course, this work would be of the greatest possible benefit to the community whom its completion would affect, and they are unanimously in favour of it. Yet, in the face of this, the Grand Jury contemptuously threw the bill aside as 'prejudicial to the interests of the district'. Why or in what way they did not condescend to say.

The tramway was subsequently built from Terenure as far as Poulaphuca, but never reached Baltinglass. During the same month, the extension of the franchise – it will be noted that *The Irish Times* used the word 'lowering' – drew comments from the paper underlining the fact that its appeal was to gentlemen and their betters, and not to their inferiors! But its defence of the Irish MPs is interesting too:

> One marked and not very pleasant feature of the House of Commons since the recent lowering of the franchise is the deterioration which it has undergone as a great national assembly. Happily there are a great many gentlemen left in it still; in fact a great majority of those who compose it retain yet that serene dignity which the noble lineage of gentle blood and adequate fortune always confer. … And yet it must be said of the few Irish members we refer to, that their proceedings, on the whole, though they have been factious and irritating, have been guided by some sort of public motive rather than by a desire for personal offensiveness. For thorough vulgarity and ill-mannered rowdyism we must look to the representatives of a few English, and perhaps one or two Scotch constituencies. It was not an Irish member who squalled and mewed like a cat, in imitation of another member, while the other was in the middle of a speech in an important debate a few years ago. It was not an Irish member who brayed like an ass in interruption of a speaker about the same time.

The freedom of the press

Our liberty depends on the freedom of the press, and that cannot be limited without being lost.

Thomas Jefferson

An aspect of education that had been exercising the minds of the Catholic hierarchy for some time was that which came to be known as the 'University Question.' The bishops wanted the government to establish a Catholic university system, and not, as proposed, a non-denominational one. As far back as June 1865, the paper had reported The O'Donoghue, in the House of Commons, moving that 'the present system of university education in Ireland prevents a large number of Her Majesty's subjects from enjoying the advantages of a university education. ... The Protestants had a university, and the dissenters had one, but the Roman Catholics, having conscientious scruples against Trinity College were practically deprived of one ...' This remark drew a response from a Mr Whiteside who said: 'Disguise it as they might, the real object of the motion was to obtain a charter for the establishment of a Roman Catholic College, and the day after this was done, a threat, already uttered, would be carried out, and the Sacraments of the Roman Catholic church would be withheld from all who sent their children to any other college'. The Chancellor of the Exchequer, winding up the debate, commented: 'Catholics should have an opportunity of receiving education in which regard should be paid to their religious opinions. If that right was denied to them it amounted to a civil disability'.

On 18 March, 1882, the imprint that had appeared in every issue of the paper since its foundation twenty-three years earlier was changed in order to announce that its premises had just been moved from 4 Lower Abbey Street to 31 Westmoreland Street. The new premises eventually comprised three separate blocks within the triangle formed by Westmoreland, D'Olier and Fleet Streets, all joined together by a warren of corridors at the centre. The Fleet Street block had formerly been a carpet warehouse and, from the first floor upwards, was a hollow hall surrounded by ornate balconies. For some unknown reason, the company eschewed the idea of taking advantage of the Fleet Street building to fix its address there – in imitation of many of the London papers – opting instead for Westmoreland Street until that frontage was sold.

The number [edition] of our paper now in the hands of our readers possesses so much of special interest for them and it is the first copy brought out in the new premises to which the printing and publishing of *The Irish Times* have been today removed. The rapid advance of the paper, and the greater responsibilities thrown upon us, compelled the enlargement of all our appliances. This necessity has been met by the erection of fresh machinery more fitted for those demands and having every latest advantage for greater speed and efficiency. In these respects all that we have desired to accomplish has been achieved.

The article went on to claim that the paper's new printing room was 'not excelled anywhere,' and that 'we have been able to secure the same extent and completeness' in the premises and conditions for those working on the production of the paper. Attention was drawn to 'the entirely new fonts of type cast for the paper', and to the fact that reports were now being received 'over our own Special Wire from our offices in Fleet Street in London, or by the public instruments of the Post Office'. Parliamentary proceedings were now being 'conducted' by the paper's own staff 'who occupy the seat assigned to *The Irish Times* in the gallery of the House of Commons':

> What the modern newspaper of the first class has become may be known from the single fact that in many of our issues, more than three-fourths of the entire news and reading matter of the number is printed from telegraphic despatches that reach us each night within the limit of a very few hours, and the amount of material which it is necessary to secure by telegraph, with great outlay and trouble, is much in excess of that used in the past.

Whenever there was little news worth commenting upon the paper turned to some general topic – today, perhaps, it might be termed 'padding'. During 1882, it described a newly developed gun that was 'likely to work radical changes and improvements in military and naval operations':

> This Armstrong 100-ton gun has put a shot into a depth of nearly two feet of wrought iron and, by the peculiar principle adopted in the multiple gun, it is believed that even greater results can be secured… The metal used is iron, lined with steel, and the weight of the piece is 25 tons. Below the line of the bore, the gun is studded with four huge udder-shaped excrescences or cylindrical 'pockets'. These pockets open into the gun at an angle, the axes towards the muzzle. The weight of the shot is … more than four times the quantity that is used for a shot of the same weight in the best gun now in use. As the ball passes the openings of the pockets, the heated gasses fire the supplementary charges one after another. It is calculated that this process greatly increases the velocity of the shot, the flight of which on leaving the mouth of the gun is four thousand feet per second, so that in less than two seconds the projectile has travelled more than a mile of space.

Another form of shooting occurred in that same year, when Lord Leitrim was murdered. The paper made the point that the horror of the event 'was triplicated' because 'landlord, assistants and horse – the entire party of men and beast – were all in one red burial blent, and shot to death almost at a hand-clap'.

Of course the motives which activated the murders can only be guessed at. But from the prolonged and wholesale disputes which Lord Leitrim had for years past maintained with his tenants, there can hardly be a doubt that the fearful crime by which he has perished, and by which two others have been hurried into eternity with him, had its origins in these agrarian troubles.

The Land Act he has regarded from the first with determined hostility and aversion, and particularly so in his Donegal estates, where it legalised the custom known as Ulster Tenant Right from time immemorial. The result of this refusing to acquiesce in the Act was that he was embroiled in ceaseless litigation with those who held from him; and refusing to accept the decision of the Land Courts, several of the cases were carried from tribunal to tribunal ending only in the House of Lords, the ultimate court of appeal in the realm, until the claimants were, it is alleged, in many cases defeated by prolonged litigation, or capitulated for want of funds to go on. The results of this chronic legal strife were that a feeling of widespread dissatisfaction and bitterness was generated amongst the occupiers of his northern estates.

Finding himself troubled, he had lately resolved upon making extensive clearances on his property, and had, it is stated, notices of evictions pending against no less than eighty-nine families in Donegal when it is certain that these proceedings had produced great and widespread exasperation, and that his life and the lives of his attendants have been sacrificed in the fierce spirit of revenge thus called into existence.

The article went on to include details of an incident four years earlier, when Leitrim deliberately

The paper's April 1878 account of the murder of Lord Leitrim made the point that 'Landlord, assistant, servant and horse – the entire party of man and beast – were all in one burial blent, and shot to death almost at a handclap'.

Until the arrival of the 'Linotype' type-composition machine, all typesetting was painstakingly done by hand. Each letter and each punctuation symbol had to be put in place individually and, after the job was finished, all these tiny pieces of metal had to be returned to their individual storage place in specially constructed drawers. These remarkable Linotype machines were introduced late in the nineteenth century and continued to be used for almost a century until the switch-over to the new electronic typesetting technology.

insulted the Lord Lieutenant, the Earl of Carlisle. The latter had been touring the west of Ireland and Leitrim took steps to prevent the Lord Lieutenant from staying, as proposed, in the inn at Maam:

> The only reason for this discourteous conduct of Lord Leitrim, by which the representative of the Queen in Ireland, with his party, was turned away from a little country wayside hotel was, it is commonly believed, that his Excellency was the representative of a Liberal Government. The letter that Lord Leitrim on that occasion wrote to his tenant, the innkeeper [Mr King], has become an historical document, and runs as follows:
>> King, – I will be obliged to you to fill the hotel with my tenants forthwith. Let every room be occupied, immediately, and continue to be occupied, and when so occupied you will refuse to Lord Carlisle and his party. If there should be the slightest difficulty as to filling the hotel and the occupation of the rooms, my desire is that you will fill each room with the workmen. But you must not admit Lord Carlisle, and consequently the rooms should be filled previous to his coming there, any orders you may have received notwithstanding. I rely on your observing my wishes to the letter. – (Signed) Leitrim.
>> P.S. – I will pay for the tenants using the rooms'.

A reward of £10,000 failed to tempt even one person to give evidence to secure the conviction of Leitrim's murderers. Jonathan Barton wrote that 'there was more than a suggestion that the constabulary did not try hard enough'.

The Irish Times published a special Sunday edition on 7 May 1882 to report two further assassinations, those of Lord Frederick Cavendish, the Chief Secretary, and Mr Thomas Burke, the Under Secretary, in the Phoenix Park, Dublin. An unusual step was taken to remove all advertisements from their usual position on the front page to make way for this news story. Cavendish had only just arrived in Dublin earlier that day and, as the paper noted, had received 'a popular ovation'.

> The news of the terrible tragedy … was received with the utmost incredulity in Dublin – people found it impossible to believe that such a deed could be perpetrated in the Phoenix Park in the broad light of an evening in May.
>
> The account of the transaction which appears to be accepted is that four men, driving on an outside car, jumped down when they saw the Chief and Under Secretary together, stabbed them, took their seats on the car, and drove off again in the direction of the Knockmaroon Gate … The Lord Lieutenant had just entered his garden in front of the [Vice-regal] Lodge when in the distance his Excellency observed a scuffle … as if there was a brawl but he gave directions that a policeman should be sent to see what it was. Little did he think that his two intimate friends were being then butchered to death before his face.

The paper published a Land League manifesto expressing pain and despair for the country as well as a statement from Michael Davitt deploring the murders. The paper's own comment was that this

The death of Cardinal Cullen, Primate of All Ireland, on 24 October 1879, was recorded by *The Irish Times* in a long leading article. In it the paper advised its readers that a detailed 'biography of the deceased Prince of the Catholic Church in Ireland is treated at length in another portion of our issue'. Note the curious positioning of the theatre notices.

had been 'an atrocity for the dark depths of which the records would be searched in vain'. Tony Gray, when editing the 125th anniversary supplement of *The Irish Times*, commented on the coverage of the murders:

> I think [it] worth considering, to dispel the notion once widely held by people who never read *The Irish Times*, that it was always fanatically opposed to nationalism in any form, and that at a drop of a hat it would blame all the nationalist parties and groups for any crime that was committed. Even [then], *The Irish Times*, though it made no secret for its preference for Imperial Rule, treated the Land League and the Irish Parliamentary Party quite seriously, and never questioned their constitutional right to take the line that they were taking.

One of the strengths of *The Irish Times*, even at this period, was its comprehensive international news-service. After the Phoenix Park murders it carried brief excerpts from continental newspapers – three mentioned here – concerning the incident:

> The bitterness in the criticism in the French press will be deeply felt. The *République Française* alludes to the last crime as 'a humiliation for the civilised world'. The *Paix* regards it as a final convulsive effort of the Nihilistic doctrines derived from Russian conspirators to prevent reconciliation … The remarks made by the Austrian press indicate that there are abroad very accurate students of Irish politics. Unanimously, horror is expressed at the cruel deed which, says the *Neue Freie Presse*, 'throws a deep shade on the Irish character'.

One month after this, the murder of another landlord was reported – this time concerning a Walter Bourke whose relations with his tenants were 'anything but good'. While the article expressed little sympathy for this landlord who had recently 'served ejectment notices with his own hands when his bailiffs refused', it criticised the murder of an unfortunate soldier travelling with him:

> We have got greatly beyond, in regarding these atrocities, a question of motive either in the general or in the particular case; it is murder by a system. … There can be no question about the fact that Mr. Bourke, who was an obnoxious landlord, and the [accompanying] Dragoon who harried nobody … are shot. A mounted dragoon could easily have escaped, and in all probability could never have identified those that lay in ambush behind a wall. His destruction was consequently not the result of fear that his survival might produce detection.

The Phoenix Park murders proved a setback for Parnell's Home Rule campaign, a situation that was further damaged as a result of his affair with Mrs Kitty O'Shea. The ensuing statement concerning Parnell made by the Standing Committee of the Catholic Archbishops was reported:[4]

---

4   *The Irish Times*, 4 December 1890.

The Catholic Archbishops and Bishops of Ireland have unanimously adopted an address to the clergy and laity of their flocks in reference to the crisis that has arisen …

They 'can no longer keep silent in presence of the all-engrossing question' which agitates Irishmen at home and abroad. That question is: 'Who is *not* to be the leader of the Irish people'. The Archbishops and Bishops affirm that Mr. Parnell is decidedly unfit for the position. They add – 'As pastors of this Catholic nation we do not base this our judgement and solemn declaration on political grounds, but simply and solely on the facts and circumstances revealed in the London Divorce Court'. Mr. Parnell has been guilty of 'one of the greatest offences known to religion and society', and its exaggerations increase greatly its 'scandalous pre-eminence'. The Bishops wish to say this without hesitation or doubt, and in the plainest possible terms: Confronted with the prospect of contingencies so disastrous, we see nothing but inevitable defeat at the approaching general elections. The weighty decision thus announced will, no doubt, exercise the largest effect. All the members of the party in London who are still engaged in deliberation, both those of one portion and of the other, will know this morning, as also will the provincial bodies, that this condemnation by the bishops is recorded, and the influence of so authoritative and explicit rejection upon the ultimate results must be commanding.

Although Parnell received messages of support from various sources, including America, as reported in the paper on 6 December, the weight of opposition to his continuing in office was against him. In some cases, as the paper reported, this was expressed with a sense of regret. One example quoted came from the Central Branch of the Irish National League which resolved that 'whilst acknowledging the past services of Mr. Parnell, the members of the Branch believe his retirement from the leadership of the Irish Party to be essential'. The paper also quoted the response to the situation by Lord Selbourne, a former Lord Chancellor, an example, some might think, of kicking a man when he is already down: 'I have never been one of those whom anybody could suppose to be disposed to defend Mr. Parnell's proceedings. … My surprise is, rather, that so many people who feel so strongly about his present moral delinquencies should have been for five years so entirely insensible to everything else in his conduct that was irreconcilable with humanity, charity and justice'.

Parnell died in 1891 and, as Robert Kee wrote, 'Any hopes for Home Rule as a 'final settlement' of Ireland's aspirations were buried with him'. Under its famous editor, C.P. Scott, the *Manchester Guardian* had initially supported Home Rule for Ireland, reporting the movement's progress in his newspaper. Scott was a friend of John Dillon, but when it appeared that Unionist opposition was implacable, he then supported the idea of excluding what eventually became Northern Ireland from Home Rule. Scott's biographer, Hammond,[5] commented that this change of stance was occasioned 'not because the problem was too difficult, but because the passions that had been excited had deprived the

---

[5]   Quoted by Geoffrey Taylor, *Changing Faces*.

Display advertisements began to be seen in newspapers towards the end of the nineteenth century, but early examples, such as the above which appeared in *The Irish Times* in 1905, were crude by today's standards.

leaders of their independence'. When, two years after Parnell's death, the Ulster Unionist Convention organised a huge rally, *The Irish Times* reported the event under these headlines and, in commenting editorially, underlined its current political stance:

ULSTER DECLARATION AGAINST HOME RULE
12,000 DELEGATES PASS THE RESOLUTIONS

The great Ulster Unionist Convention of 1892 has been held. It is only now, when the meeting has been held, that it has been possible to gain any idea of the full significance of its great dimensions. Ulster spoke yesterday with a voice which will ring through the constituencies of the United Kingdom. The demonstration not only fulfilled the expectations of those who sympathise with its purpose, but conspicuously refuted the sinister prophecies of the adversary …

The resolutions, which were passed by acclamation, were framed in a spirit of sober seriousness, and no false note of bombast or bravado detracted from the effect of the speeches. The politicians who were willing to condone the acts of the Land League, and to smile on the iniquities of the Plan of Campaign, are entitled, if they choose, to condemn the Ulstermen for declining to recognise the title of a National Parliament to their allegiance. But they can no longer affect to doubt the intense earnestness of those whom they are prepared to treat as rebels. The aspect of the gathering needed no aid rhetoric to be impressive …

Above all, it must be remembered that, though the gathering was one peculiarly of Ulstermen, they speak in this matter for loyalist minorities scattered, in greater or less strength throughout the other provinces. No sentiment was more widely applauded than the declaration that it was not part of the intention of the North to abandon their fellow Unionists in other places, and to obtain freedom for themselves at the cost of the enslavement of their brethren …

The declaration not to abandon fellow Unionists in the South, reiterated several times subsequently, proved hopelessly unsustainable.

Some interesting details about staff wages at this time emerged when some fragments of a wages book dating from this period were discovered. Scott, the editor, was being paid £5 weekly – the same as his predecessor, Wheeler, had been receiving some thirty years earlier. If this indicates something about wages in the company at the time, it may also, perhaps, say something about the stability of currency throughout this period. James Carlyle, the general manager, was being paid £4.10, while the wages of the long-serving Simington (who was to succeed him) were £4 weekly, and the cashier (later to become company secretary), R.F. Townley, was getting £3.10.

Back in the 1880s, *The Irish Times* made an indirect but important contribution to yacht racing in Ireland by playing a part in the introduction of a one-design class of sailing vessel from which grew the famous and very long-lived class of Dublin Bay Water Wags. These fourteen-foot open sailing dinghies have continued to race successfully to this day every Wednesday during the season at Dun Laoghaire, where special Wag Nights continue to be a regular feature. This all began when a Mr T.B. Middleton placed an advertisement in the paper proposing that a new class of Sailing Punts be established in Kingstown harbour, 'all built and rigged the same so that an even harbour race can be had with a light and generally useful boat …'.[6]

On 28 March, 1898, Sir John Arnott, who had purchased *The Irish Times* twenty-one years earlier, died in his eighty-fourth year at his home in Montenotte, Cork. During his

---

[6]   *The Irish Times*, 18 September 1886.

Prior to the twentieth century, illustrations continued to be comparatively rare until the technique of engraving printing blocks was perfected. Advertisers were quick to take advantage of the method in order to make their advertisements more appealing. This example appeared in the paper during May 1909.

final year as proprietor, the paper made a profit of £33,000, but now both the family title and ownership of this successful newspaper passed to his son, the second Sir John. The following day, the paper's normal, thin column rules were, once more, replaced by thick rules throughout the entire issue, denoting mourning. Almost two columns were devoted to both the news of his death and to details of his achievements throughout his lifetime:

> If the enjoyment of a vast fortune entails its rights, it also creates its responsibilities, and these Sir John always understood. It was not merely in direct acts of personal kindness and open-handed beneficence that his authority was felt. It was ever his policy to provide for the future as well as the present …
>
> The son of John Arnott, J. P., of Greenfield, Auchtermuchty, Scotland, and born in 1814, he came to Ireland at the time of Her Majesty's accession to the throne … His first enterprises were undertaken in Cork. From that city he went to Belfast and within a very few years the foundations of his prosperity were firmly established. … His energies grew with his wealth, and rapidly extended over several parts of Ireland and to England and Scotland.

The article went on to note his involvement in railway companies, breweries and steamship lines, before adding that 'in the year 1873 he purchased this journal from the

When Sir John Arnott, the newspaper's second proprietor, died in March 1898, extra thick column rules were used throughout the paper to denote mourning. In a leading article, he was described as 'the chief and moving spirit of large business organisations, and these in every case proved successful. He was director of railway and other companies, breweries and steamship lines, and in 1873 purchased this journal from the representatives of the former owner'.

SIR JOHN ARNOTT.

The history of the career of a notable fellow-citizen who for so many years lived amongst us, and with whose active life so large a measure of profit and of progress in this country is identified, claims general and profoundly sympathetic attention. Many projects subsequently, even recently, have been realised which originally were conceived in the mind of a generous and enlightened thinker, whose work lives after him, whose services will more clearly be understood than even now they are, in time to come. If the enjoyment of a vast fortune entails its rights, it also creates its responsibilities, and these Sir John Arnott always understood. It was not merely in direct acts of personal kindness and of open-handed beneficence that his authority was felt. It was ever his object to provide for the future as well as for the present. He foresaw necessities before their actual incidence, and notwithstanding the burdens of business incurred by his many enterprises, he kept a keen watch upon

representatives of the former owner'. Sir John's involvement in Cork attracted special mention, where for three consecutive years he had been Mayor. He was knighted in 1859 and created a baronet in 1896. His eldest son, who succeeded him, was then just twenty-six years old, having been born in 1872.

James Scott died just one year after the death of the paper's proprietor. To this day the newspaper's third occupant of the editorial chair remains a shadowy figure despite being described at the time as the editor 'who had steered [*The Irish Times*] through the difficulties and dangers of the Home Rule crisis in 1886'.[7]

No personal details about Scott seem to have survived, but speculation that he may have been related to the famous *Manchester Guardian* editor, C.P. Scott, is almost certainly incorrect. It has been thought just possible that he may have been connected to a Scott family running the *Galway Observer*, a paper founded in 1881 which survived until the mid-1960s.

---

[7]   *Progress of British Newspapers in the Nineteenth Century*, a handbook published in 1900.

Algernon Lockyer

1899–1907

———◦◦◦———

'The largest and most important newspaper in Ireland'

SCOTT'S SUCCESSOR WAS Algernon Lockyer who was said to have previously been editor of the *Morning Post*. While a newspaper of this title was still in existence in London and there had also been an earlier one having the same title in Dublin that had ceased publication sixty-seven years earlier, it is hard to believe that Lockyer had edited either of these papers. A more likely possibility (but by no means certain) was that the newspaper concerned was the *Morning News*, founded in the same year as *The Irish Times* but which ceased publication in 1864. As with Scott before him, very little is known about Lockyer, except that a triumvirate comprising Lockyer as editor, the second Sir John Arnott as proprietor, and the quite remarkable J.J. Simington as general manager, controlled the destiny of the company for the next eight years.

Simington, who was still involved as a director for almost two years after I had joined the staff in the late forties, had started with the company in 1879. That was exactly two decades after the paper's foundation, at a time when it continued to be printed at Lower Abbey Street, and only two years after the death of the man who was, effectively, the paper's first editor,[1] George Wheeler. Simington seems to have been born around 1862, so that he was probably about seventeen years old when he joined the staff. When he retired from the board in 1948 he had completed sixty-nine years of service with the company, making him almost certainly the longest-serving member of the staff and holder of a record now unlikely to be surpassed. A native of Drogheda, the fact that he was a Catholic proved no barrier to his advancement through the ranks of the company even at this early period. He was replaced by John O'Docherty who had joined the company in 1903, and when O'Docherty died in 1942, G.C.J. Tynan O'Mahony took his place, so that *The Irish*

---

[1]   As already noted, Dr Shaw, the first editor, held that post for only fourteen weeks.

The Fourth Estate

'The idea of the fourth estate is important in relation to the role of news in society. Thomas Carlyle attributed the term to Edmund Burke's observation that "There were Three Estates in Parliament, but, in the Reporters' Gallery yonder, there sat a Fourth Estate more important than they all". Between the seventeenth and nineteenth centuries the three estates in Britain were the Church, aristocracy and the House of Commons. Today they are the executive, legislature and judiciary. But what Burke and Carlyle meant was that the fourth estate was essentially a fourth power … which acts as a counterbalance and check to the other three estates no matter how they are defined. For them a free fourth estate was essential to good government.'

Jackie Harrison

Times had three consecutive Catholic general managers between 1903 and 1947 when Jack Webb was appointed to the position. Tynan O'Mahony, whose son, Dave Allan, became a well-known television personality, was well connected to the newspaper business, having worked for several London papers including the *Morning Post*, and his father had worked for the *Irish Daily Independent*. His wife, who had been women's editor on the *Freeman's Journal* was a sister of Katherine Tynan, the poet and writer.

To celebrate Simington's sixty years with the company, a presentation ceremony took place in 1939 when it was said of him:

> It is almost impossible to believe that this astonishingly youthful figure has been associated with our newspaper for sixty years … 'J.J.S.' retains the same sprightly step, the same jaunty tilt of the bearded chin as he looks quizzically at you over the rims of his gold-rimmed spectacles, the same alertness of mind that anticipates your next argument, and the same keenness of humour that so often expresses itself in a rollicking laugh. Watch him dashing up the stairs from the Front Office, two at a time, and you will doubt your senses. There he is, a miracle of septuagenarian youth, at his desk from early morning until late – often far too late – at night, thinking of twenty things at once and generally doing half a dozen of them, bubbling over with energy and enthusiasm … After sixty years of unceasing work, he is as active as he ever was. Every member of the *Irish Times* staff wishes him many more fruitful years in his managerial chair.

Over two hundred members of staff, and five members of the Arnott family, contributed to the presentation – a portrait of Simington painted by the artist William Conor. The attendance was reminded that Conor had already painted portraits of Douglas Hyde,

The second Sir John Arnott became the paper's third proprietor on the death of his father. Two years later, in 1900, it became a limited company with a share capital of £450,000. However, by holding all the Ordinary Shares, the Arnott family continued to control the company for more than forty years.

R.M. Smyllie and – would that Douglas Gageby had known this[2] – the Revd J.B. Armour of Ballymoney.

As a very junior clerk, I clearly recollect seeing Simington, a wiry figure, as thin as a rake and with a goatee beard who, around 1947–48 – while in his mid-eighties – was still a member of the board. The description of him ascending the long flight of stairs, two at a time, was absolutely correct although he was also able to make the more difficult descent in the same fashion. He was interested in everything. Indeed older members of the staff recalled that he had an almost school-boyish variety of interests including postage stamps, old Dublin directories, and collecting autographs of celebrities – nothing, it was said, was too insignificant to arouse his enthusiasm. Two years after his presentation, he retired as manager, but remained on the board for a further six years.

A handbook entitled *Progress of British Newspapers in the 19th Century* was published in 1901 and, in a section on the newspaper scene in Ireland, it devoted several paragraphs to *The Irish Times* which it described as

---

[2]   Douglas Gageby often quoted Armour of Ballymoney in his leading articles. The Presbyterian minister was an outspoken critic of Carson and once famously said that 'Home Rule is a Presbyterian principle'.

the largest and most important newspaper in Ireland … [it] has just been turned into a limited company. In its early days its politics were not very clearly defined but for the last thirty years it has been a moderate Conservative organ. The excesses of language too often common in Irish journalism have been sedulously avoided, and it has always maintained an excellent news service. It possesses a large circulation among members of all classes and creeds, and enjoys the support of all who have a substantial interest in the country.

In a general article about the press in Ireland, the handbook stated: 'Advertisements are the chief source of revenue for all the various journals – these being inserted in the Dublin papers at one penny per line upwards; the *Irish Times* taking the lead at a much higher figure owing to its vast circulation among the well-to-do classes'. It noted that at the time of Major Knox's death, the newspaper 'was already a valuable property' and, following its purchase by Sir John Arnott, it had 'rapidly increased in circulation and revenue'.

The 'vast circulation' mentioned was approximately 20,000, and while this did represent the largest sale in Ireland at the time, it was to be challenged by William Martin Murphy's *Irish Independent* not long after its launch just over four years later. Before that, the paper's principle competitor was the *Freeman's Journal*, with which *The Irish Times* had been striving for supremacy in sales for years. But even at this early period, as the handbook quoted above observed, *The Irish Times* 'had to face competition from the [London] metropolitan press which pours out its thousands of sheets every day'. The *Journal* appealed to the far wider Catholic audience but an unexpected intervention favoured *The Irish Times*, at least in the short term. This resulted from the launch of a new morning paper, the *Irish Daily Independent*, whose owners decided to compete directly with the *Freeman's Journal* for its readership. The *Journal* was already experiencing some difficulties because it had supported Parnell's campaign, indirectly encouraging another grouping to launch, in 1891, a short-lived anti-Parnellite paper, the *National Press*. The Archbishop of Dublin, Dr Walsh, published several letters in this new paper warning Catholics against views expressed in the *Journal*. The *Freeman's Journal* then accomplished a political about-turn in order to oppose Parnell, a move that prompted Parnell's supporters to stage a mock funeral during which copies of the *Journal* were burned and then buried in Kilbarrack churchyard. This was the confusing situation when the *Irish Daily Independent* was launched in 1895, and a decade later all this prompted the very successful – and sometimes very controversial – businessman, William Martin Murphy, to intervene on the newspaper scene, re-launching and re-naming the *Irish Daily Independent* as the *Irish Independent*.

The Irish Times kept details – very few of which have survived – recording how it was performing in competition with competing newspapers, noting the number of advertisements each paper carried. The table below indicates that both the (Dublin) *Daily Express* and the *Freeman's Journal* had been suffering from falling sales and both ceased to

So, he did

'When I want a peerage I will buy one, like an honest man.'

Alfred Harmsworth, later Lord Northcliffe

publish (in 1921 and 1924 respectively), thus opening the way for William Martin Murphy's *Independent* (launched in 1905). In circulation terms, the latter caught up with the *Times* and, subsequent overtook it:

	I. Times	*Freeman's J.*	*Independent*[3]	*D. Express*
1894	962	594	505	504
1899	848	585	428	521
1909	864	484	552	315
1919	978	391	736	264
1923	870	396	830	–

Before all this happened, the major news at the turn of the century continued to be about the Boer War. The outbreak, in January 1899, prompted *The Irish Times* to publish a long leading article closely following the British argument that the war had been forced upon a reluctant Britain by the actions of the Dutch settlers in South Africa:

England's true answer to the Transvaal is her expedition to South Africa, which in number of men and horses is the largest … which has ever left the British shores, even more powerful than that which was sent to the Crimea. Mr. Balfour spoke with great effect last night at Haddington. The war, he declared, is forced upon us 'not by men fighting for their country, but by an oligarchy fearing that the hour of their domination is nearing its end'. We have had, he added, 'war forced upon us because we have desired to see established that state of things under which alone peace is possible in South Africa'.

Speaking at Dundee last night, Mr. Asquith [the Conservative leader] said that at this very moment a state of war existed between a country inhabited by men of the same colour and blood. He had always credited Her Majesty's Government, and he did so now, with a sincere and honest desire to avoid war. It seemed incredible that the other side should strike the first blow in a conflict which could have but one issue.

---

[3]   The first two figures relate to the *Irish Daily Independent* and the remaining three to the *Irish Independent*.

The *Irish Times*, the chief Unionist organ in Ireland, which was established in 1859, has attained under the proprietorship of Sir John Arnott the premier position in Ireland. It has a circulation far in excess of any other newspaper in that country, and is also widely read throughout Great Britain and abroad.

Like almost every other newspaper founded prior to the twentieth century, *The Irish Times* placed its news on inside pages, devoting the front page to classified advertisements. Although this gave the paper a very dull, grey appearance, news did not appear daily on the front page until the 1940s. The issue depicted here is that of February 13, 1899, and also shown are the mastheads of the evening and Sunday editions published at that time.

The news during the second year of the war chiefly concerned the three major sieges of the campaign, Kimberly, Ladysmith and Mafeking, although many other place names were sprinkled through the news columns, including Spion Kopje, the Modder River and Colenso. The paper reported that during Irish enrolment in the Imperial Yeomanry 'over two hundred names are in the list of applications' and that the Royal Irish Fusiliers had just sailed for South Africa in the troopship *Avoca*. The campaign dragged on until General Redvers Buller was replaced as commander-in-chief by Lord Roberts (an Irishman) who managed to turn the direction of the conflict in favour of the British.

In an unusual step at the time, *The Irish Times* carried news on its front page on New Year's Day, 1900,[4] and included was a report concerning the fact that 'Her Majesty the Queen sent a Christmas greeting to all the Troops in South Africa'. In all, some 20,000 Irishmen served with the British forces during that war – indeed throughout much of the nineteenth century, almost one quarter of all serving soldiers in the British Army were Irish. This situation gave rise to the typically Irish comment at the time that 'the Irish fought for the Empire, the Scotch administered it, and the English took the profits'!

In 1900 a decision was made to form a company called The Irish Times Limited with a share capital of £450,000, divided into 55,000 preference shares of £5 each, and 35,000

[4]   On 7 September 1901, the *Daily Express* became the first London newspaper to publish news daily on the front page.

ordinary shares of £5 each. The names of the original subscribers were listed as follows: John A. Arnott, Bart., David T. Arnott, journalist, William Guest Lane, solicitor, Robert Stokes, chartered accountant, John J. Simington, chief clerk, Albert Hall, clerk, James Carlyle, journalist. As first trustee of the Arnott Estate, Sir John Arnott held virtually all of the ordinary (controlling) shares. The other first directors were David Arnott, Loftus Arnott, Maxwell Arnott and James Carlyle. The Certificate of Incorporation issued on 19 November, 1900 was numbered 2514.[5] Various alterations were made to the original Articles of Association during the years 1904, 1920, 1946, 1952 and, in connection with the formation of the Trust, in 1974. The Arnott family continued to play a considerable role in the company for nearly fifty years. The second Sir John became the first chairman of the Limited Company, and was later succeeded by Sir Lauriston. The Arnott control of the company did not end until until Frank Lowe was appointed chairman in 1946. Besides the daily morning newspaper, the company ran two other publications: a very short-lived *Sunday Irish Times* and the *Weekly Irish Times*, founded in 1875: the latter, which was later re-named the *Times Pictorial*, for a time outsold the daily paper, and survived until 1958.

Royal visits to Ireland were invariably accorded generous coverage. Queen Victoria's visit during April 1900 was to prove her last.

---

[5]   The Certificate of Incorporation issued to The Irish Times Trust Limited in 1974 was numbered 47802.

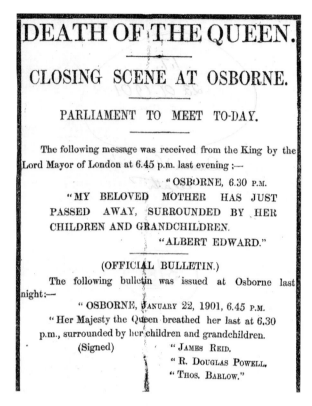

The paper's announcement, on 23 January 1901, of the death of Queen Victoria.

Large headlines heralded the arrival of Queen Victoria at Kingstown in 1900 and the report described the tumultuous greeting that awaited her as she drove through the Township of Blackrock where 'an astounding display of loyalty and enthusiasm was witnessed'. From there she arrived in Dublin where she stayed at the Vice Regal Lodge which, for the occasion, had been renamed 'Royal Lodge'. On the way 'her carriage passed the Cathedrals of St Patrick and Christ Church where the joy-bells rang in her ears'.

Barely nine months afterwards, on 23 January, 1901, the paper reported that she was gravely ill and that Dublin was 'tense with anxiety'. When she died it was reported that 'Dead Bells' were pealed at St Patrick's Cathedral. All the columns of the eight-page *Irish Times*, including the pages of advertisements, were bordered with thick black lines of mourning. No less than three of the eight pages were devoted to the news of the monarch's death, and reminders of her visits to Ireland during her exceptionally long reign.

> The Queen is dead. Since Friday night when the first official intimation of Her Majesty's illness was made known, the public mind has gradually been preparing itself for what was felt to be the almost certain event. … The news of her death will bring terrible disillusionment to millions of her subjects … By us in these islands it is probable that the full effect will not be realised for some months …

Reflecting on her long reign the paper recalled that the Crown was 'by no means popular with the masses for a time. Even as late as thirty years ago there was a party in this country, small in numbers, but considerable in influence, that made no secret of its Republican aspirations. One never hears these aspirations now'. It would seem that *The Irish Times* did not have its ear close enough to the ground and thus failed to appreciate the increasing evidence of change on the way. One piece of evidence materialised just a few days later

Exactly four years after Victoria's last visit to Ireland, her successor, King Edward VII arrived in Dublin to complete a busy programme which included the opening of the Great Exhibition at Ballsbridge. He also laid the foundation stone of the new Royal College of Science in Upper Merrion Street, a building which his successor, George V, formally opened in 1911. This attractive edifice, twice royal-blessed, is now Government Buildings.

when it reported that a vote of condolence in connection with Queen Victoria's death had been rejected by Dublin City Council by 42 votes to 35. Despite the fact that the vote was subsequently passed with abstentions, this was an indication of the changing political situation.

The coronation of Victoria's successor, King Edward VII, did not take place until more than a year and a half later when the paper was printed entirely in blue type. Around the same time, the paper reported two events with Arnott family connections, even if this was not stated. The first concerned evictions at the de Freyne Estate at Frenchpark, Co. Roscommon, where in one case a tenant's wife had to be evicted four times. The Lady de Freyne had married into the Arnott family. The second item was a report of the inauguration of the Phoenix Park Racecourse, in which the Arnotts had a significant interest.

During 1903, the company purchased, for the sum of £250, the *Irish Field*, a racing and sporting weekly newspaper that had been established nine years earlier. Sales figures for this period are not available but from the 1950s onwards, it had a circulation that hovered around 10,000 and contributed modest profits annually until it was sold a few years ago. Incidently, the *Field* was a curious organisation – a part of *The Irish Times* but also *apart* from it. It was edited for many years by Tom Atkinson[6] until Ernest Branston succeeded him as both editor and manager with a staff of one young clerk. The latter position was held for a time by Wilfred Brambell who went on to be a well-known actor – initially with Jimmy O'Dea in Dublin's Gaiety Theatre and later on television in the *Steptoe and Son* series.

ROYAL VISIT.

THE KING IN DUBLIN.

NEW COLLEGE OF SCIENCE.

LAYING THE FOUNDATION STONE.

IMPOSING CEREMONIAL.

ENTHUSIASM OF THE PEOPLE.

AFTERNOON AT PHŒNIX PARK RACES.

COMMAND PERFORMANCE AT THE ROYAL.

Their Majesties took part yesterday in the principal function included in the programme of their present visit to Dublin. At noon the first stone of the new College of Science was laid by the King in Leinster Lawn in presence of a large and fashionable assembly, composed of noblemen, gentlemen representing the different provinces, members of the learned professions, and citizens prominent in trade and in commercial life. The reception of Their Majesties along the route from the Viceregal Lodge to the place appointed for the interesting ceremony was whole-hearted and enthusiastic. It was the first occasion since their arrival in Dublin that the citizens were favoured with an opportunity of seeing Their Majesties pass through the streets, and the mode in which they crowded the thoroughfares forming the route of the Royal procession showed that they were determined to make the most of it. A... ceremony Their Majesties ret... to the Viceregal Lod... they honoured... Park ...

---

6   Not to be confused with another Tom Atkinson who later became office manager.

The launch of the *Irish Independent* in 1905 introduced a new level of competition into the Irish newspaper market. As already noted, there had been four other morning papers based in the city in close competition with each other, thus allowing *The Irish Times* to move ahead and continue, for a time, to claim that it had the highest circulation in Ireland.

William Martin Murphy is more likely to be remembered as the man who crushed the strike led eight years later by James Larkin – the notorious 1913 Lock-out. It was in 1904, having noted that three of the existing titles had been greatly weakened, that Murphy made plans to introduce his own new paper. He had long been interested in printing and had dabbled in newspapers too. When he heard that the *Irish Daily Independent* was virtually bankrupt and that the *Freeman's Journal* was considering buying it, Murphy intervened and secured the *Independent* for himself and launched his own *Irish Independent* a few months later.

While the *Irish Independent* and the struggling *Freeman's Journal* continued to battle it out for the same broad Catholic readership, *The Irish Times* continued for a time in the ascendant. But as the *Journal* weakened further, the *Independent* began to gain in strength, and soon overtook the *Times*. From the start, Murphy's declared intention was to make his paper 'first and foremost, a commercial undertaking' and a century later this might still be its motto. Fr Stephen Brown quoted Murphy's remark, adding: 'Indeed, its very essence was business. To this rather than to the popularity of its political opinions it owed its remarkable success'. Murphy directed the paper's fortunes aggressively, signalling his intent by selling it at one halfpenny, further damaging the *Journal* and then beginning to leave the *Times* far behind. A quarter of a century later saw the emergence of a new rival, the *Irish Press*, but in the meantime the *Independent* became the undisputed organ of Catholic nationalism.

The *Freeman's Journal* took two decades to expire, surviving the destruction of its Prince's Street premises in 1916, followed by a deliberate attack by anti-Treaty forces on its machinery in 1922 that proved just about the last straw. De Valera's anti-treaty party watched the *Journal's* final struggles and even considered the possibility of taking it over in order to launch its own paper, but nothing came of this. By purchasing the title and its premises for £24,000, Murphy forestalled that move, thus both ending 160 years of newspaper history and eliminating the remaining competition from that quarter – the second, but certainly not the last occasion that the *Independent* was to take this kind of preventative action. Murphy had announced in his paper's first leading article:

We believe we are right in claiming to be the first halfpenny morning paper published in Ireland and that it will contain the news of the day presented in a form which the public will appreciate as a departure from traditions of journalism which are now outworn.

According to Hugh Oram, 50,000 copies of that first issue were printed, but within a few weeks daily sales of around 25,000 were being claimed, and two years later its circulation began to exceed that of *The Irish Times*. By 1908 the circulation had advanced to around 40,000, and Murphy decided to introduce the concept of audited net daily sales, thought to have been the first paper in Ireland to do so. His pricing decision was a direct copy of what Alfred Harmsworth had done ten years earlier when he launched his *Daily Mail* in London, undercutting the opposition by selling at half the price. As Harry Greenwall wrote: 'The Harmsworth idea was to produce a penny paper for a halfpenny to give a new generation of readers of the penny newspapers the same 'advantages' that were accruing to the readers of the penny newspapers for fifty per cent less'.

In fact there is a little-known story behind Murphy's decision to adopt Harmsworth's thinking. Prior to launching the *Independent*, Murphy travelled to London to see for himself the most modern printing machinery then available, and took the opportunity to visit Alfred Harmsworth, who, eight years earlier, had launched the *Daily Mail* with astounding success. Harmsworth, who later became Lord Northcliffe, was a Dubliner, having been born at Chapelizod in 1865. Rumours of a Fenian rising prompted young Alfred's Irish mother to take her child to London, and it was there, in 1904, that the fifty-six-year-old William Martin Murphy met the thirty-nine-year-old successful proprietor of the *Daily Mail*. Murphy sounded him out about rumours that the *Daily Mail* was making plans to start publishing in Dublin. Fortunately for him, Harmsworth said he had no such plans (and, more importantly, he was telling the truth!), and thus the way was clear for Murphy to emulate Harmsworth's triumph.

Fifty years later, the *Independent* reflected on its successful launch: 'The reading public of Ireland, slow as a rule to take to any innovation, quickly recognised in the *Irish Independent* an almost entirely new departure in Irish journalism … It won respect and admiration for its scorning of sensationalism and for the honourable and impartial treatment it gave to every school of thought in Ireland'. In its centenary supplement fifty years later, John Horgan wrote about the paper's first editor, William Harrington, as a 'pioneer of what was then described as the new "tabloid" style of journalism'. Even as Horgan wrote these words in 2005, neither he nor anyone else outside the offices of the *Independent* could have been aware that plans were being hatched to launch a tabloid edition of the paper to run in tandem with the existing broadsheet edition.

Like *The Irish Times*, the *Independent* had to step adroitly – albeit somewhat less adroitly – around the changing political situation during the first quarter of the twentieth century and, along with most of the media, it condemned the Rising and called for its leaders to be punished. Both it and *The Irish Times* subsequently backed the pro-Treaty side, though not uncritically. As Horgan pointed out, the *Independent* criticised Cosgrave's government when it attempted to nationalise the railways, no doubt mindful, as he added, of its proprietor's financial involvement in several railway companies. Cosgrave was later to hit back at what he called 'one of the so-called businessmen who had been responsible for the economic disorder caused by the 1913 Lockout'.

Adopting a strong Catholic stance from the outset, and with a special appeal for rural readers, this resulted in the two remaining metropolitan morning papers, the *Independent* and the *Times*, pursuing readers in different segments of the market. If the *Independent's* market was very much the larger, the *Times* could rest easy – at least for a time – in the knowledge that its smaller market included most of the professional and business classes (the majority of whom were then Protestants) that were so vitally important for advertisers. There were well over one million Protestants in the country, of which approximately one third were living in what was soon to become the Irish Free State where the core of both papers' readership lay. Protestants were still to be found in relatively large numbers – around ten per cent of the total – in parts of Cavan, Donegal, Kildare, Monaghan and Wicklow, while numbers in some areas of Dublin – notably in Blackrock, Dalkey, Kingstown, Pembroke, Rathgar and Rathmines – the figure exceeded fifty per cent. *The Irish Times* did have a small but significant Catholic readership, part of the rising sector of Catholic professional and business class, at least some of whom, as Fintan O'Toole noted, 'formed part of the unionist constituency to which *The Irish Times* addressed itself'.[7]

Comments about *The Irish Times* at this time often referred to it as 'a Protestant paper' which it certainly was, yet the *Independent* was seldom dubbed 'a Catholic paper', even though that is precisely what it was. Stephen Brown, S.J., who made a detailed survey of Irish newspapers, may have explained why this was so when he wrote in 1937 that the Catholic press 'was Catholic without having to proclaim itself so, Catholic but not clerical'. He went on to comment on the way the situation developed during that decade:

> The two leading papers under Catholic management – the *Irish Independent* and the *Irish Press* – are rivals and vie with one another to capture the favour of the Catholic public. None of our dailies profess to be Catholic, in the sense of religious newspapers. All of them attempt to cater for the whole public, irrespective of religious affiliation. Even *The Irish Times*, which was formerly the organ of Unionism in politics and of the Protestant community, gives a good deal of Catholic news and, as a rule, avoids – at least as regards form and mode of expression – statements that would be offensive to Catholic opinion. It is much read by Catholics.

When, in 1904, the Abbey Theatre was established, the new theatrical movement was welcomed by *The Irish Times*. It continued to give its productions extensive coverage, although Fintan O'Toole thought the paper had 'a rather ambivalent relationship not just

---

[7]   In his *Irish Times Book of the Century*.

with the Abbey but with Yeats'. Nevertheless, O'Toole considered that its readership was, 'on the whole, able to identify with both the Irish literary revival and its British cultural connections'. Also in that same year the paper reported – in the stilted language originating from Buckingham Palace – the news that Trinity College, Dublin had decided to confer degrees on women:

> The following is the King's letter, authorising Trinity College to confer degrees on women:-
> Edward the Seventh, by the Grace of God, of the United Kingdom of Great Britain and
> Ireland, and of the dominions beyond the seas, King, Defender of the Faith, to all to whom
> these presents shall come, greeting.
> Whereas we are informed by the Provost and Senior Fellows of Our College of the Holy
> and Undivided Trinity, of Queen Elizabeth, near Dublin, that the Senate of the University
> of Dublin have by a large majority prayed that the degrees of the said University may be
> conferred upon women subject to the regulations and restrictions which the Provost and
> Senior Fellows of the College and of the Senate of the University may hereafter agree to
> impose …

On the same page, the paper carried a detailed report of an address given by Archbishop Walsh to a meeting at University College, Dublin on the long-running saga of 'the University Question'. He expressed (in language not very different from that which emanated from Buckingham Palace) his gratitude 'to the Jesuit Fathers for the great work that has been done by them in this place', and continued:

> We are said to be on the eve of some great reform, of something when it comes, we shall be
> justified in claiming as having brought us at last to a happy termination to the long, and as
> it seemed at times, the almost hopeless struggle in which the Catholics of Ireland have been
> engaged ever since they began to see even a distant glance of the establishment of genuine
> religious equality in Ireland. Let us, at all events for the moment, assume we are at last within
> sight of the end of all this wearisome struggling for elementary justice …
> For I know the forces that are arrayed against us, and I believe that I should have to plead
> guilty to something bordering upon presumption if I were to take any very enthusiastic view
> as to the likelihood of our witnessing, in our time, a triumph of justice over these forces that
> have so long been powerful enough to withstand its powerful onward march, a triumph
> especially over the resistance which comes from blind and unreasonable prejudice, with the
> intolerant and intolerable assumption involved in it, that if we ever are to get anything at all
> in this matter of University education, the measure of what we are to get must be, not the
> claim made out for us on the principles of right and justice, but just as much or just as little
> as the Protestant authorities of Trinity College, Dublin, and the Protestant authorities –
> Presbyterian or Episcopalian as they may be – of Queen's College, Belfast, consider may,
> consistently with their own interests, be given to us.

"THE PLAYBOY OF THE WEST."

DISTURBANCE AT THE ABBEY THEATRE.

Scenes of a most extraordinary character were witnessed at the Abbey Theatre, Dublin, last night in connection with the performance of "The Playboy of the Western World." An organised attempt had evidently been made to prevent the performance, and despite the efforts of the management and the presence of a number of police constables the interrupters succeeded in their object of preventing anybody from hearing a single word of the entire performance. The programme opened with a one-act piece by Mr. Synge, entitled "Riders to the Sea," the scene of which was a cottage on an island off the West coast of Ireland. During the course of this performance the audience was in no way turbulent, but when the curtain was raised on "The Playboy" it at once became apparent that a large section of the audience in the gallery and the back portion of the pit was determined to manifest feelings of a most hostile character. The play, which was produced for the first time on Saturday evening, has, it appears, given offence to a very large number of the Dublin community, who maintain that it is utterly untrue to life and a travesty on Irish character. The action takes place on the lonely coast of Mayo. The central incident of the piece is the glorification of a self-confessed parricide, who subsequently becomes unpopular when it is discovered that his crime is of a comparatively trivial character, and has not resulted in the death of his father. A considerable section of the audience strongly resented the notion that such a state of affairs could be taken as a correct reflex on western peasant life, and showed a determined resolve to interrupt the representation. There were, on the other hand, a great many people in the front seats who seemed to be most anxious to hear the play and judge for themselves as to its qualities; but the interrupters at the back of the theatre would hear of no attempt to ... the piece, and kept up a sust... of hissing, booing, and ... first act had been ... broke out in ... upon ...

During January 1907, performances of Synge's 'Playboy of the Western World' at the Abbey Theatre were interrupted, as the paper reported, by 'a large section of the audience in the gallery and the back portion of the pit [that] was determined to manifest its feelings of most hostile character'.

The year 1905 saw the passing into law of the Wyndham Act, the last of a series of land acts designed to deal with the worst iniquities of landlordism. While *The Irish Times* may have held a poor opinion of the land agitation that had forced the government into action, it was not a paper of or for the landlords. It was during this period that *The Irish Times* published George Russell's often quoted letter addressed 'to the Masters of Dublin'. This was a stinging commentary on the circumstances that allowed the city's notorious tenements to provide examples of some of the worst slums to be found in Europe. He was also critical of those who managed the city but who were, as he expressed it, bad citizens. As he wrote: 'we rarely if ever hear of the wealthy among you endowing the city with munificent gifts which it is the pride of merchant princes in other cities to offer. ... Those who have economic powers have civil powers also, yet you have not used the power that was yours to right what was wrong in the evil administration of this city.'

Eight years later, when Hugh Lane proposed the establishment of a municipal art gallery in Dublin, W.B. Yeats campaigned on behalf of the idea, but insufficient funding caused Lane to threaten the withdrawal of thirty-nine paintings which he proposed to donate to the new gallery. Yeats composed a poem entitled 'The Gift' and sent it to *The Irish Times* which published it. Although written against Lord Ardilaun because he had shown little enthusiasm for the gallery, the person most outraged by it was, as Roy Foster has pointed out, William Martin Murphy, the proprietor of the *Independent*. Despite the paper's readiness to publish the poet's verse and his letters to the editor, the relationship between him and the paper continued to be somewhat uneasy. Foster has also told how, during 1905, Yeats reflected on the success of twelve of his plays staged in a single season, but 'in true Dublin style *The Irish Times* tended to review them without entering the theatre, since their drama critic confessed "plays depress my spirits"'.

The year 1907 was notable for what became known as the 'Abbey Theatre Riots'. When J.M. Synge's play, *The Playboy of the Western World*, was first staged in January of that year, there were scenes of disorder for several nights occasioned by sections of the audience. Under the headline, 'MORE DISTURBANCES AT THE ABBEY THEATRE', the paper described what happened during the play's second performance, including the appeal to the audience by Yeats to give the performance a fair hearing:

> There were renewed disturbances last night in the Abbey Theatre during the performance of Mr. Synge's comedy, *The Playboy of the Western World*. In view of the disturbances that were witnessed on the previous night, unusual interest was manifested in the performance …
>
> Mr. W.B. Yeats came before the curtain and said: – 'A difference of opinion has arisen between the management of this theatre and some of our audience as to the character of the play which we are now about to produce, and as to the policy of producing it. If any of you wish to discuss with us the merit of that play or our correctness in producing it, I shall be delighted to discuss it with you, and do my best to answer your arguments. On Monday evening next I will come here to debate it with any of our audience, and I will ask you who object to it to come up on this platform and address the audience …'
>
> For a few minutes the play was listened to with comparative tranquillity, but it was clearly apparent that the interrupters were merely biding their time. A reference of one of the characters in the piece to the ministrations of 'Father O'Reilly' provoked a remark from the pit, 'What a priest-ridden fellow you are.' Hereupon some of the occupants of the stalls jumped to their feet, and hotly demanded the ejection of the interrupter. A perfect storm of groans and cheers followed, and the disorder was accentuated by a person in the stalls issuing a challenge to the house generally.
>
> Derisive cheers greeted this outburst, and both the rival factions rose and fairly glared defiance at each other. Groans, hisses and cheers were given with lusty vigour, and the din was increased by the valiant efforts of a performer on a penny trumpet, but the "music" he produced was almost completely drowned by the angry interchanges which passed between the stalls and the back portions of the pit …

Two nights later similar scenes were witnessed: 'Republican women turned out in force', and Yeats again addressed the rowdy audience. Christopher Murray, in his volume about O'Casey, wrote that 'naturally, the most authoritative version of his speech is the one published by *The Irish Times*':

'Is this', he shouted, 'going to be a recurring celebration of Irish genius? The news of the happenings of the last few minutes here will flash from country to country. Dublin has once more rocked the cradle of a reputation. From such a scene in this theatre went forth the fame of Synge. Equally, the fame of O'Casey is born here tonight. This is his apotheosis.'

The same year also saw the ending of Lockyer's editorship, and although he had held the position for only eight years, it was said of him that under his leadership, the newspaper had 'maintained its previous success'.[8]

---

[8]   *Progress of British Newspapers in the Nineteenth Century*, 1900.

John Edward Healy

1907–1934

———<>———

'Adapting to new realities'

ALMOST THREE YEARS after the launch of the *Irish Independent*, a new editor was appointed to *The Irish Times*. John Edward Healy filled the vacant editorial chair in succession to Algernon Lockyer, though neither the departure of Lockyer nor the arrival of Healy was mentioned in the paper's columns. While almost nothing is now known about his two predecessors, a few details about Healy have survived, thanks mainly to Lionel Fleming, a journalist working during Smyllie's time. John Healy had entered the Church of Ireland training college intent on becoming a clergyman, but changed his mind and, after becoming first a teacher and then a barrister, he embarked on a career in journalism instead. Described as polished in appearance with a neat moustache, he always set out for his office impeccably dressed, complete with bowler hat and walking stick, and on arrival he would exchange his hat for a skullcap. His journalists viewed him as an aloof person who almost never spoke to the junior members of his staff. Lionel Fleming, who joined the staff as a young reporter in the early 1930s, remembered that Healy addressed him as 'Mr.' in a way which 'made it clear what Smyllie and Newman (two future editors of the paper), were later parodying in their own so-constant use of that title to one another'. Fleming also recalled that Healy had certain quirky notions about editorial correctness, including his extraordinary rule that the first editorial should always comprise three paragraphs, each with twenty-two lines, while the second editorial article had to have one single paragraph of thirty-five lines! While rigid in form and outlook, and grammatically correct in every sense, Fleming considered that Healy's leaders 'set the tone for the whole paper'. Fleming also wrote: '*Laudator temporis acti* [1] is a phrase which seems to

---

[1]   One who praises past times.

me to fit him – and, indeed, a phrase that might have pleased John himself, for he was a great hand at working at least one Latin quotation into every leading article he wrote.'

Indeed, Healy did not limit himself to Latin quotations; Greek was sometimes utilised too, and he happily included, almost at the drop of a hat, references to and quotations concerning classical figures. Even when editorialising on 'The Free State Railways'[2] he could not refrain from including the following lines:

> 'Tis not in mortals to command success,
> But we'll do more, Sempronius, we'll deserve it.

Like his proprietor, Healy was a convinced Unionist and, indeed, often dined with Sir John Arnott at the family home. However, in his *Book of the Century*, Fintan O'Toole made the following point:

> The unionism of both Arnott and Healy was not that of the Protestant landlords, nostalgic for the good old days of Ascendancy rule. It was modernising, industrial and urban, anxious to see the rest of Ireland follow the lead of industrial Belfast into the twentieth century. Healy, in particular, was also sympathetic to the notion of a federalist unionism that would keep Ireland within the United Kingdom, but give it more control over local affairs. And although the Ireland of *The Irish Times* was Protestant, unionist and imperial, it was nonetheless Irish.

Lionel Fleming's opinion of Healy, that he was a man of remarkable inflexibility of mind, may be seen at least in some respects as somewhat questionable if one takes the time to read his leading articles written during and immediately after the period 1916–22. After 1922 he often termed the Free State government 'The Provisional Government', but he accepted that it *was* the one true government of Ireland, whether or not the new regime was to his liking. He was realistic enough not merely to accept it but went as far as to welcome and praise Cosgrave's infant government. This support for the new government was made much easier for the paper's editor when de Valera and his anti-Treaty group had walked out of the Dáil. As John Horgan wrote: 'A government led by W. T. Cosgrave and manned by the pro-Treaty majority was a different proposition from one which might have included de Valera himself and firebrands like Liam Mellows and Cathal Brugha … Their exclusion not only from government but – by their own action – from the Dáil itself, not only put a premium on supporting Cosgrave, but made it a more congenial task'. A newspaper supporting the Government at this time could, however, face retaliation by the anti-Treaty forces, as the *Freeman's Journal* discovered when, after

---

2   *The Irish Times*, 18 December 1932.

The 'Harlot' Speech

During 1931, the British Prime Minister, Stanley Baldwin, made a passionate speech against what he felt had been newspaper persecution, coining a phrase that was to be remembered long after the incident that had given rise to it had been forgotten. After lashing out at the methods used by certain unscrupulous newspapers – direct falsehood, misrepresentation, half truths and so on – he directly attacked the editor of the *Daily Mail*:

'I have no idea of the name of that gentleman. I would only observe that he is well qualified for the post he holds … [Concerning the statement made by him] the first part is a lie, and the second part is untrue. The paragraph can only have been written by a cad. [Although having been advised that the statement was libellous] I shall not move in the matter and for this reason: I should get an apology and heavy damages. The first is of no value and the second I would not touch with a barge-pole. What the proprietorship is aiming at is power, and power without responsibility – the prerogative of the harlot throughout the ages.'

publishing details of the inner workings of de Valera's movement, armed Republicans attacked and destroyed the paper's printing machinery.

Twenty-five years after Healy's death in the year of its centenary, the paper described him as 'one of the finest journalists ever produced by this country or any other … Under him, the paper became the organ of a fighting Conservatism – of unionism in the best sense. It can be said of the newspaper under his editorship that it fought faithfully for the retention of the Act of Union so long as there was an Act of Union to be fought for … [and thereafter] he continued to struggle for such vestiges as remained.'

A new Chief Secretary arrived in Ireland just as Healy had become editor. His name was Augustine Birrell, a man whom Healy – nine years later – was to criticise repeatedly, accusing him of utter incompetence. Even on his arrival in Dublin, he was greeted with no great enthusiasm by the paper, partly because Healy had been a critic of his predecessor:

Mr. Birrell arrived in Dublin yesterday, and will enter today upon the arduous office of Chief Secretary for Ireland. He comes among us with a handsome testimonial from his immediate predecessor who told a Liberal audience in Manchester on Saturday that Mr. Birrell's 'good sense, good humour, and conspicuous ability will enable him to understand the condition of things in Ireland.' We are quite willing to give Mr. Birrell credit for this understanding as soon as he affords us practical proof of it in his Irish administration, but we regret that we cannot regard its existence as proved by Mr. Bryce's testimony …

Part of the difficulty had arisen from what the outgoing Chief Secretary had said about recent accounts 'in this and other Unionist papers', accounts which Bryce had considered were 'grossly exaggerated'. The paper questioned the fact that just because of a single incident, 'Mr. Bryce expects the British public to be convinced of the existence of a flagitious newspaper conspiracy against the fair name of Ireland'. The article continued:

> If this is the sort of 'good sense' which Mr. Bryce attributed to Mr. Birrell we can only hope that the new Chief Secretary will begin as soon as possible to live down the unfortunate compliment with which he has been ushered into Ireland.
>
> Mr. Birrell is at least *consensus omnium*, a man of humour, and we are not without hope that this saving quality may protect him against Mr. Bryce's unhappy and dangerous theories about the condition of this country. If he has read Mr. Bryce's Manchester speech, his sense of humour ought to have informed him already that there are limits beyond which the policy of 'explaining away' becomes at once humiliating and ridiculous, and that it will be easier, as well as more dignified, to begin his career in Ireland with a resolution to find out the facts for himself.

In a special fiftieth anniversary edition published in 1909, the paper re-stated its political stance in 'supporting every national movement and all legislation that seemed likely to promote Ireland's prestige and welfare as an integral part of the United Kingdom and the British Empire'. That it had long since abandoned Knox's support for Home Rule was clear from the paper's claim that it had been 'a strong influence in directing the movement which found itself powerful enough to defeat two Home Rule Bills'. It saw the outlook for the future as very promising, and considered the Act of Union as either ideal or sacrosanct. 'We support it because it confers upon this nation a system of government which, though often far from perfect, is yet more likely to promote [Ireland's] peaceful domestic development, undisturbed by vexatious interruptions than any other which has yet been proposed'. Something of Healy's dilemma when facing up to the many changes that lay ahead is illustrated by the fact that throughout his time in the editorial chair, Gaelic terms – Sinn Féin, Dáil Éireann, Oireachtas, etc. – were always printed in italics. Almost fifty years later, *The Irish Times* wrote about how it had reported and commented upon the upheavals of that period: 'Posterity will decide how far the paper was right or wrong, prescient or short-sighted'.

When the details of the 1912 Home Rule Bill became known, Healy wrote that it was 'a thoroughly unsatisfactory compromise. It has none of the securities of the present system and none of the virtues of real self-government'. He expressed detestation of the idea of partition, and as early as 1911, when writing about the formation of the Ulster Volunteer Force, he forecast that 'two Parliaments in Ireland would perpetuate in their worst forms our unhappy differences'.

The two Irish visits of King Edward VII in the early years of the new century, and that of George V in 1911, were some kind of last hurrah for both *The Irish Times* and for the still significant remaining proportion of the population that continued to support the union. On each of these occasions the impressive street decorations, the scenes of acclamation and expressions of loyalty must have seemed, to them, reassuring. Nevertheless, the movement towards Home Rule continued its uncertain course, prompting the paper to editorialise to its own satisfaction:

> A remarkable lack of general interest in the Home Rule Bill is manifesting itself among all classes. So far as Dublin is concerned, the bill, which was heralded with so many words, has fallen like a stick from a spent rocket. Honest Nationalists, if not hostile, are lukewarm in their general approval, while Unionist businessmen openly condemn it as political trickery in which they can see no good.

Perhaps the most stunning news item during this period was that of the sinking of the ocean liner *Titanic* in April, 1912, which was reported almost with disbelief, and prompted a long leading article in the same vein:

> We cannot be surprised that the public received with something like complete incredulity the first reports yesterday morning that the giant liner was sinking off the Newfoundland banks as the result of a collision with an iceberg … The *Titanic* was appointed throughout in a way that no hotel on solid earth could hope to rival. She had suites of luxurious apartments, carried a large staff of first-class cooks, and was fitted with spacious lounges containing all kinds of costly furniture and decorations …
>
> If it be, indeed, that only 675 women and children have been saved out of the ship's immense passenger list, this is one of the supreme tragedies of the sea. The loss of the *Titanic* finally disproves the confident assertion that her system of watertight compartments made her absolutely unsinkable …

The main news published on 8 September 1913 appeared under the headline: DUBLIN LABOUR TROUBLES. This referred to the 1913 Lockout, during which, two days earlier, one man had died of injuries received, and tram services had been interrupted. The paper reported that:

> At one o'clock yesterday a big meeting was held in Sackville Street 'to assert the right of free speech'. The space between the Nelson column and the Parnell statue was filled with people who were addressed from three brakes.[3] A resolution was adopted asserting the right of free speech and trade union combination, and demanding an independent inquiry into the

---

3 Open horse-drawn carriages.

conduct of the Police. Speeches were delivered by several of the English delegates, and it was announced that a joint conference, including representatives from all the trade union organisations in Dublin would be held today with the employers.

Alongside this report there was a letter from Lady Gregory expressing disquiet about the lack of decision concerning the site for the Municipal Art Gallery and the possibility that American funding might have to be returned. Immediately above this were four verses of poetry written by W.B.Yeats, reacting to the same topic. The well-known poem was sub-headed: *On reading much of the correspondence against the Art Gallery*, the third verse of which runs:

> Was it for this the wild geese spread
> The grey wing upon every tide?
> And Robert Emmet and Wolfe Tone,
> All that delirium of the brave?
> Romantic Ireland's dead and gone –
> It's with O'Leary in the grave.

The poem was sent by Yeats to *The Irish Times* – presumably for its first publication – and was signed and dated, 'Dublin, September 7, 1913'.

Just under a year later, on 2 August 1914, the paper took the unusual step of publishing a Sunday edition to announce the outbreak of what came to be known as the Great War. Large headlines proclaimed the news: GERMANY DECLARES WAR ON RUSSIA: ULTIMATUM TO FRANCE. Most of the reports were about 'demands,' and 'mobilisations', and just one short report stated that a German patrol had been fired on by a Russian frontier guard 300 yards on the German side of the Russian frontier. In its leading article, *The Irish Times* correctly foresaw this incident as likely to 'open a new, incalculable and dreadful chapter in the history of Europe':

> All the strenuous efforts after peace have failed. The politeness of diplomatic talk is at an end. We are face to face with the certainty of war on such a scale and of a character so terrible as civilisation (if we can use the word without irony) has never yet known … Before tomorrow's issue of this newspaper is in our reader's hands fighting may have begun on the Franco-German frontier.

A few days later, with war already declared, *The Irish Times* appeared to greet the news with some kind of relief, and optimistically hoped that it would bring with it some form of longed-for unity. Unsurprisingly, it supported Redmond in his call to the Volunteers to support Britain in its struggle with Germany. At the same time, it repeatedly warned the government about 'incidents of growing militancy and of anti-British feeling,' and called on the Government to deal with what it deemed the curious and worrying complacency in Dublin Castle. Nevertheless, the paper also viewed the outbreak of the war as a rallying-point, a tremendous issue on which it hoped nationalists and unionists might unite:

The Irish Times announces the news of the outbreak of the Great War in August 1914.

We believe that the people of these kingdoms are today more cheerful than they have been at any time since the war cloud began to gather over Europe. The period of suspense and uncertainty is ended. In Ireland today the national feeling is not merely one of courage and confidence. Faced with terrible and urgent danger though we be, our hearts find room for thankfulness – even for exultation. In this hour of trial the Irish nation has 'found itself' at last. Unionist and Nationalist have ranged themselves together against the invader of their common liberties. A few weeks ago it used to be said by despairing English politicians that Ireland was two armed camps. Today she is a one armed camp, and its menace is directed against a foreign foe. Mr. Redmond's speech … gives to Southern Unionists, in particular, the boon that was hitherto denied to them – the opportunity of asserting their nationality …

We are sure that co-operation between the Ulster and Nationalist volunteer forces will now prove to be a simple and easy thing. The Nationalist army has hastened to endorse Mr. Redmond's speech. It is not only ready, but eager to unite with Ulster's army for purposes of home defence. We do not pretend that the political question of Home Rule is affected by this splendid act of union, but Sir Edward Carson and Mr. Redmond have done a noble work for Ireland. They have achieved the beginning of national reconciliation; they have opened a great door.

To assist readers trying to follow news from the war fronts, *The Irish Times*, in conjunction with G.W. Bacon Ltd, London, later published several special war maps priced at one shilling each. Commenting on the first map, the paper explained: 'Not only are the present battle fronts … very strongly marked but the furthest progress of the Allies and the Central Powers is also indicated in each case.' After two years of fighting, the news of heavy casualties on the Western Front had become almost commonplace, but even worse news then began to filter back to Ireland concerning the fate of two of the Irish Divisions in and around the infamous Somme region. At virtually the same time as the Easter Rising back in Ireland, preparations were being made to prepare the 16th and the 36th Divisions to be part of a plan to bring the war to an end by a massive strike on that front. The result was a disastrous failure, but this news was slow in coming back, as may be seen from the leading article in *The Irish Times* on July 6, 1916:

> At this moment Ulster is torn between anxiety and pride. Her 36th Division has fought splendidly, and, it is to be feared, with heavy loss. The exact locality has not been revealed … Wherever it was, the Ulstermen won immortal fame for Ulster and for Ireland. 'Their heroism and self-sacrifice', says *The* [London] *Times* 'continue to be the theme of mournful praise among their comrades in arms.' It is no secret that the 16th (Irish) Division is also within sound of the British guns between the Ancre and the Somme. Here surely, is an inspiring thought for Ireland. At home we are once more torn by political contentions. The blood of Irishmen shed by Irishmen is hardly dry upon the streets of Dublin … It is our firm belief that there need be no partition if our fighting men are given that voice in Irish affairs to which, more than any other body of Irishmen, they are entitled.

Although the First World War was a cataclysmic event for thousands of Irish families, (and for almost the whole of Europe and much of the rest of the world too), it hardly featured at all in official Irish history for more than half a century afterwards. The events in Dublin during the six days of 24–29 April 1916 saw to that. But it is equally true that the huge part played by Irishmen in the British forces at that time has been virtually ignored in Britain, while in Northern Ireland the heavy losses sustained by the Ulster division – but not those suffered by the other two Irish divisions – are still vividly recalled. Decades later, in the paper's special supplement on the Rising, Henry Harris was to write about the significant input of the Irish regiments in that war: 'By 1916, the number of Irishmen in the British Army was greater than the sum of all armies Britain had sent to the continent since the days of Elizabeth I. The Inniskilling battalion alone equalled half the numbers of Marlborough's total infantry; the Royal Irish Rifles totalled nearly as many men as Wellington had assembled at Waterloo.'

Back in Ireland, the British forces were taken totally by surprise by the events of Easter Monday, 1916. Utter confusion reigned. *The Irish Times*, that had written only six years earlier about 'vexatious interruptions', now had to report on the real thing, although a combination of censorship and the dangers posed by attempting to view what was happening resulted in very restricted reporting by the newspapers. The paper admitted that it had been unable to provide proper coverage, in the absence of which, wild rumours circulated. On the day after the commencement of the Rising, the main leading article began thus:

Latin Tags

The once popular usage of Latin tags in editorials, etc., has now largely died out. Hugh Cudlipp rather over-did it when he wrote the following: 'In an age which is neither an age of faith nor an age of reason, most men seem to live on the day-to-day treadmill of impulse: *Ad maiorem Dei gloriam* and the *suprema ratio rerum* alike give way to the sovereignty of *ad hoc.* Yesterday's belief is as obsolete as yesterday's newspaper.'

This newspaper has never been published in stranger circumstances than those which obtain today. An attempt has been made to overthrow the constitutional government of Ireland. It began yesterday morning in Dublin – at present we can speak for no other part of Ireland, for there has been an abrupt stoppage of all means of external communication. At this critical moment, language must be moderate, unsensational, and free from any tendency to alarm. As soon as peace and order have been restored the responsibility for this intended revolution will be fixed in the right quarter. The question whether it could have been averted will be discussed and will be answered on the ample evidence which the events of the last few months afford. Today we can only deal with to-day's and yesterday's facts. During the last twenty-four hours an effort has been made to set up an independent Irish Republic in Dublin. It was well organised; a large number of armed men are taking part in it, and to the general public, at any rate, the outbreak came as a complete surprise… Of course this desperate episode in Irish history can have only one end, and the loyal public will await it as calmly and confidently as may be …

The paper reminded its readers that it had, on several occasions, drawn the attention to the illegal drilling and militaristic manoeuvres which, while being carried out openly, had been ignored by the authorities. As will be seen, the paper was later to be especially critical of Birrell, the Chief Secretary, in this respect. The article ended with the prediction that 'the ordeal is severe, but it will be short'.

Although all the paper's editions were printed as usual that morning, it was not possible for them to be distributed. This was not explained to its readers until almost two weeks later when the following announcement was published:

THE IRISH TIMES
TUESDAY 25th APRIL, 1916

Owing to the disturbed state of the city on the above date, we were requested to delay the issue to the public of that day's paper when it had been already printed. The paper contains the details of the outbreak of the Sinn Fein rebellion on the previous day (Easter Monday). We can now offer a limited number of these papers for sale. The issue will form an interesting souvenir of the Irish insurrection of 1916.

Several commentators have remarked that the paper devoted more space to the Dublin Spring Show and to the war in Europe than to the rebellion, but this was hardly surprising when the imposition of martial law and censorship made it impossible to report in any detail what was happening. There was a premium on the London-based newspapers that continued to be sold in Dublin despite the fact that they were not subject to the censor's pen. Whatever about this advantage, the English press often got things wrong. For example, the *Daily Mail*, with a circulation of over two million, reported that 'Countess Markievicz has been helping the rebels and has been wounded', and on the same day it also incorrectly reported that her husband, while fighting on the Russian front, 'has lost an arm.'

Situated close to the General Post Office, both the *Irish Independent* and the *Freeman's Journal*, along with the *Daily Express*, near the City Hall, were unable to publish for several days. The main premises of *The Irish Times* escaped damage, but the company was unable to prevent the insurgents from entering its auxiliary printing office in Lower Abbey Street from which they rolled out large reels of newsprint to strengthen their barricades. This hardly mattered by the end of the week, because the entire premises and those around it were utterly destroyed in the huge fires that swept down the street.

The paper's coverage of events sometimes included amusing news items. Readers may already know something of Constance Markievicz's unlikely claim that, at St Stephen's Green, she had made an arrangement whereby each day at noon during Easter Week, a temporary truce took place to allow the ducks in the park's pond to be fed.[4] However, *The Irish Times* did report that 'Mr. Kearney, the Superintendent of the park … went about his duties as usual … The fact that his domain was frequently swept by bullets did not upset him. At regular intervals, no matter how fierce the fusillade, he always fed the ducks on the pond, and they, too, seemed equally unconcerned with the strange and exciting tumult in the park'.

Despite the imposition of censorship, *The Irish Times* not only welcomed the introduction of martial law but was later to plead for its retention. On the day the announcement was made, the paper stated that 'plain as are the Regulations to be observed under Martial Law, which we print today, we think it well to impress the necessity of a rigid observance of them on the civil population of Dublin. The censorship will permit us perhaps to say we live in times that demand that we walk with more than customary wariness …' No papers at all could be published that week on Friday or Saturday, and the next issue of *The Irish Times* (comprising only four pages) appeared on the following Monday with this notice:

---

4   See the author's volume on the Gore-Booth family.

TO-DAY'S IRISH TIMES

To-day's issue of the 'Irish Times' carries the dates Friday, April 28th, Saturday, April 29th and Monday, May 1st. The 'Irish Times' was printed daily during the insurrection until Thursday. On Friday and Saturday, although members of all staffs were in attendance, the conditions in the Trinity College – Sackville Street area made publication impossible. To-day's issue includes the news of several days, and bears the three dates for the convenience of persons and institutions that file the 'Irish Times' for reference.

This issue also carried news and comment about the ending of the Rising under large headlines: COLLAPSE OF SINN FEIN RISING, INSURGENTS SURRENDER IN LARGE BODIES and SUDDEN ORDER TO CEASE FIRE:

On Saturday, P.H. Pearse, one of the seven leaders, surrendered unconditionally with the main body of the rebels. Yesterday other bodies came in dejectedly under the white flag. Of the buildings which were seized a week ago not one remains in rebel hands. The General Post Office, save for its noble portico, is a ruin. The premises of the Royal College of Surgeons and Jacobs' factory were evacuated yesterday … It is believed that most of the ringleaders are dead or captured … So ends the criminal adventure of the men who declared that they were 'striking in full confidence of victory', and told their dupes that they would be 'supported by gallant allies in Europe'. The Dublin insurrection of 1916 will pass into history with the equally unsuccessful insurrections of the past. It will only have this distinction – that it was more daringly and systematically planned, and more recklessly invoked than any of its predecessors.

The leading article of the day described the events of the week as 'a record of crime, horror, and destruction, shot with many gleams of the highest valour and devotion'. It then added: 'We do not deny a certain desperate courage to many of the wretched men who to-day are in their graves or awaiting sentence of their country's laws'. To this it added that 'the first tribute must be paid to the gallant soldiers who were poured into Dublin, including at least two battalions of famous Irish regiments'. The paper insisted that

this outbreak, and all its deplorable consequences could have been averted. For the last year all Irishmen have known that the danger existed, and that it was coming surely and steadily to a head. Urgent and repeated warnings were given to the Government. They were neglected. The men who neglected them have accepted one of the gravest responsibilities in history. They will be called to account at the bar of public opinion – it must come soon – they will have to make their defence against a vast accumulation of damning evidence.

The crime has been committed; the explosion has occurred; and we have gained at least one advantage. We now know beyond yea or nay, the extent, the power, the motives of the seditious movement in Ireland. All the elements of disaffection have shown their hand. The

State has struck, but its work is not yet finished. The surgeon's knife has been put to the corruption in the body of Ireland, and its course must not be stayed until the whole malignant growth has been removed. In the verdict of history weakness today would be even more criminal than the indifference of the last few months. Sedition must be rooted out of Ireland once and for all ... The loyal people of Ireland, Unionists and Nationalists, call to-day with an imperious voice for the strength and firmness which have so long been strangers to the conduct of Irish affairs.

This reference to the surgeon's knife (as well as the use of the words 'punishment' and 'stern justice' in several other of the paper's leading articles), has sometimes been interpreted as a call for more executions. Healy used words carefully and did not specifically call for executions, despite some subsequent assertions to the contrary, but given its background such a demand was exactly what was expected of *The Irish Times* from several quarters. On 3 May, the paper stated that 'the country has no desire that punishment should be pushed to the point of mere revenge, but in the interests of safety, it demands that stern justice shall be inflicted upon the authors of one of the most far-reaching crimes in Irish history'. Among those who – without evidence – blamed the paper for the executions was P.S. O'Hegarty, a member of the Supreme Council of the IRB (the Irish Republican Brotherhood) who claimed that 'the army and *The Irish Times* demanded blood and they got it'.

Curiously enough, the paper's reaction to events was not dissimilar to those of the other Dublin-based papers excepting, perhaps, the *Freeman's Journal.* It stated, on the day after the last executions took place, that 'a fatal mistake has been made with these hurried trials and immediate executions' and, unlike *The Irish Times*, called for an end to martial law – which it termed a 'Military Dictatorship'. It also drew comparisons with what happened after previous rebellions: 'The fact is that the secret trials, military sentences and executions that have followed the Insurrection would never before have been legal even in Ireland at any period. Robert Emmet and his comrades were tried and condemned by judge and jury. So was William Smith O'Brien. So were the insurgents of 1867 ...'

The Dublin *Daily Express* took a more hard-line view, specifically about the trials. Referring to 'a talk of pardon' it asked its readers: 'Pardon for whom? For the misguided men who plotted and planned to set authority at defiance in an attempt to establish an "Irish Republic?" There can be no pardon for such as these ... We do not suggest that punishment should be meted out in a spirit of revenge, but simply as a stern measure of justice and as a drastic deterrent to all forms of sedition.' Here again, the word used was 'punishment,' not 'execution.' Commenting on 'the deplorable events of the past week', the *Evening Mail* stated: 'We publish elsewhere the official announcement as to the fate of some of the rebel leaders who have been tried for their crimes; and have paid the penalty with their lives. Surely they could have anticipated no other fate'.

Most of these newspaper reactions were relatively mild in comparison with what the *Irish Independent* had to say. Having suggested leniency for those involved in 'only minor parts' during the rebellion, it is not difficult to discern the hand of its proprietor, William Martin Murphy – the personification of big business and the strict employers at the time – in his paper's next statement. 'When, however, we come to some of the ringleaders, instigators and fomenters not yet dealt with, we must make an exception.' Murphy would not have forgotten Connolly's part in leading the resistance during the 1913 Lock-out, nor would he have been unaware of the fact that Connolly was now in a prison cell awaiting his fate. This scenario may well have influenced the wording that followed in the *Independent's* editorial but, like the other papers, it too held back from using the word 'executions': 'Let the worst of the ringleaders be singled out and dealt with as they deserve'. Of course it is unlikely that the military officers presiding at the courts martial required prompting from any newspaper. The badly injured Connolly, sitting on a chair, was shot two days later. When that happened, *The Irish Times* stated: 'We hope sincerely that no further executions may be found necessary, though we hope also that no convicted murderer will escape the penalty of his crime.'

For its part, *The Irish Times* seemed to be engaged in a concerted campaign to have the Chief Secretary, Augustine Birrell, sacked. Its opinion was quite widely shared because many people took this view when it became generally known that both the Chief and the Under Secretary were out of the country when the uprising took place. As Foy and Barton wrote, this was seen 'to epitomise a regime riddled with incompetence and ignorance'. Because the paper had already criticised Birrell for spending too much time out of Ireland, it must have given Healy some satisfaction when he was enabled to include the following in a report on the proceedings in the House of Commons:

SIR JOHN LONSDALE – Has the right hon. gentleman any statement to make with regard to Ireland?

MR. BIRRELL – I think my right hon. friend, the Prime Minister, will do so.

SIR FREDERICK BANBURY – May I ask whether we are to understand from the Chief Secretary's statement that he is going to Dublin?

MR. BIRRELL – If I can make arrangements.

MR. ASHLEY – Will the right hon. gentleman say why he ever left Ireland?

MR. BIRRELL – I do not think the Chief Secretary is always pinioned in Ireland, as far as I know.

Shortly after this, Birrell, who had been under enormous pressure to do so, tendered his resignation, admitting to Parliament that he had underestimated the Sinn Féin movement. Healy felt that his frequent criticisms concerning the Chief Secretary had now been more than justified:[5]

---

5   *The Irish Times*, 5 May 1916.

Mr. Birrell's resignation of the Chief Secretaryship, like so many acts of the present Government, has come too late. It is a public blessing but it has been purchased at a terrible cost to Ireland … Within the last few months the steady preparations for an armed uprising in Ireland have been visible to the naked eye … Mr. Birrell, the Government, and the British public received a thousand warnings. Mr. Birrell and the Government took no notice of them … and now the expected has happened. The monument to Mr. Birrell's Chief Secretaryship is a stricken city, a heavy toll of loyal and innocent life, and the disgrace and ruin of thousands of wretched young Irishmen whom a firm Irish Government would have protected from their own folly. …

We shall gladly barter all Mr. Birrell's brilliancy for a firm hand in Dublin Castle. We cannot afford another insurrection in Ireland. On Wednesday the Prime Minister, Mr. Birrell, Sir Edward Carson and Mr. Redmond all urged that no needless severity should be shown in stamping out the embers of the recent outbreak. The whole of Ireland will endorse this sentiment. As Sir Edward Carson said, this is no occasion for vengeance … By all means, let justice be tempered with mercy. But the leaders of the insurrection must be made incapable of further mischief. The conditions which made it possible must never be permitted to recur.

Part of Birrell's defence had been that he was anxious (as Brian Barton has pointed out) 'to contain, and not provoke, Irish extremists'. Birrell had taken the view that if some pre-emptive move had been made against what he assumed was the rump of the Irish Volunteers – that section which did not follow Redmond – it might have caused unknown problems. Healy, for his part, did not allude to any of the Chief Secretary's difficulties, so that his editorial comments were all the more sharp and bitter:

Mr. Birrell is witty, eloquent and learned. He would have been admirable as a professor in one of those ancient universities where scholarship is not inconsistent with indolence. Unfortunately he was sent here, not to teach literature, but to rule Ireland. The task required strength, watchfulness and industry, and he was wholly unfitted for it. He governed without open discredit for so long as no difficulty arose which his permanent officials could not solve, but his very weakness soon created difficulties that could only be met by the wisest, strongest statesmanship. The disaffected elements in Ireland discovered quickly that there was no guiding hand at Dublin Castle. They began to plot the downfall of the British rule in earnest, and, when Mr. Birrell treated the menace as a jest, their confidence and audacity increased.

Birrell's resignation was quickly followed by that of the Under Secretary, Sir Matthew Nathan, and then by the Lord Lieutenant, Lord Wimbourne. *The Irish Times* commented on the latter:

The Government of which he was titular head failed to meet a swarm of difficulties many of them created by itself … and it was not to be thought that when Mr. Birrell and Sir Matthew Nathan had fallen, Lord Wimbourne could escape … We submit that at least two qualifications should be regarded as indispensable in the new Viceroy. In the first place, he ought to be an Irishman. The members of the late government were not Irishmen … An Irish Viceroy would never have allowed the recent insurrection to come to a head. In the next place, the new Lord Lieutenant ought to be a soldier.

Such a person, the paper thought, having presided over the transition from martial law to civil law, 'would be able to transmit the spirit of military administration to the civil instruments of the State'. However, at a time when emotions were extremely taut it continued to be important that reactions should be tempered with moderation. Healy must have been stung when the *Freeman's Journal* made accusations about his editorial call for dealing with the leaders of the Rising to be punished – not least because the *Journal* had used the same word. He responded[6] by drawing attention to the fact that:

Ten days before the outbreak, [the *Freeman's Journal*] was still exhorting its readers to ignore the coming danger … It said that the seditious movement was making no headway in Ireland. 'Our Sinn Feiners' it declared, 'are not half so numerous as the conscientious objectors in Great Britain.' It needs some little hardihood to resume dogmatism after so recent and so disastrous an experiment in prophecy … The *Freeman* is equally in error today, though with less excuse. Confronted, amid the ruins of Prince's Street [where its badly damaged premises were situated] with the fruits of its timidity and nervelessness, it is timid and nerveless still.

On 6 May, the paper reported the Prime Minister's comments about General Maxwell. As General Officer Commanding in Ireland, he had been instructed by the Government to quash the rebellion, and sanctioned to inflict 'the extreme penalty as sparingly as possible, and only in the cases of responsible persons who were guilty in the first degree'. It was Maxwell's interpretation of this instruction that caused so much controversy.

The Prime Minister's statement to the House of Commons concerning casualties was reported on 10 May. The figures given were as follows: Military, 124 killed and 388 wounded; R.I.C., thirteen killed and twenty-four wounded; D.M.P., three killed and three wounded. The then estimate of casualties among the insurgents was sixty-five killed but no figure for wounded was stated, nor was any figure given for the number of civilians killed, although that figure was reckoned a day or two later at around 140. The paper reported on the structural damage done to the city centre, and it commented upon the state of the Four Courts and its contents. The damage to the Record Office was relatively

6   *The Irish Times*, 6 May 1916.

The caption for this photograph read: 'Business as usual. A news-vendor resumes business among the ruins'. Taken just after the ending of the 1916 Rising, the lone figure is seen standing on the corner of Henry Street beside the badly damaged General Post Office.

slight, and its comments upon this situation contrast strongly with what it had to say about the same building just six years later:

> At the Four Courts, the officials are 'taking stock' of the records, and so far as the examination has gone remarkably few documents are reported missing. Much anxiety was felt as to the safety of the valuable papers, etc., in the Record Office, and it is reassuring to be able to state on the best authority that the contents of that office have suffered little injury. No important records are known to be missing, but several bundles of papers have been removed in a crumpled and crushed state. Many of the windows were smashed and every locked receptacle was broken open. A few baskets of Wills more than twenty years old, were carried out by the rebels to assist in fortifying outposts, and some of the contents of these baskets have been recovered as far away as Greek Street, at the rear of the building.

Under the headline SIR JOHN MAXWELL AND THE CLERGY, the paper published the text of a letter written to the Catholic Archbishop of Dublin, as well as Dr Walsh's reply. Maxwell had thanked the Archbishop for the services rendered by his clergy during the rebellion and was anxious to receive the names of those clergy known to him who had been involved in 'special gallantry.' Dr Walsh replied:

Dear Sir John Maxwell,

In reply to your letter of Monday, I beg to thank you for the gratifying testimony to the fidelity of our clergy in the discharge of their duties during the recent troubles in Dublin.

I have been much struck by your request to be furnished with the names of clergy in special gallantry and devotion that I might bring to your notice. But I quite concur with your view that services desiring high praise are practically universal. Many such cases have, of course, come to my knowledge … but I feel that it would be invidious to treat their cases as if they were exceptional.

Again thanking you for your kindly letter, I remain your faithful servant,

William J. Walsh,

Archbishop of Dublin.

On the same day, *The Irish Times* published an advertisement inserted by its competitor, the *Freeman's Journal*, requesting its agents and subscribers to send in fresh orders 'as owing to the complete destruction of our premises and books [this information] will not be accessible for some time'. As noted earlier, there was 'no love lost' between the two rival newspapers, but this was an early example of how newspapers quickly overlooked old animosities when a serious problem had struck one of their number. All the newspapers at the time were carrying advertisements inserted by business houses announcing details about alternative or re-opened premises.

When *The Irish Times* published a special supplement during March 2006, in connection with the ninetieth anniversary of the Rising, the introduction commenced with the following words:

When we talk of the Easter Rising, as we will do in this 90th anniversary year and even more so on the 100th anniversary in 2016, we are talking about two quite distinct things. One of them is, in the simplest sense, a myth. It is a story to which great significance has been added by the meanings that people wish to read into it. This Easter Rising is, depending on one's point of view, the founding act of a democratic Irish State, a historic act of treachery, a mandate for any un-elected group to take up arms in the name of the Irish Republic, a supreme expression of unselfish idealism. It is bitterly contested, both by those who wish to lay claim to its legacy and by those who abhor it …

John Edward Healy had been faced with the unenviable task of steering *The Irish Times* through this difficult period as well as the half-dozen or more years that followed. For part of that fateful week he had virtually the entire field to himself as the editor of the only newspaper in the city in a position to continue publishing for all but a few days. The trade magazine, *Newspaper World*, subsequently paid tribute to Healy and the staff of the paper for its coverage 'of the memorable week when the continuing rifle and Maxim gunfire in the Westmoreland Street area made it impossible to venture around. Members of the several departments in the office were in attendance on each day but the paper was not published on the Friday and Saturday'. A special edition of *The Weekly Irish Times* was published on Saturday, 29 April to provide a very detailed overall view of the events. This was later followed by an even more comprehensive publication of 250 pages entitled *The Sinn Fein Rebellion Handbook*, still widely regarded as an important source book.

Arguments about who made the correct political decision during the years 1914-16 will almost certainly never be resolved. Was Redmond right to support Britain in return for a promised Home Rule, or did Pearse make the correct decision to challenge Britain in armed rebellion? As already briefly mentioned, a third person holding a different view stood in the wings but has since been all but forgotten – George Russell, who saw himself as an authority on a future Irish settlement. His aim for a form of Dominion Home Rule found no support from either Sinn Féin or from the parliamentary nationalists. He had set out his thinking in an extraordinary series of lengthy articles published by *The Irish Times*.[7] The paper made a point of informing its readers that it took no responsibility for Russell's views, but Healy's decision to publish them in three consecutive issues reflected great credit on the editor and his newspaper. Shortly afterwards, Russell reprinted his *Thoughts for a Convention* in pamphlet format, arguing for Home Rule while remaining a British Dominion. The range and depth of Russell's *Thoughts* was quite remarkable, as were some of his predictions:

> I now turn to Ulster and ask if the unstable condition of things in Ireland does not affect it even more than Great Britain. If it persists in its present attitude, if it remains out of a self-governing Ireland, it will not thereby exempt itself from political, social and economic trouble … Everything that happens in one quarter will be distorted in the other. Each will lie about the other. The materials will exist more than before for civil commotion, and this will be aided by the powerful minority in the excluded counties, working in conjunction with their allies across the border.

The Irish Times welcomed the Home Rule Convention called by Gladstone in 1917, and expressed anxiety at the many delays and about the composition of its participants, agreeing that 'a body of well selected Irishmen will be better fitted for the task than any body of Englishmen'. It predicted, ominously, that 'it would be folly to have any confidence in success'. The Convention finally got under way in an attempt to bridge the gap between Sinn Féin and the Ulster Unionists, but the task proved impossible, causing Russell to predict that he could 'hear the whistle of bullets in the street [and see] the gutters filled with blood'. Horace Plunkett, who had supported Russell (and may have

---

[7]   Published on 7, 8 and 9 October 1913. In a chapter contributed to Boyce and O'Day's volume on *Ireland in Transition*, Nicholas Allen suggested that Russell's choice of *The Irish Times* seemed 'at first an odd one', but he added that Russell 'was popularly understood to be a fair analyst of his opponents, a quality that may have commended him to *The Irish Times*'.

used his influence to persuade Healy to publish Russell's detailed essays), subsequently acknowledged that the southern Unionists 'would have accepted their proposals had Ulster come in'.

Meanwhile, the European War continued its four-year course with catastrophic casualties on all sides. Just one month before it ended, a German submarine torpedoed the mail boat, *Leinster*, which sank with the loss of almost 600 lives shortly after departing for Holyhead. On 12 October, the paper commented:

> When such calamities happen, the first estimates of loss are often exaggerated. In this case, unhappily, they prove to have fallen short of the dreadful truth. The official figures are given in the Lord Lieutenant's telegram to the King. The *Leinster's* full complement of passengers and crew on her last voyage was 780 men, women and children. Of these, 193 have been saved and 587 are dead. Germany's latest crime has been one of her greatest, but all the aspects of this Irish tragedy are not wholly dark … In his message to the Irish public, Lord French pays tribute to the gallantry of the rescuing craft, and to the courage and unselfishness of all who faced – and in most cases met – death on the doomed ship. The country will endorse most heartily his praise of the conduct of the Irish mail packet service during the four years of war. Captain Birch died exactly as we had known that every man in the service, from the highest to the meanest, would be ready to die. Lord French reminds us that the crew of the *Leinster*, and those brave postal workers who died in one awful blast, have fallen as gloriously in the great cause as any sailor or soldier in the war. The manner of their end honours Ireland, and Ireland owes to their memory, and to the needs of those who depended on them, a debt which must be paid in full …

Exactly one month later, on 12 November, 1918, *The Irish Times'* main leading article, headed 'Laus Deo', expressed relief that the so-called 'war to end all wars' had ended. Indeed, the paper not only did not use the term, but actually stated that 'no student of history will dare to say that war is ended for ever':

> Yesterday morning, Germany accepted Marshall Foch's terms of armistice, and before noon the last gun had been fired on the western front. The agonies of four years and three months are finished, the war has been ended on conditions which guarantee, as Mr. Asquith said yesterday, that it cannot be resumed …
>
> Among crowds rejoicing in our cities yesterday were many to whom the flags and shouting must have brought a renewed and poignant sense of bereavement. Their dearest lie in France or Gallipoli or under the North Sea, and they may have been tempted to ask is victory worth the price? … To them and to those who mourn them, our debt is eternal and unpayable. Of one thing, however, we can be certain. The Allies' aims in entering the war have been wholly fulfilled and an intolerable menace to the world's freedom and peace has vanished into thin air.

The sense of peace in Ireland was short-lived. The War of Independence soon put an end to that, with dozens of daily shootings and as many reports of reprisals filling the columns of the paper. On 20 August 1920, it reported the shooting dead of an RUC district inspector at Lisburn:

> Telegraphing from Lisburn last night, our correspondent says:- Today, shortly after one o'clock, District Inspector Oswald Ross Swanzy, Royal Ulster Constabulary, was shot dead on the public street in Lisburn when returning from worship in Christ Church Cathedral. The foul deed was witnessed by a large number of the congregation. As Mr. Swanzy was turning the corner near the Northern Bank, three men suddenly dashed forward and fired three shots at him. The District Inspector fell, and three more bullets were fired into him as he was lying on the ground.

Every year afterwards, until the fifties, his family inserted a notice in the 'Roll of Honour' column of *The Irish Times*, a column introduced during the Great War where memorial notices of Irish servicemen killed in the conflict could be inserted by relatives on the anniversary of their deaths. With the passing of time, the number of such announcements diminished and these notices subsequently appeared under the more general heading 'In Memoriam'.

The aftermath of the Great War, the Rising, the War of Independence and the Civil War resulted in huge problems for *The Irish Times*. It described the opening of the Dáil in August 1921 as a 'hollow farce'. The event did, however, present the paper with an opportunity 'to meet Sinn Féin in the flesh and to see [for itself] the men whose names have become household words throughout the country, and around whose figures popular legend has woven a web of almost mediaeval romance'. The report continued:

> Shortly after the scheduled hour, the crowd sprang to its feet, and the tall figure of Mr. de Valera could be seen striding through an avenue of clapping hands and agitated bodies. He was followed by his colleagues of the Sinn Féin ministry in Indian file, and Michael Collins' name was the signal for an outburst of applause, which, however, was silenced quickly by the volunteer stewards. Mr. Collins' appearance upset all the preconceived ideas of one who had known him only through the newspapers. He is tall with a slight leaning towards *embonpoint*, and, with a great mass of jet-black hair, gave one an impression of an almost Falstaffian geniality. Unless his looks belie him, Mr. Collins has a good sense of humour …
>
> When Mr. de Valera got up to speak everybody held his breath. What was he going to say? His first few sentences were terse and to the point, and one was impressed by the excellency of his delivery. 'We are not Republican doctrinaires', he exclaimed, and a flash of hope lit up the atmosphere. But it soon disappeared. Speaking with great emphasis and obvious sincerity, Mr. de Valera soared into the realms of pure theory and lofty idealism. One felt that, like

Yeats's poet, he was hiding his head amid a crowd of stars; and reality began to dissolve in the quickening flow of his eloquence. One's thoughts were carried back to the frosty January morning in the clock room of the French Foreign Office when President Wilson was making his famous speech at the opening of the Paris Peace Conference. One had the same impression of moral fervour and passionate sincerity and the same unwelcome conviction that disillusionment lay in store. As a shrewd observer of human affairs remarked on that occasion when the American President resumed his seat, '*C'est magnifique*; but it is not hard tacks'.

The paper's reference to Michael Collins's appearance and to his sense of humour were, to be followed one year later (almost exactly to the day) on August 21, 1922, by an announcement regretting his death. The paper wrote of the killing of General Michael Collins, Commander-in-Chief of the National Army, fatally wounded during the Civil War in an ambush by anti-Treaty forces as he drove through north Cork to visit his mother:

> His death is a disaster for Ireland. Irishmen the world over will mourn him … That he should have met his tragic end at Irish hands is the darkest feature of this national calamity … Like his friend and teacher, Arthur Griffith, General Collins was a firm believer in the destiny of the Irish people and its fulfilment through the medium of the London Treaty …

Sparked off by strong disagreements over the terms of the Treaty secured in London, the Civil War was, if anything worse than all the horrific events that had gone before. Collins was only one of many who died in this conflict that pitted Irishmen against Irishmen. Another death, that of Erskine Childers was, as Fintan O'Toole expressed it, particularly poignant for *The Irish Times*

> because it summed up the tormented passage from empire to independence that the country as a whole, and indeed, the paper itself, had followed since the beginning of the century. Executed as a Republican die-hard in November 1922, Childers had begun the century as an English imperialist and had supported many of the same causes as *The Irish Times*. In an editorial on his death, the paper noted that he had 'fought against the tyranny of the Boers', and that 'many years ago, in a brilliant book [*The Riddle of the Sands*], he foretold the German attack on the liberties of Europe, and when his vision was fulfilled, he defended those liberties on sea and in the air'. Even now, while supporting his execution as a grim necessity, the paper could not deny Childers the praise due to 'an idealist, a thinker of high thoughts, and a brave man'. Faced with the cruel blighting of the hopes which the century had begun, the paper could only ask, 'What is the mysterious difference which sometimes, in ardent minds, perverts the ideals of freedom from a blessing into a curse?' It was a question to which the previous decade of almost universal violence had supplied no answer and which would be asked again in the coming times.

Another casualty of the Civil War, albeit in a different category, was the total loss of the irreplaceable contents stored in the Public Record Office. J.J. Lee took the view that the decision of O'Connor, Mellows, Traynor and Brugha, the anti-treaty leaders involved, to coop themselves up in the Four Courts building was tactically inept. But even leaving that charge aside, it was surely a gross act of mindless carelessness to use this building as a defensive fortress, thus putting at risk its precious contents – irreplaceable records of seven hundred years of Irish history. The destruction of the building and its contents drew this comment from *The Irish Times*:

> If there is an Elysian field for beautiful buildings, Dublin's General Post Office, her Custom House, and her Four Courts will keep sad company there. The destruction of the Four Courts is at once the heaviest and most tragic of these losses. Last week, the [Four] Courts were a monument to the taste and ambition of eighteenth-century Irishmen. Today their blackened ruins are a monument to the selfish folly of a small minority of a later generation. The explosion which destroyed our great treasury of legal and public documents has torn whole chapters out of Irish history and has involved some of the country's most important business in costly confusion. The full responsibility lies, of course, with the men who offered a reckless defiance to the authority of the Irish Government and the will of the Irish people.

The Civil War period was a very difficult one for all the newspapers. Most of them, one way or another, had to face threats from the Republicans or directives from the Government, each anxious that its side would be accorded advantageous reportage. One of the early signs that *The Irish Times* was trying to adjust to the newly-emerging political circumstances was demonstrated in an editorial that commented: 'For the first time in our history a Government using force to put down an insurrection has had the overwhelming support of the common people'.

Because Republican threats were mostly made in rural areas where sales of *The Irish Times* were weakest, it was less affected in this respect than the other titles. Although the *Freeman's Journal* had made a remarkably quick recovery after suffering considerable damage during the Rising, it was deliberately attacked by armed Republican forces during the Civil War and, as Professor Lee wrote, 'they showed their respect for freedom of the press by destroying the paper's printing machinery'. Incredibly, it actually managed to get going again but, sorely weakened, it was finally killed off by competition from the by now powerful *Irish Independent*. *The Irish Times* was to comment in its centenary supplement on the manner of its own coverage of the events of Easter Week and the period that followed:

> There is no occasion to manufacture excuses for *The Irish Times's* attitude towards the Rising in 1916. The paper represented not merely Unionist opinion, but official Nationalist opinion

as well; it was only afterwards that the Nationalist Party changed its outlook – in concert, certainly, with a growing proportion of the people. It continued to preach the cause of moderation on all sides. All the time, it strove to avert the terrible tests of strength which it foresaw as almost inevitable, and which became real in 1919. It refused to believe that the appeal to physical force could not be postponed by wise statesmanship … Its hopes began to languish with the failure of the Irish Convention of 1917, and died as the temper of the country rose.

The article cited Healy's positive attempts at reconciliation, 'both as Editor of *The Irish Times* and as London Correspondent of *The Times*, along with Sir Horace Plunkett and a representative of *The Times* newspaper whose identity has never been revealed'. These attempts at reconciling Irish aspirations with the realities of traditional unionism came to nothing. The article also made the point that during the 'Black and Tan' War, Healy refused to accept a guard over his own house or at *The Irish Times* and, summing up, concluded: 'Probably no journalist in the history of this century had so much excuse for weariness. It must not be forgotten that he had lived through all the strains of two civil wars, as well as that of a great one.'

It is certainly true that the turn of political events was not to his personal liking, and it cannot be denied that, at least in certain respects, he was slow to adapt the paper to the new circumstances. However, at a time when most of his readers shared his view, he had to be careful not to antagonise them, and so found himself walking something of a political tightrope. In his favour, it must be said that he did accept the Treaty when it came, and he did continue to support it during the Civil War. He also accepted the newly-elected Government as the true Government of Ireland and he went on to praise the workings of the new Dáil. Furthermore, he correctly identified some of the problems likely to arise in the event of partition. When partition became a reality, he noted that, in the meantime, 'it gave the six counties of Ulster their recognition as an independent unit, which had to be consulted, and could only be united with the rest of Ireland by persuasion and of its own free will'. That was more than eighty years ago, but it has taken almost as long for Healy's sentiment to become widely accepted. The other side to his character showed when he warmly applauded the clause in the draft Constitution which was to make the Oath of Allegiance compulsory on members of the Dáil.

Writing in his *Book of the Century* about the post-Independence period, Fintan O'Toole commented on the editor's references to partition and to the North generally:

Once the Union was gone, the ideal of the editor, John Healy, was 'a united, liberal-minded prosperous Ireland, an enthusiastic member of the Commonwealth, cherishing its links with Great Britain and the Empire'. But he also warned in his editorials that the only way to 'achieve unity was through peaceful co-operation, and cautioned that a policy compounded of 'half overture and half obloquy' would succeed merely in evoking the old war cry of 'No Surrender'. In many ways *The Irish Times* remained an ambivalent presence. On the one hand it was still rooted in a declining imperial world; on the other hand it was so anxious to be respectful of the new state and constructive in its criticisms that its defence of minority rights was rather muted.

It is quite obvious that Healy disliked and distrusted de Valera. 'What would happen', he wrote, 'if the Republican Party should succeed in defeating the forces of the Free State and succeed in establishing a *de facto* Republican form of government? The answer is easy. British troops would be hurried back to Ireland. The old warfare would be renewed on a more dreadful scale than ever. Hundreds of thousands of young Irishmen and Englishmen would perish, and when the inevitable end came, Southern Ireland would be a wilderness, without communications, property or commerce, and incapable of recovering within the next hundred years'. This now reads as an almost 'over the top' reaction. Fintan O'Toole viewed Healy's direction of the paper as a determination that it should play a constructive role in the new state. This was despite the fact that the official culture of the Free State remained, as he wrote, 'pious and conservative', adding that *'The Irish Times* was inclined to accept the reality that the Catholic Church would have a dominant role'.

One positive way it supported the government was its endorsement of the newly adopted policy towards the restoration of the Irish language (although it objected to making it a compulsory subject in the schools). However, it was not exactly helped in continuing its more general support when censorship and divorce laws were introduced. The paper balanced all this by continuing to declare its commitment to the Commonwealth and to some of the concessions that had been made to the British connection. Before the Treaty, the paper became strongly anti-partitionist, viewing any development that might lead to the setting up of two parliaments as the worst possible outcome. When that actually came about, it then hoped – a forlorn hope – that Sir James Craig, the Northern Prime Minister, would eventually take his place in a united Ireland parliament. Perhaps the paper's greatest difficulty at this time was caused by the State's subsequent failure to respond sympathetically to its small Protestant minority, much less take account of the opinions of the northern majority.

In the introduction to his book of essays on aspects of the press in Ireland and Britain, Simon J. Potter wrote that 'many of the chapters … present, for the first time, essential background material on the history of Irish newspapers and journalism. Nevertheless, there remain gaps in our knowledge that this volume has been unable to fill. We still lack a basic understanding of the subtle and changing attitudes expressed by the Dublin *Irish Times* for example …' Another person who wrote about the problems faced by *The Irish Times* in the handling of events around this period was Terence de Vere White.

Commenting on the Imperial Conference, he noted that the paper was not alone in having difficulties in adjusting to the changed circumstances: '*The Irish Times*, always quite as impartial in politics as the London *Times*, was enthusiastic at the part which the Free State had played in Commonwealth affairs. But, in Ireland as a whole, there was no enthusiasm.' Conor Brady, who occupied the editorial seat more than sixty years later, credited Healy's editorial performance during not only the turbulent years of the Great War but also through the upheavals that created the two states on the island of Ireland by 'adapting the newspaper to new realities'. He went on to acknowledge that while the paper declined commercially under Healy (and even further under Smyllie), it continued to maintain high editorial standards. Brady also had this to say about the paper's stance under Healy's editorship during the early days of independence:

> It railed against the climate of censorship and repression that was sponsored by the Cumann na nGaedheal government. Yet it supported that government in its economic policies and its firm law-and-order stance against those who remained unreconciled to the Treaty … It opposed legislation that prohibited divorce and that added heavy penalties for anyone supplying contraceptives.

What the paper termed 'the tangle which the problem of divorce created in the Free State legislature', was the subject of a long editorial during 1925. In it the paper[8] took the view that the Dáil had sought to deprive the subjects of the Free State of a right that was guaranteed by the State's Constitution and was inherent in citizenship of the British Empire. When this matter came before the Senate, the chairman, Lord Glenavy, ruled it out of order on the ground that the Constitution could not be altered by mere resolution of Parliament.

> We recognise the enormous and painful difficulties of the situation. On the one side are the Free State citizen's guaranteed right to rebuild his life after a disastrous marriage, and the deep conviction of many citizens that the exercise of such right is no offence against the Divine Law. On the other side are the clear teachings of the Church of the large majority of the Irish people. It is a fact that the members of this Church regard divorce as sin, and it is a fact that no legislation in the Free State Parliament is possible without their consent. The problem then of reconciling the minority's constitutional freedom with the dictates of the majority's conscience is by far the most delicate problem that this State has been, is, or ever is likely to be, confronted. Yet it must be solved if the Free State's very name is not to be a lie, if a rankling sense of injustice is not to be a canker at the very root of progress, and if the nation's hopes for a united Ireland ever are to be fulfilled.

[8]   *The Irish Times*, 12 June 1925.

The paper devoted two columns to Yeats' speech on the question of divorce made on that same day to the Senate. He had begun by stating that he had no doubt 'that the party in this House which desires to prevent divorce will prevail …'

> We are a tolerant nation and the circumstances are very special that urge us to interfere with one another's rights or liberties. Left to themselves, Dail and Senate would have found an easy solution.
>
> If the profound desire of the Irish people for unity between North and South is ever to be fulfilled; if North and South are ever to enter into some political association, the North will certainly not abandon any right which it already possesses. It seems to me clear that if you show that southern Ireland is to be governed on Catholic ideas alone, if you pass laws that the Protestants consider oppressive, you must give up all thought of unity …
>
> This question came before the Committee that drew up the Irish constitution. That Committee was urged to make marriage indissoluble, and it refused. But that refusal expressed the political mind of Ireland. Now you are asked to reverse the decision of the Committee by men whose minds are not political but religious. You are urged to it by men whom, I admit, it must be exceedingly difficult for the Catholic members of this House to resist …
>
> If you legislate upon such grounds, there is no reason why you should stop there. There is no reason why you should not forbid civil marriage altogether, seeing that civil marriage is not marriage in the eyes of the church, and that it is just as much immorality according to that view as the remarriage of divorced persons is according to men like Dr. Byrne. Nor do I see why you should stop at that, for we teach in our schools and print in our books many things which your Church condemns. In fact, once legislate on purely theological grounds and there is no form of religious persecution which cannot be justified, and I am not entirely certain that there are not men in Ireland today who will urge you to it …

Another commentator, Conor Cruise O'Brien, when writing about what he termed the 'Free State sectarian legislation', added:

> The only daily paper that had opposed this new legislation in any degree had been 'the paper' – *The Irish Times*, especially after the crass administration of the literary censorship began to drive many Irish intellectuals, writers and artists into a sort of interior emigration. It was to 'the paper' that these people, many of them Catholics, turned. If they lived in the country, and were cautious, they had their *Irish Times* delivered in plain wrappers.

But the fact of the matter is that much of what *The Irish Times* had in the past stood for was being gradually eroded or was already gone. And a very significant segment of its readership had already gone too – gone away – and its remaining potential readership was already being further eroded. As Professor Lee pointed out, while the 1922 Free State Constitution had no sectarian bias, there certainly was an 'underground,' and largely

July 1927 saw two very large funerals in Dublin, those of Kevin O'Higgins and Constance Markievicz. At the latter, photographed above, large crowds lined the streets and eight cars were required to carry the wreaths.

unacknowledged situation where 'the Catholic archbishop of Dublin insisted to Cosgrave that the Catholic Church had not merely the right, but the duty, to control Protestant consciences'.

During 1926, encouraged by a deputation of Catholic bishops, the Minister for Justice, Kevin O'Higgins, appointed a Committee on Evil Literature. This was to be the first step leading to the Censorship of Publications Act which O'Higgins – murdered a year later by Republicans while he was walking to Mass – did not live to see. John Horgan commented on the resulting Act: '*The Irish Times* went some distance in its attempt to reconcile its liberal Protestant ethic and its demonstrably middle-class concerns. Public opinion and 'old fashioned manliness' were more effective censors than legislation, it suggested.'

In its issue published on Monday, 18 July 1927, *The Irish Times* carried (on the same page) reports on both the murder of Kevin O'Higgins and the funeral of Constance Markievicz. In its coverage of the O'Higgins murder, the paper included the text of a Pastoral Letter written by Archbishop Byrne which had been read at all Masses in his archdiocese. Calling the deed 'this cowardly assassination,' Dr. Byrne added that the circumstance 'has aroused a deepened horror amongst our Catholic people. When the victim was stricken down, he was on his way to perform the usual Sunday duty of a Catholic – to assist at the Holy Sacrifice of the Mass'. The Very Rev. Canon Breen, P.P.,

Booterstown, to whose church O'Higgins had been walking when gunned down, was also reported in the paper as condemning the action: 'The poor man retained his consciousness almost to the last … and he forgave even these murderers.' Under a separate headline, 'National University Condolence,' the paper reported – without comment – a resolution of profound loss 'being passed at a meeting of the Senate of the National University of Ireland at which Mr Eamon de Valera (Chancellor) presided'.

The paper's report of the funeral of Constance Markievicz noted that 'the wreaths were numerous [and] were carried in eight motor tenders'. Large numbers of people marched in the funeral procession which included five bands, one of the sections being composed of members of the Workers Union of Ireland led by 'a red banner which bore an inscription in Russian. This emblem was said to have been presented to the Irish workers by the workers of Moscow.' Fifty-five years later, the near convergence of the funerals of Markievicz and O'Higgins prompted Conor Cruise O'Brien to write: 'At the latter were the massed ranks of respectability, at the other the rabble.' If this remark seems rather harsh, perhaps the Latin tag – *Interdum vulgus videt*[9] – got it more nearly right.

The Irish Times continued to be cautious about de Valera, an unease that deepened when, after re-naming his party 'Fianna Fáil,' he decided to re-enter active politics to contest the 1927 General Election. As Healy commented: 'The main issue is between the Government party and Mr. de Valera's Fianna Fáil. The one offers the electors an imposing record of good work coupled with a constructive programme for the future; the other can point to nothing but a depressing career of futility, while its plans for the future are as vague as they are impractical.' A month later, the paper carried the news that 'Mr. de Valera's Party will take the oath and enter the Dáil tomorrow. This unanimous decision, which was announced after midnight, was the result of a long conference of Fianna Fáil deputies in Dublin yesterday.' During the course of a lengthy statement the party stated that 'its members will not acknowledge any allegiance is due to the English crown. It has, however, been repeatedly stated, and it is not uncommonly believed, that the required declaration is not an oath; that the signing of it implies no contractual obligation, and it has no binding significance in conscience or in law; that, in short, it is merely an empty formula which deputies could conscientiously sign without being involved, or without involving their nation, in obligations to the English crown.'

When the Dáil reassembled next day, the newly elected Fianna Fáil deputies entered the chamber after signing 'the empty formula'. The party's stand-off had, after five years, abruptly ended. *The Irish Times* reported the reaction of Captain Redmond, leader of the National League, who said: 'It is impossible – and it would be foolish – to attempt to ignore the significance of this event. It means that the representatives of something like

---

[9]   Sometimes the rabble sees what is just.

one-third of the electorate who recorded its vote at the recent general election have decided, with or without reservation, to avail themselves of constitutional methods for the attainment and the protection of their ideals. That in itself is an immense gain for the cause of constitutionalism as distinguished from revolutionism'.

The paper's long-running feature, *An Irishman's Diary*, was introduced in that same year, and may well be the oldest of its kind in journalism. Although begun during Healy's editorship, it is generally accepted that Smyllie – Healy's assistant and successor – devised the idea. He contributed to its first columns, always under his own personal pseudonym, *Nichevo*.[10] For many years the column was made up of miscellaneous items contributed by the reporting staff who wrote under the umbrella-pseudonym of *Quidnunc*, and it was only later that a single journalist wrote the entire column. One of these was Seamus Kelly who occupied the column's special *Quidnunc* chair for three decades. When writing the *Diary* column for the paper's centenary edition, he recalled that it was not true, despite what some people thought, that R.M. Smyllie had been a founder member of *The Irish Times*! Kelly went on to list some of the principal early *Quidnuncs*: G. Tynan O'Mahony, Alec Newman, 'Jap' Power, Lionel Fleming, Patrick Campbell, Brian Inglis and Tony Gray.

At the end of July 1928, the paper reported under large headlines: AN IRISH VICTORY IN OLYMPIC GAMES. DR. O'CALLAGHAN WINS THE HAMMER-THROWING EVENT. In fact, the report began: 'British, Irish and Dominion athletes shone in the Olympic Games yesterday, the crowning achievement being Lord Burghley's magnificent win in the final of the 400 metres hurdles. The 100 metres was an Empire victory, first, second and fifth places going respectively to Canadian, English and South African runners.' It was not until the third paragraph of the report that the Irish win was mentioned: 'The only other event of importance, the hammer throw, was won by the Irishman, Dr O'Callaghan, of Kanturk, who came into prominence this year at the Irish championships in Dublin … His throw yesterday at Amsterdam was 51.39 metres (168ft. 7ins.), or .10 metres better than the Swede, O. Skoeld, who was second.'

A now forgotten regular feature in the paper from the late 1920s was entitled *In The Northern Capital*, a miscellany of news items concerning the North, presumably an early attempt to broaden the paper's appeal. A typical example, in the issue dated January 2 1931, included details about new orders for the shipyards and plans to install a giant dock there at a cost of £300,000. There were also short reports about a proposal to increase housing subsidies; the forthcoming Belfast Municipal elections; and an account of the completion

10   Tony Gray claimed that Smyllie told him that *Nichevo* was the Russian equivalent of 'I don't know, who cares?' Roughly translated from the Latin, *Quidnunc* means 'What now?'

A very unusual way to address an envelope! Posted in England during October 1928, it successfully reached its destination despite the distracting but clever drawing depicting most of the passengers seated on a tramcar reading *The Irish Times*.

of the work in connection with the huge Silent Valley reservoir in the Mourne Mountains.

John Healy may have hoped that things had settled down as the paper entered the 1930s, but three more significant happenings were to intervene before he vacated the editorial chair in 1934. The first was the introduction of a third daily paper into the metropolitan newspaper market. This was the *Irish Press*, founded by de Valera, who carefully structured the paper in a way that ensured that he, and not the Fianna Fáil party, controlled its destiny. Its first editorial acknowledged the contributions 'made by the 10,000 Irish men and women, here at home and beyond the seas who have made this great enterprise possible … inspired by no hope of gain'. Ironically, the founder had ensured that these last four words were to prove all too true.

The new paper adopted as its motto 'The Truth in the News', and quickly achieved sales in excess of 100,000, an impressive figure, already close to that of the *Irish Independent*. *The Irish Times* continued to keep its circulation figures close to its chest but

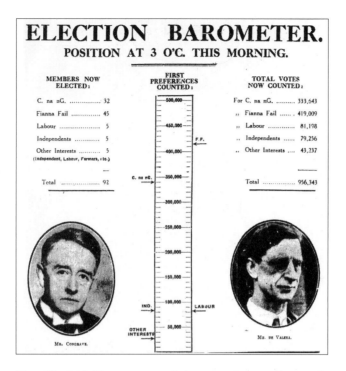

ELECTION BAROMETER.

POSITION AT 3 O'C. THIS MORNING.

MEMBERS NOW ELECTED:		FIRST PREFERENCES COUNTED:		TOTAL VOTES NOW COUNTED:	
C. na nG.	32			For C. na nG.	333,643
Fianna Fail	45			,, Fianna Fail	419,009
Labour	5			,, Labour	81,198
Independents	5			,, Independents	79,256
Other Interests	5			,, Other Interests	43,237
(Independent, Labour, Farmers, etc.)					
Total	92			Total	956,343

MR. COSGRAVE.   MR. DE VALERA.

How *The Irish Times* announced the not-quite-complete results
of the 1932 general election which saw Fianna Fáil entering
government for the first time.

its sales were probably, even at best, less than a third of that of the new entrant to the market. Appealing to a different readership, the *Press* would not have been seen by the *Times* as a direct competitor, so it comes as no surprise that John Horgan was to write that '*The Irish Times* gave it a patrician welcome, and even reprinted an extract from its first editorial. The *Irish Independent* carried on as if the *Irish Press* did not exist: and edited-out references to the paper in its reports of speeches of Fianna Fáil politicians.' In one particular sense, the *Independent* did *not* treat the *Press* as if it did not exist: by manipulating its strong connections (through its Murphy proprietorship) with the railway companies to prevent, initially, the new paper from using the special newspaper trains. This move caused the *Press* huge distribution difficulties in dispatching its paper to the provinces where most of its readership was to be found.

The second big problem Healy had to overcome was how to treat the arrival of the Fianna Fáil party into power after it won the 1932 elections. John Horgan commented that, after the election, *The Irish Times* qualified its opposition to the new administration. It did this by demonstrating a willingness to 'at least give Mr. de Valera a chance to show that he might not live up to the picture of him as a socialist ogre, with which they had earlier regaled its readers'. He also noted that de Valera 'had come to the compromises necessary for the administration of a country despite his many reservations, while *The Irish Times* came to terms with a political party whose antecedents it regarded as radically subversive, but which was now in government'. As the election results had trickled in, it soon became obvious to the paper that de Valera's party had done well:

> In contrast with the election of September 1927, the *Cumann na nGaedheal* party has fared badly and the *Fianna Fail* party has fared well. Mr. Cosgrave and his colleagues, even with the help of all the Independents, cannot control the fortunes of the next Free State Government … In most other respects, the outlook is obscure. The *Fianna Fail* party certainly cannot win such an independent majority as would be adequate backing for the drastic and revolutionary policy to which it is pledged.

The Irish Times took some crumbs of comfort from the fact that de Valera had no option but to form a coalition with the Labour Party.[11] It hoped that 'as the price of office, Mr. de Valera must be prepared to bow his crested head, and tame his heart of fire …' With a majority of not more than eight votes over the opposition, the paper felt sure that:

> From the outset, Mr. de Valera's course will be anxious and difficult … Certainly, some of his larger and more daring plans must be postponed. It is, perhaps, a reasonable prediction that the main items that the Labour Party will allow him to tackle in the coming session will be the abolition of the oath of allegiance, the repeal of the Public Safety Act, and the repudiation of the land annuities …
>
> He has convinced himself that the oath is not an essential part of the Treaty, although Article 4 of the Treaty begins with these words: 'The oath to be taken by Members of Parliament of the Irish Free State shall be in the following form.' Mr. de Valera's optimism assumes the British Government's easy compliance in the abolition of the oath, and, therefore, of the whole Treaty. He ignores the fact that by such abolition, the Free State would cease to be a Dominion of the British Commonwealth, and would forfeit tariff preferences. He argues that, if England is the Free State's best customer, the Free State is England's best customer, forgetting that, while England has a hundred customers, the Free State has only one …
>
> As for the land annuities, he blandly refuses to believe that the English people, like Buffon's wicked animal, will defend themselves when attacked. In effect, Mr. de Valera's faith in England's generosity, magnanimity and powers of self-sacrifice is far greater than our own …

Healy's long leading article went on to allow more than a hint of praise for the new head of State and, indeed, for his newspaper, and concluded on a hopeful note:

---

11   *The Irish Times*, 23 February 1932

To-day, Mr. de Valera is on the eve of office, and he must have a fair chance to redeem his promises, which embrace work for all, and the creation of a State that shall be at once Christian and prosperous. We add with pleasure that Mr. de Valera's tone and his newspaper's tone in this hour of their triumph, are beyond reproach … The price of this adventure may be high, but perhaps, the result will justify it. In Hans Andersen's story a costly pageant was needed for the discovery that the Emperor had no clothes.

De Valera, as expected, went ahead with his decision to inform the British Government that the oath of allegiance was being abolished and, at the same time, gave notice that he intended to withhold the land annuities. These annuities, which dated back to the Land Acts of more than a quarter of a century earlier, were the repayments for the loans provided by the British government after tenants were enabled to purchase outright the lands they had rented. De Valera's decision to withhold the annuities – worth some £3 million a year – resulted, as *The Irish Times* predicted, in British retaliation. How to treat this story was another of Healy's important editorial decisions, and he took the view that de Valera had made a serious tactical mistake. In a subsequent editorial he predicted that de Valera's 'dreams of utter independence for the Free State … his lofty notion of the British character forbids him to think that England would resent either the removal of the oath of allegiance or the retention of the land annuities'. Healy was right. Britain introduced penal tariffs on Irish agricultural imports, the beginnings of what came to be known as the 'Economic War'. Healy, with some difficulty, went as far as he could to take the Irish side but warned that such 'meddling' would result in real distress, which it did, especially to those of the farming community who had no other outlet for their produce. Healy's reaction to all this was to look northwards and to question the sincerity of de Valera's stated aims in connection with unifying the country:

> While President de Valera in the South is doing everything in his power to banish all signs of the British connection … the people of the North are moving precisely in the opposite direction. How can Irish unity be achieved in such circumstances? The North, at least, is honest in this matter. It has no desire for unity and its spokesmen do not hesitate to say so. In the Free State, on the other hand, unity is in everyone's lips … yet everything that has been done in the in the twenty-six counties during the last twelve years … has had the effect of widening the already yawning gulf between Dublin and Belfast.

Expressing concern for the retention of some kind of link with Britain, one of the paper's editorials quoted Griffith's suggestion about Irishmen joining the British Empire with their heads held up as citizens of a mother country. Such a move, the paper thought, might have given unity a real chance. It then added: 'The man above all others who could have brought about that condition of affairs is Eamon de Valera. We freely admit that no

A group of Dublin newspapermen photographed in the old boardroom of *The Irish Times* in 1939 following a presentation to the paper's manager, J.J. Simington, seen seated in the centre of the picture. Also present (from left): J.C. Dann (of the *Evening Mail*) representing the Dublin Newspaper Manager's Committee, J.C. Dempsey, advertisement manager of the *Irish Press*, J. Beggs, manager, *Evening Mail*, and J. Donohoe, manager, Independent Newspapers.

encouragement ever was given by Belfast, but statesmanship makes its own opportunities. We believe, indeed, that there is still a chance.'

On 2 May 1932, the paper reported a scientific experiment in the space of just sixteen lines – because its significance was not fully understood at the time – under a single column headline: THE ATOM SPLIT. YOUNG DUBLIN DOCTOR'S PART IN DISCOVERY:

> After nearly three years work with special apparatus at the Cavendish Laboratory, Cambridge, two young men – Dr. J.D. Cockroft and Dr. E.T.S. Walton – under the direction of Lord Rutherford, the eminent scientist, have succeeded in splitting the atom. Dr. Walton, the younger of the co-workers, is an Irishman and comes from Dublin.… Lord Rutherford describes the result of the experiment as a discovery of great scientific importance. 'It is difficult,' he added, 'to say to what this discovery may lead'.

Another hugely important event took place one month later which *The Irish Times* announced under three-column-wide headlines: THE EUCHARISTIC CONGRESS OPENED. IMPOSING CEREMONY AT THE PRO-CATHEDRAL. PAPAL LEGATE AND EIGHT CARDINALS PRESENT. Describing the Congress as 'the greatest gathering of dignitaries of the Church that Ireland has ever seen', the paper went on to report that 'rarely if ever has Dublin had so many visitors within its boundaries as there are in the city at present. Yesterday the streets were so congested that it seemed as if the population had already been doubled.' The colourful scenes at the opening Mass at the Pro-Cathedral were described in detail:

> East and West met and mingled in common worship. White, black, yellow, all races were one in their common religion. With the Church dignitaries there were also present many lay members of the Vatican court wearing their picturesque uniforms. John Count McCormack was wearing a brilliant scarlet uniform, with broad sash – the court dress of his office as Private Chamberlain to the Pope. Sir Thomas Grattan Esmonde was also in court dress of black and gold.
>
> The arrival of the Papal Legate was a stirring sight. Headed by a cross-bearer, the visiting cardinals walked slowly up the nave, each Prince of the church attended by his suite, and at the end of the procession came the Papal Legate, surrounded by the members of the Vatican Court in their colourful uniforms. Slowly and stately to the tune of accompaniment of the hymn *Ecce Sacerdos Magnus*, the cardinals proceeded to the altar, and then when he and the other cardinals had taken their seats on the thrones the assembled congregation burst spontaneously into the hymn *Veni Creator*.

The Irish Times had, of course, changed and it was continuing to change its outlook to meet the new realities. During 1973, Owen Sheehy Skeffington wrote about the paper at that earlier period:

> When Unionism in the 26 counties was left to the mercy of the Paddies ... its principle journal, *The Irish Times*, the stern, unbending, popular voice of Unionism, was forced to keep its coldly intolerant eye on the new state in which it survived. Its primary consideration until the early 1950s was its Protestant readership whence came its advertising revenue. Its politics in international affairs were British Conservative; in Irish affairs it remained severely critical of the de Valera government. Because of its Protestant and Unionist readership, it naturally thought more of Northern Ireland than did the other journals, but its position was defensive and nostalgic rather than topical. Without relaxation of its Unionism, it did open its columns to dissident nationalists whose radical criticisms of 26-county government and society made them unwelcome in Catholic-run newspapers. It was not widely read in Northern Ireland, where from the first there was little interest in the 'Southern Unionists' abandoned in the Treaty settlement. But slowly it did build up an increasing readership among 26-county liberal Catholics, who found its acid criticism more congenial than the cloying conformism of other prints.

A few years later, John Horgan described how Healy 'had engineered a relatively positive approach for his former proto-Unionist paper to the new constitutional arrangement, as well as a more lukewarm one to Mr de Valera's accession to power'. Fintan O'Toole subsequently summed up the paper's position thus:

> In many ways, *The Irish Times* under Healy remained an ambivalent presence. On the one hand it was still rooted in a declining imperial world; on the other hand, it was so anxious to be respectful to the new state and constructive in its criticisms that its defence of minority rights was rather muted … It was still suffused with nostalgia for the lost world of British Ireland.

O'Toole saw a link here with the elderly staff still employed by the company. These included J.J. Simington, the paper's manager, who had been with the company since 1878, and Bill Coyne, the company's voluble porter, who had served not only in the Great War, but in the Boer War before that. Other long-serving staff included Ned Duncan who served in the accounts department until failing sight in his mid-seventies forced him to retire. There were at least two veterans in the Case (printing) Room – Ned Smith who could vividly recall the earlier fire in November, 1919, and Patrick Cullen, – also with over fifty years' service – who arrived each day at the works department wearing a bowler hat. To these names must be added that of Healy himself who was born around the same period as Simington, becoming editor of the paper in 1907. In all, John Edward Healy edited the paper for twenty-seven years, making him the longest-serving editor of *The Irish Times*. When he died 'in harness' in 1934, his assistant for the previous sixteen years, Robert Smyllie, succeeded him.

Robert Maire Smyllie

1934–1954

—⟶∙◦∙⟵—

'Eternal vigilance is the price of impunity'

ROBERT SMYLLIE WAS one of the most influential editors of *The Irish Times*. It is important to make this statement at the outset because he has so often been caricatured as a figure of fun or, worse still, an inebriated, shambling clown. Patrick Campbell, Brian Inglis and Tony Gray, each of whom served under him, have projected him thus, and this reputation has survived to obscure, at least partially, what he actually achieved during his twenty years in office. In appearance, he was enormously overweight and wore small, round spectacles that gave him an owlish appearance. Campbell remembered him as 'one of the last of the old-style editors'; to his way of thinking, the business of the proprietors of a newspaper was to appoint a man whom they felt they could trust and leave him to get on with the job. Campbell, who also recalled that his own mother sang duets with Smyllie at the Dublin Arts Club, has left us with this picture of the man:

> When it is possible [today] to work on the lower slopes of a national newspaper without discovering which of the scurrying executives is the editor, I count myself fortunate to have served under one who wore a green sombrero, weighed twenty-two stones, sang parts of his leading articles in operatic recitative, and grew the nail on his little finger into the shape of a pen nib like Keats.

Brian Inglis, like Campbell, did recognise some of Smyllie's achievements when he worked for the paper. Indeed, Smyllie played a significant part – but got little thanks for doing so – in training both men in the journalist's art, enabling each of them to carve a career as successful journalists in London. Inglis was to write, in a contribution to the centenary edition of *The Irish Times*:

Anybody who passes his formative journalistic years in that establishment never, in a sense, leaves it … *The Irish Times* provided, in the best sense of the cliché, a liberal education. My first mentor was a reporter so ancient that his first mark-up had been to cover the [1870–71] Franco-Prussian war.

Lionel Fleming was to write that after Healy's death, the staid atmosphere in the editor's room changed. He was almost certain, however, that the directors had misgivings when they appointed Smyllie, and had probably only done so 'because they had little room to manoeuvre'.

Before he came to Dublin, journalism was already in Smyllie's blood; his father, also Robert Smyllie, founded the *Sligo Times* in 1903 and continued as its proprietor until it folded at the beginning of the Great War. When that happened, Smyllie senior moved to Belfast where he joined the *News Letter* as its assistant editor. Before this, in 1912, the young Smyllie went from Sligo Grammar School to Trinity College, Dublin and, during vacation two years later, he obtained a holiday job as a tutor to a wealthy American. They travelled to Germany, and when the war broke out, his employer, as a citizen of a neutral country, returned to the States but Smyllie, travelling on a British passport, was interned. His four years' imprisonment were spent in Ruhleben, a civilian internment camp near Berlin, among a large group of people of various nationalities and from different walks of life, many of them intellectuals. The name of the camp, as it happened, seemed to reflect Smyllie's new circumstances, for the German phrase 'in Ruhe leben' may be simply translated as 'living in peace'. With nothing better to do, he read widely, attended organised camp lectures, talked with fellow prisoners about Central Europe in general, and he quickly picked up a good working knowledge of German as well as some French. It has been suggested that the camp provided the young Smyllie with a better, more rounded education than was obtainable at any university.

With the foregoing in mind, it is interesting to look back at the coverage provided by the paper during the first days of the Great War. On 3 August 1914, *The Irish Times* reported on the plight of tourists stranded in Germany at the outbreak of hostilities. Of course it knew nothing of Smyllie's plight, let alone that he was to be one of the paper's most notable editors. Its reportage on that date recorded that some 10,000 people arrived at various London railway stations from all parts of the continent: 'They are probably amongst the last that will be able to get to England. Thousands of English people are stranded in France, Germany, Austria, Italy and Belgium, with only a slight prospect of reaching these shores … One of the travellers stated that nearly 1,000 passengers had been stranded on the quay at Boulogne. … An English traveller who returned yesterday from Rotterdam described the city as being in the greatest excitement. Men fought and women fainted … The Germans have forbidden Europeans to cross the frontier by train or motor car …'

Although R.M. Smyllie continues to be regarded by many as one of the great editors of his day, it is thought that the directors were reluctant to appoint him to the position but saw no suitable alternative candidate. His two decades in the chair were to have a huge influence on the paper's future despite his addiction to drink and the fact that he has sometimes been portrayed as little more than a figure of fun.

When released in 1918, Smyllie returned to Sligo to discover that his father's newspaper had closed, with serious consequences for the family's fortunes, one being that it was now impossible to complete his college education. At this point, he decided to see if he might obtain a job with *The Irish Times*. Healy interviewed him and was immediately struck both by Smyllie's wide knowledge of European politics and history, and his competence in speaking German and French. A short time later, Smyllie returned to Europe to attend the Paris Peace Conference on behalf of *The Irish Times*.

When the conference at Versailles was convened, it transpired that newspaper reporters were to be kept at a distance from the proceedings being conducted in secret. This development worried Smyllie, because he sensed that if Healy became aware of it, he would be recalled to Dublin. As Tony Gray wrote: 'So Smyllie played two cards. He began immediately to send Healy what today would be called 'feature articles', then known as 'specials'. Smyllie's 'specials' were descriptive pieces covering everyday life in post-war Paris. He also fleshed out details of the surroundings in which the official communiqués were issued in order to add a touch of colour to the drabness of their diplomatic formality. Smyllie's second 'card' concerned the rumours that were then floating around Paris about a delegation from Sinn Féin that was expected to demand a hearing at the conference. This was on the grounds that the war had been triggered off by the refusal of one great power, the Kaiser's Germany, to respect the rights of one small independent nation – Belgium. Sinn Féin wished to argue that it had a right to put forward the case of Ireland, another small independent state, whose rights had been thwarted by another aggressive power, the British Empire. Smyllie did his best to convince Healy that this new development was likely to bring a potentially interesting Irish angle to the international conference.

In fact, it did no such thing. The victorious powers at the end of the Great War did not – nor were they likely to – admit the representatives of those who had not only dangerously interfered with the prosecution of the war, but had both voiced support for, and had secured assistance from, the now-defeated Germany. Sean T. O'Kelly was not even given a hearing and returned to Dublin – as did Smyllie, whose editor was hardly surprised at this turn of events.

Recognising Smyllie's talents, Healy appointed him to be his assistant editor, and to write both general feature articles and leading articles on European affairs. He rated his new assistant highly enough to send him to the British Commonwealth conference and to the League of Nations in Geneva. It is impossible at this remove to discern how much Smyllie influenced Healy's tentative moves in changing the paper's policy towards the new State. Smyllie was, however, able to build on this, thereby attracting a gradually growing number of liberal business and professional Catholics to the paper. An early signal that change had already begun was demonstrated by the paper's moderate reaction to the death in 1920 of Terence MacSwiney, Lord Mayor of Cork, who died while on hunger strike in London:

> We can expect no agreement of public opinion concerning the merits of Alderman MacSwiney's death in Brixton Jail. … We cannot even expect any serious attempt by either side to understand the other side's point of view. Nevertheless we may ask those for whom the late Lord Mayor of Cork is now a martyr to try to appreciate the other side's point of view. One thing Irishmen of all parties will concede to Mr MacSwiney's memory. He was a brave man who, for the faith that was in him, endured a terrible ordeal with dignity and patience. He willed his own death, but willed it unselfishly for a cause which he believed worthy of the price. We maintain strongly that the end did not justify the means, yet … such a death as Mr. MacSwiney's must inspire all generations to sorrow.

'Bertie' Smyllie was appointed editor in June 1934 following Healy's death, but he had been acting as editor for at least a year beforehand, throughout Healy's long illness. One of his first important editorials appeared seven months later on the vexed subject of the land annuities:[1]

---

[1]   *The Irish Times*, 11 February 1935.

When the Free State Government decided to withhold the land annuities from Great Britain, thus opening hostilities in the economic war, we ventured to predict that in the long run the game would prove not to have been worth the candle. It was not until 1927, just before Fianna Fáil entered the Dáil, that they discovered the startling fact that the Free State did not really owe the land annuities at all. Every farmer in this country knew – and knows today – precisely what the land annuities are. They were never part of the public debt, they are merely a private obligation on the tenant-purchaser to pay his former landlord for the possession of his holding. The Free State Government – and for that matter, the British government also – simply acted as an agent, collecting the money in Ireland, and passing it on to the British Treasury for distribution in the form of interest to the holders of Irish Land Bonds …

The mid-thirties saw the continuation of de Valera's 'Economic War' during which Britain, predictably, retaliated by imposing crippling taxes on Irish agricultural produce. During the 1934 annual Dublin Spring Show, six hundred farmers called a meeting to draw attention to their plight. *The Irish Times* commented:[2]

The Free State farmer actually is in an impossible position. In the old days he paid his annuities punctually and to the full, and did not care particularly what happened to the money when it left his hands. Then he sold his cattle, his butter and his eggs to Great Britain for a good price, and was one of the most independent persons in Western Europe. All that has been radically changed by Mr de Valera's 'economic war'. Now the farmer is required to pay his annuities and his rates as formerly; but he has no longer a free market in Great Britain. On the contrary, the British Government, in consequence of President de Valera's blank refusal to pay the land annuities, has imposed a series of penal tariffs against Free State goods which is paralysing trade between the two countries.

During the previous twelve months the British government collected over £4.5 million by means of the special duties. Every penny of this had been paid by Irish farmers over and above the land annuities they had paid to the Irish Government, but which de Valera had chosen not to pass on to Britain. The leading article made it clear that *The Irish Times* continued to have qualms concerning de Valera and his party:

We do not suppose that President de Valera will pay the least attention to yesterday's resolutions. He has acquired the autocratic mentality which regards all criticism as impertinence. Nevertheless we believe that yesterday's meeting will do some good. It will serve to bring before the notice of the ordinary citizen the fact that the farmers are in a very bad way and that their plight is attributable entirely to the incidence of the 'economic war.'

---

[2] *The Irish Times*, 3 May 1934.

Portrait of R.M. Smyllie, editor, 1934–54, by the well-known Irish artist, William Conor (1881–1968).

Also during 1934, the paper carried a detailed report about the Free State's new Minister Plenipotentiary to the Holy See, Mr. W.J.B. Macauley. Addressing the Pope, Macauley spoke of 'the great affection of our people which has inspired Your Holiness to acquire such a profound knowledge of our history'. This enabled him to understand 'in the most intimate way how very largely that history has been determined by the unwavering fidelity of the Irish people to the Church of Christ'. Smyllie had continued Healy's policy of providing generous coverage to news of special interest to the paper's growing Catholic readership. It continued:

> The representative of Your Holiness in Ireland will have given you the fullest account of the manner in which my government has followed the teachings of the Holy See in its policy of social reconstruction, and of its efforts to enable the whole people to take their proper place in an ordered Christian civilisation. Our relations of unfailing filial devotion towards the Holy See in the past give the best guarantee for similar relations in the future, and I beg Your Holiness to believe that I shall do all that lies in me to continue the good work of my predecessor.

Around this same time the paper reported that Leon Trotsky, the deposed leader of Soviet Russia, had sought permission to reside in the Irish Free State. The Irish Government, in a statement issued by the Government Information Bureau, responded to representations made on Trotsky's behalf stating that 'it would be quite impossible'.

The news of the abdication of King Edward VIII prompted Smyllie to write about the implications this would have for Ireland in his main leading article in the paper on 12 December 1936:

> The final act in the moving drama of Britain's monarchical crisis was staged last night, when His Highness Prince Edward broadcast his farewell to his people over whom he had ruled for less than a year …

Although the entire Commonwealth has been grievously distressed by the abdication of King Edward, all the Dominions – with one exception – have taken immediate and unambiguous steps to legalise the situation, and to recognise the former Duke of York as his lawful successor. The exception, we need hardly say, is the Irish Free State. President de Valera and his Government always seem to be 'different' on principle. They easily could have followed the lead of the other Dominions, and have introduced simple legislation to meet the changed condition of affairs, thereby facilitating the difficult task of His Majesty's Government in the United Kingdom, and helping in some degree to lighten the blow that has fallen on the Empire; but President de Valera does not do things that way. He seized the opportunity with almost embarrassing haste, to take advantage of the new position for his own purposes. Yesterday in Dáil Eireann two bills were introduced and are being rushed through with unprecedented speed. One of these measures deals with internal, the other with external affairs. By implication one of the bills recognises the new King, although recognition is accorded in a most absurdly involved and roundabout way, defining His Majesty as the person who would have succeeded to the throne if King Edward had died on Thursday. The other bill anticipates the new Constitution by the removal of the King's name from the Free State's fundamental law, and the final abolition of the Governor General's office. The whole arrangement is typical of President de Valera's confused processes of thought, and yet it is not without subtlety. So far as the domestic affairs of the Free State are concerned, there will be no King in the future … but in external affairs – such matters as diplomatic and consular representation, for example – the King will be recognised as head of the Commonwealth, so long as the Free State deigns to be associated with the other Dominions.

Two days after this leading article appeared, the main news of the day was headlined: DAIL'S MOST REMARKABLE SESSION. ACCESSION OF NEW KING RECOGNISED. BUT HE WILL HAVE NO PART IN INTERNAL AFFAIRS. The paper's report on the passing of the Executive Authority (External Relations) Bill in the Dáil recorded that it was passed by eighty-one votes to five, Fine Gael voting with the Government. The report continued:

In explaining the bill, President de Valera said that it provided that the Free State's diplomatic and consular representatives in outside countries will in future be appointed on the authority of the Executive Council, and that every international agreement concluded on behalf of the Free State will be concluded by or on behalf of the Executive Council.

But another section of the Bill provides that as long as the Free State is associated with the Commonwealth Nations, and so long as the King, recognised by them as a symbol of their co-operation, continues to act on their behalf for the appointment of diplomatic and consular representatives, and the conclusion of diplomatic agreements, the King so recognised is authorised to act on behalf of the Free State for the like purposes when advised by the Executive Council to do so.[3]

---

[3]   As John W. Wheeler-Bennett pointed out, 'the Dublin government gave no formal assent to or dissent from the Act of Abdication,

Printing Press Destroyed

A huge fire destroyed about one-quarter of the premises of *The Irish Times* and all of its printing machinery during September 1951. The following are a few of the news items carried in the last edition to be printed on the old press:

King George VI had hurried back to London from a curtailed holiday at Balmoral for medical treatment.

The racing driver, Stirling Moss, scored his third consecutive win in Ireland at the Dundrod circuit.

The attendance at a Memorial Service for RAF veterans in St. Patrick's Cathedral, Dublin, was told they should be proud of the Air Force motto, *Per ardua ad astra*, because it was coined by Dr. L.C. Purser, former Vice-Provost of Trinity College, Dublin.

A Belgian ship with cargo for both Dublin and Cork was diverted to Cork because of a strike in Dublin. Unfortunately, the cargo destined for Cork had been stowed beneath the cargo for Dublin.

St. Peter was tipped to win the 4.30 that afternoon at Edinburgh.

Commenting on these events, the historian, John Wheeler-Bennett, wrote that de Valera had thus 'at last achieved the realisation of that formula of the "external association" of Ireland with the British Crown, to which he so tenaciously adhered, in fair weather and foul, and in the face of all possible difficulties, ever since he had propounded it to Mr. Lloyd George in the Anglo-Irish negotiations of July 1921'.

Two important transport events occurred simultaneously during 1936. The world's largest ocean-going liner, the *Queen Mary*, sailed on its maiden voyage to America, and Aer Lingus inaugurated its first two flights to Britain – to Liverpool and Bristol. The report mentioned that the Bristol flight carried five passengers, and the only freight on board was 'a parcel of copies of *The Irish Times* for delivery to London'. It continued:

Before the Aer Lingus machine, *Iolar*, left for Bristol, it was blessed by the Army Air Corps' chaplain, Rev. William O'Riordan, as it stood on the tarmac outside its hanger. The Minister for Industry and Commerce, Mr Sean Lemass, who was among the group at the aerodrome for the inauguration of the services, wished the enterprise every success and said he hoped these services would be the first of many linking Ireland with other centres in Britain and the continent.

but indicated that it did not desire the United Kingdom Act to be extended to the Irish Free State'. Irish diplomatic representatives then continued to be accredited in King George's name and bore his Letters of Credence.

The first cryptic crossword appeared in the paper during April 1943, and since then well over 13,000 similar puzzles have followed in the same series.

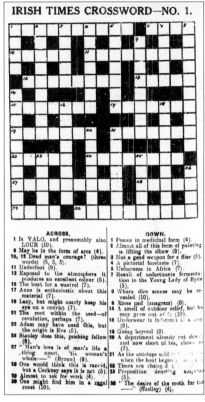

IRISH TIMES CROSSWORD—NO. 1.

Another report on that same day concerned the forthcoming visit of Herr von Ribbentrop, 'Chancellor Hitler's Ambassador-at-large', as guest of Lord Londonderry on his estate at Mount Stewart, near Newtownards, Co. Down. A statement issued from Berlin was quoted as saying that the visit would be purely a private one.

The year 1936 also saw the commencement of the long-threatened Spanish Civil War, and Smyllie sent Lionel Fleming to cover it. *The Bell* described Fleming's reports as 'some of the most factual, balanced editorial analysis to be found in Europe. Even if *The Irish Times* was still, in essence, "a Protestant paper", this allowed it to follow events in a measured way, uninfluenced by the Catholic Church.' Fleming later recalled that the *Irish Independent,*'ever the faithful mouthpiece of the Church, sent a man to Franco's side to describe the fearful threat to Christianity which Franco was now countering'. This view of the situation was broadly endorsed by John Horgan, who pointed out that the strongly Catholic *Independent*, 'as might be expected, adopted a strongly pro-Franco line, making much of reports of atrocities by Republican forces against priests and nuns'. However, as the earlier experience in Ireland had shown, civil wars inevitably result in the most appalling atrocities on both sides, so that one-sided reporting merely resulted in slanted news.

The outbreak of the Spanish Civil War has been viewed by some as the real beginning of the Second World War. Hitler and Mussolini sent contingents to aid Franco in a Fascist alliance, and the war drew Irish participation to both sides of a conflict that more than matched the horrors of the civil war in Ireland fifteen years earlier. Father Stephen Browne, the Jesuit author of *The Press in Ireland*, commented that both the *Irish Independent* and the *Irish Press* 'are anxious to capture the support of Irish Catholic sentiment. … In the recent conflict in Spain the *Irish Independent*, alone among the metropolitan dailies, took definitely the side of the Spanish national army against the Socialist-Communist-Anarchist combination. Alone it gave the Irish public the full facts about the persecution of the Church and the atrocities against priests and nuns.' *The Irish Times* found the situation very confusing. 'For some time', it editorialised, 'it has been impossible to discover what has been happening behind the battle-smoke in Spain'. Given the thinking of that time, it was inevitable that Smyllie had to face up to threats made by a number of advertisers that a boycott would be imposed on *The Irish Times* if he continued thus to report the war. Fleming recalled being told that after a priest had visited the editor's office on a similar mission, Smyllie expressed himself in song:

> For once I had an Orange cat
> and he sat beside the fender,
> and every time the Pope passed by,
> he'd scream out 'no surrender'.

Writing about the paper's earlier days, Fr Brown – quoted above – thought it had played an important part in Irish life from the start:

> … and has consistently remained the organ of the Protestant interest in Ireland, its politics being Conservative or Unionist. It steadily opposed all the national movements. It afforded a platform and a rallying ground for all those, Catholics as well as Protestants, whose first allegiance was to England or whose principal preoccupation was the maintenance of the existing order … The two leading papers under Catholic management – the *Irish Independent* and the *Irish Press* – are rivals and vie with one another to capture the favour of the Catholic public.

As specified earlier, he noted that no national daily paper actually professed to be Catholic 'in the sense of religious newspapers … Even *The Irish Times*, which was formerly the organ of Unionism in politics and of the Protestant community, gives a good deal of Catholic news and, as a rule, carefully avoids, at least as regards form and mode of expression, statements that would be offensive to Catholic opinion. It is much read by Catholics.'

While it was only to be expected that *The Irish Times* was often under scrutiny concerning its Protestant origins, the antithesis of this was that the *Irish Independent's* ultra-Catholicism was generally accepted as the norm. The problems faced by the former in adjusting to the new political-religious situation are now well understood, but those of the Independent are hardly ever considered, much less criticised. A notable exception occurred when John Horgan perceptively pointed to what happened when, a decade later, Dr Noel Browne resigned as Minister for Health after a combination of the Catholic hierarchy and a section of the medical profession opposed the introduction of his Mother and Child scheme:

> The *Irish Independent*, which might have been expected to weigh in heavily behind the bishops and the medical profession, maintained an unexpected editorial silence. Although it would not have been widely known or remarked on at the time, the reason for this was in all probability the fact that the Chance family, which was represented on the board, had some

fifteen years earlier informally adopted the young Noel Browne, then an orphan, and paid for his university education. Ideology and practical politics dictated that they could not support the stand he had taken, but neither would they allow their papers to attack him.

Writing during the mid-forties in *The Bell*, Vivian Mercier noted how *The Irish Times* – and its readership too – 'that had supported the established English government whether it was Liberal or Conservative, at once took to supporting the established Irish Government led by Mr Cosgrave. However, with the eclipse of Fine Gael and the long period of Fianna Fáil's supremacy, during which time Mr de Valera's government had become even more firmly established than Mr Cosgrave's ever was, *The Irish Times* has been put in a quandary.' The quandary was, of course, the paper's misgivings about de Valera's policies that it saw as strengthening rather than weakening partition. It took several years for Smyllie to adopt a generally conciliatory line towards de Valera. In 1937 he wrote: 'We are glad to admit that in many ways President de Valera's government has confounded its former critics, including ourselves; that it has acted fairly and uprightly towards political and religious minorities, and that its ministers, on the whole, have done their job conscientiously and well'. This thinking was reinforced after the 1938 General Election, when the paper expressed its satisfaction that de Valera had been returned to power.

During August of that year, under the headline MONTREAL WELCOMES THE IRISH TIMES, the paper reported the arrival there of a seaplane from Foynes[4] carrying a supply of its edition printed the day before. There were scenes of excitement, especially among the Irish immigrants in that city 'where surely no Irish paper was ever in such demand before. Hundreds were disappointed, and those who were lucky enough to secure a copy at the modest price of ten cents treasured the souvenir.'

During that same fateful year, de Valera sorted out two of the outstanding problems between Ireland and Britain. The first concerned the so-called 'economic war', settled on generous terms when Britain waived its remaining claims on the land annuities, amounting to almost £100 million, in return for a single payment of £10 million. De Valera succeeded in persuading Britain to cede the treaty ports, a quite remarkable achievement considering the developing aggressiveness being displayed by Adolf Hitler in Nazi Germany.

The success of the paper continued to be hindered by a dangerously small readership but, despite this, Smyllie is on record as having claimed that, proportionate to the population of Britain, its sales were the equivalent of more than double that of the London *Times*. The crash in Protestant numbers between 1911 and 1923, which was followed by a continuing decline, made it clear that if the paper was to survive, it would have to shake off any remaining perception that it was Protestant-oriented. In doing so, however, it

---

[4]   Foynes seaplane base lay almost directly across the Shannon estuary from the future Shannon Airport.

needed to ensure that this could be done without, at the same time, alientating that still important readership segment. Despite the lingering perception, *The Irish Times* never went as far as *The Observer* which – at least until the forties – included in its Articles of Association a stipulation that 'every director of the company and every managing director, editor or business manager must be of the Protestant religion, and if he ceases he shall *ipso facto* vacate his office.'

Even after the arrival of the *Irish Press* in 1931, the *Irish Independent* continued to dominate the newspaper scene, although Donat O'Donnell, writing in *The Bell*, stated that sales of the *Independent* initially dropped from about 150,000 to around 120,000. John Horgan made an interesting observation when he noted that in 1927 the Catholic hierarchy entertained the idea of starting a church-owned newspaper. However, as he wrote:

> The generally obsequious approach of the mainstream press, notably the *Irish Independent*, towards the Catholic Church, had made the creation of a specifically church-owned news-paper an unnecessary extravagance … As late as 1955, as the *Irish Independent* prepared to celebrate its fiftieth year in existence, it wrote to a number of senior Catholic churchmen inviting them to contribute special messages for an anniversary supplement. (Churchmen of the other denominations do not appear to have been similarly invited, such was the narrowness of the paper's cultural and social focus).

Archbishop McQuaid of Dublin responded to the aforementioned invitation, saying that the paper had been marked by its 'policy of distinctive loyalty towards the Church'. However, at the paper's centenary in 2005, no reference was made to this greatly treasured remark in the section on 1955 events in a specially published supplement. John Whyte noted[5] that during this period, the Catholic church appeared to have no problems whatsoever: 'Ecclesiastical news seemed like an unbroken round of successes – churches built, missions established, congresses held' – but, he added, there were a few dissenting voices, specifically naming both *The Bell* and *The Irish Times*. He said that the *Times* 'was the main alternative voice … which offered a forum for differing views. … But it had a small circulation, appealing to a particular segment of the population. The other three dailies – the *Irish Independent*, the *Irish Press* and the *Cork Examiner* – were totally circumspect, as was Radio Éireann.'

Throughout the first half of Smyllie's tenure, the paper averaged between twelve and sixteen pages per issue. It continued the curious custom, adopted by most newspapers dating from the nineteenth century, of filling the front page with advertisements so that the news often commenced on either page three or four, and, like all the other papers, it was produced using late nineteenth-century technology. *The Irish Times* adopted the even

---

5   During the course of a Thomas Davis lecture series broadcast by Radio Éireann. See J.J. Lee, *Ireland, 1912–1985*.

more curious idea of placing the sports news at the front end of the paper commencing on page two, a move all the more strange because its coverage of sport was, to put it mildly, not especially good.

During the 1930s, when improved technologies allowed for greater use of photographs, a decision was made to appoint an art editor – not to report on the arts but simply to take charge of the growing photographic department. Until then, it had been under the control of the chief photographer, George Leitch, who had learned his trade in the Royal Air Force and who was by far the best-known cameraman in town. Management, however, decided to appoint Kevin Collins – a non-photographer – to the new post. Leitch, who may have had an axe to grind, told the story that after Smyllie ordered a one-week suspension of Collins for mixing up names in a photo caption, Collins approached the editor saying that he was not attempting to defend himself, thus prompting Smyllie to ask:

'Well, what the hell do you want then?'
'It's just that I've heard you have suspended me for a week'.
'That's right', Smyllie said.
'Well I was wondering if you would make it a fortnight, sir; I was thinking of going to West Cork, and it's hardly worthwhile going for a week'.
Smyllie laughed, so the story went, and told Collins to take a fortnight's holiday.

Smyllie, even while he was Healy's assistant, had already begun spotting young talent for the paper's reporting team and Alec Newman was his first 'find'. Lionel Fleming, who was the second, was taken on by Smyllie despite the fact that he had no journalistic experience. That happened when, as Fleming recalled, mounting the stairs leading to Smyllie's room, he heard what sounded like part of the last movement of Beethoven's ninth symphony. Nearing the great man's office, Fleming recognised that the words being sung were not those of the well-known *Ode to Joy* but a bawdy improvisation composed by Smyllie:

Down the hall the butler wandered,
bent on sodomistic crime,
For the parlour maid was pregnant
for the forty-second time.

According to Fleming, what followed was the briefest of interviews. 'Be here tomorrow. Three guineas a week'. Hailing from West Cork, Fleming quickly noticed that Dubliners invariably mispronounce the city's foreign street names – for example, Dorset Street is rendered 'Dor*set*', Amiens Street becomes 'Ay-me-ins' and D'Olier is changed to 'Dough-leer' Street, and so on. He recalled that, for his first assignment, he was told to go to West *More* land Street. It was only when he saw Gardaí dragging some men into a van outside the front office door that it dawned on him that the incident he had been sent to cover had occurred 'in what I always pronounced as Westm'land Street'.

Among the other bright young stars hired by Smyllie were Harold Browne, Brian Inglis, Alan Bestic, Jack White, Tony Olden, Seamus Kelly, Bruce Williamson, Patrick Campbell, Dan Duffy, Gerry Mulvey, George Burrows, Cathal O'Shannon, Michael McInerney and the brothers Ken and Tony Gray. This strong editorial team had no equal in Ireland at the time, although a number of these 'discoveries', after refining their skills with the paper, went on to London to further their careers. Fleming joined the BBC, and Jack White, who had initially hoped to do likewise, eventually joined the new Irish television service. Tony Gray went to the *Daily Mirror* before joining the ranks of the freelancers, while Paddy Campbell disappeared to join the *Sunday Dispatch* before becoming a noted television personality, largely on the basis of his serious speech impediment.

Brian Inglis, who was one of Smyllie's later appointments, joined the paper in 1939 and has left a brief record of the Dickensian state of the paper's premises, a state which remained unchanged a decade later when I joined the company. The newspaper was operating out of three separate buildings, fronting on to D'Olier Street, Fleet Street and Westmoreland Street respectively. All three were linked together at the centre, and as Inglis wrote: 'Between them a network of passages had been constructed – the more confusing in that there were no signs showing which way to go. The editorial staff in those days went in through the main Westmoreland Street door past the counters where people were putting in advertisements or collecting replies.' He described the route to the editorial departments (then in the D'Olier Street building), reached by a wide staircase from the front office to the first-floor level. The warren of offices was accessed by yet another flight of stairs, 'all dingy and depressing', and one arrived at the reporter's room which 'had one telephone and one toilet … It was not my idea of a newspaper office; nor were its inhabitants like newspapermen.' Inglis wrote that Smyllie 'liked meeting distinguished men, but he could not be bothered to seek them out; they had to come to him, in *The Irish Times* office – or, if they had been well advised, in the Palace Bar, where he held daily court'.

Patrick Campbell's *My Life and Easy Times* was replete with anecdotes about Smyllie, and when it was belatedly published, in 1967, it was given a scathing review in the paper by Mary Holland. She said it made for 'a grey, soporific and blurry book' and she was especially critical of what Campbell had to say about Smyllie. She wrote: 'He emerges as a figure in a string of anecdotes, mouthing colourful language, but there is no feeling of the man himself, or of what he did in making a newspaper which was at once unmistakably Irish and yet rose above the parochialism of the rest of the Irish press.' Holland reminded readers that Sarah Purser had said 'he is educating us all' when he was reporting in a column called *The Courts day by day,* 'and was moved to write with real passion of the suffering of others'. Holland posed the question: 'What happened?' and said that the

From left: Arthur Burgess, long-serving company secretary and director; Barbara Dickson, one of the first of the paper's women journalists; and Bill Coyne, porter and part-time switchbord operator, who had fought both in the Boer War and the Great War.

answer is in the title of this book and in one sentence: 'It would always be indolence, not fear, that would dictate my retreat from the top of the ladder. I knew what my function is only too well – the simple one of having a nice, easy time.' In that book, Campbell described how he informed Smyllie of his intention to leave:

> Then I told Smyllie I was going. He was very angry. 'God damn it!' he shouted. 'I teach you young bastards how to be newspapermen, and then you go flying off to London the first chance you get'. Then he calmed down. He was a generous man. 'All right', he said, 'Go'. But there was still bitterness in his voice when he said, 'And I hope it keeps fine for you.'

When things did not work out right for Campbell the ever-indulgent Smyllie agreed to take him back, but it was not long before he decided to depart once more to accept a post with one of the London Sunday titles. When told, Smyllie's reaction was to remark: '*The Sunday Dispatch* is a shuddering awful newspaper. The thought of a member of *The Irish Times* working for it pollutes my mind.' Both of Campbell's skulking departures, without so much as a 'thank you', had understandably infuriated Smyllie. There is no record of what Smyllie thought of Brian Inglis' subsequent exit, but it certainly infuriated Hubert Butler, one of Ireland's most enduring and distinctive writers, whose letters to the editor were a regular adornment to the columns. Butler was extremely critical of Inglis' decision to leave Ireland because, as Roy Foster noted, Inglis was leaving 'to become an important London journalist instead of staying in Ireland and showing that the Southern Protestant tradition could provide more exemplars of an Irish way of life than the handful of country crocks, retired British servicemen, civil servants and suburban car salesmen in whom the spirit of contemporary Anglo-Ireland has its incarnation'.

Éamon de Valera, as Taoiseach, attended the Institute of Journalists' annual dinner in January 1939, prompting the paper to comment two days later:

> On two occasions Mr de Valera has paid a delicate compliment to this newspaper. At an Ard-fheis of the Fianna Fail party – was it in 1937? – he said that, when in doubt about a topic for a speech, he examined *The Irish Times*, and never failed to find something. The second occasion was at Saturday night's dinner of the Institute of Journalists when he remarked that this newspaper 'always gives me inspiration'. Courtesy demands courtesy. Let us hasten to assure Mr de Valera that he seldom makes a speech which does not serve as an inspiration to the Press; and that is a tribute which not everybody merits or receives. Looking at the matter in this light, the Premier may be able to answer a question which he himself posed on Saturday night. At the Institute of Journalists' annual dinner this time last year, he raised the question of the freedom of the Press. He was surprised – so he admitted on Saturday – to perceive that this journal, while finding no fault with either the matter or the manner of his speech, was moved to inquire why it had been delivered at all. Mr. de Valera wonders at our suspicion. The answer is, of course, that Mr. de Valera suffers from one of the inconveniences of his position. A private individual may say as he pleases, and say it as often as he pleases, about the freedom of the Press or anything else; but a leading statesman must expect his lightest words to be raked with a fine-tooth comb. Who knows whether the most apparently casual remark proceeding from a Premier may not be the thin edge of the wedge?

When W.B. Yeats died – also in January 1939 – the news not unexpectedly caused the paper to comment editorially, quoting the poet's own words, 'We were the last romantics', adding that his death in France closed a chapter in the history of Irish letters:

> The world has lost not only the greatest Irish poet, but the greatest poet writing in the English language. He joins the great company of the poets who died in exile – Shelley and Keats and Rupert Brooke – and this is an enhancement of the loss which Ireland has incurred. That his remains will be permitted to lie permanently in France we doubt; his fitting resting-place is in the religious peace of a great cathedral. His tomb ought to be in Dublin's St. Patrick's, close to that of Swift. Of the company of Swift he would be proud, and the Ireland of the coming days will be as proud of W.B. Yeats as it is today of the great Dean …

For almost half a century W.B. Yeats laboured to bring a new soul into the country he loved with a deep and burning devotion. If he spurned the older political balladry for wrong reasons, he was, nevertheless, surely right in his instinct that pure poetry never could flower from the hybrid stem of a political movement devoid of ideals … When his inspiration led him towards poetic drama he brought verse back to the stage, and it gave to Ireland the beginnings of that drama for which the country has come to be revered in all parts of the world, and the Abbey Theatre is his splendid monument.

As the Spanish Civil War came to a close, the British prime minister, Neville Chamberlain, was desperately negotiating with Hitler over his demand that the Czech-Germans be incorporated into Greater Germany. *The Irish Times* confidently predicted[6] that there would be no European war:

> We need not inquire too closely into the details of yesterday morning's agreement at Munich. Suffice it to say that the method of peace has triumphed over the method of war, and that the remarkable scenes in London last evening, recalling the frenzied demonstrations of Armistice Day nearly twenty years ago, illustrate in vivid fashion, the relief that has been felt by the people of the whole civilised world …
>
> As we think, two men, above and before all others, have been responsible for the fact that Europe enters the month of October at peace instead of war. Both of them have not hesitated to make heavy sacrifices for the sake of those many millions of innocent lives … One of them is Neville Chamberlain; the other, Edward Benes …

The unfortunate President Beneš had been given little option but to agree to cede a large slice of his country, Czechoslovâkia, to Nazi Germany. Hitler had insisted that the Sudetenland, largely populated by German-speaking Czechs, be incorporated into the Greater German Reich, having successfully achieved the *Anschluss* – the incorporation of Austria – a year earlier. Chamberlain had brokered the deal and commented that Czechoslovakia was 'a far-off country about which we know little.' *The Irish Times* appeared to take a similar view:

> From the moment when Herr Hitler spoke at Nuremberg the issue was clear. The rights and wrongs of the Sudeten Germans' case against Czechoslovakia did not matter. What did matter was the fact that Germany possessed the mightiest armaments in the world; that its leader had set his heart on a certain object, and that he was determined to go to any lengths to secure it …
>
> What shall we say of President Beneš for whom the heart of humanity is bleeding today? Since the crisis began, Edward Beneš has been subjected to unparalleled provocation. He has

---

[6]   *The Irish Times*, 1 October 1938.

been reviled and abused in the coarsest and vilest terms not only by Herr Hitler and Field-Marshal Goering, but also by the whole controlled Press of Germany, which has depicted this valiant and high minded statesman as a cunning criminal, seeking to embroil the world in a suicidal war. He hardly could have been blamed by history if he had given way to the popular clamour and led his nation to an epic fate; but Edward Beneš has a conscience and no man … has deserved better of mankind.

As events were to prove, Hitler's designs on Eastern Europe were not settled by the acquisition of Austria in March 1938 nor by the Sudetenland in the autumn of the same year. Despite stating in a speech at the time that 'it is the last territorial claim that I have to make in Europe', barely six months later, the Nazis seized most of what remained of Czechoslovakia, the first territorial acquisition where it could not be speciously defended as incorporating areas mainly inhabited by ethnic Germans. Then, after snatching the city of Memel and its surroundings from Lithuania, Hitler made it clear that Poland was next on his shopping list. On 2 September 1939, after German troops invaded Poland, *The Irish Times* commented that

although technically Great Britain and Germany are still at peace, it looks now as if nothing short of a miracle can avert a European war … Twenty-four hours ago, we expressed the hope that, though the situation looked black, Herr Hitler might hesitate at the last moment, and peace would be saved. The sequence of events is soon told. The British government had been making strenuous efforts to induce Hitler to deal directly with the Poles regarding the future of Danzig and the 'corridor', and at one time it seemed as if Mr Chamberlain's tireless efforts might bear fruit. We now know that from the very start, Herr Hitler had not the least intention to negotiate with the Poles, or, for that matter, with anybody else …

Yesterday morning at dawn, German troops crossed the Polish border. Polish towns were bombed by the German Air Force, and Herr Hitler informed the Reichstag, which was specially convened for the occasion, that he had decided to speak to the Poles in the language which they had been using against Germany for some time past. Danzig [which had been declared a Free City after World War One],[7] was proclaimed solemnly to have been re-incorporated in the Reich, and Europe once again was presented with an accomplished fact.

Some may have viewed it as surprising that the paper welcomed the government's decision to declare its intention to remain neutral:

For the moment, at any rate, we in Ireland have the good fortune to be remote from the turmoil of Europe's strife, and every night pray to God that this happy condition of affairs may continue … [The Government's] first and paramount duty is to take immediate steps

---

[7]   Douglas Gageby, whose father-in-law, Sean Lester, had been appointed to administer the Free City on behalf of the League of Nations, was the author of a book on this subject.

to secure – so far as they are able to secure – the safety of our Irish State. At present it is virtually defenceless. In the shadow of universal disaster every Irish citizen worthy of the name will stand four-square behind his government, and will be ready to defend the national interest with his money, his labour, and, if necessary, even with his life.

When stating that the paper approved of de Valera's policy on neutrality, Smyllie added that 'in all circumstances of internal and external affairs, it is the only feasible policy for Eire. Yet it would be absurd to pretend that the people of its country can remain indifferent to the fortunes of Great Britain as, say Nicaragua. For one thing, there can be very few families in Eire that have not some relatives or friends in one or another of the British services.' Tom Garvin described 'neutral Eire' as a pretence where nothing was happening: 'Ireland felt like a rather down-at-heel sitting-room with a large hippopotamus sitting in the corner while everyone pretended it wasn't there.' The English historian, John Wheeler-Bennett, commented that de Valera actually had no choice but to decide on neutrality, suggesting that had he attempted to sway his countrymen towards war, he would have failed, even to the extent of having a civil war on his hands. As he expressed it, 'Ireland at this juncture, with characteristic paradox, would rather fight than go to war'.

His four-year internment in Germany had widened Smyllie's knowledge of European history and left him better equipped than any other Irish editor to comment on the massive events now taking place. In addition to his German experiences, he had returned to Europe during the mid-thirties to visit Czechoslovakia and later wrote a series about his experiences in the province of Ruthenia which was subsequently reprinted in booklet format. This territory was at the furthest eastern tip of the country, still very primitive, and inhabited by a people closely related to Ukrainians – indeed, the Soviet Union seized the province for itself at the end of the war. Smyllie was well-fitted to comment on Hitler's manipulation of German wrongs resulting from the First World War in order to lead his people towards his promised 'Thousand-Year Reich', as well as his promise to provide *Lebensraum* – living space for Germans in the lands to the east. Smyllie saw parallels between Ireland and Poland, and at one point, assumed that his readers were as familiar with European history as he was:

In this tragic hour, the thoughts of all Irishmen, whatever may be their political views, will turn with deep feeling to the agonies that are being suffered by the people of Poland. There has been much in common between the histories of our two nations, and no Irishman can think without sympathy of the days when

> Hope for a season, bade the world farewell,
> And freedom shrieked – as Kosciusko fell!

During both world wars, *The Irish Times* published war maps to enable readers to follow the battle lines. This photograph, taken in June 1944, shows one of the front office windows in Westmoreland Street dispalying a new war map in connection with the "D-Day" landings in northern France.

Just how many readers, one wonders, were aware that Thaddeus Kosciusko was a Polish general who fought courageously – but in vain – against the armies of Prussia and Russia in 1794? As events were to prove, Smyllie was correct to point out that history was about to be repeated. Even as its armies tried desperately to counter simultaneous German attacks from the north, west and south, Poland was stabbed in the back a few weeks later when the Soviet Union invaded from the east.

Before the Second World War was a day old, a German submarine sank the liner *Athenia* 250 miles north-west of Donegal. *The Irish Times* headlines next morning read: SUBMARINE WARFARE RULES IGNORED? ATHENIA TORPEDOED AND SUNK. 450 PASSSENGERS TO ARRIVE IN GALWAY TODAY. The paper reported that the ship had been sunk without warning, fifteen hours after Britain had declared war on Germany. On its way to America with over 300 American passengers fleeing the war, it had called at Belfast, where it had also taken Irish passengers on board. A Norwegian tanker, with 450 rescued passengers, was reported to be heading for Galway where 'the Irish Government had taken steps to have them attended to, and when they arrive doctors, nurses and ambulances will be waiting to convey them to hospitals in the city'.

As the war progressed, the paper found itself the target of the newly-appointed censorship board, and Smyllie developed a particular dislike for Frank Aiken, Minister for the Co-ordination of Defensive Measures, whom he once described as 'unintelligently impossible'. Smyllie was to carry on his personal guerrilla war with Aiken and the censorship department for the rest of the war. Whether he liked it or not, censorship was strictly imposed, not only to ensure that the belligerents were in no doubt that Ireland was, indeed, neutral, but also to suppress any possibility of internal divisions. Douglas Gageby reflected that censorship in Ireland 'was more heavy-handed than in any other neutral', citing the example that when snow fell during early May of one of the war years, the censors insisted that the news should not be published 'because it was military information'.

The censorship restrictions imposed upon *The Irish Times* were more severe than those imposed on the other papers if only because it made no secret about which side in the war the paper favoured. Brian Girvan has written that the then secretary of the Department of External Affairs, Joe Walsh, disliked *The Irish Times* for what he saw as its support for the British side of the war, taking the view that the paper's 'dearest wish is to bring the British back'. The censors expunged much of Smyllie's perceptive views on Central Europe, though he famously managed some small victories. One of Smyllie's tricks was to slightly change a news story – just sufficiently to cause the censor to miss the point while allowing his readers to see that point. After John Robinson, a journalist with the paper, joined the Royal Navy, his ship was sunk by the Japanese but, luckily for him, he was rescued. On hearing about this, Smyllie arranged the insertion of a small news item informing readers that 'the many friends of Mr. John Robinson, who was involved in a recent boating accident, will be pleased to hear that he is alive and well'. His most notable success had to await the end of the war. The front page of the paper announcing the news was decorated with a series of photographs of the principal war leaders, all arranged in the shape of the letter 'V' (for victory).

On several occasions, the opposition parties in the Dáil made it clear that in their view censorship was being applied too strictly. Under a three-column headline during 1942, the

Front page news. The paper's editions published on 21 April 1941 saw *The Irish Times* finally (after 82 years) making the decision to place news daily on the front page. The reluctance of so many newspapers to make this change now appears inexplicable – even the *Manchester Guardian* continued to use the front page for small advertisements until eleven years later. Perhaps more curiously, the *Guardian's* decision to change was not delayed by its commercial management but by its editor, A.P. Wadsworth.

paper reported that a motion in relation to censorship had been defeated. The wording of the motion read: 'That the Dáil is of the opinion that the censorship is being used at present unduly to restrict free speech and prevent the natural expression of public opinion in this country. Effective measures should be taken forthwith to ensure an administration of censorship powers which will command the confidence of our people.' Mr de Valera defended the actions of the censorship board whose task was, he said, 'the most difficult of all tasks of war time, because it had to parry the weapons which the belligerents were using against each other'. The motion was defeated by fifty-six votes to thirty-two.

The complexities of the policy of neutrality were nicely demonstrated by de Valera during that same year when he ordered the instant despatch of fire brigades from Dublin and elsewhere to Belfast in order to fight the fires resulting from a series of heavy German bombing raids on the city. A quarter of a century later, Owen Sheehy Skeffington commented on the decision:

> For the first time, one sees evidence of a genuine sense on the part of both the 26 counties and the minority in the 6 that the island was a total community in that the woes of some were the woes of all. When the Germans bombed Belfast, Mr de Valera's reaction was immediate. Every effort of his remarkable statesmanship in these years was strained to the maintenance of Eire's security away from the global holocaust; but these were his people the Germans were killing, unionist and nationalist, Catholic and Protestant. Instantly he gave orders and through the night of 15–16 April 1941 the fire brigades of Dublin, Dun Laoghaire, Drogheda and Dundalk went northward to the rescue of blazing Belfast. The second major raid, on 5 May 1941, brought the same response. At long last Dublin had shown some claim to speak for all of Ireland and the claim was none the weaker because Mr. de Valera's aid for the north was weapons of peace.

The Irish Times opened a fund for Belfast refugees who had been bombed out of their homes, raising over £3,000 in two days, with money reaching this newspaper at the rate of over £50 per hour. De Valera addressed a meeting at Castlebar: 'Speaking in public for the first time since the disaster in Belfast, I know you would wish me on your behalf, and on behalf of the Government, to express our sympathy with the people who have suffered there. In the past, and probably at present, a number of them did not see eye to eye with us politically. But they are our people, their sorrow is our sorrow, and I want to say that any help we can give them will be given wholeheartedly, believing that were the circumstances reversed they would also give their help wholeheartedly.' Curiously, while de Valera was in Castlebar to speak about food and turf production, *The Irish Times* carried a long leading article about turf production but made no comment on the Taoiseach's remarks about the Belfast air raids.

One month later, a large headline announced the news: 'GERMAN BOMBS DROPPED ON DUBLIN' and the details covered almost half of the paper's front page. Initial reports indicated that at least thirty people had died and over eighty had been wounded. A considerable section of the North Strand area had been badly damaged, early indications suggesting that some 300 houses had been demolished or damaged:

> All around the 1,000 yard line which three of the most destructive of the four bombs were dropped, work was proceeding yesterday to clear up that swathe of devastation which the explosives cut across the Ballybough and North Strand areas …

There were rumours that Germany had deliberately targeted Dublin in this manner to demonstrate its displeasure over de Valera's intervention when Belfast had been bombed

The scene after a German plane had dropped a stick of bombs on the North Strand area of Dublin in May 1941. Thirty people were killed, many more were injured and over three hundred houses were destroyed or damaged.

only weeks earlier. In all, German bombs were later dropped on more than half a dozen locations around the country for which no satisfactory explanation seems to have been forthcoming, much less for the sinking by U-boats of several Irish vessels despite being clearly marked as neutral merchant ships.

After a British bomber crashed in the Wicklow Mountains during 1941, *The Irish Times* reported in detail that the Irish Army – including an army band – had taken part in the funeral ceremony when the four dead airmen's bodies were taken to St Mary's Church, Blessington for a burial service. The army additionally arranged for shots to be fired at the graveside and the Last Post sounded. Presumably the censor allowed this coverage on the basis that the Government treated the dead of all the belligerents with equal respect.

While a number of staff members had joined the British forces, others opted for a different course. Patrick Campbell joined the Irish Naval Service, Seamus Kelly joined the army, and several more served in the Local Defence Force – George Hetherington, Tony

Gray, and Alec Newman, as did Lauriston Arnott who had fought with the British army during the First World War.

Although the paper had, on a few important occasions, placed news on the front page, there seemed to be a reluctance to make this a standard feature until 21 April. The reluctance of so many newspapers – especially those founded during the nineteenth century – to make this change now appears inexplicable. Even the *Manchester Guardian* continued to use the front page for small advertisements until eleven years later. Perhaps more curiously, the *Guardian's* decision to change was not delayed by its commercial management but by its editor, A.P. Wadsworth.

Two crucial battles proved to be the turning point in the Second World War – Stalingrad and El Alamein. By March 1945, the German position was hopeless but its army fought on. In the East, Russian forces reached the German frontier and in the West they had been driven back across the Rhine. On 5 March, *The Irish Times* reported that Cologne was 'a heap of rubble' and that Dresden had been 'wiped out'. About the latter, it reported that 'the town area is devoid of life. A great city has been wiped from the map of Europe … Now we can only speak of Dresden in the past tense.'

On 2 May, the main news of the day was proclaimed in a headline that occupied the full width of the front page: HITLER'S DEATH ANNOUNCED IN BERLIN. ADMIRAL DOENITZ NEW FUEHRER SAYS STRUGGLE WILL GO ON. Quoting German Radio, it stated that Hitler 'had fallen at his command post', although earlier the radio had claimed he had been 'fighting in the midst of hard-pressed Berlin garrison'. Neither version proved correct. After calling on his troops to fight to the last drop of blood, he left them to get on with it and committed suicide. Two days later, the paper reported the news that 'the Taoiseach and Minister For External Affairs, Mr de Valera, accompanied by the Secretary to the Department of External affairs, Mr. J.P. Walsh, called on Dr Eduard Hempel, the German Minister, last evening to express his condolence.' Smyllie very perceptively elaborated on the news of Hitler's death:

For the last ten years, and particularly since the outbreak of the war, Adolf Hitler had an almost uncanny instinct for that mysticism which plays such a vital part in the German character, and it was this mystic quality that raised the Führer to such a pinnacle of national hero-worship. Now that he is dead he can have no heir, for none of the remaining German leaders has been able to exert his peculiar appeal. His death must make a terrific difference to the future of the war by Germany. It must be remembered that every fighting German man took a personal oath to the Führer … but the death of their leader coming, as it has come, at a moment when their military fortunes have reached their nadir, cannot but tear the heart out of their resistance.

Smyllie was greatly irritated by the actions of the Censorship Board during the Second World War and went to some lengths to circumvent what he judged to be some of the irrational decisions forced upon him. He achieved his final success on May 8 1945 when the main news of the day was about the ending of the war in Europe, and small photographs of the principal allied war leaders were arranged on the front page in the shape of the letter V (for victory).

The war in Europe formally ended on 5 May 1945 and *The Irish Times* editorialised that

> for most practical purposes, the war in Europe is over … Details are lacking concerning the manner of the German surrender. During the past few days all sorts of rumours have been rife … The total collapse of the German army in Italy has removed the last chance of a prolonged struggle in the so-called 'Southern Redoubt'. Salzburg, within a few miles of Berchtesgaden, has fallen into American hands. General Patton's troops are also on the Brenner Pass … In the East, a certain amount of fighting continues. Berlin is a city of the dead … and the plight of Berlin's remaining inhabitants must be appalling …
>
> Germany's defeat is even more overwhelming than it was in 1918; but as Field Marshall Smuts said in San Francisco the other day, victory is not enough. While the ruins of National Socialist Germany are still smouldering, the work of rebuilding must begin without delay.

When the Germans formally capitulated, there were huge celebrations in Britain and elsewhere. Dublin witnessed, as the paper reported, 'the hoisting of the Union Jack and the Red Flag over the main entrance of Trinity College … attracting the attention of some hundreds of people'. This provoked a counter-demonstration organised by students from University College who produced and burned a Union flag. Eventually Gardaí with drawn batons dispersed the crowd but not before some windows of *The Irish Times* office were smashed by stones. Just over a week later, Churchill spoke on radio about the war and broke silence on the question of Irish neutrality:

Owing to the action of Mr de Valera, so much at variance with the temper and instinct of thousands of Southern Irishmen who hastened to the battle front to prove their ancient valour, approaches which the Southern Irish ports and airfields could so easily have guarded were closed by hostile aircraft and U-boats. This was indeed a deadly moment in our life, and if it had not been for the loyalty and friendship of Northern Ireland, we should have been forced to come to close quarters with Mr de Valera or perish forever from the earth.

However, with a restraint and poise to which, I venture to say, history will find few parallels, His Majesty's Government never laid a hand upon them – though at times it would have been quite easy and quite natural – and left the de Valera Government to frolic with the German and later with the Japanese representatives to their hearts' content. When I think of these days I think also of other episodes and personalities. I think of Lieut. Commander Esmond, V.C.; Lance Corporal Kenneally, V.C.; Captain Fagan, V.C., and other Irish heroes I could easily recite, and all the bitterness by Britain for the Irish race dies in my heart.

Three days later, on 17 May, the Taoiseach replied in measured terms to Churchill's criticisms in a radio broadcast, the text of which was published in *The Irish Times*:

Certain newspapers have been very persistent in looking for my answer to Mr Churchill's recent broadcast … I know the reply I would have given a quarter of a century ago. But I have deliberately decided that it is not the reply I shall make tonight. I shall try not to be guilty of adding any fuel to the flames of hatred and passion, which, if continued to be fed, promise to burn up what is left by the war of decent human feeling in Europe.

Allowances can be made for Mr. Churchill's statement, however unworthy, in the first flush of his victory. No such excuse could be found for me in this quieter atmosphere. There are, however, some things which it is my duty to say. I shall try to say them as dispassionately as I can. Mr Churchill makes it clear that in certain circumstances he would have violated our neutrality and that he would justify his action by Britain's necessity. It seems strange to me that Mr Churchill does not see that this, if accepted, would mean that Britain's necessity would be the whole moral code and that when this necessity was sufficiently great, other people's rights were not to count …

That Mr Churchill should be irritated when our neutrality stood in the way of what he thought he vitally needed, I understand, but that he or any thinking person in Britain should fail to see the reason for our neutrality I find it hard to conceive …

Mr Churchill is proud of Britain's stand alone after France had fallen and before America had entered the war. Could he not find it in his heart the generosity to acknowledge that there is a small nation that stood not for one or two but for several hundred years against aggression; that endured spoliations, famines, massacres in endless succession; that was clubbed into insensibility, but that each time on returning to consciousness took up the fight anew, a small nation that could never be got to accept defeat and has never surrendered her soul?

The Irish Times did not attempt to make the point that de Valera appeared to have given, as 'the reason for [Ireland's] neutrality', that Ireland had endured several hundred years of aggression inflicted by Britain. The paper simply commended the Taoiseach for his use of language that was 'as temperate as it was dignified':

> Mr. de Valera has his faults as a statesman and politician; but he has one outstanding quality. He is a gentleman. Never in the course of a long public career has he been either rude or discourteous; and his broadcast on Wednesday night was a model of good manners.

Office space was so limited at this time that many of the commercial day staff worked in offices that were used at night by the editorial staff. My advertising job entailed working in the room that, at night, became the subeditors' department. On the morning after a dozen or so senior Nazis, who had been adjudged guilty of serious war crimes, had been hanged, there was the usual basket on the desk containing photographs considered, but rejected, for inclusion in the previous night's paper. That morning it contained eleven grisly photographs of Ribbentrop, Kaltenbrunner and the other Nazi leaders dangling on the end of the hangman's rope.

The war certainly enhanced Smyllie's reputation as an exceptional editor, but it is an inescapable fact that there was another side to his character. Tony Gray has suggested the possibility that the directors were never entirely happy about his performance: 'Nobody in the office', Gray wrote, 'would have denied for a minute that he was a brilliant man, far larger than life, a personality who dominated every company in which he ever found himself. But he was also a man utterly unamenable to any form of discipline whatever, and completely incapable of appreciating any of the problems concerning the distribution, circulation and management of the newspaper.'

Frank Lowe had been invited to join the board of directors during the mid-1940s. A successful businessman, he soon realised that the remaining Arnott brothers on the board, whenever they were short of money, were prepared to sell portions of their shareholdings to him. They found a ready buyer in Lowe who was subsequently appointed chairman in 1945 when he, in turn, invited the brothers Ralph and Philip Walker, as well as his own adopted nephew, George Hetherington, to become directors too. The second Sir John

Lawrence Knox's daughter presenting a portrait of her father, the founder of *The Irish Times,* to Frank Lowe, chairman of the company, in 1945.

Arnott had already died and his brother Lauriston succeeded to the title and remained on the board until 1958, after which the Arnott control of the paper finally ended. One story concerning Sir Lauriston illustrates how little some of the Arnott family knew about the business of newspapers. During a discussion about a forthcoming special supplement, when Tynan O'Mahony told the directors that perhaps it could be set in Cheltenham (a typeface used in the paper), Arnott questioned this, asking 'Why can't we set it ourselves?' Jack Webb related a similar incident after Sir Basil Goulding was invited to join the board a few years later. During a discussion about raising the price, several of the directors expressed concern that the paper's sales might be adversely affected. Goulding, however, put forward a completely impractical suggestion: 'Why don't we bring out two editions, one consisting of fourteen pages at the old price, and a larger one of twenty-four pages selling at the increased price'?

Even if he disapproved of his methods and habits, Lowe appears to have had a healthy respect for Smyllie. For his part, though, there can be little doubt that Smyllie detested Lowe because of his tight control on the paper's admittedly slender finances. As Tony Gray wrote: 'It always irked [Lowe] that all the journalistic departments ever seemed to do was spend money, often in quite large quantities. He could never grasp the fact that it was the editorial content of the paper which made people buy it and advertise in it.'

Smyllie could sometimes make extraordinarily unexpected decisions, perhaps none more so than that to invite Brian O'Nolan to write – in Irish or English (or both) – for the paper. Anthony Cronin took the view that Smyllie wanted to demonstrate that his newspaper 'was not against the Irish language but only against the chauvinism and hypocrisy that went with it', and went on to speculate that Smyllie must have seen that this new contributor was ideally fitted for his purposes. The connection had actually commenced in 1939 when O'Nolan took part in a lengthy correspondence – writing initially under the pseudonym Flann O'Brien – concerning a review of one of Frank O'Connor's plays. Intrigued by what he considered was an unusually inventive writer, Smyllie invited O'Brien to contribute a regular column under yet another of his various pseudonyms, Myles na gCopaleen. Hoping that he would become internationally famous, O'Nolan was later to simplify this to Myles na Gopaleen – much to the regret, as Cronin noted, of some of *The Irish Times* journalists 'who liked the pedantry of the eclipse of the genitive'.

But, before all that, the young O'Nolan had entered University College, Dublin and joined one of the debating societies. His fellow students included Vivion de Valera, son of the well-known father and later to become head of the Irish Press Newspapers, and also James Meenan who, in 1974, was to become one of the original Governors of the Irish Times Trust. Meenan may not have paid much attention to O'Nolan at the time but he did write about the L & H:

> This most heterogeneous congregation, reeling about, shouting and singing in the Hogarthian pallor of a single gas-jet … It was certainly a disorderly gang but its disorders were not aimless and stupid, but often necessary and salutary. It could nearly be claimed that the mob was merely a severe judge of the speakers.

The result of Smyllie's invitation was the long-running Cruiskeen Lawn series, the first of which, appearing during October 1940, took the form of a discussion about the revival of the Irish language. In it he considered that if *The Irish Times* was printed entirely in Irish, 'there would not be a word about anything but food and drink … The Irish would be full of *cainnt na ndaoine*, excerpts from *seádna, corra-cainnte, sean fhocla and dánta díreacha* and would embody examples of *béarla féinne* and even *énbhéara* or bird dialect'. Despite Smyllie's wishes the column subsequently virtually abandoned Irish. Thirteen years later, O'Nolan resigned his civil service job, probably because his superiors would have become aware that his pseudonym did not disguise the real person and were, therefore, concerned about his numerous attacks on well-known people, especially Ministers and senior civil servants. As a consequence, he thereafter lacked a steady income, a situation that forced him to try to broaden his literary output, but only with limited success.

His column, especially during the earlier period, was often brilliant and very funny, though, as ill-health and other problems beset him, his writing could be laboured and repetitive. Readers came to enjoy his references, written from his imagined address in Santry Court, to 'the Brother', and to other featured characters including Keats and Chapman, whose imagined adventures together provided Myles with opportunities to arrive at excruciating puns. At one period, his zany sense of humour led him to invent a book-handling service for wealthy people who lacked either the intellect or the desire to read books. The 'service' would undertake to write comments into supplied books, underline sentences and so on in order to provide the owner's shelves with the appearance of being well-used. Even more bizarre was his idea of providing an escort service for similar people, arranging ventriloquists to accompany them to important functions where they would provide highly intelligent comments about art, music and literature. But there was also a dark side to some of his writing. Tom Garvin made the comment that 'behind his brilliant and scarifying wit lurked a deep sense of cultural despair'.

A shrinking number of people now remember his columns. Fewer still recall the regular visits of this dour-looking figure to the paper's Front Office, almost always wearing a heavy, black overcoat and broad-brimmed black hat, looking neither left nor right as he proceeded with his latest 'copy' to the wooden letterbox affixed to the wall labelled 'Editor'. Constantly under financial pressures, and not helped by his drink problem, he sometimes became querulous, fighting with Smyllie and with Jack White, the features editor. White (and later, Brian Inglis too) sometimes had to visit O'Nolan to placate him if some words were deliberately omitted from a contribution, for fear of libel. On one occasion, after a ten-month absence, Douglas Gageby, then joint managing director, intervened to pacify 'Myles' over one particular long-standing quarrel. O'Nolan's health deteriorated – he was often seriously ill – further curbing his writing and, after Gageby became editor, the paper continued to pay him even when he was unable to supply his twice-weekly column. Brian O'Nolan died in April 1966. Anne Clissmann thought that only Donal Foley, writing *Man Bites Dog*, 'corresponded in any way to the mixture of fantasy, nonsense, irony and inversion which Myles used to attack the idiocies of bureaucrats, the pretensions of idealists, the lunacy and danger of certain social attitudes'. Summing up, she also perceptively noted:

> As a final example of Myles's transcendence, and in an ironic reversal of the mood of the last years, *The Irish Times* on the day after O'Brien's death was still printing the latest articles as if the passing of the man who had written them was quite irrelevant to their continuance.

Around this time, a satirical cartoon published in *Dublin Opinion* depicted the editorial department in *The Irish Times,* as Vivian Mercier described it in *The Bell*: 'Practically everybody down to the office boy wears a top hat. The only works of reference in evidence are *Burke's Peerage* and *Who's Who*. The chief activity evident is engaged in by two elderly gentlemen who appear to be swopping melancholy reminiscences of the days of the Viceroys. There's no sign of an editor but a caller inquiring for him is being told: 'He's either gone down to Sackville Street or out to Kingstown'. Mercier's own view was that the paper 'had the virtue of a clear-cut and intelligible policy, which is more than can be said of any of its contemporaries'. He disagreed with the notion that – even at this time – the paper appealed only to Protestants. He pointed out that it contained 'church news for Catholic readers' and specifically drew attention to the paper's recent coverage of the Pope's address to Catholic medical practitioners. According to his calculations, the *Irish Independent* used 79 words in its report; the *Irish Press* 137, and *The Irish Times* 267 words. Mercier then continued on the topic of who actually read the paper:

> The price, three pence at present, means … that most of its readers are at any rate in fairly comfortable circumstances. In spite of what the *profanum vulgus* may think, its readers must be in the main orientated towards Ireland rather than England …
>
> *The Irish Times* has rendered a service to this class by finding for it compromise formulae, which have made the passage from Unionist to 'ex-Unionist' to Fine Gael supporter, to Fianna Fáil or Labour supporter seem natural and honourable instead of a hideous betrayal of tradition. Its leadership has thus helped the Protestants of Eire to retain an influence on the affairs of their country which is still all out of proportion to their numbers …
>
> It would not be right, however, to give the impression that only Protestants read *The Irish Times*. Slowly but surely it is becoming the organ of the entire professional class, Protestant and Catholic … [who] likewise appreciate the fact that *The Irish Times* addresses itself to an educated public.
>
> The paper also manages to represent the left wing of the so-called Ascendancy, so that a great many of its readers must follow it a little breathlessly as it boxes the compass, ever moving a few points further away from the true or fixed North of Unionism. They must frequently be shocked by its liberalism, though I doubt if many of them ever go so far as to withdraw their subscriptions. As far as social legislation is concerned, it is well to the left of the Fine Gael party – and most of Fianna Fáil too. In fact, it has been maliciously said that *The Irish Times,* in its anxiety not to appear Green, has turned more than a little Pink – if some of its readers do not positively see Red.

It was around this time that *Dublin Opinion* coined the phrase 'The Old Lady of Westmoreland Street', no doubt inspired by an earlier one adverting to the *New York Times* – 'the Grey Lady of Forty-third Street'. But long after *Dublin Opinion* ceased publication, and even after *The Irish Times* had sold its Westmoreland Street façade, the *Irish Independent* revived the idea. Lacking the originality of either of the former, it began referring to 'The Old Lady of D'Olier Street', giving the impression that Middle Abbey Street was competing with a decrepit old dowager rather than against a better-equipped and far more more up-to-date member of the distaff side. Back in the 1940s and 1950s, however, *The Irish Times* continued to be very much a minority newspaper, especially outside the metropolis, where most newsagents ordered exactly the number of copies they were certain they would sell. As often as not, the names of the regular customers would be written on the copies reserved for them, and it was not unusual for these copies to be stored out of sight beneath the counter. Michael McConville has mentioned that C.S. Andrews, whom J.J. Lee described as 'a notable civil servant', once drew up a list of what he saw as 'Protestant offences'. Included among them were 'travelling inside [downstairs in] trams instead of on top [and] reading *The Irish Times*, which was then a committed Unionist newspaper'. In his best-selling book, *Angela's Ashes*, Frank McCourt recounted his experience when he applied for a job in Easons' Limerick branch office. The manager informed him that 'we distribute *The Irish Times*, a Protestant paper, run by the Freemasons of Dublin … We take it to the newsagents but we don't read it. I don't want to see you reading it. You could lose the Faith, and by the look in those eyes you could lose your sight.' Intrigued by all this, the young McCourt brought a copy home. When his mother saw him reading the *Times*, she told him that he was lucky that his father was not there to see what he was doing. If he had, she ventured, he would have said: 'Is this what the men of Ireland fought and died for, that my own son is sitting there at the kitchen table reading the freemason's paper.'

After World War II had ended, Smyllie was approached by Norman Ashe – a glider pilot during the war – with the suggestion that he and Tony Gray (who was acting as 'Quidnunc' at the time), might fly over the invasion beaches and the bomb-damaged cities of Europe taking aerial photographs for the paper. Gray was to supply the covering text, and wrote later that what was being proposed was that they would be the first private pilots to fly over the war zones almost immediately after the war. As Gray pointed out, the operation would entail considerable expense at a time when *The Irish Times* had been taken over by what he termed 'an extremely parsimonious outfit of hard-headed Dublin businessmen'. Hard-headed businessmen or not, both the board and Smyllie agreed to authorise the project which resulted in a twelve-part illustrated series entitled 'Europe as the Crow flies'.

During May 1947, the paper carried the strange headline across four columns of the front page: MUIRCHU LOST ON HER WAY TO THE SCRAP HEAP. Formerly the British gunboat, *Helga*, which had shelled Liberty Hall and other targets during the 1916 Rising, it had since then become the flagship of the Defence Forces naval service. It had just left its base at Cobh for a final journey to a Dublin scrap-yard, when it shipped water and sank near the Tuskar Rock lighthouse. One reason for the story's prominence in *The Irish Times* was the fact that one of its reporters, Brian Inglis, had come on board at the last moment as the thirteenth person to do so and had, perhaps as a consequence, brought the ancient vessel ill luck. A Welsh trawler rescued all on board the ship.

Fianna Fáil lost power in 1948 for the first time in sixteen years. The new coalition Government embarked upon a plan to establish an Irish news agency, a move seen by some journalists as government interference. Politicians, however, continued to view partition, rather than the economy or the high emigration rates, as the nation's most pressing problem, so when a Commission on Emigration and Other Population Problems was set up in 1948, *The Irish Times* welcomed the move as 'a brave departure'. The paper saw it as 'a break with the ostrich-like behaviour of many patriots, who boast of the people's will to freedom, while ignoring the truth that the people's chief will, as revealed by the emigration statistics, is to clear out, bag and baggage, from the land their fathers strove for'.

Ireland became a Republic in 1949 – as did India – but unlike India, Ireland left the Commonwealth. As Dr Kenneth Milne observed, there was 'evident discomfort' among the readership of *The Irish Times* – most of whom were then Protestants – not least because the terms of the constitutional settlement of 1922 concerning Commonwealth and Crown had been discarded unilaterally.[8] Costello's announcement of the decision in far-off Ottawa (without as much as a hint of a referendum) was described by J.J. Lee as 'perhaps the most inept diplomatic exhibition in the history of the State'. Smyllie's reaction was, however, quite remarkably restrained:

> The birth of a new Republic was welcomed throughout the country. In celebrations centred upon Dublin where a 21-gun salute was fired from O'Connell Bridge by men of the 19 Field Battery … The tricolour flew from shops, business premises and public buildings, while in the suburbs the Papal flag flew from many buildings …

Many messages of goodwill from around the world were included in the paper's news columns, and heading the list was that sent by King George VI. After pointing to the close relations between the two countries, he added: 'I hold in most grateful memory the services and sacrifices of the men and women of your country, who rendered gallant assistance to our cause in the recent war, and who made a notable contribution to our victory. I pray that every blessing may be with you today and in the future.' Under the

---

[8]   Dr Kenneth Milne, historiographer of the Church of Ireland, writing in a chapter contributed to Stephen White's volume about Protestant reactions to political change in Ireland

headline, PRAYERS FOR THE REPUBLIC, the paper carried a short report about a Service held in St Patrick's Cathedral:

A special Service of Intercession for the Republic of Ireland was held in St. Patrick's Cathedral, Dublin, yesterday morning. It was conducted by the Rev. J.W. Armstrong, Dean's Vicar, and the Rev. Beirceart Breathnach, who recited prayers for the Republic in Irish … The music included a hymn of Saint Columba, set to a traditional Irish air. The Service was marked by the use of the new State prayers. The versicle, 'O Lord, save the King,' has been replaced by 'O Lord, guide and defend our rulers'.

While the Church of Ireland had officially recognised the new situation, many of its adherents – the bulk of whom were readers of *The Irish Times* – saw this latest development as one more example of the State disregarding some of the earlier guarantees designed to take account of their distinctive attitudes to political events. As Terence Brown expressed it:

The Protestant minority in the settlement of 1922 had reason to feel that some of what it esteemed in the Union of Britain and Ireland remained secure or had been satisfactorily reformulated. Its political experience over the next twenty-six years was one of systematic attrition of its political desiderata. In general terms anything in which they put their political faith was to disappear over two and a half decades: the Oath of Allegiance to the Crown, the right of appeal by Irish men and women to the Privy Council, representation as of right in the Upper House of the Irish Parliament, which had been guaranteed in the settlement of 1922, [and] Irish membership of the British Commonwealth of nations …[9]

During this whole period, most of the newspapers in Ireland continued to be very cautious as to how they expressed their views. Terence Brown, already quoted above, alluded to this situation when he wrote: 'Regrettably most Irish journalism … contented itself with the reportage of events and the propagandist reiteration of the familiar terms of Irish political and cultural debate until these categories became mere counters and slogans … Irish journalism therefore comfortably reinforced the prevailing sense that Ireland, marked, as the nationalists constantly stressed, by distinctive social, religious and linguistic forms, was somehow different from the rest of the world …'

By today's standards, pay throughout the forties and fifties was extremely low so that the papers' directors were commonly seen as a bunch of Micawbers even though it was fairly obvious that the company's finances were precarious indeed. After my appointment as company secretary, I found an entry in the board meeting's minutes book dating from a few decades earlier in which it was recorded that the directors had sanctioned a salary

[9] In a paper commissioned by the Forum for Peace and Reconciliation.

increase for me of seven shillings and sixpence per week. I wondered how long they had agonised over the matter. Pay rates for some senior clerks were as little as six or seven pounds a week and, despite having no less than two unions, many journalists were faring only slightly better. Both of the journalists' unions were still British based; the Institute of Journalists dated from 1884, having been founded more than a decade before the National Union of Journalists which eventually replaced it.

The death of George Bernard Shaw in November, 1950, coincided with the Papal Proclamation of the new dogma of the Assumption of the Virgin Mary 'in body as well as in spirit, into Heaven'. *The Irish Times* reported that the attendance at the ceremony was thought to have been the largest ever in Christendom, but it devoted almost as much space to details about Shaw's long life:

> Bernard Shaw was Irish without being Gaelic, British without being Saxon; he blended the two in admirable proportions. Never forgetting the land of his birth, his defence of Sir Robert Casement, and his plea for the lives of the leaders of 1916, will ever be remembered by his countrymen.

The paper recalled that at his wedding, Shaw wore a suit of old clothes in such a ragged condition that the Registrar took him to be a beggar, and nearly married the bride to the immaculately-dressed best man. Also reported was the medical advice given to him to eat meat, despite which he continued to be a vegetarian. Shaw's riposte was quoted: 'My Will contains directions for my funeral, which will not be followed by mourning coaches, but by herds of oxen, sheep, swine, flocks of poultry, and a small travelling aquarium of live fish – all wearing white scarves in honour of the man who perished rather than eat his fellow creatures.'

A few years earlier, Smyllie made an editorial decision that took no account of the greater good of the company. When John Hershey's account of the horrors resulting from the atom-bombing of Hiroshima in 1945 was published, Smyllie secured the serial rights and ran the entire piece in a single issue of *The Irish Times*, that of 31 October 1946. Although an extra-large print order had been arranged, all copies of that day's paper were sold out by lunch-time. Had he discussed the matter with the board, or even with the circulation staff, he would have been persuaded to serialise it over an entire week.

The year 1950 was famous, at least as far as *The Irish Times* was concerned, for the 'Liberal Ethic' controversy. Now almost forgotten, it was surely the most extraordinary correspondence ever to appear in the Letters columns of the paper, indeed, perhaps in any newspaper. It occupied so much space that, on several days, advertisements were held over. Once again, it was typical of the thinking on the editorial side of the house during Smyllie's reign that this decision was made without reference to staff members in the advertising department who, of course, had to face irate customers the following day. A small announcement explained the situation to readers:

HELD OVER
No classified advertisements have been inserted to-day
owing to pressure on space. All advertisements for
insertion to-day will be carried forward to Monday next.

The correspondence began after a Catholic theologian, Professor Féilim O'Briain, suggested that there was a continuity between the liberal critics of the church and communist totalitarianism. He compared the position 'at its most innocent and futile,' to some letter in *The Irish Times* about 'priest-ridden Irish' or 'the domination of the clergy'. At its most ruthless, he found its most vigorous expression in the 34 prelates imprisoned in, or exiled from behind the Iron Curtain, and claimed that Socialists and liberals agreed with free love, the artificial prevention of births, abortion and divorce.

Dr Owen Sheehy-Skeffington was the first to respond, causing Hubert Butler[10] to describe him later as a humanist, and 'as we know, he once engaged in what must have been the longest newspaper war ever waged in Ireland in defence of the Liberal Ethic'. Sheehy-Skeffington accused Professor O'Briain of sweeping generalisations. Brian Inglis joined in, and the topic gradually broadened into a series of side issues including censorship and the subject of Article 44 of the Constitution. A Dr Heffernan noted that Father O'Briain had instanced the massacres of members of his Order in the Spanish Civil War and questioned if he would attribute the acts of the Spanish Inquisition three hundred years earlier, to liberalism. The Rev. W.G. Proctor intervened to provide a Protestant view, to contrast with the Catholic and liberal opinion already expressed. His letter ended by making the point that 'this discussion on the liberal ethic should thus be recognised as a three-cornered one, not as hitherto appears, only between Catholicism and liberalism'. Many of the letters appeared over pseudonyms, a practice abandoned by the paper not long afterwards. One of these accused Father O'Briain – whose extremely long letters jousted with all of his many opponents – of giving 'a brilliant display of inductive, deductive and seductive logic'. Dr Sheehy-Skeffington returned several times to the correspondence, observing that, as he wrote: 'Yet, once more, Father O'Briain prudently avoids defending most of the positions at which his fire has been returned. Upon nine of the points on which I joined issue with him in my last letter, he has no answer to make. This has been his method throughout, and it hardly makes for a close-knit controversy.'

---

[10]   David Krause, in the *Irish Literary Supplement,* described Butler as 'an eloquently moral, enlightened and intellectually militant Irishman who uses words as his weapons'.

Seven weeks after the report of his lecture had provoked the controversy in *The Irish Times*, Father O'Briain's last letter on the subject appeared. Shortly afterwards, the paper reprinted most of the correspondence in a booklet running to 90 pages, six of which carried O'Briain's final letter. 'Clericalism is a figment of bigoted and ignorant imaginations', he wrote, adding: 'If it has any existence, it simply indicates a system in which a majority of people accept, willingly and deliberately, the membership, teaching and discipline of the Catholic Church … The fact that so many liberal and socialist correspondents object to this spiritual submission shows how soon liberty would wither away did they get control.' At the end of this letter came the time-honoured editorial formula: 'This correspondence is now closed.' In fact, one more letter ensued, addressed – not to the editor – but to the manager of the paper, from the same Very Rev. Professor Felim O'Briain, OFM. whose views had initiated the controversy, in which he wrote: 'I should be grateful if you would convey to the editor an expression of my gratitude for the courteous and impartial manner with which he presided over the controversy. I had no idea that the discussion would arouse such interest.'

By far the most important debate during 1951 concerned what came to be known as 'the Mother and Child controversy'. The Minister for Health, Dr Noel Browne, had attempted to introduce reforms to the health services but met with resolute opposition from both the Catholic hierarchy and sections of the medical profession. However, on 12 April, under the headline 'DR. BROWNE REPLACED BY MR. COSTELLO', the paper reported that Dr Browne had resigned, thanking the 'many hundreds of doctors who had offered to participate in the Government's Service'. As these offers had been made in confidence he had, he stated, all the records relating to them destroyed. When Browne commented: 'As a Catholic I accept the rulings of their Lordships the hierarchy without question', the paper remarked that the Catholic Church seemed to be 'the effective government of Ireland'. Before bowing out, Browne passed copies of his correspondence with bishops and politicians to the media. Editors were hesitant to use the material because this was technically a breach of the Official Secrets Act but, as Browne himself later wrote:

> This correspondence consisted of sixteen letters from myself, Seán McBride, John Costello and members of the hierarchy. We had been warned that the government might attempt to place an embargo on their publication, but Smyllie, an editor with genuine liberal beliefs, had promised me that if such an embargo be attempted, at the risk of going to prison, he 'would publish and be damned'.

According to John Horgan, other editors then followed in 'a remarkable breach not only of the criminal law but the polite conventions of political journalism which had obtained hitherto'. Browne, however, wrote that: 'As to the media, we were supported by the then liberal *Irish Times* which had a relatively small circulation. The mass circulation Independent Newspapers suppressed our side of the story and the de Valera Irish Press Newspapers did the same.' *The Irish Times* subsequently commented on the aftermath:

> A gallant fight has ended in defeat … [Browne's] tragedy is that he failed to perceive the extent and power of the forces that were both openly and covertly arrayed against him.
>
> It was dangerous enough that his 'Mother and Child' scheme aroused the fierce hostility of a considerable part of the medical profession; it was fatal when his views came into collision with the Roman Catholic Hierarchy. With a united Cabinet on his side, he might have prevailed against the doctors … but … he was left to fight a single-handed battle when once the Church entered the arena. Thus, not for the first time, progress is thwarted …
>
> This newspaper has not been uncritical of the ex-Minister's proposals, and holds no brief for his particular scheme. Our sorrow is that he has not been permitted to fight it out on its own merits …

As Fintan O'Toole was to point out many years later, *The Irish Times* played an important part in making this controversy a testing-ground for Church-State relations, but further revelations about interventions by the Catholic hierarchy came to light when the State Papers for 1951 were released under the thirty-year rule. It transpired that, in 1945, Archbishop McQuaid effectively persuaded the Government to drop its proposed legislation on child adoption. Among the documents newly made public was a letter sent to the Archbishop by the Attorney General during 1951, just before another attempt was being made to introduce a bill to regularise the adoption system. The Attorney General enclosed, in his letter to McQuaid, an advance copy of a speech in which he was going to denounce *The Irish Times* as 'a bitterly anti-Catholic paper'. He proposed to add that 'it is my earnest hope that the State will never by legislation imperil the immortal soul of a single child to satisfy the well-meaning but misguided views of those who advocate legal adoption'.

More than half a century later, further details relating to the background of these events were revealed in an article written for the paper by John Bowman[11] concerning several extraordinary approaches made by Seán MacBride to Archbishop McQuaid. MacBride and his new party, Clann na Poblachta, had done well during local elections in 1947 and he immediately wrote a servile letter to the Archbishop. The latter was informed that MacBride had just become a public representative 'for a portion of Your Grace's Archdiocese' and wished to pay his humble respects 'and to place myself at Your Grace's disposal'. He added that he would 'always welcome any advice which Your Grace may be good enough to give me and I shall be at Your Grace's disposal should there be any matters upon which Your Grace feels that I could be of any assistance'. Thanking MacBride, the

DR. BROWNE REPLACED BY MR. COSTELLO

Minister's Scheme Killed By Hierarchy Ruling

THE TAOISEACH HAS TAKEN OVER THE MINISTRY OF HEALTH FROM DR. NOEL C. BROWNE, WHO HAS RESIGNED, WITH EFFECT FROM MIDNIGHT LAST NIGHT. HIS RESIGNATION WAS HANDED TO THE TAOISEACH YESTERDAY AFTERNOON AND, SHORTLY AFTERWARDS, MR. COSTELLO WENT TO THE PRESIDENT AND ADVISED HIM TO ACCEPT IT. LAST NIGHT DR. BROWNE ALSO WENT TO THE PRESIDENT AT ARUS AN UACHTARAIN AND SURRENDERED HIS SEALS OF OFFICE.

One of Dr. Browne's last official acts was to announce that the free Mother and Child Health Service without a means test, which the Government had decided to introduce in June, 1948, had been rescinded. He also announced: " As a Catholic I accept the rulings of Their Lordships the Hierarchy without question." A new scheme—with a means test—will now be necessary.

Dr. Browne also announced his thanks to the " many hundreds " of doctors who had offered to participate in the Government's Service. As these offers had been made in confidence he had, he stated, all the records relating to them destroyed. The headquarters of the Clann na Poblachta Party will receive his letter this morning resigning from the organisation.

The resignation of Dr Noel Browne as Minister of Health, following the 'Mother and Child' controversy, was the main news story on 12 May 1951.

Archbishop assured him that he would not 'fail to take advantage of your generous suggestion that you are at my disposal …'

Bowman's *Irish Times* article then quoted MacBride's response in which he wrote that he did not deserve 'the thanks which Your Grace so graciously gives me, for in writing to Your Grace I was but doing what I considered my very first duty'. It was 'with no sense of false humility that I say I shall stand in need of help and guidance in the discharge of my new duties. Accordingly, I trust that Your Grace will not hesitate to call upon me at any time to impart such advice, formally or informally as may from time to time occur to Your Grace.' Bowman then added the following comment:

> Any supporters of MacBride who might wish to excuse this rush to ingratiate himself with McQuaid on the grounds that he was a political neophyte fresh from the triumph of a famous bye-election victory, will find no solace in MacBride's repeat performance after the general election a few months later.

The resulting letter was, if anything, even more fawning than those written earlier. It seems likely that the Archbishop's responses to this correspondence must have encouraged MacBride to make use of this open door to attempt to persuade McQuaid to denounce

Dr Noel Browne, whose Mother and Child scheme had effectively destroyed his political party. As Bowman pointed out in his *Irish Times* article, MacBride insinuated that Browne, whom he loathed, had, in an election leaflet, claimed that the Children's Hospital in Crumlin represented his own achievement rather than McQuaid's. Unfortunately for MacBride, the Archbishop 'had no intention of wandering into this minefield, and especially at MacBride's prompting'. While most people were aware of the strong clerical influence brought to bear on governments throughout this period, few could have envisaged the vista so clearly exposed in this single newspaper article. Commenting upon these interventions, Sheila Chillingworth wrote:[12]

> It was fortunate that R.M. Smyllie, editor of *The Irish Times* from 1934 to 1954, believed it was his duty to keep the Irish public informed of such controversies. By articles and, above all, his correspondence columns he performed a vital service to the Protestant community in Ireland. During the Mother and Child controversy, *The Irish Times* was the first paper to publish all the State correspondence about it. Gradually 'the Protestant paper' became essential reading for Catholics also.

Brian Inglis had already made the same point some four decades earlier when addressing a student meeting in Trinity College in February 1967. Stating that the college had introduced him to nationalism, he added that he was a nationalist, not by temperament, but by conversion:

> I should like to see Trinity doing very much what *The Irish Times* has done. It broke through by allowing 'Kingstown' to be called 'Dun Laoghaire' and that annoyed a lot of readers. Now it has broken out all over, put up its price, and not only retains its old readers but has created a new class of reader including the Catholic bishops who formerly would not be seen dead with it and are now prepared to flourish it under their arm.

On 16 September 1951, the next day's issue number 29,363 of *The Irish Times* very nearly did not get published. I had gone home for lunch as usual, and as I left to return to the office, my next door neighbour, an inveterate joker, called out: 'You needn't bother going back, the place is on fire!' I laughed and continued on my way, but when I reached College Green I could hear fire brigade units arriving noisily and saw clouds of black smoke ahead. Half of *The Irish Times* Fleet Street building was ablaze, and the firemen began desperately to try to prevent the flames spreading into the other buildings. The section on fire contained the huge printing press, the Linotype typesetting machines and the entire stock of the company's printing machinery. Coincidentally, this printing press had been

---

[12]   In a chapter contributed to Stephen White's *A Time to Build*, 1999.

This photograph, taken a few hours after the company's printing plant had been destroyed by fire in September 1951, shows staff working in the old Westmoreland Street front office by candle-light because the electricity supply had not yet been restored. Staff members in the picture (from left): 'Paddy' Bassett, Dermot James, Leslie Sibbald, Jim Reid (standing outside the counter), and Marjorie Homan.

purchased second-hand thirty years earlier after the company's previous press had also been destroyed in a fire. Even as I watched the flames, I could hear the sounds of the heavy Linotypes crashing through the burning first floor on top of the rotary press that occupied both the ground floor and the basement. A short distance away, in the basement and ground floor of the D'Olier Street building, lay a brand new printing press, still being assembled and due to be commissioned in less than two month's time. Nothing could save the old press, so all the efforts were now directed at protecting the new one.

The almost-ready new press was duly saved, but in the meantime the paper had no workable printing machinery. Offers of help came from Independent Newspapers, the Irish Press Group, the *Evening Mail*, the *Belfast Telegraph* and several provincials also offered assistance. Jack Webb, as general manager, settled for the *Mail*, whose press would be readily available at night and whose page size, unlike those of the other two Dublin groups, was the same as *The Irish Times*. Miraculously, a paper was scrambled out next day. The main front-page news was about the near calamity of the previous day:

> Yesterday's fire, which is reported in this morning's issue, has caused grievous material damage to *The Irish Times*. It requires us to offer both apologies and thanks … Today's is an 'emergency' issue but there is every reason to believe that within the next day or two it will be possible to produce at least some close approximation to a normal issue of the paper … *The Irish Times* this morning, and for some mornings to come, may not display its familiar appearance, but its spirit will be unchanged.

Most of the commercial staff had to work for several hours without electric lighting in order to process the advertising content for the paper, and even if the paper's entire photographic archive had additionally been lost, the main thing was that no one was killed or badly injured. Just under two months later, the paper was able to announce:

> After an absence of 57 days, *The Irish Times* has today returned home. Last night the rollers of the company's powerful new printing press whirled into action to produce thousands of copies of the first complete edition of the paper to be printed in *The Irish Times* building since the fire of September 17th …
>
> It would have been sad, indeed, if the paper had not been able to maintain continuity of production now that the 100th anniversary of its foundation is only a few years ahead. No doubt it will recall with pride in 1959 the fact that it did not miss production.

The completion of the installation of the new Hoe & Crabtree rotary press, costing £85,000, meant that, for the moment at least, the paper had the most up-to-date press in the world, capable of turning out 160,000 newspapers an hour if run at maximum speed. The new machine was three floors high with a then novel facility for stopping the press instantly in the event of a 'paper-break'. One of the firms wishing to be associated with the occasion was the Leinster Engineering Company, whose advertisement was headed 'Well Done':

> It is with feelings of admiration and pride that we pay tribute to the fine achievement of *The Irish Times* in making such a speedy recovery from the extensive fire damage to their premises. Admiration at the energy and enterprise of *The Irish Times* in publishing a daily paper since the fire under difficult conditions; pride at being privileged to assist in repairing the damage to precision printing machinery, and in installing the huge new Hoe printing press on which today's *Irish Times* was printed in the reconstructed Westmoreland Street premises. We are happy to associate ourselves with this important event and we extend our best wishes to *The Irish Times* for the future …

De Profundis

Under this headline, meaning 'out of the depths', *The Irish Times* printed an extraordinary report during June, 1951.

A grim variant of the old fable of Rip Van Winkle was produced recently in Poland. It seemed that workers were clearing away rubble and bomb damage near Gdynia, when they discovered two German soldiers who had been entombed in a bunker for no less than six years. The Germans had been trapped inadvertently when their own sappers blocked the bunker in the course of the retreat from Russia. Originally there had been six entombed men. Four died in the bunker, and one of the remaining pair fell dead when he reached the light. The survivor whose beard and hair reached to his knees, was astray in his mind, and lost his sight when the unaccustomed sun touched his eyes. Large stores of food and wine in the bunker enabled him to hold onto life; and Polish doctors now are trying to restore his sight. There is some prospect of success, in so far as he has been able to provide his age and the fact that he is a Berliner.

Jack Webb, mentioned above, had joined the company as an advertising representative, canvassing for the paper's property section. During his first few years, in the aftermath of the Second World War, few houses were changing hands, but the market recovered in 1947. Suddenly, the paper was carrying more property advertising than all the other advertising put together and word went round that his salary and commission – running at over £1,200 per year – was greater than the salaries of the directors. The latter acted with alacrity when Tynan O'Mahony unexpectedly died, and Frank Lowe offered Jack Webb the job as general manager, emphasising that for a young man this was a chance to achieve a substantial promotion. In response to his question, Webb was told that his salary would be £800, to which he said that he would be mad to accept a twenty-five per cent cut. Lowe was ready for this and told Webb his current earnings were not under discussion and if he chose to remain in his present job it would be on a flat salary of £800. Webb had no choice but to accept the 'promotion'. Immediately after this, Berkeley Vincent, Senior, who had been Office Manager, was offered Webb's former job in charge of property advertising, but unlike the other half-dozen 'reps', he was placed on a fixed salary designed to ensure that it came nowhere near that of the directors. Lowe must have thought this an astute arrangement, but the surge in the property market ebbed away as quickly as it had come, with the result that Vincent, unlike his fellow representatives, was assured of a steady income no matter what the state of the advertising market.

A few years before all this, the company employed its first circulation manager, Phil Myers, a quirky Yorkshire man who always greeted fellow members of the staff with a cheerful 'Top of the morning to you'. Given the climate of that period, there was not much anyone could do about promoting sales of the paper, but it was surely even more problematical for an Englishman who never fully understood how differently Irish people thought. If he is remembered at all now it is because in September 1950 he launched an in-house monthly news sheet called *Under the Clock*, the masthead of which featured a depiction of the company's famous timepiece. The first issue included a photograph of Tony Gray and Norman Ashe at Collinstown airport 'on the point of their departure for their epic flight', an event already mentioned in this chapter. Subsequent issues consisted of references to company developments, reports from the various departments and pen pictures of various members of staff. It continued to be published until March 1952, but a number of issues during Autumn 1951 had to be produced using a copying machine following the fire that had destroyed the paper's entire stock of printing machinery.

Writing about Smyllie in *The Leader* a few years before he died, Brian Inglis recalled that he could be infuriatingly casual in routine matters: 'To answer letters is his agony; to lose them is his delight. His small office is crowded with dust-laden articles awaiting acceptance (or rejection), and letters awaiting reply. It is commonly believed that some of these date back to his appointment as editor in the thirties'. Smyllie's last few years were dogged by ill-health, almost certainly the result of alcohol poisoning, though he also suffered from diabetes. During bouts of illness, he sometimes worked from home, receiving members of staff at his bedside. Tony Gray remembered being summoned to the editor's house in Pembroke Park, where he had to join those who had arrived before him, including William Morrison Milne, the chief sub-editor, Alan Montgomery, the chief reporter, and Tynan O'Mahony, the then general manager.

Smyllie subsequently moved house to Killincarrick, near Delgany, sixteen miles from Dublin, and reached by a very infrequent bus service in the post-war years. He quickly adopted the habit of going home at night on the last Number 84 bus due to depart from the nearby quays at 11 pm. The story has been told that one evening, when Smyllie was delayed by some late-night crisis, there was a timid knock on his office door. A head appeared – that of the conductor of the last Delgany bus – who was pleading with him to come quickly as its departure was already overdue. The crew dared not leave without him!

Tony Gray's earlier reference to the board of directors during the late forties as 'an extremely parsimonious outfit' was not entirely without merit, but it took no account of the financial problems facing the company. Brian O'Nolan, in a letter written to Brian Inglis, who had since become editor of *The Spectator*, referred to what he termed the 'petty instructions from certain directors who make prams and who should properly be in them'.

Cartoons began to feature regularly in the paper during 1953 with 'N. O'K's' neat single-column sketches appearing on the front page. This example, his very first effort, appeared on 13 April of that year, and was a comment on the controversy concerning 'The Bowl of Light' (*alias* 'The Thing', or even 'The Tomb of the Unknown Gurrier'), installed on O'Connell Bridge, Dublin in connection with the inauguration of the Tóstal festival.

"Somebody flung a brick at it last night—they've narrowed it down to the animal gang or the Arts Council. . . ."

This was a rather obscure reference to Philip Walker whose company, Walker's of Liffey Street, acted as agents for, among other things, radios, bicycles and prams, whose brother, Ralph, was to succeed Frank Lowe as chairman of The Irish Times Ltd. O'Nolan must have known that many companies at that time were struggling to survive because, although Ireland had been sheltered from the worst aspects of the war, trading conditions during the post-war period continued to be abysmally poor. Tom Garvin thought that this period of stagnation both encouraged and fed a 'moral and social conservatism,' which came to be viewed 'with a certain fatalism and what amounted to complacency and even complicity'. In this situation, the paper's main source of income, its advertising volume, was running at a very low level, so that the company's profits were either minimal or, in some years, non-existent.

When King George VI died in 1952, it carried a report concerning comments made by the Fine Gael leader, John Costello, about the late king's last message to Ireland. Costello had said: 'It is right that we should recall the message – and the generous terms of the message – on the occasion of the External Relations Act – a message of goodwill sent on his own behalf and on the behalf of the British people'. A year later, the coronation of Queen Elizabeth II was marked in Dublin by picketing at the British Embassy by the

Ralph Walker became chairman of the Irish Times Limited in 1959 on the death of Frank Lowe, and continued to hold the post for fourteen more years.

Anti-Partition Association, and by the absence of representatives of the Government from a garden party held by the British Ambassador.

The year 1953 also saw the inauguration of the now almost forgotten *An Tóstal* festival which got off to a bad start. The centrepiece decoration on O'Connell Bridge, Dublin, named 'The Bowl of Light', turned out to be 'a tawdry contraption' which was quickly and without ceremony dumped in the River Liffey, leaving behind the concrete base which Myles na gCopaleen labelled 'The Tomb of the Unknown Gurrier'. The event struggled for a number of years and, in 1957, in an attempt to boost it, an international theatre festival was added to the programme. When this idea was repeated a year later, a whole series of difficulties arose starting with Archbishop McQuaid's refusal to have Mass celebrated in Dublin's Pro-Cathedral to mark the opening of the festival. Sean O'Casey withdrew his specially commissioned play, *The Drums of Father Ned*; a production of James Joyce's *Ulysses* was cancelled, causing Samuel Beckett to withdraw his play as a mark of protest. *The Irish Times* condemned the cause of this disaster:[13]

---

[13]   *The Irish Times*, 15 February 1974.

In his day, George Leitch was Dublin's best-known photographer. He learned his trade with the Royal Flying Corps and liked nothing better than covering the annual Rugby Football international matches. In this picture he is seen arriving back in Dublin from a New Zealand Rugby tour in company with two attractive young women (he was also good at that) whom he had just presented with grass skirts.

No evidence has been adduced that either of these productions contains a hint of obscenity or of blasphemy; yet pressure has been brought to bear against both of them from high places, and the [festival] Council has kissed the rod … The primary function of An Tóstal has been to attract visitors to Ireland. It has not been a conspicuous success in that regard but the introduction of a theatre festival last season commanded international attention … Next year's Tóstal Council will be well advised to submit its programme to the Archbishop of Dublin in advance of publicity if it is to avoid a similar wastage of money and effort …

The same year also saw the introduction of another long-running series, entitled *Thinking Aloud*, a feature still appearing every Saturday after more than fifty years. Lesley Whiteside recalled that it all started after Jack White had met the Rev. A.H. Butler, then Church of Ireland rector of Monkstown parish, who, when asked by White, suggested that if a weekly religious item was about to be started, George Simms would prove an ideal contributor.

Dr Simms subsequently became Archbishop of Armagh and the column eventually came to be written on alternate Saturdays by a Catholic and a Protestant clergyman.

One of the stories related by Tony Gray in connection with the editor's later years concerned Smyllie's arrival back in his office during mid-evening only to discover that all or most of his senior editorial staff had gone missing. He was not amused when he eventually discovered that the group had left the office to attend a party at the Brazilian Embassy. So, when Newman arrived back, the editor addressed him in his customary fashion:

'Mr. Newman, sir,' adding, 'I understand you have been at some promotion or other at the Brazilian Consulate'.

'Yes, Mr. Smyllie, sir, that is correct'.

'And not only you, but also the Chief Sub-Editor, the News Editor, the Art Editor, and every shuddering executive of this shuddering newspaper?'

'Yes, Mr. Smyllie, sir. That is correct'.

'I am determined to ensure that this promotion, whatever it was, receives absolutely no free publicity in *The Irish Times* tomorrow. Kindly note that as of this moment, all dagoes[14] are banned from the pages of this newspaper'.

'*All* dagoes, Mr. Smyllie, sir?

'All dagoes, Mr. Newman'.

A few days after the above conversation had taken place, Smyllie had forgotten all about it. But Newman hadn't.

When Smyllie came in, he was far quieter than usual as he ferreted his way through the early proofs, clearly looking for something. At long last he spoke.

'Mr. Newman, sir. You haven't seen the proofs of the Pope's speech, by any chance, have you?' The Pope had that morning made a highly controversial pronouncement on some matter of international interest.

'Yes, Mr. Smyllie, sir, I have, naturally.'

'Well, where are they? They don't seem to be in my set of proofs.'

'No, sir, of course they're not. Because I killed the story on your instructions, Mr. Smyllie, sir.'

'What on earth are you talking about, Newman?', snapped Smyllie, all formal politesse forgotten in his sudden anger.

'Don't you remember, Mr. Smyllie, sir? Only the other night you banned all dagoes from the pages of this newspaper. By my reckoning, his Holiness is a dago, is he not? Ergo, Mr. Smyllie, sir, I killed the story.'

There were endless stories about the man. One such appeared in an unsigned article published in *Marketing Opinion* during 1982, which claimed that Smyllie kept a bottle of Scotch whisky in a filing cabinet under the letter 'S'. Another claimed that, following a

---

[14] Men of Italian, Portuguese or Spanish origin.

An amusing interlude snapped by an *Irish Times* photographer when An Taoiseach, Éamon de Valera, was opening Booterstown National School in March 1957. Archbishop Simms (on his left) obviously enjoyed the moment too.

confrontation with de Valera over censorship, Smyllie made a point of calling to the Taoiseach on his way to a Freemason's meeting complete with his Mason's regalia.

During Smyllie's last years as editor, the chaotic state of his office was the cause of increasing concern on the part of the board. The directors decided to appoint Harold Brown, whose service with *The Irish Times* had been mainly in the sports department, as news editor. Brown, seen by the directors as a clear-headed, no nonsense Northerner, was given the impossible task of introducing some discipline into the conduct of the editor's office. If he succeeded even to a limited extent this was, as Lionel Fleming later recalled, because Alec Newman switched his allegiance from his boss, Smyllie, to Brown. While the intention was to strengthen Newman's position, Newman began to think his own position was being threatened. The move ended tragically when, just a year later, Brown was found dead in his closed garage, sitting in his car with the engine running.

Smyllie's health continued to be a matter of concern. Alec Newman had been Smyllie's assistant for several decades and, naturally, regarded himself as editor-in-waiting. However, he was viewed by the management as too much in the same mould as Smyllie, and he was also seen as lacking the undoubted editorial flare of 'R.M.S.' Jack White then fell under the directors' spotlight. He had been sent to smarten up the London Office, a feat that he accomplished quickly and efficiently, and his daily *London Letter* became one of the paper's most popular features. Frank Lowe recalled him to Dublin, inviting him to spend a weekend in his house at Howth. Smyllie was greatly frightened when he heard that White had stayed with the chairman, thinking that the board was about to ditch him. Alec Newman, waiting in the wings for his elevation, had good cause to be worried too; now in his mid-forties, his hopes for promotion would disappear if Jack White got in ahead of him. The board made an initial manoeuvre appointing White to be features editor, a completely new post, placing him in charge of all the editorial content of the paper excepting the news, sport and the leading articles, a move widely seen as grooming him in readiness to succeed Smyllie. In fact, White, who would almost certainly have made a very good editor, never got his chance, eventually leaving to join the newly established Irish television service.

The news of Smyllie's death, on 11 September 1954, came as no surprise to those close to him. He had been hospitalised with increasing frequency and had also spent several periods convalescing. Although Donal O'Donovan wrote that the names of those who attended the subsequent funeral 'read like an Irish *Who's Who*', it was Tony Gray who noted the names of some who did *not* attend. The latter included the President, Seán T. O'Kelly, the Taoiseach, John Costello, and the leader of the Opposition (and proprietor of the *Irish Press*), Éamon de Valera.

Lionel Fleming did give Smyllie credit for his 'achievement of reconciling *The Irish Times* with Irish points of view and Irish aspirations, and doing this without hypocrisy, or the abandonment of standards, or any wavering of the paper's friendship for Britain. The voice could still be critical, but it asserted itself as an Irish voice.' Bruce Williamson, later to be deputy editor himself, summed up the man's two decades thus:

> It was a marvellous interlude, that period with Smyllie, but it was no way to run a newspaper. Certainly, as time went by, it became clear that this enclave of magnificent Bohemianism was totally unsuited for a modern newspaper. The thing that always surprised me was that the paper survived. But it survived an awful lot of people, and that's why today, no matter what happens, I'm sure that one of the last institutions to go down will be *The Irish Times*.

Alec Newman
&
Alan Montgomery

1954–1961 & 1961–1963

———➤●⬧●←———

Newman: 'A perfect foil for Smyllie'
Montgomery: 'Guinness was good for him'.

R.M. SMYLLIE died after twenty years in office, and Alec Newman succeeded him despite the fact that many had thought that Jack White was more likely to be chosen by the board. The board was to regret that it had not moved faster. Bruce Williamson, who was later to be deputy editor of the paper, was to write of Smyllie's successor:

> Two more dissimilar characters could hardly be imagined – Smyllie with his blunt directness, Newman with his gentle and slightly pedantic ways; Smyllie … basically a loyalist, Newman already edging towards republicanism. Yet in a sense they were as complementary to each other as Don Quixote and Sancho Panza. They were always bickering in a good-humoured and often in an extremely comic way, but between them they did the paper a great deal of good.

Another *Irish Times* journalist, Brian Fallon, Literary Editor and Art Critic, wrote of Newman that 'though a decent and cultured man, he lacked both the popular touch and the ponderous flair coupled with the massive personality of his predecessor. His editorship saw the paper slip further in prestige and readership, challenged increasingly by the *Irish Press* under an able editor, Jim McGuinness. It was not until the mid-1960s that the energy and radically new outlook of Douglas Gageby brought *The Irish Times* back on an even keel, though inevitably on a different course'.

Smyllie's huge presence continued to be felt even after he had died. Tony Gray remembered writing what he described as a fairly controversial leading article which, as usual, was submitted to the editor for approval. After reading it, Newman handed it back with the comment: 'I don't have the slightest problem with it but you know that the editor would never have let it pass.' Along with most of the senior editorial staff, Newman continued to refer to the deceased Smyllie as 'the Editor'.

Alec Newman had been a schoolmaster at the High School, Dublin, and when a classical scholar at Trinity College, Dublin, he had been invited by John Healy to write occasional articles and reviews for the paper. Newman gave up teaching in 1930 when offered a full-time position in the editor's office, writing leading articles and assisting generally with the paper's production. As a child living in Belfast, Newman remembered the rioting and shootings in that city, events that later led him to become a nationalist, thus influencing, to some degree, Smyllie's adroit adjustments of the paper's political direction. Now, after almost twenty-five years assisting, he was fully in charge for the first time. Unlike his two predecessors, he did not have to face huge political changes – indeed his tenure of office was marked by a period of relative calm apart from a short campaign directed by the IRA against British Army establishments and the RUC in Northern Ireland. Some idea of the fairly general passive support given by the majority in the Republic at this time to the IRA was demonstrated when, in January 1957, two of its members were killed in an attempt to bomb Brookeborough police barracks in Co. Fermanagh. Commenting upon the subsequent events when the State papers for that period were released, *The Irish Times* quoted from Bowyer-Bell's book, *The Secret Army*.

When the bodies of Seán South and Fergal O'Hanlon were carried across the Border their transmutation from young men to martyrs began. There began a week of all but national mourning. Crowds lined the route of South's funeral cortège to Dublin. Larger crowds came to pay their respects. Mass cards began to pile up and overflowed. Town councils and County Corporations passed votes of sympathy, not only for South and O'Hanlon, but also for their cause … At midnight on January 4th, 20,000 people, including the city's mayor, were waiting for the hearse. The next day a great silent procession of 50,000 followed the casket to the grave.

Newman not only had to deal with the opening of that earlier IRA campaign, but also to direct the paper's coverage of – to sample two extremes – a general election defeat for Fianna Fáil and the arrival of myxomatosis in Ireland. Not unexpectedly, given that Newman had been Smyllie's assistant for two decades, the change of editorship produced

Loftus Arnott was the last member of the family to be appointed chairman of the company (1940–45) although his brother, Sir Lauriston (photo right) continued to serve as a director until he died in 1957. His death brought to an end the Arnott management connection with *The Irish Times* that had lasted for just over eighty years.

little evidence of change in the paper's policy, although Bruce Williamson was to express the view that Newman edged the paper further from its former unionist stance. Commenting on a remark made by the German Ambassador at this time criticising the standard of journalism in Irish newspapers, Professor Lee wrote that *The Irish Times* had become

> … a paper of genuine quality, but only when the potential readership had expanded, thanks to educational change. It had never, it is true, pandered to popular passions. A number of notable newspaper columns, in English or Irish, subsequently emerged, like those of Desmond Fennell in the *Sunday Press*, Anthony Cronin, Liam de Paor, Seán O Riordáin, and Brendan Ó hEither, as well as the 'Beocheist' column in *The Irish Times*, or Conor Cruise O'Brien in *The Irish Times* and the *Irish Independent*, which sought to address issues of enduring importance.

Alec Newman must have been pleased when, in 1955, his newspaper was awarded a 'highly commended' certificate in an annual competition organised by *Printing World*, open to all newspapers in Britain and Ireland, although it was only the first of many. The paper was later to feature even more strongly in another annual award scheme, confined to Ireland, for press photographs.

In October of that year, Archbishop McQuaid made known his disapproval of a planned football match between the Republic of Ireland and Yugoslavia. *The Irish Times* reported a predictable reaction from Mr Harry Midgley, the Northern Ireland Minister of Education, who called the intervention 'one of the most monumental pieces of clerical interference yet seen … This justified', he added, 'the attitude of those who believed that the Hierarchy still worked on the presumption that they were not only the controllers of faith and morals, but of every other field of human activity in what was to them a clerical state. And we have it on the authority of the Roman Catholic Bishop of Cork [the Most Rev. Dr. Lucey] that the Roman Catholic Hierarchy in the Republic are the final arbiters of right and wrong, even in political matters.' This short-lived controversy prompted a number of readers to write to the paper on the topic, one of whom mentioned that 'it is barely a month since we entertained here in Dublin a team of Russian astronomical scientists. They were wined and dined and … personally received by our President, Premier and other leaders. Yet, throughout it all, I do not recall one single protest from any quarter.' The football match went ahead, but no members of the government attended and the Army Band, due to provide music, was discreetly withdrawn. Unofficial Ireland was represented by an attendance of 31,000, but there was some consolation for the government and the bishops; the Yugoslav team won 4–0.

Arguably one of the worst examples of clerical intervention at this time was probably that which happened in 1957. However, it was not the Government that was put under pressure but the tiny Protestant population of a small village in Co. Wexford. *The Irish Times* reported its beginnings during late May of that year:

> Because of a boycott by Roman Catholics in Fethard-on-Sea (population 100) Co. Wexford, the Church of Ireland school and its eleven pupils are without a teacher; Protestant shopkeepers and dealers in the area are doing little business and one man is seeking police protection for his family.
>
> The school closed on 15 May when its Catholic teacher was advised by a number of women in the village that 'it would be better for her if she did not give any more lessons.'
> The Sexton [caretaker – also a Catholic] of St Mogue's Church … was advised by her neighbours to give up the duties she had been carrying out there for a number of years.
>
> The boycott began on Monday 13 May, when local people announced their intention of staying away from village shops owned by Protestants. Its cause was the disappearance on 7 April of Mrs Sheila Cloney, and her two children, Eileen and Mary, aged six and three years. Mrs Cloney, who is the wife of a local farmer, Mr Sean Cloney, who is a member of the Church of Ireland, married Mr Cloney, a Catholic, in London, in 1949 …

It seems very curious indeed that the initial report in *The Irish Times* made no mention of the part played in the incident by the local Catholic clergy who (and not 'a number of

Newspaper Preferences

My parents were Labour voters … My father read de Valera's *Irish Press* every day, backwards, that is, he started with the back page's sport and moved steadily in reverse order to the front page, largely ignoring, I suspect, whatever scraps of foreign news the paper saw fit to carry in those days. He was never an *Independent* man; I heard an acquaintance of his one day referring to that paper with a contemptuous snort: 'The *Independent*? Ha! – full of horses and dead priests.' *The Irish Times*, of course, did not enter our field of vision. The *Times* was the choice of what my mother still referred to, with a sort of curtsy in her tone, as the 'Big House'.

John Banville,
in a contribution to *The Lost Decade*,
edited by Dermot Keogh and others.

women' as reported in the paper) instigated the boycott. A few weeks later, however, it described the boycott as 'undemocratic, unchristian and in every way detestable'. Father Allen and his curate had informed Mrs Cloney that young Eileen must not be sent to the Protestant school but to the Catholic school in the village. She refused and when the boycott commenced she disappeared with her two children. What followed was that the few dozen Church of Ireland members in the locality were made the subject of a nasty general boycott. Hubert Butler, who wrote about all this in detail, thought that Bishop Staunton of Ferns would intervene and 'put an end to what was becoming a national scandal'. That did not happen; indeed, Bishop Browne of Galway described the boycott as 'a peaceful and moderate protest'. When the Taoiseach, Éamon de Valera, was asked to intervene, he was unable to do so but described the boycott as 'ill-conceived, ill-considered and futile for the purpose for which it seems to have been intended'. Almost three decades afterwards, Butler (a frequent contributor to the Letters columns of *The Irish Times*) returned to the subject, commenting: 'Today the idea of neighbourly love has been diluted till it covers all humanity. We grieve for distant events and people with sympathy as thin and ephemeral as the newspaper in which we read about them.' Dermot Keogh was to write: 'How much out of step were such expressions of intolerance with official thinking and with public opinion in general.'[1] Another writer, John Banville, was thinking mainly about censorship when he contributed a chapter to *The Lost Decade*, but his thoughts might easily have embraced the wider scene during the 1950s:

---

[1]   In a paper commissioned by the Forum for Peace and Reconciliation.

What continues to surprise me, when I look back like this, is how docile we were, how grimly accepting of the status quo … From the start, de Valera set out to conduct a carefully prepared political experiment … The republic which he founded with the aid and encouragement of [Archbishop] John Charles McQuaid, was unique: a demilitarised totalitarian state in which the lives of the citizens were to be controlled not by a system of coercive force and secret policing, but by a kind of spiritual paralysis maintained by an unofficial federation between the Catholic clergy, the judiciary, and the civil service.

Banville might also have been writing about what came to be known as the Tilson case, where the husband of that name, prior to his 'mixed' marriage, agreed to have any children of the marriage baptised as Roman Catholics. After changing his mind, he removed them to a Protestant orphanage thinking that, in common law, as head of the household he was within his rights. The courts, however, returned the children to their Catholic mother. Commenting on this case and that of the 'Mother and Child' controversy, Dr Kenneth Milne wrote that both 'were seen to give credence to the allegation that Home Rule was, indeed, Rome Rule'[2].

McQuaid's strong views, though apparently not universally seen as strong at the time, were sometimes the target of criticism from *The Irish Times*, even before he was appointed Archbishop of Dublin. Back in 1934, Catholic bodies expressed concern when an athletics meeting was being planned at which it was proposed that both men and women would be taking part. On that occasion he reportedly is said to have called the decision 'un-Catholic and un-Irish'. John Cooney has told the story of how an *Irish Times* journalist faced up to a threatening McQuaid. The occasion was a Conference of Convent Secondary Schools at which, when the Archbishop was addressing some 300 nuns, he paused suddenly to ask if there were any journalists in the hall:

> Peader Cearr of the *Cork Examiner*, when he made himself known, was told the meeting was private, and he was ordered to walk down to the podium to hand his notes to the Archbishop. Denis Coughlan of *The Irish Times* quietly left the hall but was spotted by McQuaid in the hallway … McQuaid approached him and harshly demanded his notebook. This time, Coughlan looked 'the terrifying figure in the eye', and told him, 'No'. Explaining that he had been invited officially, Coughlan said his notes were not his to surrender as they were the property of the newspaper. If His Grace wished, he could take the matter up with the editor. He refused to give him his name but showed his invitation from the Dublin Diocesan Press Office. Muttering that there must have been a mistake, McQuaid flounced away in a rage …

2   In a chapter contributed to Stephen White's book *A Time to Build*.

The two continental visits made by Smyllie during the late thirties resulted in a series of articles appearing under his pen name, 'Nichevo', and each was published in booklet format. On his first trip, which has been already briefly mentioned, he went to Ruthenia, then forming the most eastern part of Czechoslovakia. The publication describing his travels was entitled *Carpathian Contrasts*. After his visit to the Dordogne in 1938, the resulting booklet was entitled *By the Banks of the Dordogne*, and advertised as 'Nichevo at his best, with many illustrations, price three pence'. Later, in a similar vein, Jack White's series *Italy in a Fortnight*, was especially successful, selling 5,000 copies.

After the war, and continuing for several decades, *The Irish Times* published quite a considerable number of longer articles in booklet format. Besides a reprint of the 1950 *Liberal Ethic* correspondence, another from this period was *Wealth from the Land*, reprinted from a series of eighteen articles that had appeared in the paper during 1953. Contributors included Brian Inglis; M. J. Costello (who had become General Manager of the Irish Sugar Company); James Dillon, a former Minister for Agriculture; and Thomas Walsh, the then current minister. Walsh summed-up the series with the comment: 'There has been a striking increase in the last few years in the amount of serious public discussion of our agricultural problems. The series of articles in *The Irish Times* is the latest and one of the best examples'.

Another booklet comprised the series, *P.R. in Ireland*, written by Proinsias Mac Aonghusa, a remarkably detailed account of how Proportional Representation had worked in Ireland, and included details of all the general elections from 1922 to 1957, and G. Duggan's *Northern Ireland: Success or Failure*. Peter Byrne's series on *The Irish Athletics Split*, covering the saga which had been running for the best part of three decades (1935–1963), was also reprinted, as were several written by Michael Viney during the 1960s – *No Birthright, Growing Old in Ireland* and *The Five Per Cent*. While researching *The Five Per Cent*, Viney interviewed Dr Simms, then Church of Ireland Archbishop of Dublin who, as Lesley Whiteside has recorded, told him: 'I don't think of [my people] as a minority – and I hope they see themselves as a part of a world-wide communion … After all, Christians at large are in a minority.' Perhaps he made the point because he was not over-enamoured with the title of the series, a detailed survey of Protestants in the Republic. Viney's *No Birthright* series, a study of the Irish unmarried mother, was considered quite daring at the time. Today, Michael Viney is usually regarded as a perceptive observer of the natural world and things ecological; it is easy to forget that when he joined the paper, he was writing on social and similar issues. Viney gave up his secure and very successful job and departed from his Dublin suburban home to live on a wild Connemara shore where he and his wife embarked on a life of near self-sufficiency. His weekly column is now among the longer-running features in the paper, and he has since published several books based on his Saturday writings.

Reverting to the paper's booklets, *The Irish Times* also produced a number of promotional publications – *Focus on the Irish Market* was published in 1949, and *Some Facts and Figures about the Republic of Ireland* appeared in 1951, and was later updated in 1955. Several selections from Donal Foley's weekly *Man Bites Dog* articles, dating from the early 1970s, were among the last to be published in booklet format. Quirky in style, the following brief extract may give perhaps a hint that the series owed something to the late, lamented Myles na gCopaleen:

> Massive redundancies will take place in the Roman Catholic Church in Ireland when Ireland enters the European Community in January. The redundancies are foreshadowed in a rationalisation plan published today making the Church a viable religious unit in the Market. The plan was prepared by the Most Rev Dr Mansholt, Bishop of Brussels, at the request of the Irish Management Institute.
>
> Approximately 100,000 Irish Catholic heads are expected to roll as a result of the Mansholt axe. 'There are far too many Catholics in Ireland', the report bluntly states, 'The religious power houses in Ireland could be run by half the number of people running them at present. What is needed is spiritual automation, with more use of the country's hot line to Heaven.'
>
> Some of the Catholics who will suffer redundancy may find an outlet in the upsurge of vocations which the market will bring, according to the Mansholt plan. 'The deployment of the new vocations is a vital matter for the religious community as a whole. They may have to find work in Germany and other religious community centres.' The report urges the immediate recall of all Irish missionaries abroad, because of the 'dissipation of Irish spiritual assets involved'. The abolition of sin was considered in the plan but rejected on the grounds that such a drastic recommendation would have a bad effect on the morals of the country.

The most unusual booklet in the entire series was that which had the longest title: *Summary of Evidence submitted in the Case of Gibbings and O'Dea and Co. Ltd.* during 1949, of which almost 1,000 copies were distributed. Running to more than thirty pages and issued 'with the compliments of *The Irish Times*', the introduction referred to the following account of a recent libel action concerning an advertisement carried by the paper for O'Dea's, the manufacturers of O'Dearest mattresses, a case that was 'of widespread interest'. O'Dearest mattresses were the subject of one of the longest-running advertising campaigns, appearing every Saturday for many years, only in *The Irish Times*. Each advertisement consisted of a cartoon above an amusing limerick, one of which, Mr Robert Gibbings, an artist and writer, did not think amusing. He complained that the advertisement appearing on 25 June 1949 contained a caricature purporting to be a portrait of himself relaxing on a mattress in a caravan, over a verse:

This advertisement for O'Dearest mattresses is an example of that company's very long-running campaign featured on the front page of the paper every Saturday for several decades.

'In a caravan writing', said Bob
'Can at times be a wearisome job,
Then it's nice to enjoy
One's O'Dearest nearby
So completely cut-off from the mob'.

When the libel case was heard, the jury decided that the advertisement was not defamatory. Damages were assessed at nil, and the defendant's costs were covered.

Perhaps, in a very different way, the most interesting of all the reprints published by *The Irish Times* was a slim hardback volume of poetry. In 1944, Smyllie had the idea to ask Donagh MacDonagh to choose from the range of verse that had appeared in the newspaper throughout the previous decade during which he had decided to include verse in the weekly *Book Page*. As Smyllie explained in the preface, he initially intended to publish the collection privately but changed his mind when he saw what he called 'the result of MacDonagh's labours'. In his introduction, the latter made the point that while some Irish poets write impeccable English, their writing has a slightly wild quality which is recognisably non-English. He described his selection as 'a cross-section of the Irish poetry of the past ten years', during which few Irish poets had not been represented in its

Brian O'Nolan, better known by his pseudonym, Myles na gCopaleen, contributed a long-running series, *Cruiskeen Lawn,* for the paper during the forties, fifties and sixties.

columns. The volume, *Poems from Ireland,* ran to just over 100 pages and included poems by more than forty Irish poets, including Austin Clarke, Rhoda Coghill, Patrick Kavanagh, Cecil Day Lewis, Louis MacNeice, L.A.G. Strong and W.B.Yeats. Also included were three poems from the Irish by Myles na gCopaleen, including the little '*Domforcai fidhbaidac fál*':

> A hedge before me, one behind,
> A blackbird sings from that,
> Above my small book many-lined
> I apprehend his chat
>
> Up trees in costumes buff,
> mild accurate cuckoos bleat,
> Lord love me, good the stuff
> I write in a shady seat.

Donagh McDonagh wrote to Gageby ten years later to suggest a second volume, but nothing came of it, although the paper did publish several books of poetry many years later, including one in 2002. This comprised a selection based upon a response given by more than 3,500 readers to vote for their favourite poem. Writing in that book's *Foreword,* the paper's literary editor, Caroline Walsh, remarked 'how established is the tradition of publishing poems in *The Irish Times.* The fact that not just this newspaper, but also Irish newspapers in general, publish so much creative writing as a matter of course, is often remarked on as unique at international newspaper conferences.' Sharing sixty-ninth place among the '100 most nominated Irish poems' was Yeats' *Under Ben Bulben.* Not many people are aware that the often-quoted lines, subsequently carved on his headstone in

Drumcliffe churchyard, were seen publicly for the first time when the poem was published in *The Irish Times*:

> Cast a cold eye
> On life, on death,
> Horseman, pass by!

Donal O'Donovan, like Viney, was another journalist who 'changed horses' in mid-life. Assistant editor during the 1960s, he left the company to become PRO for the Bank of Ireland – no one could have doubted that the pay was better there. But the pull of journalism drew him back into freelancing for *The Irish Times*, doing casual subediting work until the chief subeditor, Donald Smyllie, (R.M.s' younger and much more conventional brother) offered him a permanent position. He became editor of the *Irish Review and Annual*, and began writing the weekly *People in Business* column, and also wrote what were seen by J.J. Lee as pioneering analytical articles representing a new level of sophistication in public economic comment.[3]

Mention of the *Review and Annual* serves as a reminder that it dated from the early thirties, and was published as a supplement at the end of each year. Tabloid in format, and running to 64 pages, all the preparation work was done on the premises of *The Irish Times*, but the finished product was, until the 1950s, printed under contract by Helys of East Wall Road. A few years later, it was printed in a broadsheet format, but this proved unsatisfactory, and it was subsequently published in three or more parts as separate supplements over a number of days. Its actual demise was so gradual that its final ending was hardly noticed, as its main features were simply incorporated into the paper itself throughout the last week of the year. It seems that the Institute of Public Administration saw the resulting gap and, in 1966, began to publish its very successful *Administration Year Book and Diary*.

On the surface, the paper's circumstances seemed to be well settled but, internally, there was a growing concern that the paper's future was in serious doubt. While both the Independent and Press newspaper groups – each with a morning, evening and Sunday publication – appeared to be riding on a wave of success, *The Irish Times*, basically a one-paper outfit, continued to find its position very insecure. As John Horgan observed:

> The major problem faced by *The Irish Times* was the narrowness and vulnerability of its operations. Its presses … were idle for most of every day, and completely on Saturdays … It had only two other publications. One was the weekly *Irish Field*, dedicated to the horse–racing and breeding industries … the other was the *Times Pictorial Weekly*, which had been started in 1941.

---

3   In a 1978 Radio Éireann Thomas Davis lecture.

The daily paper continued to struggle to lift its circulation figure above the 33,000 mark at a time when both of the other two metropolitan dailies were running at or very near 200,000. Profits were, at best, around the lower end of five figures in the better years and, during those other years (about one in every three or four), simply non-existent. The directors groped around for some means of reviving the company's fortunes and thought they had found what they had been seeking in 1957. An entrepreneur, J.J. McCann had, eight years earlier, launched what approximated to an Irish version of the BBC's *Radio Times*. This was his *Radio Review* which, with no opposition, continued to be very successful, tempting him to try his luck at entering into the Sunday newspaper market. The outcome was a deal agreed between him and the paper's directors whereby they took over the radio publication and agreed to print and publish the proposed Sunday paper. Unbelievably, they also agreed to appoint McCann managing director of the company. Considerable, if muted, antagonism was directed both towards McCann and the staff he brought into the company, and also because of the fact that the door which, as long as anyone could remember, had a notice stating 'Board Room', was suddenly changed to 'J.J. McCann, Managing Director'. Clearly, he wanted everyone to know who was now in charge, and began with a gross act of philistinism by dumping the entire set of bound volumes of *The Irish Times*, running from 1859 to 1956, because he needed the admittedly large room space for more practical purposes. Perhaps he had taken his cue from Harry Bartholemew, chairman of the *Daily Mirror*, who had ordered the destruction of its entire archive of four million photographs along with massive cutbacks in its library of press clippings. Hugh Cudlipp recalled that, as a result of the clippings' cull, 'a damned silly machine' was installed in the cuttings' library into which journalists were obliged to peer into a projector on the principle of the 'what the butler saw' machines on seaside piers. Thanks to McCann, this also happened in *The Irish Times*' library.

Continuing to clear the decks of anything else that might be in the way, McCann closed the *Times Pictorial* to concentrate resources on the new *Sunday Review* which was launched with the expectation that it should achieve sales of around 200,000 – the target figure to run at a profit. This new sister newspaper was as different to *The Irish Times* as chalk is to cheese, and was deliberately aimed as far down market as those comparatively straight-laced times would allow, (loosely based on a certain Dame Violet Markham's dictum that 'virtue is not news'). This, in turn, serves as a reminder about an apocryphal story that the College of Heralds in London, when approached to provide a motto for Lord Riddle of the *News of the World*, responded with the suggestion *humanum nihil a me alienum puto*.[4]

---

4   Roughly translated, meaning 'nothing human is alien to me'.

The new brash and breezy Sunday tabloid got off to an encouraging start, achieving a circulation figure of 100,000. The entire cost of its expensive launch was, of course, funded from the very modest resources put aside earlier to boost sales of the daily, the future of which was dependent upon expanding its own readership. For the moment, however, all resources were poured into the new publication, but try as they might, McCann and his staff were unable to lift the sales of the *Sunday Review* to a point where it would break even, let alone make a profit. As more and more money continued to be directed at the troubled tabloid, there was growing animosity among members of the staff of *The Irish Times* who now feared that McCann's paper was not only likely to fail, but could drag the daily down with it.

The new paper's first editor, G.H. Gray, was later replaced by John Healy who introduced a new feature, his 'Backbencher' political column, and there were plans to add a colour supplement, but the resources were simply not available. The *Sunday Review* did achieve one notable first when its edition on 3 December 1961 included the first printing of a Rotogravure full-colour advertisement to appear in any Irish newspaper. Although the methodology was complicated and prone to breakdowns, this innovation then became a regular feature in both the Sunday and the daily paper. The process involved pre-printing the colour section (prepared by Hely's), and re-reeling the paper rolls prior to the newspaper's run. Although never thoroughly satisfactory, it served its purpose for a time. The *Independent* followed suit, but went to the additional expense of installing its own gravure machine, and continued to use it long after the *Times* had moved on to an integrated colour press.

Having gained a Sunday publication, even if it had yet to prove its worth, the directors turned their attention to the possibility of adding an evening title to the company's stable. *The Evening Mail* had gone into a steep decline following the launch of the *Evening Press*, and the *Times'* directors seized the opportunity to purchase the ailing title, convinced that they could reverse its fortunes. What they had to reckon with was the fact that the *Evening Press*, (the principle cause of the *Mail*'s difficulties), was being edited by a highly successful and ambitious editor, Douglas Gageby. However, the deal went through and the newly acquired *Mail* was turned into a tabloid which seemed for a time to have been a successful transmutation. But revamping a newspaper is always a dangerous undertaking: if existing readers do not like the way their familiar newspaper has been changed, and if the changes do not bring a significant added readership, the experiment is certain to end in disaster. The real problem was that the company simply did not possess a deep enough pocket to sustain the necessary subsidisation of the *Mail* as well as that of the struggling *Sunday Review*. Had the situation been otherwise, each might have succeeded but, hampered by the company's small capital base, the bold adventure ended in disaster, an ending brought about by the realisation, just in time, that a continuation would sink *The Irish Times*. The

Alec Newman had the invidious task of following in the steps of R.M. Smyllie. Partly because of this and the board's perception that the paper was not making progress (although crucially, the company was unable to provide adequate resources to make this possible), he was cruelly sacked without warning.

opportunity to sell the *Radio Review* title to the new radio and television service had been taken in October 1961; the *Mail* was closed on 19 July 1962, and the *Review* followed the same road a year later on 24 November. As for *The Irish Times*, it had been almost bled dry. McCann departed, the Boardroom sign was reinstated, and Ralph Walker, already a director, was appointed as chairman.

The inauguration of the State's first television service presented all the national newspapers with a formidable competitor, not only in the field of news gathering and presentation but because the station very quickly began to capture huge swathes of advertising, seriously impacting on their advertising revenue. The situation was so serious that neither the Independent nor the Press groups permitted the new service to make use of their libraries' stock of news clippings and photographs. Curiously, *The Irish Times* allowed open access to its own records, a resource which was of enormous help to RTÉ until it began building up its own library.

While all this had been happening, Alec Newman continued as the editor of a daily paper with extremely limited resources. Until the arrival of Douglas Gageby, the paper's editors took little or no interest in mundane matters such as advertising volumes, circulation figures and trading profits (or, more to the point, losses). As for the paper's sales, there was a general editorial view, actually expressed by Smyllie some years earlier, that its then circulation of just over 30,000 was 'about the right sort of circulation' for a newspaper such as *The Irish Times*. If Newman shared this view, this notion, as well as the succeeding period of relative calm, may have lulled him into a sense of false security. The directors saw things differently, starkly aware that the paper had to improve its sales or perish, and they began to question if Newman was capable of effecting this turnaround.

Although he had been a perfect foil for Smyllie, and was highly regarded as an exceptionally literate journalist, he lacked the drive and leadership required of a successful editor. The board belatedly came to the decision that he was out of his depth and proceeded to act with uncharacteristic swiftness and brutality. As Hugh Oram described it: 'When the bomb-shell struck, a shaken Newman emerged from a meeting of directors to tell fellow journalists that "the bastards have got me". He had been sacked coldly and clinically, in the best newspaper style, with no thanks for thirty years of loyal service. He spent the rest of the few years remaining to him writing for the *Irish Press*.'

Bruce Williamson, a gentle giant who had shared the same office as Newman, was so incensed at the treatment meted out to his colleague that he resigned in protest. Happily (certainly for the future of *The Irish Times*), after honourably making his point, he resumed his place, and eventually became one of Douglas Gageby's four deputies and, although it was never actually stated, his most senior deputy editor.

In London, Rupert Murdoch denied that he made a speciality of sacking his editors, and once wrote to Harold Evans, when he was editor of *The Times* (and had just been voted Editor of the Year by Granada Television), stating:

> I have to admit I have a reputation for firing editors, but the facts do not support it … I have only ever sacked one editor, of *The Australian* – although I admit I sacked him twice. I suggest that is evidence of a forgiving nature!

It seems that in this respect editors are like football managers; when newspaper tyrants don't get the results expected of them, then their editors get the sack. As G.K. Chesterton once wrote: 'Editors live under the shadow of The Three Fears – Fear of Misprints, Fear of Libel, and Fear of The Sack.'

The author, Leslie Montgomery (1873–1961), had two very slender connections with *The Irish Times*. Better known by his pen name, Lynn Doyle, who wrote short stories mainly about Ballygullion, his first so-called 'connection' with the paper came about when he resigned from the Censorship Board in protest over its workings. He went on to write a strong letter to the paper, sparking off a correspondence which caused Seán O'Faoláin to write also, referring to the censors as 'Smuthounds'. Over the years, the paper had been

Alan Montgomery worked twice as an editor for the company. After the *Evening Mail* was purchased, he was appointed editor of that newspaper but the venture was doomed from the start. Later, following Alec Newman's departure, Montgomery was appointed editor of the daily paper, only to leave the post on discovering that the brewing firm, Guinness, was prepared to pay him more to act as their P.R.O.

critical of the censorship board, but perhaps never before were these criticisms as strongly worded as the write-up which was sparked off by the publication of the first official listing of banned books in 1930:

> Our first comment is that the authors of the condemned books will receive hearty congratulations from their friends. English publishers will play up keenly to this advertisement which the wisdom of the Free State Legislature has put gratuitously at their service … Now all these books will be the subject of tea-time talk and will line the pockets of passengers from Holyhead to Kingstown.
>
> We do not say or believe that a majority of educated and intelligent Irish people will wish to read indecent books or will make any effort to obtain them. In all countries, however, there are large numbers of people, idly curious or actively vicious, whose taste runs towards unhealthy literature; and for such people in the Free State, the Minister's ban, whether just or unjust, will act rather as a stimulus than as a prohibition.

During the same year that Leslie Montgomery died, his son Alan succeeded the unfortunate Newman. Alan Montgomery would have featured in a roll call of Smyllie's journalists, if such a list had ever been drawn up. Most of the other names have since been all but forgotten: John Collins, Hugh Curren, Jim Lawlor, John Mulloy, Christy Redmond

A 1951 photograph of the directors of The Irish Times Limited. From left: Douglas Gageby and George Hetherington (joint managing directors), John A. Robinson, Arthur Burgess (company secretary), Ralph Walker (chairman), Philip Walker (his brother), and Howard Robinson who was not related to the other director of the same name. A framed portrait of Lawrence Knox, the paper's founder, may be seen on the right of the picture.

and Paul MacWeeney (the last of these recalled starting work with the paper at £1.17. 6d. a week). McWeeney also remembered a really ancient reporter called Stoddart (his name was actually T.A. Stoddart), who ceased to be the paper's financial reporter only when he died in office at the age of 92. Fragments of an old wages book also listed some of the senior executives at an even earlier time, including James Carlyle, the general manager, J.J. Simington, who succeeded him, Arthur Townley and Albert Hall, two company secretaries, and James Scott who was then the paper's editor.

Alan Montgomery had, in fact, joined the staff in 1936, when many of the above-named journalists were still working for the paper, and at a time when most of the journalists were not unionised. Despite this handicap, the National Union of Journalists, just a few weeks after his arrival, secured what was regarded as a landmark victory when it won for its members a six-day week. Besides inheriting the editorial chair, 'Monty' inherited a period of relative political peace.

Montgomery's recollections of journalism during that period were unhappy. He cited several happenings such as journalists arriving late to cover some court case and buying carbon copies of other journalists' reports 'for the price of a pint'. Worse still, he claimed that he could remember journalists emerging from court and being bribed to ensure that a particular case was not reported.

A number of significant events took place during his first year as editor. The Soviet Union put the first human being into space; Ireland applied for membership of the EEC; John F. Kennedy became president of the USA; and RTÉ commenced its television broadcasting service. The year 1962 saw the IRA calling-off its border campaign; Ireland becoming a member of the UN Security Council; the opening of the second Vatican Council, the Unionists winning another Northern Ireland election and Fianna Fáil, too, winning yet another general election – but only just. Seán Lemass, had succeeded Éamon de Valera, but he was forced to lead a minority Government, a serious set-back for the party. His leadership carried it through a series of crises, causing David Thornley, a prominent political scientist, to write in *The Irish Times*:[5]

> Since 1959 Mr Lemass has worked wonders with a Fianna Fáil party that owed himself, in contrast to de Valera, no sense of instinctive loyalty. He has rejuvenated an ageing party, injecting it with new vigour, and over the whole apparatus hangs the supremely gifted leader, – not in the Dev mode, but a superbly gifted political tactician.

John Healy, who had boarded *The Irish Times* after the sinking of the *Sunday Review*, was to write of Lemass, a decade later, that he was the most professional politician of his time but to J.J. Lee, he was 'no hero'. The professor thought Lemass 'lacked de Valera's rapport with the adoring faithful, and even the easy familiarity with the populace of his successor, Jack Lynch'.

Ireland continued to be a relatively backward country, but its situation would have been greatly worsened but for the safety valve of emigration, and when the *Programme for Economic Expansion* was launched in November 1958, *The Irish Times* predicted that its success or failure would be 'measured by the emigration figures'. The census of 1961 told its own story: a further decline in the population figures, down almost three per cent to approximately 2.8 million, the lowest-ever recorded figure, while that of Northern Ireland, at 1.4 million, was up almost four per cent. Lemass had succeeded the elderly de Valera in 1957 after many years of waiting in the wings, but despite his talents there was little he could do to stop wholesale emigration. Although he was Taoiseach for only seven years, his record in office in many other respects ensured that he would be well remembered. As *The Irish Times* was to lament,[6] 'he came to power too late, he left power too early'. It also quoted Lemass when he bowed out: 'It is time I passed on. I don't want to become a national monument around the place'.[7]

---

5 *The Irish Times*, 1 April 1965.
6 *The Irish Times*, 12 May 1971.
7 Ibid, 12 May 1971.

Second best is not good enough

"The *Manchester Evening Chronicle* was compelled to close, although it had a circulation of over 250,000, which was two-and-a-half times that of the average circulation of provincial evening newspapers in Britain. This large sale and the paper's manifest popularity with a great number of readers proved useless in attracting advertising because it consistently ran second to the *Manchester Evening News*. As a result its advertising revenue fell to a level where it was operating at a loss of over £300,000 a year … If you can only run second you might as well not run at all."

Francis Williams, a former editor of the *Daily Herald*.

It seemed that Alan Montgomery had an exceptionally easy time while editor of *The Irish Times* but, apart from Shaw, who had lasted only two weeks, no other editor of the paper held that post for such a short time, less than two years. Montgomery's appointment had come about only because Jack White, who was being groomed for the post, suddenly departed for the bright lights of the country's new television service. Just two years later, Montgomery was asked by the well-known brewing firm of Guinness to chair an interview board to select a new PRO for the company, but none of the interviewees were deemed suitable public relations material. Montgomery, realising that the pay for the job was considerably better than what he was getting as editor, promptly applied for the position and got it. As he departed, nodding heads in the editorial department agreed that Guinness was good for him.

After enjoying two decades of retirement, Alan Montgomery died in 1996, aged 84. Perhaps he influenced several other departures to non-journalist positions around this time: Martin Sheridan, an editorial assistant, went to Córas Tráchtála, the Irish Export Board, and Noel Fee left for the Irish Sugar Company. There is a possibility that Montgomery's early departure also pre-empted a move by the directors to replace him. Like Newman, he was an excellent journalist but in increasingly competitive times something more than that is required of an editor. The paper needed a visionary, dynamic leader, preferably one who had already demonstrated his ability. The directors didn't have to look very far for the answer to their problem because the answer was literally staring them in the face from across the boardroom table!

Douglas Gageby

1963–1974

—➤●◄—

'The outstanding editorial achievement of the century'.

DURING THE PERIOD of retrenchment that followed the *Sunday Review* and *Evening Mail* closures, the board of directors had made two crucial decisions. George Hetherington (who had indirectly influenced this author to join the company sixteen years earlier) decided to approach Douglas Gageby with an invitation to join *The Irish Times* as its joint managing director, but Gageby, immersed in the successful *Evening Press*, initially declined the invitation.

Born in Dublin but reared in Belfast, Gageby was a Protestant nationalist who, after studying in Trinity College, Dublin, served for two years from 1943 in the Irish Army during 'the Emergency', where he was assigned to the Intelligence Corps. Following the end of World War II, at the instigation of Seán MacBride, the Government set up the Irish News Agency. Conor Cruise O'Brien wrote afterwards: 'We had acquired a highly competent journalist staff including, as editor, Douglas Gageby, who later became editor of the *Evening Press* and who later still became the most successful editor of *The Irish Times* in the second half of the 20th century.' By 1954, the INA was employing more than forty, but it was closed three years later.

Gageby moved to the Irish Press Group during that same year and he went on to play a most important role in the setting up of the *Evening Press*. Such was the thoroughness of the planning at Burgh Quay that he was actually appointed editor of the new paper one year before the publication of its first issue. No Irish newspaper, before or since, has been launched with such remarkable success, quickly overtaking the long-established *Evening Herald* and mortally damaging the even older and rather staid *Evening Mail*. Describing the three morning papers at this time, Gageby said that each paper's respective political outlook was easily defined. As he expressed it: '*The Irish Press* was clearly on the side of its founder, Eamon de Valera; The *Independent* aligned itself roughly with the former

Cumann na nGael party, but did not openly commit itself; *The Irish Times* enjoyed taking its pick.' A joke circulated during this period about an Englishman who, while on holiday in the West of Ireland asked a group of locals in a pub about the three national newspapers. When one of the men explained that the *Irish Press* was 'Dev's' paper; *The Irish Times* was the Protestant paper; and the *Independent* was the priest's paper, a second man intervened to say: 'No, no, the *Indo* is not the priest's paper, it's the priest's housekeeper's paper.'

When Douglas Gageby was approached for a second time by *The Irish Times*, this time with a dangling carrot of an offer of a seat on the board, he decided to accept the offer. As he described it himself during a television interview in 1988, he decided to agree 'after fairly cautious probing on both sides'. He was appointed joint managing director, a post he initially shared with George Hetherington. When Hetherington resigned in May 1962, Gageby became managing director and, after Montgomery's sudden departure just one year later, he was appointed editor. Another decision crucial to the future of the company had been made by the board two years earlier: Major T.B. McDowell was invited to join the directors. He had served in one of the Irish regiments in the British Army both during the closing stages and during the aftermath of World War II. Assigned to the Army Legal Service and qualifying as a barrister, he took his army title with him, as he was entitled to do, and joined Great Universal Stores in 1955, which then had many branch outlets in Ireland. The subsequent invitation to join the board of directors of *The Irish Times* must have been something of a high-risk proposal involving, as it did, the purchase of one-fifth of the Ordinary shares of a company with a less than impressive trading record. McDowell accepted the risk.

One of his first tasks was the unpleasant one involving the closing down of the *Evening Mail* before it bankrupted the *Times*. Months later, when the company was in danger of running completely out of money, he acted as executioner of the *Sunday Review*. Donal O'Donovan, who was features editor on the daily paper, later recalled an occasion when, while acting as stand-in for the editor, he was interviewing Seán MacBride when McDowell arrived unexpectedly in the office. Taken aback, O'Donovan introduced MacBride by saying: 'This is Major McDowell, our new hatchet man.'

The demise of the *Sunday Review* virtually coincided with the assassination of President Kennedy, and this earth-shattering news was one of the first major stories to face the new editor. The news was reported by *The Irish Times* on 23 November 1963 under a bold headline that stretched across the entire front page: KENNEDY IS ASSASSINATED. It recorded that the president had been shot 'by a hidden assassin armed with a high-powered rifle' and had 'lived for about 35 minutes after a sniper cut him down as he drove through Dallas'. Part of President de Valera's subsequent address on television was also reported: 'During his recent visit here [in Ireland] we came to regard the President as one of ourselves … We were proud of him as being one of our race and we were convinced that

Douglas Gageby, photographed shortly after his retirement, was uniquely appointed editor of the paper on two occasions. One of his own journalists, Patsy McGarry, wrote of him after he had died, that he had taken 'a niche newspaper with a narrow tradition and made it an indispensable instrument for those who wished to be informed in mainstream Ireland'.

through his fearless leadership the United States could continue to increase its stature amongst the nations of the world ...'

This duo, Gageby and McDowell, was to become the means whereby *The Irish Times* was extricated from a state of terminal decline. It is hardly an exaggeration to state that, between them, each acting in a very different way but crucially, both in tandem, they succeeded in setting the paper on its long road to recovery and all that followed from that. It was an extraordinary stroke of good fortune, in October 1963, that Montgomery's unexpected departure opened the way to appoint Gageby as editor. His years both as joint managing director and as managing director were, in themselves, critical too, giving Gageby an insight into the complexities of running what is, essentially, a clumsy beast. None of his predecessors in the editorial chair had either any knowledge of, or any real interest in, what happened outside the editorial department. So while the situation of the company continued to be critical, at least the omens were good.

The picture began to brighten with the first tentative signs of a very slight increase in sales which, by 1966, had almost reached the 45,000 figure. When Jack Moore, one of the Company's advertising representatives, proudly told his counterpart in the *Irish Independent* this news he was laughed at, hardly surprising when sales of the latter stood at nearly four times that figure. Laughable though it may have seemed, that same figure represented an extraordinary turn-around in a very short time; sales had shot up by approximately one-third from just under 33,300 in four years. As already mentioned, the paper's circulation figures were traditionally kept secret; the actual figures were never even recorded in the board minutes books. I once made a trawl of such references as could be found concerning the paper's sales prior to having them publicly audited by the Audit Bureau of Circulations (ABC) in London. During the paper's first few months, sales reached approximately 8,000 copies per day, and around 10,000 by 1860 and, after that, the few references found provided similarly generalised figures. In 1899 the company was claiming to have 'the largest circulation in Ireland' and by 1911 the circulation figure was said to be 'larger than at any time since the critical weeks of the Boer War'. The arrival of the *Irish Independent* obviously damaged sales but, even so, circulation during 1920 was said to be 'larger today than at the outbreak of the late war'. Seven years later, following a price reduction by the *Independent*, sales were 'slightly diminished', and although the directors hoped that the figures had then 'reached rock bottom', during 1929 a further 'slight decrease' was recorded. Things began to improve slightly during the early thirties, after which total silence seems to have been ordered until the decision to join the ABC was taken two decades later.

The paper's gradual recovery received a severe setback in 1965 as a result of a general printer's strike which lasted ten weeks. This was the first serious stoppage since 1934 when, in July of that year, five issues were missed. An earlier strike had occurred during 1920, when a dispute concerning trade discounts put the paper off the streets for almost a month, causing the *Irish Newsagent* to comment that it was 'the first appearance of a strike in our trade in Ireland'. The 1965 strike was a great deal more serious, stopping the production of all the Dublin-based newspapers and additionally affecting forty-six commercial printing houses. When a settlement was reached on 11 September, the paper reported that the total loss suffered by the industry was as yet not estimated but was known 'to be very great'. Despite the board's shabby treatment of Newman, and the paper's reputation for low wages, the company's attitude to its staff was generally regarded as paternalistic. Throughout the stoppage, rumours had been circulating that *The Irish Times* was about to 'go to the wall', and these stories began to gain currency during the prolonged strike. A group of Dublin businessmen, concerned about the possibility that *The Irish Times* might sink without trace, wrote to the company secretary, Arthur Burgess, offering financial assistance, should it be required. A similar offer was made to the Dutch

Seamus Kelly was 'Quidnunc' (writing *An Irishman's Diary*) for many years and was also the paper's theatre correspondent. He is seen here taking part in the filming of 'Moby Dick' in which he had a major role. *(Photo: Courtesy of Warner Brothers).*

newspaper, *De Tejd*, when it ran into financial difficulties, and it was actually rescued from closure by a group calling itself 'The Friends of *De Tejd*'.

The company's Annual Report for 1964 had claimed that 'the tide is on the turn', a situation that owed much to the closing down of the *Evening Mail* and the *Sunday Review*. During the two previous years, it had suffered losses of £20,000 and £8,000 respectively, and shareholders were beginning to get used to receiving no dividends. However, the turning tide of 1964 saw a profit of £30,000, dropping back to £24,000 a year later, partly as a result of that year's prolonged strike. The final settlement of that strike reduced profits to £17,000 in 1966 but the real turning of the tide, which included a circulation figure of close to 50,000, came in 1967 when, after clearing all the arrears of dividends, the company was able to announce a profit of almost £50,000.

Part of the paper's new success arose from a determination to broaden its agenda, appointing circulation representatives in key areas outside Dublin. George Miskimmins, who serviced most of Ulster, had an uncanny knack of appearing to know, or to know of, almost anybody living in the province. His presence there, and those of the others in Cork, Galway and elsewhere, paid dividends in promoting sales which continued to move steadily upwards. On the editorial side, the paper began to report proceedings at four parliaments: those at Dublin, Belfast, London and Strasbourg; and a range of specialist writers was recruited whose contributions, and those of the regular staff, began to be recognised when a decision was made to publish the writer's by-lines. Names like George Burrowes, John Horgan, Dennis Kennedy, Michael McInerney, Donal O'Donovan, Michael Viney, Dick Walsh and a dozen others became familiar to readers. McInerney must be rated as the doyen of political reporters at the time, so when Éamon de Valera died, he was called upon to summarise the late statesman's life, a summary that some readers may have felt managed to gloss over some of the dead leader's more controversial actions.[1]

> Mr de Valera dominated Irish Politics for fifty years, and he occupied the centre of the stage in the most eventful period of Irish history. He was loved, hated and feared during his lifetime … There were times that we all stood up and cheered the nobility of his utterances; there were, of course other times … The death of a great statesman is also a time of retrospect and assessment as well as for deserved tribute …
>
> The quest for Irish freedom dominated and completely absorbed the man from 1909 onwards … During the fifty years, it was his hand and mind which determined militant and political advance after the national movement had been shattered and torn in 1916 … From 1922 to 1926, however, was the one period when his leadership was inadequate to prevent the national debacle, but forces were unleashed obviously beyond his control and perhaps the Civil War was the inevitable consequence of a divided army and people.
>
> Ireland's finest hour was followed by its darkest night but it must be said for de Valera that it was he who, after our Gethsemane, set the nation finally on the positive march again with his masterly exposition and analysis of the country's political situation in May 1926, an effort which founded Fianna Fáil. Through the thick political jungle he saw the Oath of Allegiance as the single obstacle to national advance. The new party threw its tactical programme overboard, entered the Dáil, abolished that oath, the appeal of the Privy Council, secured the evacuation of the [treaty] ports, the financial agreement, the new Constitution and the ultimate agreement with Chamberlain which led the way for neutrality in the Second World War …

An important development at this period was Gageby's decision to appoint Donal Foley as news editor. Between them, they searched for and found additional new writers: Nell McCafferty from Derry, and Maeve Binchy from a school classroom. They joined the news team, along with others including Mary Cummins, Mary Holland, Mary Maher, Nuala O'Faoláin and Olivia O'Leary. It seemed that Foley had a particular penchant for

---

[1]   *The Irish Times*, 29 August 1975.

identifying female talent so the paper had significantly more women journalists than was the case in any of the other newspaper groups. Foley's editorship of the weekly current affairs column in Irish, *Tuarascail*, and his *Man Bites Dog* column were other significant contributions made by him to the paper.

As a junior reporter, McCafferty was despatched by Foley to cover the happenings at the minor courts that were otherwise hardly ever mentioned in the newspapers. Her 'in-your-face' reportage was widely acclaimed; indeed, not noted for her shyness, she actually claimed that the paper's prestige rose as a result of this series:

> It was all about how some buck-ignorant District Justices in the law courts at the Bridewell maltreated petty criminals and social derelicts who appeared before them – often without legal representation because there was no Free Legal aid in the early seventies. The column was a roaring success, especially among the snobbish upper ranks of the judiciary … The liberal *Irish Times* and its liberal readers loved the column too … The paper's prestige rose on the backs of the column's defence of the same.

She became annoyed with the paper's legal advisor, Terence de Vere White, when he advised the paper against fighting a libel suit, initiated by a judge, concerning one of her columns. In White's opinion it would have been unwise to fight a case against a member of the judiciary, so an apology was published and no money changed hands.

It was during 1967 that David Marcus came up with the idea of asking one of the newspapers to commence a weekly feature to promote new Irish writing generally, but especially to revive the Irish short story. Not surprisingly, he decided to approach *The Irish Times* but, as Ray Burke wrote:

> He went into D'Olier Street early one morning to try to meet the editor, and then realised that daily newspaper editors were hardly ever in their offices before mid-day, so he went to the Silver Swan pub … Marcus fell into conversation with Sean McCann, features editor of the *Evening Press*, and told him why he was in town. McCann, who had recently commissioned Marcus to write a series of articles, persuaded him not to go to *The Irish Times* with his idea, but to go home and await his call. McCann called that night, inviting him to meet Coogan.[2] Marcus put his idea to Coogan and the deal was signed in half an hour.

The new weekly *Irish Press* feature was an instant success, usually occupying a full page, and attracting writers like Benedict Kiely, Patrick McCabe, John McGahern and John Banville (who was to join *The Irish Times* Book Pages' staff more than a decade later). That *The Irish Times* failed to acquire the feature at the time was due to a most unfortunate turn

---

[2] Tim Pat Coogan had been appointed editor of the *Irish Press* two or three years earlier.

of affairs, but some would see it as even more unfortunate that the feature was not adapted or even copied after the demise of the *Irish Press*.

The year 1966 saw the fiftieth anniversary of the Easter Rising, and the IRA arranged a preliminary celebration by blowing the top off Nelson's Pillar in the heart of Dublin. The statue and about one third of the Pillar was reduced to rubble, leaving the authorities with the problem of deciding what to do with the substantial remaining two-thirds of the familiar monument. On 14 March, the paper's city (late) edition carried the headline, CROWDS CHEER AS ARMY BLOWS UP NELSON PILLAR: 'There was a crack as of a giant whip; a blue flash with a red core, and that was the end of the Nelson Pillar at exactly 3.30 am today'. The paper also reported that there had been a last-minute attempt to halt the demolition by members of the Royal Institute of Architects of Ireland who applied unsuccessfully for an injunction to a High Court judge at his home. Additionally, a sculptor, Mr. Michael Biggs, failed in his attempt to save the inscriptions on the pillar's plinth, which he said were one of the finest known examples of Regency lettering. As the paper's headline attested, the large crowd assembled to watch the demolition showed little sympathy for the pillar or its lettering: 'People sang and danced as they waited for the count-down and there was a great deal of cheering and clapping when the pillar fell.' A striking photograph taken at the precise moment of the blast illustrated the page one report.

The actual anniversary of the Easter Rising was marked by *The Irish Times* with a special supplement. Among the contributors were a number of historians, including Owen Dudley Edwards, Nicholas Mansergh, Owen Sheehy-Skeffington and Conor Cruise O'Brien. This last, who had started writing for the paper during his student years, was still contributing articles at this time. It was written of him that: 'No one had such style and wit whether speaking or writing. He was a performer *par excellence*, and whether one agreed with him or not, his rapier thrusts at opponents was high entertainment.' Under Gageby, the paper had abandoned whatever was left of its vestigial support for unionism, so that O'Brien's strongly held views and the forthright manner of much of his writing was not at all to Gageby's liking and was to lead to difficulties between the two. O'Brien's views about post-independent Ireland on its fiftieth anniversary are clearly illustrated in the following extract:

My generation grew into the chilling knowledge that we had failed, that our history had turned into rubbish, our past to 'a trouble of fools'. With this feeling it is not surprising that the constant public praise for the ideals of Pearse and Connolly should have produced in us bafflement rather than enthusiasm. We were bred to be patriotic, only to find that there was nothing to be patriotic about; we were republicans of a republic that wasn't there. Small wonder that Pearse's vision of an Ireland 'not free merely but Gaelic as well' did not convince us. Pearse died, not for an island, or part of an island, but for a nation; an entity with a distinct culture based on its own language. The nation for which he died never came to life. Culturally, Ireland remained a region, or rather two regions, of the English speaking world …

When the answer to Pearse's 'not free merely but Gaelic as well' turned out to be '75 per cent free and 0.6 per cent Gaelic' it proved impossible for Pearse's followers to either accept these figures or to alter the realities they represent. A desperate game of let's pretend followed; Ireland is Gaelic – is not Gaelic the first official language? Ireland is free – does not the Constitution declare that the national territory consists of the whole island and its territorial seas? The realistic, as distinct from the fantastic, provisions of the Constitution are in force 'pending the reintegration of the national territory'. [Such reintegration], always unlikely … couched in language inspired by Catholic theology and purporting to bind the Protestant majority in Northern Ireland who were never consulted in the matter at all.

O'Brien went on to claim that 'Connolly's Worker's Republic is as far off as ever', adding that 'The *Irish Independent*, which in 1916 continued to call for more executions until it got Connolly', remained 'the paper of the Catholic bourgeoisie'. O'Brien continued to write for *The Irish Times* until suddenly, in March 1986 and without any public explanation, he ceased his regular contributions and began writing for the *Irish Independent* instead. O'Brien detailed what had actually happened in his own *Memoir*, where he described how he and Gageby 'had been moving in opposite directions with regard to religion and nationalism'. Despite this, O'Brien averred that he had greatly admired Douglas Gageby as an editor:

> When he invited me to write a regular column for *The Irish Times* I took this as the greatest implicit compliment that had ever been paid to me, professionally … I heard from one of Douglas's colleagues that he often swore when he read my copy. He may have sworn but he always printed it, unchanged, and that was all that mattered. After I had been writing for *The Irish Times* for some years I received an offer from the *Irish Independent* to switch to them …
>
> I hesitated before accepting the *Independent's* offer. I was not at all worried about moving a little down market, and reaching a lot more readers. What worried me was that if I left *The Irish Times* and if the *Independent* dropped me, I would have nowhere to go.

One story that went the rounds was that when the *Irish Independent* got wind of some disagreement between O'Brien and Gageby, it offered him a fee that was multiples of what the *Times* had been paying him. (O'Brien had written that the *Independent* 'was a lot richer than *The Irish Times*'.) So when he telephoned Gageby to ask if he was prepared to match the much higher fee that he was now being offered, Gageby immediately said: 'No'. The intended inference of the abrupt response being (rightly or wrongly) that he was glad to have found a way to stop O'Brien writing for the paper. Some of the elements of this version may not be correct but it cannot be denied that Gageby's thinking, especially about the North, differed hugely from O'Brien's.

Douglas Gageby was, of course, a self-confessed 'romantic nationalist', and O'Brien was not the only person to conclude that this clouded his judgement concerning Northern Ireland and, to a lesser degree, about England. Several English-born journalists, including Kevin Myers and Bruce Arnold, felt strongly that he disliked them because of their Englishness, and both felt that tensions originated from their very first encounter. But Gageby's northern roots pulled at his heartstrings, not in the direction of his family's unionism as might have been expected, but further back in history to the United Irishmen, a movement originating at once as nationalist, northern and Protestant. Fionnuala O'Connor, one of the paper's experienced northern journalists has described how, every so often, Gageby would travel to Belfast during the height of the northern paramilitary campaigns in order to visit the very strong team of reporters he had stationed there. Something of his 'romantic nationalism' comes through her writing:

> He said the same things [to us] each time, or so I remember. Why didn't we write more cheerful pieces? Would one of us not go and climb Cave Hill, for God's sake, and write about Jemmy Hope and Tone and the meetings under Napoleon's Nose? We could have done more in that direction, but such ideas seemed jarringly out of place at a time of political deadlock and hundreds of killings taking place every year.

Bruce Arnold, who had joined *The Irish Times* in 1961, admired what he termed its old-fashioned objectives, bridging the divide between Britain and Ireland and between North and South – 'things loathed by Gageby', he wrote.[3] Accepting that Gageby had done much to stabilise the paper, he took the view that this had been achieved at some cost to its identity. Wesley Boyd, who joined the paper from the defunct *Northern Whig* in 1963 thought, for example, that Gageby's political thinking caused him to misread the likely consequences of the meeting between Captain Terence O'Neill and Sean Lemass in January 1963. Professor Lee has described this move by O'Neill as 'one of the most perilous enterprises in statesmanship [in an attempt to] persuade a triumphalist ascendancy to begin treating its hereditary inferiors as its contemporary equals'. Boyd thought that Gageby saw this historic meeting as a positive development, indicating a wind of change in unionist thinking, and wrote that he and his fellow northern journalist, Dennis Kennedy, who was long experienced in reporting from there, tried to advise their editor that Ulster unionism had *not* changed, but was determined in its purpose of the retention of the union. As if to prove the point, O'Neill was forced to resign shortly afterwards. Dennis Kennedy, for his part, also saw certain events in a different light from his editor, and has recalled that every so often his articles had to be 'modified' or given what he

---

3   See Andrew Whittaker's book for this and further comments made by Bruce Arnold, Wesley Boyd and Kevin Myers about Douglas Gageby's editorship.

considered 'poor presentation'. In an *Appreciation* published just after Gageby's death, Kennedy credited Gageby for developing the paper's unmistakable personality. He, too, noted that Douglas was 'in his own words, a romantic nationalist', adding that 'it was romantic nationalism which coloured his and his paper's approach to the Northern issue, though he kept its columns open to opposing views, including mine, however heretical he found them'.

Owen Sheehy-Skeffington, when commenting on how Gageby viewed the Northern 'troubles', used the word 'sentimentalism' rather than 'romantic' to make a similar point. He thought that, during the sixties, the paper was more radical on the North than when writing about the Republic and, when referring to Gageby, he wrote:

> The editor's Protestant origins made for greater sentimentalism respecting long-standing Catholic leaders than their characters and achievements merited, but on Unionism and the Orange Order, *The Irish Times* proved itself a grim and well-informed adversary …
>
> Having broken with the sectarianism which animated his co-religionists in his native Belfast he proved much more remorseless and searing in his analysis than many a Catholic in the north, and infinitely more concerned than most Catholics in the south … He brought an endurance to his crusade which persons who had not made such a radical cleavage from their own kind lacked … In some respects this was to the newspaper's advantage, and to the advantage of the educational process it was trying to achieve. Its line was not predictable; its exceptionally good information, taken with the former point, brought increasing numbers to read it on Northern Ireland, north and south of the border; it offered Unionists a choice of weapons, irony and onslaught, and most frequently of all, the simple recital of fact.

Undoubtedly, the paper lost a portion of its northern unionist readers at the time because of Gageby's dislike of Unionism and, in so doing, it also lost some of its influence there. Writing about him after his death, *The* (London) *Times* remarked that 'his sermons [editorials] to Ulster Unionists to find their future in a united Ireland … reached few of them as *The Irish Times* was no longer much read in Northern Ireland …' Statistically, the loss of these readers seems to have been compensated by gains among northern nationalists, but to those who had stopped reading it, it must have appeared to them that their newspaper not only did not understand their position but saw no reason to sympathise with them either. The paper was, in fact, actually reflecting the view of the majority in the Republic which was, to put it mildly, ambivalent – as illustrated by a poll at the time that showed forty per cent of respondents in the Republic being sympathetic with the motives of the IRA, if not with its actions.

However, Gageby was, without any shadow of a doubt, demonstrably a great editor, and his political outlook, whether one agreed with it or not, effectively completed the tentative moves made earlier by Healy and Smyllie to change the paper's stance. As Fintan O'Toole observed:

There was an opportunity to broaden the paper's base and give it an ever more central position in Irish life by recognising the increasing importance of women, and of the young, and of a more independent strain of Catholicism with little time for blind faith, unquestioning obedience, or direct church interference in political decisions. Gageby responded to these opportunities with detached coverage of debates within the church, with the more sceptical and irreverent coverage of politics … and with the increasing prominence of young women journalists.

Another very different criticism voiced by some readers concerned the paper's limited coverage of sport, and some linked this with Gageby's lack of interest in the subject. If the connection could be proven, it would beg the question as to why he allowed the paper to be perhaps the only newspaper in Ireland or in Britain to publish sports news at the front end of the paper. Nevertheless, it was a fact that the sports journalists were almost always seriously cramped for editorial space, and the sports editor for most of this period, Paul McWeeney, often arrived at the afternoon editorial conference seeking a quota of three pages in the next day's paper but had to leave with an allocation of two.

In 1968, *The Irish Times* recorded record-high profits at £76,000, while its circulation had passed the very significant figure of 50,000. The Northern Ireland 'Troubles' had begun, resulting in the paper devoting even greater space to news coverage from that quarter for what would be over two decades of murder and mayhem. For the reporters on the ground, their work was often difficult, dangerous and very unpleasant. Reporting and commenting upon the aftermath was almost as bad.

One such event was the notorious bombing of the Abercorn Restaurant in Belfast. The following day the paper commented:[4]

Two legs gone, one arm sheared off, an eye lost – all in one young female body. That equals someone's idea of patriotism in Ireland in 1972. Of what are the victims of the Abercorn explosion a symbol? Of Ireland's march to independence, unity and dignity among the nations? Of Orange insistence that Ulster will remain British? It hardly matters at all. All are shamed … the Abercorn explosion was not relevant against the British Army; it was not relevant against the British government, except that it showed the sick society which exists in the North. This attitude presupposes that a better one is in the making. Is it in the competence of anyone who could plant that bomb to bring about a better society?

Despite this and other leading articles written in a similar hard-hitting style, the paper sometimes appeared uncertain how to deal with the Northern conflict. On occasions it seemed to mirror, if only in a very vague way, the general ambivalence then held by a large

---

4   *The Irish Times*, 4 May 1972.

A group of 'Foley's Babes' as they were known, because Donal Foley was responsible for recruiting many young women journalists. Included in the photograph (from left) are Maeve Donelon, Nell McCafferty, Mary Maher, Geraldine Kennedy, Gabrielle Williams, Christina Murphy, Mary Cummins, Caroline Walsh and, seated centre, Renagh Holohan.

percentage of the general public about Sinn Féin and the IRA. Majority feelings in the Republic may not have been pro-IRA, but long-held views about the downtrodden Northern Catholic minority coupled with a latent historical hatred of the British Army produced, what were at best, mixed messages, some of which spilled over to the comment columns of *The Irish Times*.

During May 1970, in what came to be known as 'the Arms Crisis', two Fianna Fáil Ministers, Neil Blaney and Charles Haughey, were dismissed by Taoiseach Jack Lynch, and were subsequently arrested on charges of conspiring to import arms and ammunition. Expounding on the situation, the paper actually saw Irish unity as likely to be achieved 'within the foreseeable future'. This optimistic view, presumably as seen by Douglas Gageby, was deemed likely to come about because 'forces in Britain and the weight of our EEC membership must render the Border anachronistic in a relatively short time … The change must come; it may be rapid; it will be peaceful. Harold Wilson [the British prime minister] is not so foolish as to think that the 1920–21 arrangement has been other than a failure.' A year later, as the British tried to hold the line between the opposing northern factions, the paper editorialised that what was being witnessed were 'all the tactical errors that are made on the routine road to a [British] withdrawal'. When commenting on the events of Bloody Sunday, the paper expressed the view that it 'was as if Britain, shorn of her empire, has been able to concentrate in the small area of the six north-eastern counties of Ireland all the talent for arrogance, blindness and malevolence that an imperial Power in decline manifests when faced with a small but determined people'. This 'end game of Empire' thinking was to crop up again when the Ulster Workers' Council strike prompted the British prime minister to declare, notoriously, that the people of Northern Ireland spent their lives sponging off both Westminster and British democracy, a remark resented almost equally by nationalists and loyalists. It prompted *The Irish Times* to declare that 'in all the shame that Britain has suffered at the hands of her departing colonials, this lying down to the bigots of Belfast ranks high in infamy.'

Such inferences prompted some to regard Gageby as being 'soft on the Provos', yet an examination of the paper's editorials during some of the most appalling paramilitary violence in Northern Ireland seems to refute the allegation. One of the worst sequences of atrocities inflicted by the IRA occurred when nineteen bombs were exploded in various parts of Belfast in a single day. *The Irish Times* responded thus in an editorial on the day that followed:[5] 'Throughout the 32 counties Irish men and women should ponder how a virulent Nazi-style disregard for life can lodge in the hearts in our fellow countrymen.'

Could it really have been true, then, that Gageby was 'soft' on the IRA? Hardly so. But such a perception may have come about because he was certainly supportive of the then main nationalist party, the SDLP and, in particular of its leader, John Hume. Hard-line unionists at the time saw little difference between the SDLP and the political wing of the IRA so this may have been a factor. The imputation that he was 'hard' on unionists may also have played some part in the perception. For his readers in the Republic, however, their main worry was that the Troubles could easily spill southwards, even if, for more than a decade, they were ignorant of the realities of the paramilitary campaigns. Conor Brady has written about what he termed 'Gageby's own journey of discovery':

> His outlook changed as atrocity and counter-atrocity pushed the boundaries of inhumanity ever further back. He understood the poverty, the deprivation and lack of opportunity that drove people from both communities into the arms of the paramilitaries. But he did not hesitate to condemn any political activities that were not wholly peaceful.

He was the first *Irish Times* editor to fully appreciate that the editorial department could not, on its own, produce a successful newspaper. In this he was quite unlike Lord Bracken who, while chairman of the *Financial Times*, averred that 'the capital of a newspaper

---

[5]   *The Irish Times*, 22 July 1972.

consists of the brains of its journalists'. Gageby's thinking had, as already mentioned, been greatly influenced by his experiences with the Irish Press group and by the fact that he had joined *The Irish Times*, not as its editor, but as a joint managing director. From that latter experience especially he had gained an overall view of the company, a perspective almost unique among newspaper editors at the time.

Haughey's resignation in 1992 caused Mary Holland to comment in a style that seemed to almost match that of some of Smyllie's editorials; all that was missing were a few Latin quotations:

> It is difficult to imagine when we will have another Taoiseach (or a speech-writer) who looks to one of Shakespeare's most sublime tragedies to sum up more than three decades in public life. Mr. Haughey had quoted from the last scene of Othello:
>> 'I have done the state some service; they know't. No more of that.'
> A few hours on and we were already a long way from Shakespeare and much, much closer to Patsy Kline. It seemed a pity that he hadn't a chance to finish Othello's final plea for a fair press:
>> 'I pray you in your letters
>> When you shall these unlucky deeds relate,
>> Speak of me as I am; nothing extenuate,
>> Nor set down aught with malice.'

When Pope Paul published his encyclical *Humanae Vitae* in 1968, there were those who saw it as an example of the Catholic Church being out of touch with its flock. *The Irish Times* reported the response made by the Rev. James Good, Professor of Theology at University College, Cork: 'I have no doubt that the document will be rejected by the majority of Catholic theologians and by Catholic lay people. For my own part, as a teacher of theology, philosophy and medical ethics, I cannot see my way to accepting the teaching on contraception put forward in this document.' The paper editorialised that the encyclical was essentially a reiteration of the Church's claim to be the one true interpreter of the moral law.

January 1970 saw the editor of the *Irish Independent* being abruptly sacked. Louis McRedmond had joined the Independent group in 1956 and after serving at various editorial levels was appointed editor in 1968. It seems that his attempts to move the newspaper upmarket did not meet with the directors' approval, and his replacement – after only two years – resulted in a staff walkout. McRedmond, a greatly respected editor, asked his journalists to limit the walkout to twenty minutes in order not to damage the paper. Interviewed on RTÉ television, he said that the appointment of his replacement indicated management's intention to make the *Independent* a 'pop paper', not the kind of paper he thought it should be. When interviewed subsequently, the new editor said that he hoped to make the *Independent* a popular, but not a 'pop' newspaper. *The Irish Times* commented in a leading article about the possibility of forming a Press Council, stating that such a body

> might encourage newspapers to be more forthcoming about themselves. Lack of this is a fault common to most newspaper organisations … In the goldfish-bowl society of today this is perhaps in need of revision. Thus, Mr. Louis McRedmond was recently fired from his post as editor of the *Irish Independent*, fired with despatch and no ceremony. He appeared on R.T.E. to say that he had been given no reason for his dismissal, yet the paper he formerly edited has not, at this writing, announced his departure.

The circulation figures for *The Irish Times* continued to grow, with sales topping the 60,000 mark by 1971. It had now ceased to be uncomfortably placed between the *Irish Independent* and the *Irish Press*, that particular role gradually being assumed by the latter publication which was becoming financially disadvantaged and had an ageing readership which it seemed unable to rectify. After control passed from Éamon de Valera to his son Vivion, and more particularly, after the death of the latter, it began to suffer increasingly from poor management/staff relations, a factor that eventually proved fatal for the entire group.

Although the circulation figures of *The Irish Times* continued to improve, the financial situation remained poor. A casual office encounter at this time illustrates the seriousness of the problem then facing the company. One day, after three or four years during which no salary increases had been possible, the directors unexpectedly announced that a general staff pay increase of one per cent was about to be made. I met Bob Booth, publications sales manager, in a corridor on my way to the despatch office that afternoon and asked him what he thought of the imminent increase. He frowned before he replied: 'You know, I'd rather do without that one per cent and then be sure the company would still be here in a year's time.' He did not say five years, or ten years; the future was as uncertain as that. Yet, somehow, there was no sense of low staff morale, unlike the attitude at the troubled *Daily Telegraph* during the seventies when Bill Grundy commented in *The Spectator* that morale was 'so low that you have to go down to the basement to find it'.

Ireland joined the EEC in 1972 and the paper's political correspondent, Michael McInerney, wrote:

> In the Irish political sense the million voters have resolved decisively all the problems that have faced the Taoiseach, Mr. Lynch, swamping Aontacht Éireann, the Fianna Fáil dissidents, and other 'Republican' parties and groups, and they have also illustrated a nation's utter disapproval of the militant wings of 'Republicanism'.

Joining the Common Market was seen as an important step towards pulling the country out of a protracted period of stagnation. Only five years earlier, gross national product was half the average for Western Europe. McInerney had commented on the setback that Ireland's accession to the Common Market had posed for the IRA and Sinn Féin because the latter had campaigned strongly for a 'no' vote. However, despite appealing to voters 'to heed the pleas of the internees', the public response to Sinn Féin had been a resounding 83 per cent majority in favour of becoming part of what was to become the European Community.

Meanwhile, over in Middle Abbey Street, Tony O'Reilly had gained control of Independent Newspapers for £1 million, a company which, twenty-five years later, would have assets worth over five hundred times that figure. He has steadfastly maintained, convincingly, that he gives the editors of his many newspapers freedom to act without interference, although Fintan O'Toole took a more jaundiced view when he wrote in his *Ex-isle of Erin*:

> Nobody seriously doubts that his influence, however passive, is pervasive … In refusing him permission to take a majority stake in the *Sunday Tribune*, the Competition Authority pointed out that his proposal for an editorial charter would have very little real effect … 'The editor may exercise self-censorship, deliberately or unconsciously. There may be direct interference by the proprietor, or influence may be imposed in more subtle ways, and an editor may take heed of the proprietor for fear of losing his job.'
>
> [During 1994] the *Independent*'s two directors on the *Tribune*'s board supported a successful motion to sack the paper's editor, Vincent Browne, who had attacked the *Sunday Independent* in print over the Bishop Casey affair. This was a reference to what was purported to be a *Sunday Independent* interview with Bishop Casey, an interview that, as the paper later admitted, had never taken place.

Bruce Hanlon, in a contribution to Belsey and Chadwick's book on media ethical issues, wrote that the London *Independent* somewhat piously suggested that the ideal situation is 'for newspapers to be owned by people solely interested in an economic return on their investment'. Those who acquired titles for reasons other than profit, the paper argued, 'inevitably used their purchases to peddle political and commercial influence'. That was in 1991, before O'Reilly additionally moved to get a foothold in *that* newspaper too, and it is interesting to note that it subsequently appeared to have got its 'ideal' proprietor. During his short period as editor of the London *Independent*, Andrew Marr became familiar with O'Reilly, and recognised that O'Reilly had wanted the London *Independent* under his belt because owning a British national newspaper 'would put him in the big league. And with the *Irish Independent* doing very well, he thought he could work the same magic in Britain … We knew he was pro-European, as the Irish tended to be, and at one remove from the British Establishment. As tycoons went, he seemed made to measure for the [London] *Independent*.' After Marr left the paper, he remarked that O'Reilly 'had always been a kind and charming boss'.

Lord Thomson was another proprietor who claimed that he did not interfere with his editors. He told the Royal Commission on the Press how he discussed matters with Denis Hamilton, the editor of the *Sunday Times*: 'I have my views on various questions and I make sure he knows them but I never see them in the paper unless he agrees with them.' Thomson stated in his introduction to John Goulden's book about newspaper management that his aim as a newspaper publisher had always been 'to create profitable newspapers whose editors were free from pressures, either internal or external. I believe that financial strength and commercial stability are the best guarantees of a free press.' Perhaps it would be too unkind to express that thought in another way; that as long as the papers were making money, Thomson was not over-concerned about their content. When Lord Beaverbrook, as proprietor and editor-in-chief of Express Newspapers, was giving evidence to the same Royal Commission, he was much more direct. When asked what happened on occasions when his editors took a different view from his own, Beaverbrook replied: 'I talk them out of it.'

Even in cases where a proprietor declares that he never interferes with his editors' duties, and even where he is no longer in a position to do so, his influence may yet come into play. The death in 1991 of Robert Maxwell, in strange circumstances, was a case in point. On the following day, Maxwell's 36-page *Daily Mirror* devoted fifteen pages to the news, replete with effusive tributes, etc. No mention whatever was made of the enormous financial problems facing his media empire which many assumed were closely related to his death. Virtually every other British newspaper detailed these problems, and Maxwell's loyal journalists, who had suppressed the truth behind the huge debts, then discovered that over £350 million had been removed from their own company pension fund. Cecil King of the *Daily Mirror* is well remembered for that paper's outburst directed against the British prime minister, Harold Wilson, 'ENOUGH IS ENOUGH'. The headline was spread across page one of the paper in huge capital letters after the editor was allegedly instructed to do so by his proprietor.

O'Reilly's acquisition of Independent Newspapers was, it could be argued, wholly beneficial for the group, resulting in its extremely successful expansion into a wide range of media, both within Ireland and most notably abroad. Historians are fond of posing the question: 'what if?' So, the biggest 'what-if' in an Irish newspaper connection must surely be what if circumstances had been different and McDowell had backed the *Independent* horse and O'Reilly had put his money on the *Times*?

Intriguing as that scenario might be, it is necessary here to return to the reality of the 1970s, when there had been three separate newspaper stoppages involving the *Irish Independent* and the *Irish Press* in addition to a further general stoppage by printers in 1972. Under the umbrella of the Dublin Newspaper Managers' Committee, a long-standing agreement had been in force between the three Dublin-based groups providing that whenever a trade union targeted one member and caused a stoppage, the other two members stopped publishing also. The purpose was to prevent the unions attacking one group in order to gain a similar advantage from the other two. The downside for *The Irish Times* was that, in the space of little more than twelve months it had been unable to publish on several occasions through no fault of its own. Staff/management relations in the company were good, whereas those in the *Irish Press* were poor, and the situation was no better in the *Independent*. Worse still, on at least one occasion, the other two groups had come together to cobble an arrangement before notifying Arthur Burgess, company secretary of the *Times*, of what they were doing. Irked by this succession of events, and anxious to publish the news that the country had just got a new government the previous day, *The Irish Times* withdrew from the 'one out – all out' agreement. The paper explained the situation to its readers, that its directors had decided it had 'an obligation to the public which overrides all other considerations'.

Annual profits for the company during the decade 1963–71 continued at a dangerously low level. In 1963 it had recorded a loss and during five of the ensuing eight years profits never exceeded £40,000. The problem resulted from escalating costs while the company's main source of income – advertising – had remained static, but the situation was to change dramatically in 1972 and 1973. This represented a remarkable achievement, but McDowell viewed the results with caution, aware that with profits beginning to run at this level the company was suddenly exposed to the attentions of predatory proprietors.

He decided that some form of trust would have to be formed as a safeguard and set about seeking advice and information from every possible quarter. McDowell began discussing the various options and studying the experiences gained by the relatively small number of publishers that had already gone down that road. He visited, among others, *The Guardian*, *The Observer*, *The Scotsman* and the *New York Times*. *The Guardian*, controlled since 1914 by the Scott Trust, was a notable example, widely viewed as one of the most enlightened of its kind, under the terms of which C.P. Scott, the paper's legendary editor, was given complete editorial freedom. *The Observer* was also highly respected even if, according to Hugh Cudlipp, the terms of its trust 'rigidly excluded a Jew or a Catholic from the editorship of that newspaper'. *The Scotsman*, under its editor Alastair Dunnett, was praised by Sir Linton Andrews, then vice-chairman of the (British) Press Council, because of its 'scholarly care and integrity in its editing'. John C. Merrill (who quoted Linton Andrews concerning *The Scotsman* mentioned above) described the *New York Times* as 'the aristocrat of the American press'. The *NYT*, incidentally, is controlled by the Ochs Trust which, like the Scott Trust, was named after its proprietor.

The internationally-known French newspaper, *Le Monde*, though not operating under a trust, had a built-in safeguard – its *minorité de blocage* – in the form of a veto power to prevent it from being taken over. In addition, its staff had a degree of control over policy-making decisions and a forty per cent share in the profits. A dissenting voice among proprietors was that of Lord Camrose who, when chairman of the *Daily Telegraph*, declared that he had little faith in newspaper trusts:

> Some newspapers today have created trusts, intended to ensure the future ownership and control shall not pass into the hands of undesirable proprietors who might change the character of the papers. I do not feel that such legal instruments are necessary or that they will achieve their purpose.

Nevertheless, that paper's subsequent proprietor, Lord Burnham, was to write that when it was founded, 'the first step taken by the proprietors was to tie up the partnership arrangement so that no member of the family could dispose of his interest in the *Daily Telegraph* without the consent of all'. A similar prohibition concerning the sale of shares by the directors of *The Irish Times* had been in force under the terms of the articles of association ever since it had become a limited company in 1900. However, the real concern now being considered was the possibility that a hostile takeover would probably result in *The Irish Times* being turned into a 'popular' newspaper to maximise the new owner's profits on his investment. This was no idle threat, as had been demonstrated just a few years earlier, when Lord Thomson had purchased *The Times*, despite the fact that J.J. Astor had set up a controlling trust when he bought *The Times* in 1922. Thomson shocked those who regarded that august journal, widely regarded in Britain as a national institution, when he decided to make it go at least a degree or two downmarket. Thomson's style was soon to be followed by Maxwell, and there were others in the wings who would not hesitate to reshape their acquisitions in order to maximise returns from their investments. Tom Baistow, a veteran Fleet Street journalist, once famously described as 'Yobspeak' the kind of headlines that would result when their new editors 'turned to bingo and jingo in the battle of sagging sales'.

Among the many experts in both Ireland and Britain whom Tom McDowell consulted was Arnold Goodman, one of England's leading lawyers who, twenty years earlier, had set up his own London practice, Goodman Derrick & Company. Besides his involvement in many landmark legal actions, he had acted as an emissary representing the British government in negotiations with Rhodesia and, as chairman of the (British) Newspaper Publishers Association, had played a key role in negotiations between proprietors, government and unions. Perhaps most importantly, Goodman was chairman of the Observer Editorial Trust. McDowell additionally made good use of his many connections carefully built up over the previous decade with some of the most senior newspaper personages, not only in Fleet Street, but in the wider British press as well. In Dublin, he sought advice from, among others, George Overend, senior partner with the well-known legal firm, A & L Goodbody, and with Robin Lewis-Crosbie at Stokes Kennedy and Crowley. Fortuitously, as it happened, the majority of the members of the company's existing directors at the time made it known that they were interested in relinquishing their seats on the board.

Fifteen months of negotiation and planning, drafting, redrafting and re-redrafting resulted in a comprehensive and, it has to be said, complicated form of trust with a view to purchasing (or otherwise acquiring) the shares in The Irish Times Limited. After gaining control of the company, its memorandum and articles of association were amended to include a series of new objectives including the following:

> To publish *The Irish Times* as an independent newspaper primarily concerned with serious issues for the benefit of the community throughout the whole of Ireland, free from any form of personal or party political, commercial, religious or other sectional control.

As already mentioned, the stilted and legalistic wording was, in the circumstances, unavoidable, so that the stated means of achieving the above continued in the same vein and included an editorial policy with the following set of objectives:

> The support of constitutional democracy expressed through governments freely elected.
> The progressive achievement of social justice between people and the discouragement of discrimination of all kinds …
> The promotion of peace and tolerance and opposition to all forms of violence and hatred …
> The promotion of understanding of other nations and peoples …

The document went on to lay down the principles governing the publication of *The Irish Times*, principles which, when so publicly announced, might well have been seen as a stick with which all future editors could be beaten:

> That news shall be as accurate and comprehensive as is practicable and be presented fairly.
> That comment and opinion shall be informed and responsible, and shall be identifiable from fact.
> That special consideration shall be given to the reasonable representation of minority interests and divergent views.

The newly amended articles of association included an important provision thought to be almost unique among newspapers – the provision that 'any person holding the office of Editor of *The Irish Times* shall *ipso facto* become a Director of the Company. Any person so becoming a Director shall on ceasing to hold the office of Editor *ipso facto* cease to be a Director'.

The trust and interventionism

"I do not believe that owners of newspapers can divorce themselves from some responsibility for the general tone and indeed particular activities of their paper. I have no respect for those owners who when faced with some gross breach of taste, shrug their shoulders and say it is a matter for the Editor ... I merely put it on record that I probably lean a little more towards interventionism than some of my colleagues and I feel that the Trust should both keep itself well informed about what goes on in the paper, as it does at present, and should not feel inhibited from expressing its views."

Jo Grimond,
former leader of the British Liberal party,
who had joined the *Guardian* Trust Board.

The language of the trust articles was, of course, a language common to the articles of other trusts too. Andrew Marr wrote of what he termed the *Observer*'s 'rather wonderful fence-sitting principles' including one stipulating that the paper should help to 'destroy the social injustices of an ill-balanced society without creating a sluggish conformity and a dull inertia'.

Directly after the second meeting of the trust board had been held, the final meeting of the old Irish Times Limited board took place, clearing the way for the new set-up. The news of the establishment of the trust, when announced on 5 April 1974, though broadly favourable, received some mixed reactions. The *Irish Independent* initially reported the move with little comment except to calculate that its own earnings compared with that of the *Times* rated the value of the ordinary shares at £1,665,400, whereas the price actually paid had been slightly lower, at £1,625, 000. The *Cork Examiner* thought that the details concerning the trust were very confusing, and for the benefit of its readers summarised it all, as it reported, in plain language:

> The simplest way to explain it is that at the top of the pile there will be a number of Governors. The cash flow from *The Irish Times* will be used to develop the newspaper itself. Any surplus will be used to pay off the £2,005,000 owed to the Investment Bank of Ireland and to the shareholders as rapidly as possible ... Any surplus over and above this will be used for charitable purposes, although what these 'purposes' are will be have yet to be defined ...

The main leading article in *The Irish Times* characterised the move as a reaffirmation of the independence of the paper, and continued by saying:

It is a guarantee to those who produce *The Irish Times*, to those who read *The Irish Times* and to those who are otherwise associated with *The Irish Times* that it will continue as before. Moreover, it is an assurance that an Irish institution is completely protected from outside takeover or control …

Today is a very big day, not only for *The Irish Times*, but also for journalism and the newspaper business in Ireland. The full ramifications of yesterday's announcement may not become clear for some time. Journalism benefits. The newspaper-reading public benefits …

Andrew Whittaker, the paper's business editor, took a somewhat critical view of some aspects of the arrangements, notably the timing of the deal. The deal had enabled, he wrote, the holders of the preference shares (the former directors) 'to benefit from a substantial mark-up of their share prices on the day, thus diminishing the capital gains tax they would pay upon realisation of the sale of their shares (should they accept the offer of redemption at par) in some six weeks time'. He did, however, quote Major McDowell as saying that the directors who had sold their shares (to the trust) had signed the transfers to a trustee more than six months earlier. Whittaker noted that the sale of the shares was costing just over £2 million, the sum being borrowed from the previous directors' interests (£380,000) and from banks (£1,625,000). He quoted a statement, made by the banks involved, that if the company made annual profits of about £400,000, the borrowings could be paid off in about five years. In fact profits were already beginning to run at this level, although no one foresaw at that stage the serious downturn that would follow during the next three years.

Several later publications, including the *Sunday Independent, Business and Finance* magazine and *Hibernia* also voiced some criticism. The first of these called the move 'an extraordinarily ingenious exercise in having your cake and eating it'. An anonymous reporter wrote that the trust had been launched 'on a wave of public relations euphoria',

Dr Thekla Beere, who was one of the original Governors of The Irish Times Trust, has been described by Homan Potterton as 'one of the most distinguished Irishwomen of the twentieth century'. She was also a Governor of the Rotunda Hospital; President of the Public Services Organisation Review Group; President of the Irish Film Society; Chair of the Commission on the Status of Women and a founder of An Óige. After graduating in law from Trinity College, she joined the civil service and, in 1959, rose to become the first ever Secretary of a Government Department (Transport and Power).

adding the comment already made by Whittaker about the timing of the deal, but without including McDowell's explanation. *Business and Finance* magazine welcomed the news that the future of *The Irish Times* as an independent newspaper had been 'made more secure by the setting up of the trust'. It summed up the position: 'While it can be argued that the price was not over-generous, neither was it giving a great deal away.'

Some of the comments made at the time represented barely disguised point scoring while one or two may have resulted from the confusion caused by the complexities of the details. Decades later, after referring to the serious decline in advertising volumes during 1975, one writer[6] stated that 'management at *The Irish Times* responded rapidly by establishing The Irish Times Trust.' In fact, the trust had been formed a year earlier, not because of a downturn but because profits had risen dramatically during the two previous years, exposing the company to a hostile take-over. The serious consequences of the 1975 downturn were significantly mitigated because the Bank of Ireland, while concerned that the company was initially unable to meet the loan repayments' timetable, held its hand because of the special regard it had for the newspaper.

The general reaction, however, was positive. Three decades later, Conor Brady was to write that the setting up of the trust 'was Tom McDowell's brainchild', and had

> secured the continuing independence of *The Irish Times* from external takeover. It provided the newspaper with a valuable charter of aims and objectives – an editorial *vade mecum* – that has stood the test of time.
>
> It also allowed the [outgoing] directors to take their profit from the success and effort of the previous decade. Significantly, it enabled Tom McDowell to remain in charge of the newly defined institutions – the company, the Trust and a charitable 'Foundation' which in reality only operated on paper.

Much of the negative response concerned how well the former directors had done out of the deal, and the almost unassailable position McDowell had secured for himself as chairman and chief executive. There was later criticism concerning the subsidiary company, The Irish Times Foundation Limited, with its provisions to support various charitable projects when, after more than a decade, these undertakings remained 'an unfunded aspiration'. However, these comments failed to take into account references, made when the trust was originally announced, to the establishment of a charitable foundation which would ultimately benefit from the profits of the business. Perhaps the word 'ultimately' should have appeared in italics for the benefit of commentators in a hurry. In fact, The Irish Times Foundation was in place mainly as a stop-gap should The Irish Times Limited cease to operate. In that event, the company's considerable assets would be administered by the foundation in compliance with the objects as set out in its memorandum and articles.

---

[6]   Mark O'Brien, in his book about the *Irish Press*.

Anyway, accusations that the trustees had failed to do anything to help charitable causes overlooked the fact that The Irish Times Limited set aside sums each year to help what might be termed 'good causes'. Maybe it was unfortunate that it was not deemed practical to devise a method whereby these latter allocations might have been channelled through the foundation company, thereby answering the criticisms more directly.

Unfortunately, mid-way through 1974, when profits were heading for an all-time high, what came to be known as the Gulf Crisis resulted in a huge recession throughout the western world. Inevitably, newspapers were severely affected and, in the case of *The Irish Times*, the timing could hardly have been worse. Already deeply in debt following the launch of the trust, it found itself unable to make the scheduled repayments. Had it not been for the forbearance of the bank (which, to its credit, held its hand because it did not wish to see the paper disappear), the whole scheme could have ended in disaster.

At the time, few recognised the enormous amount of thought and work incurred by McDowell in not only putting the trust in place, but in his careful choice of Governors (directors) to oversee its workings. As already mentioned, Conor Brady credited him with being the trust's 'brainchild', and with being responsible for its 'remarkable construction'. He also praised those same Governors for being 'without exception people with a genuine sense of public service'. The original concept worked well, even when the company was experiencing financial difficulties, especially when the Bank of Ireland became anxious about the debt repayments and pressed hard to secure for itself a place on the board. McDowell succeeded in resisting the move with considerable ingenuity. Criticisms became more commonplace a quarter of a century later when, because circumstances began to change, there seemed to be a reluctance to amend what some considered to be certain outdated aspects of the trust.

For well over a decade (although the sequence was to change), monthly board meetings of The Irish Times Trust Limited were held on a set morning, followed in the same afternoon by a board meeting of the operating board, The Irish Times Limited. The trust Governors were then also directors of The Irish Times Limited along with senior management. During the interval between these meetings, the members of the two boards had a buffet lunch together enabling all to talk informally to each other. Before each trust meeting ended, as secretary, I would telephone the editor to invite him to join the members to enable them to speak with him on editorial matters. Then, in the same way, the managing director would likewise attend the meeting so that accounts figures, etc., might be discussed in detail. Brady's comments on this procedure are worth noting:

> The Governors were all assiduous readers of the paper and one had to be *au fait* with the content across every section in order to maintain one's position in what could sometimes be an extended dialogue …

Overall, the Trust worked well. In 16 years as editor, I never once came under any untoward pressure in regard to editorial content or policy … The columnists often came in for fire. I frequently found myself having to defend opinions that I did not share – or at least defending the right of someone to express these opinions. But in the end I was always told to 'carry on' as I thought best. Tom McDowell was unfailingly protective. He frequently reminded Governors that whereas they might have a month to think about an issue, the editor often had to make a decision in a few minutes.

During very stringent times in the seventies and early eighties, every department in the company was directed to operate within an extremely tight budget. Almost without exception, all the other departments carefully complied while Gageby's (editorial) department invariably overran its budget allocation. Given the difficult background, McDowell and the Governors exercised a remarkable degree of understanding because of their accepted thinking that the content and presentation of the newspaper was all-important. The heads of the other departments, it must be said, felt that Gageby 'got away with murder'.

I had been appointed company secretary of The Irish Times Limited shortly after the trust was set up and four years later, from 1978 until my (early) retirement, I became company secretary of The Irish Times Trust Limited, and throughout this entire period I continued to act as McDowell's personal assistant. This latter appointment had dated from the mid-sixties, well before any thought had been given to the idea of forming a trust, so that both before, during and after the trust was established, I had an inside view of almost all that was taking place.

Conor Brady wrote that 'Tom McDowell was – is – a man of great complexity. He could be considerate to a fault. In our years of working together, his gestures of kindness to me and to my family were innumerable. So it was with other members of the extended *Irish Times* organisation … Tom's pleasure in giving help to those in need of it was palpable and genuine.' I endorse this view without reservation, claiming that nobody knows the truth of it better than I, having worked closely with him for almost three decades. His two-roomed department consisted of the boardroom where he worked, and an outer office where, after the formation of the trust, a small staff included the two company secretaries. Throughout the house, this department was known, for obvious military reasons, as 'The Bunker'. Although he was generally known, and usually addressed as 'Major', in many ways he was not most people's idea (nor was Douglas Gageby) of an ex-military man. True, he was a disciplinarian and expected the highest standards of people who worked for him; he once told me that, in the army, if one had been out all night on manoeuvres, one would be expected to be on parade next morning at 9 o'clock. I never forgot this nugget of information because, a few weeks earlier, I had

---

A National Institution

What I was trying to do was to make the [*Daily*] *Telegraph* a national institution without the awful connotations that the expression normally carries – that's to say, an institution that is respected and admired and which would leave the world poorer if it were not there. It sounds awfully boring but I regarded it as my life's work – that's all.

Baron Hartwell,
Chairman and Editor-in-Chief, *The Daily Telegraph*.

---

returned from a holiday in southern Austria, travelling day and night for 48 hours by ship and train and, having arrived in Dun Laoghaire just two hours earlier, I was at my desk at nine o'clock.

He was well aware that he was not always the easiest person to get on with, indeed he once told me that he would not work for himself! However, as Brady has written, he could be, and often was, kindness itself. When I was hospitalised and seriously ill with cancer in 1979, nobody outside the immediate family was more attentive to my situation, although Douglas Gageby, too, showed his concern, bringing me books and fresh fruit from his garden. While I was recovering from the debilitating treatment, Tom McDowell presented me with what I continue to regard as a very special book – A.P. Wavell's *Other Men's Flowers*. This remarkable collection of poetry was assembled by a most unlikely person – a British field-marshal, and was published at a most unusual time – during the Second World War. On the book's first blank page the chairman penned a message that I continue to cherish along with the book itself: 'Dermot, This anthology has given me much pleasure over many years, and I send it to you now, following our conversation this morning about true values in life. Best messages for a rapid and complete return to full health not just for the sake of yourself and your wife but also for *The Irish Times*. Your contributions to the paper and to both the Trust and the Company have been of the greatest assistance in our achievements over the years – not only officially but also to me personally. – TBMcD.'

Working in 'The Bunker', I was conscious of its remoteness, more apparent than real, from the rest of the house and in order to counteract this, I regularly took the opportunity to visit members of the staff rather than telephone them. Paul Tansey who worked with the paper during the sixties and early seventies, remembers what he called Gageby's 'mooching around', explaining that D.G. 'was an early exponent of managing by walking around', dispensing encouragement and, occasionally, criticism. Conor Brady adopted this

Benny Green, who was virtually the paper's unofficial advertising manager, photographed during 1948. The calendar, plainly visible behind him, was one of a series published in this unchanged style for more than thirty years.

same concept and was to write later how he engaged in what he termed 'MBWA – management by walking around'. In my case, however, it was 'IBWA – *information* by walking around'. These casual encounters enabled me to stay in touch, personally, both with individual staff members and with the broader picture of what was happening in the various departments, and sometimes when problems developed I could advise the chairman, to enable these difficulties to be tackled before they became serious.

As might be expected, I viewed the formation of the trust as a very positive step, a view that was shared by almost the entire non-editorial side of the company. In-house reservations tended to come from some of the journalists. This may seem strange given that they were likely to benefit more directly, not only because of the trust's recognition of the importance of the paper's content, but also because of its undertaking to ensure the paper's independence. Important to *all* the staff was the fact that while profits were not a primary objective of the trust, it did recognise the need to be profitable, and saw to it that the bulk of the paper's profits were utilised to re-equip and to continue to develop *The Irish Times*. With no shareholders in the conventional sense, the paper could, if it chose, pursue policies that might adversely affect profits without worrying about shareholders whose only interest in the company might be the size of their annual dividend. While I recognised that the trust was not perfect, and few thought it was, it certainly was a very positive development.

The experience of other newspapers which operated trusts was interesting. C.P. Scott, the greatly respected former editor of the *Manchester Guardian*, (the paper dropped the word 'Manchester' in 1960), has often been quoted, although one point made by him is seldom now heard: that there are two 'sides' to a newspaper. Between the two, he wrote, 'there should be a happy marriage, and the editor and the business manager should march hand in hand, the first, be it well understood, just an inch or two in advance'. Writing about its own problems in 1966, the *Financial Times* editorialised: 'There is a good deal of unpalatable truth in the claim that, to be independent, a newspaper has to be commercially successful.' After it became profitable, it is significant that *The Irish Times*, by far the smallest of the three Dublin-based newspaper groups at the time, became the first to completely re-equip with the most up-to-date new production technology then coming on stream. Being in the vanguard might have been expected from by far the wealthiest group, the Independent Newspapers, but for reasons best known to itself, it did not begin to seriously invest in new technology until after both the Times and Press groups had completed their own re-equipment.

An important component of new technology was the development of web-offset printing, opening up the possibility of much greater flexibility and the use of colour printing. In 1973, a well-known newspaper design consultant, Alan Hutt, was forecasting that 'newspaper design is likely to be profoundly affected by the developing new printing techniques, particularly web-offset'. He quoted another print expert, Chris Irvine, who was then predicting a major newspaper revolution because 'offset is likely to allow newspapers greater freedom and the greatly improved print quality and stunning colour already enjoyed by the magazines'. These predictions proved correct, although the early offset presses were slow-running and this initially delayed the take-up by the newspapers. During the mid-sixties, the *Shropshire Sun* and the *Reading Evening Post* were among the first to avail of what proved to be a revolutionary printing development that completely eliminated the smells, noise and dirt associated with the old hot metal technology. Indeed, when Douglas Gageby returned from an inspection of Roy Thomson's brand-new state-of-the-art print facility at Hemel Hempstead, and told staff at *The Irish Times* that 'you could eat your breakfast off the floor of the case room [print room]', his remarks were received with utter disbelief.

Ever since Victorian times, newspapers had been printed by the old hot metal technology, and most of the print preparation was executed by printers in what was known as the case room where the overseer had what was almost certainly the most stressful job in the business. For decades, Jack Cairns, a thin white-haired man, operated from what looked like a signal box in the centre of the large room, surrounded by Linotype and other printing machines, controlling the flow of 'copy' coming simultaneously from the advertising department downstairs and from the editorial department upstairs. If his team failed to cope, the paper would miss the lorries shared by the three newspaper groups. The company owed a huge debt to him and to his successors for their part in the nightly miracle that produced each day's newspaper. There were many others like them engaged in various activities throughout the house, people who never got recognition for their efforts. Examples included Paddy Fitzpatrick in the despatch department, who knew in his head the precise route taken by every newspaper parcel to its destination in a newsagent's shop, and Brian Kavanagh who knew everything that needed to be known about the paper's circulation. Then there was Barney Coughlan in Accounts, Jim Cooke in charge of the 'Works', who had a big say when a new press was about to be ordered, along with accountant Derek McCullagh. Benny Green joined the staff as an office boy in 1921 and became a key member of the advertising staff, preparing the paper's daily 'dummy'. This involved allocating spaces for the next day's paper, around which the editorial copy was due to be fitted: a task that Dick English subsequently inherited. There were many others, unfortunately too many to list here, who often worried themselves sick to ensure that the complex task of assembling a daily newspaper was completed successfully and on time. One other person should be mentioned, Charles Mullock, who possibly came closer than anyone else to Simington's record of sixty-nine years in the company. Charlie joined the staff in 1929 and was cashier for twenty years before being appointed company secretary in 1967, retiring seven years later. However when the chairman asked him to stay on as a member of his own small staff, Charlie did so until 1987, thus completing a remarkable service of 58 years with *The Irish Times*.

New technology was about to dramatically change the way newspapers were produced but, in the meantime, following an escalation in oil prices between 1973 and 1976, inflation in Ireland soared to 26 per cent. The inevitable consequence was a near collapse in the advertising market, and *The Irish Times,* along with all the other newspapers, was forced to tighten its belt and, painfully, reduce its pagination. The weekly *Education Times*, launched two or three years earlier, was closed during this period of retrenchment. Edited by John Horgan, it had been remarkably successful in all but one respect: it had failed to attract the expected advertising.

There was considerable surprise – even dismay – when Douglas Gageby announced his intention to retire in 1974, stating that he wished to devote time to writing. Although he had served just eleven years in the editorial chair, so much had been achieved that his period in office had seemed much longer. The board was suddenly faced with having to make a quick decision about replacing a man who, on the face of it, seemed irreplaceable.

Fergus Pyle

1974-1977

———————⟫●⟪———————

'Replacing the irreplaceable'

WHEN THE DIRECTORS announced that the new editor was to be Fergus Pyle, the news was received with mixed feelings. No one doubted his ability as a journalist, but in the same way that an excellent teacher may not always prove to be a good school principal, neither does an excellent journalist necessarily make a good editor. Presumably, the board decided that the only way to find out was to appoint one of its most experienced and reliable journalists and hope for the best.

For all kinds of reasons, including personal expectations, few newly-appointed editors receive 100 per cent support from their fellow journalists and Pyle quickly found that his appointment was not met with approval by most of his colleagues. He had originally joined the staff on a one-month trial period thirteen years earlier, the year that Alec Newman had been sacked. He later succeeded Donal O'Donovan as features editor, and he became the paper's first resident Belfast correspondent when the decision was made to set up a full-time office in Belfast. (*The Irish Times* was the first Dublin-based newspaper to do so.) Pyle's appointment as Northern editor to strengthen the paper's already comprehensive coverage of the north brought him into general prominence for the first time. One of his first assignments there involved covering several Civil Rights marches that ended in bloodshed. Later, after being sent to Paris, he went to Brussels to cover European news, proving an excellent, meticulous and widely-travelled journalist. Donal O'Donovan wrote of 'his lively, accurate and cosmopolitan style of writing'.

It was while he was in Brussels covering the EEC. that he got a totally unexpected telephone call to come back to Dublin to take the editorial chair. Jim Downey and Dennis Kennedy were appointed assistant editors at this time, so with this strong team in place,

The Art Of Sacking Editors

Despite the fact that he knew nothing about journalism, Arthur Baxter, who had been a piano salesman, was taken on by Beaverbrooke for his *Daily Express* in 1918. Ten years later, Baxter had become editor-in-chief and, five years after that, Beaverbrooke appointed the young Arthur Christiansen to share Baxter's position. Baxter was furious, as is evident from Beaverbrooke's recollection of the ensuing dialogue:

Baxter:	'In that case I resign.'
Beaverbrooke:	'In that case I accept your resignation.'
Baxter:	'In that case I withdraw it.'
Beaverbrooke:	'In that case I ask you to vacate your office …'

the board hoped all would be well for the future. Fergus must have accepted the appointment with mixed feelings; flattered, but probably aware that he was stepping into what was, for him, totally unknown territory.

Major news stories during his editorship included the abduction of the Dutch businessman, Dr Tiede Herrema, whose paramilitary kidnappers threatened to kill him unless three republican prisoners were released. They eventually surrendered and released their hostage unharmed. Also occurring during this period were the extraordinary circumstances that resulted in the resignation of President Cearbhall Ó Dálaigh as a result of a perceived insulting remark made in 1976 by the Minister for Defence, Patrick Donegan. The minister's intemperate remark followed Ó Dáilaigh's decision to send the Emergency Powers Bill to the Supreme Court before signing it, a saga later documented in detail by Risteárd Ó Glaisne.[1] *The Irish Times* commented:

> The implications of the Donegan affair go very deep. It will be very strange indeed if a Taoiseach who so rightly condemns subversion allows a Minister – one of the Ministers, too, most closely concerned with the security of the state – to remain in office after offering an outrageous insult to the President. Apologies are not enough. Until Mr Donegan resigns, the Government's own respect for the institutions of the State must be in question. This affair, which carries in it possible seeds of a constitutional problem, is a most urgent matter demanding action to restore public confidence.[2]

[1]   In his biography of President Ó Dálaigh.

[2]   Three decades later, a somewhat controversial account of these events appeared in an article by Jim Duffy in *The Irish Times*, 24 October 2006 which, in turn, prompted a response from former Judge Donal Barrington taking issue with Duffy, appearing in *The Irish Times*, 2 December.

Fergus Pyle, when appointed editor, had a very 'hard act' to follow. Few journalists would have relished the idea of succeeding Douglas Gageby and, although Pyle was a gifted and skilled journalist, this move was to end in failure.

Another major story in 1976 concerned the so-called 'Heavy Gang' saga, arising from the paper's investigation into allegations of police using threats and brutality in order to extract statements or confessions from arrested suspects. After six weeks, the paper's team of reporters had assembled what was a shocking story which, because of the fact that the journalists were aware that it was a mixture of hearsay and evidence, could not be sustained should it be challenged in court. Fergus Pyle took a brave decision to take responsibility should any legal action ensue, but fortunately no legal challenge resulted.

While hardly a major news item, the so-called 'Lissadell Affair' was one of the longest-running sagas to occupy the paper, especially in the *Letters to the Editor* section. The saga commenced when Michael Gore-Booth succeeded to his father's title and to the Lissadell Estate on the death of his father in 1944. Unfortunately, he was adjudged of unsound mind and made a Ward of Court, so that the estate was administered on his behalf by the Solicitor General for Wards of Court. All went well for about a decade during which time Michael's sister, Gabrielle, was unofficially appointed manager. Later, various changes in the administration of the estate were made, many of which were not to Gabrielle's liking. Because of her frequent complaints, Mr Justice Gerald Maguire, acting as Committee of the Estate, informed her that he had appointed a manager to run the estate and she was not to interfere in future, nor was she was permitted to inspect the accounts. She became increasingly suspicious as timber, stock and equipment began to be sold off, as she argued, at rock-bottom prices, and a lengthy war of words ensued. This, in turn, became a matter of interest to the media, especially to *The Irish Times* which began reporting the developing saga in some detail. Eventually Terence de Vere White, the paper's literary editor and a former solicitor, was despatched to Co. Sligo to see the situation for himself and to talk to the Gore-Booth family's solicitors. After his visit he reported that he had spoken to

The British Journalist

You cannot hope to bribe or twist,
thank God! The British journalist,
But, seeing what the man will do
unbribed, there's no occasion to.

Humbert Wolfe, *The British Journalist*

Mr Charles H. Browne, of the firm of (alas that Dickens had never heard of it!) Argue and Phibbs of Sligo. I expected Mr Browne, as man to man, to warn me that Miss Gore-Booth tended to exaggerate. Far from it. If she had laid about her with whips, Mr Browne resorted with scorpions. He even had a tale to tell of attempted murder of a witness for the Gore-Booths …

De Vere White's sympathetic article resulted in an extended correspondence being published in the paper over a period of many months. By far the most interesting were several letters written by Mr Justice Cahir Davitt, a retired President of the High Court, who took the unusual decision to respond in this way to criticisms made by Gabrielle Gore-Booth and by others of his judgement. In one of his letters, Davitt made the point that the matter was a hugely complicated one, not easily understood by members of the general public, adding that

the whole story is to be found in the files of the matter now extending back over twenty-five years. Part of the other side of the story can be found in my judgement … Perhaps your readers [this remark was addressed to the newspaper' editor] would like an opportunity of hearing it. I have no objection to the judgement being fully reported should you, Sir, see fit to do so, and if the President of the High Court should give the necessary permission.

The Irish Times secured the necessary permission and published Davitt's judgement in full, prompting Mr T.A. Finlay, S.C. (later to become Chief Justice) to write:

It might well be that this publicity showed up some anachronism in the procedures of the administration of the Wards of Court. To lawyers like himself, who knew the fierce integrity and abiding common sense of Mr Justice Davitt, who had tried the issues arising between the relatives of the Ward and the Committee in that particular case, it was unthinkable that an underlying suggestion of a perversion of justice in that case, as distinct from some frailty in the method of administration, had any grounds at all.

While allegations that timber, stock and equipment had been sold off at give-away prices was hotly disputed, it certainly was a fact that all but 400 hundred acres of the old estate were sold to the Land Commission against the wishes of the family. The long-term result of this decision was that Lissadell would never again be a self-sustaining estate.

The already poor state of the famous old mansion, threatened by a leaking roof, became steadily worse, and it seemed that it was heading for a terminal decline. In the end, it resulted in the family's decision to sell the estate and there were brief hopes that the Fianna Fáil-led government would purchase the family home of Constance Markievicz – a founder member of the party – for the State. There followed a further extended correspondence in *The Irish Times* but the government decided not to purchase the property. The affair eventually came to a close when the estate was purchased by private owners who announced that they were committed to completing the restoration of the house and to keeping both it and the estate open to the public.[3]

It was during his short period as editor that Pyle spotted a talented cartoonist, Martyn Turner, whose work then began to appear as an adornment in the paper's columns and has continued to do so for the past thirty years. Around the same time, Michael Viney decided to leave the comforts of suburban living for a life of near self-sufficiency in farthest Connacht, from where he began his weekly contributed articles, *Another Life*, for *The Irish Times*. Within four years he was to publish two books based on this series which were far removed in both content and style from what he had been writing earlier for the paper.[4]

Another contributor to the paper during this period was Pat Liddy, whose fine-line drawings of Dublin buildings were a regular feature, most of them featuring what he called 'the often undeservedly less well-known buildings and institutions' rather than 'their more famous neighbours'. Like Viney, he republished a wide selection of examples from his *Dublin Today* series in more permanent form in 1984, a volume[5] that inspired an even more ambitious work published by Dublin Corporation sixteen years later as part of its celebration of the Millennium.

When, during the late 1970s, the respected Dr. Simms announced his intention to retire as the Church of Ireland Archbishop of Armagh, the news was widely received with disappointment. This cultured man, a Gaelic scholar, and an authority on the Book of Kells was not, as noted in an *Irish Times* editorial, always fully appreciated in the North.[6] This prompted Lesley Whiteside to comment that the editorial had 'picked up Bishop Hanson's criticism that all the major denominations in Northern Ireland had bartered

---

[3]   The story is told in greater detail in the author's book about the Gore-Booth family.
[4]   *Another Life*, and *Another Life Again*.
[5]   *Dublin Today*, 1984.
[6]   *The Irish Times*, 11 February 1980.

Many would agree that Martyn Turner is almost certainly the finest cartoonist ever to work for an Irish newspaper. Seen here as depicted by himself, he was originally taken on by Fergus Pyle.

their integrity in return for the support of their people'. She realised that this had been done in order to make the point 'that Dr. Simms had absolutely refused to take on the semi-political role in which bishops tend to be cast'. The editorial continued:

> Some of his own flock did at times demur at his quiescence, as they thought, and contrasted him with 'more outspoken' prelates. He was criticised at times as being too much on the establishment side; he was mistrusted by some in the North for his Irish cultural leanings and his devotion to the ecumenical movement. But George Simms went his way. The words of Isaiah might typify his approach: 'In quietness and confidence shall be your strength'.

Meanwhile, Fergus Pyle's editorship of the paper was in serious trouble. It had became apparent that he lacked both the authority and the drive required to maintain the position, and the regular comparisons being made between himself and his highly successful predecessor made life even more difficult for him. Given time, all this just might have been overcome but, instead, he had the misfortune of suffering from several appalling strokes of bad luck.

The first was the worsening of the political situation in the North, which coincided with the Ulster Workers' strike and all the mayhem that followed, but worse was still to come. During Gageby's decade, the paper had gone from strength to strength, widening its coverage not only of the north but also into the other provinces, notably the west. The number of editorial staff had been greatly increased following the recruitment of a group of specialist writers, some of whom quickly became household names. Advertising revenue was buoyant and the paper's circulation figures had risen steadily from around 50,000 to just short of 70,000 – almost double that of fifteen years earlier. Gageby had scarcely left the premises when the Arab-Israeli war broke out, and the resulting huge increase in oil prices brought an economic downturn to the entire western world. In Ireland, advertising volumes, the most important source of the paper's revenue, plummeted. Profits dropped significantly and, during the next three years, almost half of Gageby's circulation gains were eroded, the actual figure dropping to 61,791. Barely three years after appointing Pyle, the board took the most extraordinary decision to ask Gageby to return as editor. Gageby agreed to his now well-remembered 'Second Coming'. It was a terrible blow for Fergus Pyle's prestige, but unlike poor Newman, he was treated humanely, being appointed editorial director on favourable terms by Tom McDowell, and he continued to write leading articles, and greatly enjoyed his role as a kind of roving European correspondent.

For Pyle, the final irony in this unhappy saga unravelled when, just after Gageby had returned, the severe economic crisis suddenly ended. Advertising prospered once more and the paper's circulation resumed its upward trend. Douglas Gageby had fortuitously avoided a downturn that even he, with all due respect, would have been unable to counteract.

Two decades later, when I heard that Fergus Pyle was hospitalised with cancer, I brought him books about France and Germany, countries we both knew well, and from which he had so often reported with insight and a rare style. He died shortly after, in 1997, aged 61.

Douglas Gageby (2)

1977–1986

———◦∘◦———

'Out of the shadows and into the light'

AFTER DOUGLAS GAGEBY had reoccupied his editorial seat, the worldwide oil crisis ended, but the North continued to be wracked by the twin paramilitary campaigns. In Dublin, despite the IRA's bomb-blast that killed the British ambassador and a young female Northern Ireland Office civil servant, large parades were taking place in the city in support of that organisation, illustrating the ambivalent attitude of many in connection with the northern violence. There was much criticism of the media because of a feeling that the graphic coverage of the so-called 'armed struggle' was actually encouraging more of the same. There was sympathy for a suggestion that the paper should consider playing down the worst of the violence. The term used, 'cutting-off the oxygen of publicity', was coined by Margaret Thatcher when she introduced a ban on the broadcasting in Britain of utterances by supporters of terrorist organisations. As Paul Gilbert has written[1]: 'Although the political advantages to a government from this sort of reporting restriction may be great, its potential for causing harm is considerable … Weighing the benefits and dis-benefits of such policies along utilitarian lines, is however, notoriously difficult and uncertain … It is hard to see how a policy which has this consequence can, in general, be to the public good.'

So, while the idea of voluntary censorship was, not unexpectedly, deemed impractical, the matter had been given serious thought. This was at a time when, as stated earlier, the Economic and Social Research Unit carried out a survey on attitudes within the Republic concerning the IRA, and found that just over forty per cent of the respondents sympathised with the organisation's motives, if not its actions. As all the terrorist groups

---

[1] In a chapter contributed to Andrew Belsey's and Ruth Chadwick's book on ethical issues in journalism.

discovered, the publicity resulting from an act of terror was often of equal value to them as the deed itself. One could argue further that even where some gross act of terrorism had failed, the subsequent media coverage provided the perpetrators with useful compensatory publicity. It was with this kind of thinking in mind that Conor Cruise O'Brien, when Minister for Posts and Telegraphs, made a number of statements about paramilitary violence that were so uncompromising that they drew the ire of all the political parties, including his own. He was especially critical of the media coverage being given to Sinn Féin, and his concerns about RTÉ's television coverage of violent events in the North led him to champion the idea of re-broadcasting BBC television rather than proceeding with the establishment of a second RTÉ channel, but this was without success.

It may appear strange that the notion of what might be termed 'self-censorship' was even considered by *The Irish Times*. While it is true that newspapers at times agree to special requests from the Gardaí to refrain from publishing reports that could hinder their investigations into serious crime, the idea of actually initiating non-reporting in general is, of course, anathema to responsible news organisations. Sometimes, as Paul Hoch noted, non-reporting resulted from union intervention, and 'freedom of the press' was qualified to mean '*their* freedom of the press'. He instanced what happened during the apartheid controversy in the seventies, when the London branch of the National Union of Journalists voted not to report the England versus South Africa cricket matches. During that same year, some of the London-based print workers refused to print newspaper stories attacking them and their union. Perhaps the most notable example of top-level decisions occurred during the thirties when the entire British media studiously avoided any mention of King Edward VIII's liaison with the twice-divorced Mrs Simpson. It was only after *The Times* made an oblique reference to a 'marriage incompatible with the Throne' that the *Daily Mail* decided it could no longer hold back:

> Until this week the *Daily Mail* rigidly refrained from commenting on or publishing news of this situation. We have been in full possession of the facts, but we resolved to withhold them … This course we took with the welfare of the nation and Empire at heart.

The fact that readership of *The Irish Times* in Northern Ireland had never been very high led Tom McDowell to quip that everybody in the North seemed to have read the paper but very few ever bought it! Conor Brady, however, claimed that it was the only newspaper with a significant readership both North and South, and that even if its sales in Northern Ireland continued to be relatively small, it was read there 'almost exclusively among the senior political, administrative, clerical, educational and business cohorts'.

> It has always had a voice – and sometimes an influence – in Northern Ireland that is disproportionately greater than its circulation. Policy and decision-makers regard it as

important reading. Its coverage of the Troubles and the associated political processes have been widely acknowledged. Even in circles that are inimical towards Dublin and the Republic it is generally regarded with some respect.

Gageby continued a strong editorial policy of committing what amounted to disproportionate resources to cover events in Northern Ireland. It almost seemed as though it was his response to what Conor Brady later termed the half-century of partition that had created a condition of widespread ignorance in the Republic about the realities of life in the North. Gageby deserves credit for the strengthening of the northern coverage which had followed the meeting between Terence O'Neill, the Northern Premier, and the Taoiseach, Sean Lemass, although the significance of this meeting was overshadowed by the street violence that later erupted. Gageby saw great potential in the founding of the Social Democratic and Labour Party (SDLP), and held John Hume in special admiration. Incidentally, Fintan O'Toole credited *The Irish Times* with being instrumental in first bringing the 27-year-old John Hume to public attention back in 1964, a move by Gageby that initiated an enduring friendship between the two men.

These final years of Gageby's stewardship saw further investment in the paper's editorial content and, in particular, its coverage of the Arts, 'from highbrow to nobrow.' Coupled with this, it became actively involved in supporting the Arts through a number of award schemes, including literature prizes announced in 1988, and followed by The Irish Theatre Awards scheme which was inaugurated in 1996.

During October 1981, Ken Gray, the paper's administration editor, wrote a memo to Douglas Gageby about the possibility of commissioning a history of *The Irish Times*. He recalled that some years earlier Michael McInerney, the paper's political correspondent, had expressed an interest in undertaking the task, but had died before getting the opportunity to attempt it. Ken had already discussed the possibility with his brother, Tony, remembering that he had been responsible for editing the paper's Centenary Supplement twenty-two years earlier. Tony Gray had been freelancing in London for many years, and approached Heinemann's, the book publishers, whose reaction to the idea was positive, suggesting that the proposed book might run to about 350 pages, centered largely on the editorships of Healy, Smyllie and Gageby.

Tom McDowell discussed the matter with Douglas Gageby and with Louis O'Neill, and when he asked my personal opinion I replied that such a project was long overdue. Indeed, I thought it was lamentable that the paper had never even set up its own archive. Unsurprisingly, the general consensus was that Gray should commence working on the idea, interviewing older members of staff and surviving pensioners in order to record what they remembered of earlier events. It was then formally agreed that Tony Gray should commence three months research for a consideration of £3,500 sterling on the understanding that copyright of all the material produced would rest with the company.

Louis O'Neill, who resigned as managing director in 1999 after being head of the non-editorial side of the company's management for over two and a half decades.

Gray proceeded to record interviews with current and former staff members after which he was given the go-ahead to commence work on the paper's files. Thereafter, at three monthly intervals, his contract was renewed with further payments while he worked on the Smyllie years, the text of which he eventually submitted to allow his work completed thus far to be assessed. Management, for financial reasons, decided that the company was unable to commit itself to continuing with the proposed history, but hoped that circumstances would soon change sufficiently to reverse the decision in time to complete the work in time for the paper's 125th anniversary. At that point Gray was informed by Douglas Gageby that the project was being halted 'for reasons of which you are aware', adding that the unfinished work 'will therefore be laid aside for consideration when the time does come'. A final cheque for £1,750 was enclosed with the letter. Seven years later, when nothing further happened, Gray sought, and was given permission to use the material he had already collected on Smyllie to write a book about him, which he completed in 1991.

Reference has already been made to Gageby's admiration for 'Armour of Ballymoney', a Presbyterian minister who had espoused Home Rule. Some voices expressed reservations about Armour because most of what is known about him derives from a biography written by his son who, it has been alleged, 'airbrushed' certain details from his account of his father's life. Curiously, Douglas Gageby does not appear to have considered a perhaps more reliable name to illustrate northern Protestant support for a united Ireland, for example Denis Ireland. Aside from anything else, his occasional letters to *The Irish Times* decrying sectarianism and 'the humbug of partition' should have brought him to Gageby's attention. Under the heading, 'Law, order and the church', he and his wife wrote towards the end of 1968 about the silence of the Protestant churches following a political murder:

Sir,– Since the political murder in Malvern Street, Belfast, in the summer of 1966, my wife and I have been waiting for a pronouncement from the Protestant Churches in Northern Ireland – a statement so loud and clear that no-one can evade the message.

Minor voices have spoken out, but our Northern Church leaders, theological and episcopal, have not. One recent pronouncement (on which you commented) amounted merely to a muddying of the waters. Indeed, for the last two years Westmoreland Street has thought more accurately, and spoken more convincingly, than either Armagh or Assembly buildings, Belfast.

With acknowledgements and thanks from two Ulster Protestants, one Church of Ireland, one Presbyterian, we remain, Yours etc.,

Denis Ireland,
Mary Ireland.

One of the biggest news stories during the next decade concerned the murder of Lord Mountbatten near his Sligo holiday home in 1979. The IRA demonstrated how ruthless it could be when the hidden bomb additionally killed the 83-year-old Lady Brabourne, along with one of his twin grandchildren, the 14-year-old Nicholas Knatchbull, and the 13-year-old Paul Maxwell from Enniskillen who looked after the boat. Two years later, another tragedy, which later became known as the Stardust Disaster hit the headlines. This involved the deaths of forty-eight young people in a horrific north Dublin dance hall fire, the consequences of which rumbled on for a quarter of a century.

During 1983, a young journalist, Geraldine Kennedy, was making a name for herself as a result of a number of exclusive political stories she was writing at the time for the *Sunday Tribune*. Senior figures in Fianna Fáil, unable to discover her sources for some of the matters raised by her about the party and about Charles Haughey in particular, decided to take action. When, as a consequence, both Kennedy and another journalist, Bruce Arnold, discovered for themselves that they were the targets of illegal telephone-tapping, they sued for compensation and won their case, establishing the principle that the constitutional right to privacy extended to the use of telephones. As *The Irish Times* editorialised:

There are, however, some fundamental planks in a democracy any tampering with which must be seen as extremely grave. One of these is the political independence and reliability of the police force. Any serious questioning of that weakens the citizen's trust in the instruments of the State – a trust that is essential for the proper conduct of parliamentary democracy.

Another related plank is the citizen's right to assume that his privacy is not to be invaded by authority unless he or she gives reasonable cause for that authority to suspect he or she is involved in crime or subversion. In this, as in many other respects, the journalist is the representative citizen, the one who asks questions on behalf of the ordinary person in the street …

Now the Government confirms that these fundamentals have been tampered with … it is the duty of this Government to make sure that nothing of the like happens again, or can happen again.

A year earlier, after a brief period in opposition, Charles Haughey became Taoiseach once more after narrowly winning the 1982 General Election and after having foiled a bid for the party leadership by Desmond O'Malley. *The Irish Times* wrote:[2]

Mr Haughey wins on numbers, but loses credibility … Not one good thing has come out of this convulsion in Fianna Fáil; nothing good for the party, of course; nothing good for the general political establishment of the Republic.

It may be said that what we have seen over the last few days is democracy at work. If so the point is made that some of the human material we have in our public life does us, and the system, less than justice. We are not the only ones to have cabals and splits and personal confrontations; but it would be hard to think of an example of another small European country, dreadfully in debt, frightened for the future, in which the law of vendetta could be allowed to burn so recklessly and fiercely at so dangerous a point.

Presumably the Fianna Fáil administration will go on, now more than ever, as a one-man committee. But how Mr Haughey can live with colleagues who spread not only dissatisfaction with his management of the party and the State, but disparagement of his personal qualities, is hard for those outside politics to understand …

Despite the above, several journalists, including Bruce Arnold, Jim Downey and Kevin Myers have commented upon Douglas Gageby's friendship with John Healy, leading to a feeling that Gageby was unduly influenced by him, and a number of them felt that this extended to his opinion of both Charles Haughey and Fianna Fáil.

From time to time *The Irish Times* had campaigned for the preservation of Dublin's architectural heritage, but some of this endangered heritage, given its British connections, evoked little more than muted concern. Queen Victoria's monument had presided in front of Leinster House from 1907 until 1948, when it was removed to the Royal Hospital, Kilmainham. In October 1986, while *The Irish Times* was still in the process of appointing a new editor, the government donated Victoria to the city of Sydney, Australia, minus several surrounding bronze figures. When the magnificent Kenure House near Rush was demolished, *The Irish Times* reported that the explanation was, simply, that it was 'a victim of apathy, neglect and dry rot'. It was also a rare example, as the paper noted, of a substantial house that had long been in Catholic ownership, its first Master having once been described as 'the only dangerous Papist in Ireland'.

During the early eighties, the British newspapers began to make serious inroads into the Irish market though, fortunately for *The Irish Times*, most of the successful intervention was at the expense of the lower end of that market. Hugh Carnegie, writing in the *Financial Times*, noted the trend:

---

²   *The Irish Times*, 7 October 1982.

Saga of Le Sage

'It is difficult to say precisely how long Le Sage [subsequently Sir John Le Sage] was Editor of this newspaper ... He went to Marseilles to meet Stanley on his return from the discovery of Livingstone; he was at Chiselhurst for the death of Emperor Napoleon; he 'scooped' the death of Palmerston; he interviewed Sitting Bull; he was in Egypt for the bombardment of Alexandria; and was the first to tell Lord Derby that Disraeli had ordered the British Fleet to enter the Dardanelles without the knowledge of his Foreign Minister. In exchange for this news he not unnaturally had the first information of Lord Derby's resignation'.

Lord Burnham, when Managing Director of the *Daily Telegraph*

By convention, national newspaper industries are strongly import-resistant; but not so in the Republic of Ireland. Walk into any newsagent in Dublin and you will find more British titles on sale than Irish ... For some years the British tabloid dailies have been helping themselves to a big slice of the Irish market with little sign of a challenge ...

With a much smaller total output than the British papers, unit costs are higher ... and other high costs ... have pushed up cover prices to the point where the Irish papers are more expensive – not just than the British tabloids but than the British broadsheets as well.

Carnegie noted that *The Irish Times* was then priced at £0.55 compared with *The Times* (London) at £0.40, and that Irish newspapers had to 'struggle to maintain their share of advertising against what they regard as unfair competition from the monopoly State broadcasting outlet, RTÉ'.

During 1984, when, writing for the paper's 125th anniversary supplement, James Downey alluded to the greed and stupidity that had 'wreaked physical havoc in the capital city and elsewhere' before he went on to comment on Northern Ireland:

When the North exploded, *The Irish Times* covered developments more authoritatively and comprehensively than any other newspaper. One hesitates to blow one's own trumpet too loudly, even on an occasion of congratulation such as the present, but it is both fair and necessary to mention that *The Irish Times's* Northern coverage was an important factor in gaining and enhancing its international reputation ... It has been consistently enthusiastic for developments that offered hope and progress, like the efforts of Terence O'Neill, the Sunningdale Agreement and, latterly, the New Ireland Forum.

Downey left *The Irish Times* in the autumn of 1986 and began writing for the *Independent*. Meanwhile, he ended this article with the comment that 'few who now read these words will survive to see the bi-centenary of *The Irish Times*; most however, can hope to live long enough to read the paper on its 150th birthday … With a bit of luck, and a lot of hard work, *The Irish Times* will be reflecting, recording, encouraging and innovating as enthusiastically as ever.'

Towards the end of 1985, the paper contributed a strong submission to the recently appointed Commission on the Newspaper Industry – this was in addition to that made by the National Newspapers of Ireland (NNI) of which it is a member. There was some emphasis on the matters coincidentally mentioned in the *Financial Times* article quoted above, and the extent of that competition was demonstrated by a comparison of sales figures. These showed that sales of British newspapers compared to those published in Ireland was at a ratio of 1:3. Also emphasised was the major role being played by the indigenous press in the Irish economy compared to the negligible contribution made by 'the imports':

> Imported newspapers provide almost no Irish jobs, and make a dramatically smaller contribution to the exchequer. They contribute little to our culture and cannot provide comprehensive coverage of Irish events …

Jim Cooke, who retired during 1996, spent his entire working life in the company's production department, finally becoming Production Director. He is seen here with Major T.B. McDowell, Chairman and Chief Executive, following a retirement presentation.

On occasion, British newspapers have sold at quite incredible prices in Ireland. The *Sun* has been offered for 25p and even 10p. *The Sunday Times* has sold for 50p. In this last instance, the newsagent paid News International [the publisher] just 15p per copy. The sum doesn't even cover half the cost of the paper on which the newspaper was printed.

The Irish newspapers united to plead for the implementation of seven recommendations, including a ban on below-cost selling; the removal of VAT; the phasing out of RTÉ's license fees; and the implementation of a draft Bill (drafted by NNI, incidentally) to overhaul the outdated laws of defamation. Almost the only reaction to all this at the time was the reduction of VAT to 13.5 per cent. During Gageby's second year back at *The Irish Times*, M.H. Consultants considered these and other problems. As quoted by John Horgan, part of their report expressed the view that there was 'scope for only three Dublin dailies; one at the top of the market (*The Irish Times*), one in the middle (where there are currently two, the *Independent* and the *Press*) and one at the lower end of the market (where there are currently no Irish papers)'. Writing about the tabloid invasion, Horgan noted the effect that some of these papers were having on the papers of the Independent group. Whereas the *Star* and the *Sunday World* were being produced with colour, the *Independent* was still using old rotary presses that were necessitating frequent maintenance and could only print in colour using the slow Rotogravure method. He commented that:

> … [the *Independent*] could not print colour as part of the normal printing operation, so that colour advertisements or photographs had to be pre-printed, with necessarily long lead time. The *Irish Independent* managed to get a colour photograph of the Irish cyclist, Stephen Roche, on its front page after he won the Tour de France in 1987; but keen-eyed observers noticed that it was a photograph taken earlier in the race.

By 1986, Gageby had nearly exceeded the agreed length of his return to the editorial chair by almost a decade and, as Conor Brady wrote, 'there was a sense among some of the staff that the modern *Irish Times* could not thrive without Douglas Gageby. It was seen so much as his creation, there was a sense that it would not work without him.' However, even if some people may be sorely missed, no one is indispensable, and an announcement appeared in the paper:[3]

GAGEBY TO RETIRE AS EDITOR.

Mr Douglas Gageby has announced his intention to retire as editor of *The Irish Times*. His decision, which was conveyed to the Chairman and the Trust Governors some weeks ago, has been accepted with regret. Mr Gageby has been Editor of the newspaper from 1963–1974

---

3   *The Irish Times*, 12 November 1986.

"Well, Douglas, what do you think"? Tom McDowell unveiling a specially commissioned portrait of Douglas Gageby to mark his retirement as editor in 1986.

and from 1977 to the present. Now that the changeover to photo-composition and full colour web-offset printing has been accomplished successfully with the installation of the most up-to-date printing press in the country, Mr Gageby has indicated that he believed a new guiding hand would be appropriate and that he should make way for another hand. Mr Gageby has agreed to continue as a director of the company. He also has agreed to continue to edit the newspaper while a successor is sought …

During his second decade, the entire production process had been changed from what had been basically Victorian technology to the new electronic technology; this was a huge operation involving the changeover from 'hot metal' production to photo-composition and full colour printing. The scale of these developments had caused him to postpone his second retirement, a decision that was of enormous importance to the company. This was especially so when one considers the catastrophic consequences that resulted from Rupert Murdoch's attempts to railroad his staff at Printing House Square, London, into the state-of-the-art facility prepared for them at Wapping. Murdoch pushed too hard and the print unions reacted by going on strike for eleven months. As Bruce Page wrote: 'The vast Metropolitan Police presence – like nothing seen before at a single industrial site – swamped the pickets … It did not take long for the frustrated print workers and their allies to become involved in violence, often on a disgraceful scale.' The print unions fought hard to hold their long-held position which, in London especially, had resulted in gross over-manning. In the case of *The Daily Telegraph*, of three new printing presses installed during the sixties, two were hardly ever used and one was never used at all. Murdoch eventually broke the power of the print unions with the expedient of using non-union labour to man the presses he had installed at Wapping seven years earlier. Thus, a new word, 'Wapping', entered the English language. That there was no 'Wapping' at D'Olier Street was a tribute to patient and humane discussions conducted over a long period until all had been agreed. Indeed, the changeover was so successfully completed that readers were quite unaware of what had happened. Gageby's decision to remain in office until all this was accomplished was a huge bonus for the company.

Some years earlier, in a volume edited by him, Louis McRedmond, a former editor of the *Irish Independent*, paid the following handsome tribute to Douglas Gageby:

> Although the success of the *Evening Press*, for which he was responsible, would have been sufficient for him to earn a special place in the history of Irish newspapers, his remarkable resuscitation of *The Irish Times* must rank as the outstanding editorial achievement of the century.

Douglas Gageby (second from left) with Bruce Williamson, Tom McDowell, Jim Downey, Conor Brady and Ken Gray.

From left: Donal Foley, one of the paper's most successful news editors, died in 1981. He had a good eye for spotting talented young journalists, many of whom joined the staff because of him. Mary Holland was for a time one of the paper's best-known women journalists and especially noted for her commentaries on Northern Ireland. She died in 2004. Dennis Kennedy, who disagreed with Douglas Gageby's stance on Northern Ireland, but gave him credit for keeping the paper's columns open to opposing views.

Douglas Gageby enjoyed more than fifteen years of retirement, until the death of his wife, Dorothy, in September 2002, which came as a huge blow. He had already been unwell, and the combination of his own illness and this tragic event forced him to retreat to a nursing home. He passed away on 24 June 2004, in his 86th year, and his death notice in the paper stated that 'as he wished, a private family funeral has taken place'. Although he had been ill for some time, the news that Gageby had died seemed almost unbelievable. His name will go down in the history of Irish newspapers as one of the greatest – arguably *the* greatest of all the Irish editors.

An impressive *Celebration of the Lives of Douglas and Dorothy Gageby*, held in one of the halls of the Royal Dublin Society shortly after Douglas died, drew an impressive attendance. Among a number of speakers who addressed the attendance between a number of recitations and musical items were: Daniel Berman, Dr. Garret FitzGerald, John Hume, M.P., Geraldine Kennedy and Mary Maher. Kennedy, as current editor, recalled being interviewed by Gageby in 1973, and described how he had

… moved the paper from the margins to the mainstream of Irish public life. It was a huge achievement and he made it seem so effortless … He believed in fair and honest reporting and keeping the clear distinction between facts and commentary.

As a Protestant republican espousing the spirit of Armour of Ballymoney – who never featured in my school curriculum – he recognised the vision of the young John Hume. He sent John Horgan off to Rome to cover the Second Vatican Council; introduced a Women's Page to give expression to the emerging women's movement; and gave a young generation of journalists their heads … And his great motto was that tomorrow is another chance to get it absolutely right, to produce the perfect paper …

Mr Gageby left behind a great newspaper, a beacon of independent and trustworthy journalism in a world of conglomerates, cross-selling and so-called synergies.

Maeve Binchy, one of his protégés, wrote that she never called him anything except Mr Gageby. 'When he asked me to call him Douglas, I could never do it. He was too important'. She also recalled that 'he was handsome, he was confident at work, he was happy in his home life, he was courageous and was dragging the paper into modern times. No wonder that so many of us were mad about him'.

After Gageby's death, Patsy McGarry wrote of how, many years earlier, he had interviewed Gageby for the *Irish Press* and remembered being told about his days spent among people of enormous talent there, and how he added that 'you could say that it made me'. But McGarry also remembered his achievements with *The Irish Times*.[4]

> He took a niche newspaper with a narrow tradition and made it an indispensable instrument for those who wished to be informed in mainstream Ireland … But not only did he successfully reposition *The Irish Times*, there was the manner in which he did so. He insisted on the very highest standards in journalism and writing and established those exacting aspirations which remain integral to the tradition of the newspaper and a constant challenge to all of us who work here … In our globalised world what Douglas Gageby imbued in his journalists has a deep relevance today, and on a grander scale, than in his halcyon days as editor of *The Irish Times*. The values he espoused are timeless. So, therefore, is his legacy.

He was once asked during an RTÉ Radio interview if he felt proud each morning when he looked through that day's paper. Gageby disagreed instantly, saying that at morning conferences the same questions were asked almost every day: 'How did we manage to make that mistake? Why was that item not put on the front page? Who wrote that stupid headline?', and so on. Charles Wintour, an editor with Beaverbrook's Express Group, once made a similar comment, saying that while there might be times to enjoy success, 'at other times there is little but the sour taste of failure – errors of judgement, lack of drive, sloppy

---

4   In a chapter contributed to Andrew Whittaker's book about Gageby.

writing, glaring inaccuracies, muddle in communication, stories missed'. Maeve Binchy was to touch on this point too: 'There never was such a thing as "Today's Paper"; there was the one we had written yesterday which, according to him, was full of faults and mistakes and unbelievable oversights.' She thoughtfully ended her tribute by hoping the Gageby family would know 'how many of us got a great and exciting start in our writing lives under his editorship. And how proud we were to be part of the time when he took our newspaper out of the shadows and into the light.'

In retirement, Douglas Gageby had continued to contribute a daily column to the paper, *In Times Eye*, under the pseudonym 'Y'. He loved Germany and France and had a good command of both languages; he and Dorothy had a property at Argelès-sur-Mer on the Côte Vermeille, 'the Vermillion coast' of the blue Mediterranean overlooked, in turn, by the Pyrénées Orientales. They also acquired a retreat in Co. Meath where he watched kingfishers and planted oak trees and translated much of what he observed into his daily nature column. Having made a rule that journalists should write under their own by-line, it was ironic that Douglas wrote this feature anonymously! As his health failed, his colleagues encouraged him to edit a selection of these contributions for re-publishing in book format and this was completed shortly before his death. I remember calling to see him at his Rathgar home where he cheerfully received me although he was clearly unwell. As I took my leave, he went back into the house and returned with a bottle of red wine. He never changed. Some time later, now in a nursing home, I heard that he had 'taken a turn for the better'. Armed with a bottle of red wine – I wanted to re-pay an overdue compliment – I called to see him but was asked, twice, to wait for a while. On the third occasion, a nurse came back to inform me that he was not very well and suggested calling back another time. He never got the wine, but these few lines of verse[5] may, perhaps, provide a poor and very belated substitute:

> Almighty God will surely cry,
>   'St. Michael! Who is this who stands
> With Ireland in his dubious eye,
>   And Perigord between his hands.
> And on his arm the stirrup-thongs,
>   And in his gait the narrow seas,
> And in his mouth Burgundian songs,
>   But in his heart the Pyrenees?'

---

[5]   By Hilaire Belloc.

Conor Brady
1986–2002

———⇒>●<⇐———

'When I became editor, a web was a place where spiders lived,
a net was a thing that trawlermen caught fish in …'

WHEN, IN AUTUMN 1986, Douglas Gageby's retirement date was announced, plans were put in motion to find a successor. For obvious reasons, most of the staff hoped that his replacement would be found in-house rather than outside of it, but the latter was a distinct possibility because the post was being advertised, additionally, in *The Guardian* and the trade magazine, *UK Press Gazette*. *The Irish Times* made the point that 'this is believed to be the first time a national newspaper had sought an editor through public advertisement, and is in accordance with a decision taken by the Board of The Irish Times Ltd in 1982'. It also took the opportunity to reprint an outline of the objects of the trust and listed details about the current governors. The advertisement attracted a very interesting response; many of the names would have been very widely known, especially among journalists, but to reveal their identities, even now, would constitute a serious breach of confidence. In this respect it is interesting that while the articles specifically state that directors undertake to 'observe strict secrecy respecting all transactions of the company', no such rule applies to the company secretary.

The formal appointment procedures for an editor of *The Irish Times* stipulate that whenever such a vacancy occurs the directors shall appoint as editor a person qualified to be a director of the company under the articles of association. The person chosen shall be 'suitably qualified for the office and … shall have been previously approved in writing by the Chairman'. As chairman and chief executive, Tom McDowell played a key role in the appointment process, initially setting up a selection committee, and devising a complicated but effective interview procedure. Perhaps uniquely among newspapers, there was also an editorial committee which acted, in effect, as a 'negative sieve' on the candidates.

Because of the numbers involved, an 'In and Out' system was adopted to avoid the possibility of any one applicant seeing another – either arriving or leaving the venue, which was one of the Dublin clubs. As each arrived, they waited with me in an ante-room pending the departure of the previous candidate. These interviews narrowed the applicants down to two in number and, as is now known, Conor Brady emerged as the new editor. The appointment was announced in the paper on 16 December 1986:

NEW EDITOR OF THE IRISH TIMES.

> Mr Conor Brady has been appointed Editor of *The Irish Times* ... Mr Brady has been a deputy editor of *The Irish Times* for the last two years and was appointed to the Board of Directors of the company in December 1985. He grew up in Tullamore, Co Offaly, and was educated at Cistercian Abbey, Roscrea and University College, Dublin. At UCD he obtained BA and MA degrees in History and Political Science ...

Brady subsequently admitted that his appointment was not initially popular with all the paper's journalists, but if some were surprised at his appointment, I was not. Apart from my personal knowledge of him and of his abilities, I had seen each of the written applications, all but one of which ran to three or four pages – brief and to the point. The application submitted by Brady was on a completely different plane; a prospectus running to over seventy pages including appendices setting out why he saw himself as suitable for the post, and evincing both his vision and his plans for the future of the newspaper. By any standard, and certainly compared to other submissions, this was a blockbuster.

He was to write later about another interesting aspect of his appointment. On meeting Fr Dermod McCarthy, administrator attached to Dublin's Pro-Cathedral whom he knew well, Brady was asked if he had received 'any communication from any of our people?' Puzzled at first, Brady then realised that what was meant by the term 'our people' was in fact the Catholic hierarchy, and he replied 'no'. He admitted that he had not given the matter any thought whatever, but now began to mentally contrast what he thought was 'a lack of reaction' to the many messages of goodwill he had received from Protestant church figures. Reflecting on this, he wrote:

> There had been some focus on the fact that I was the first Catholic to be appointed as editor in a newspaper and organisation that were traditionally seen as Protestant-dominated. It was not an especially significant matter within the newspaper itself, and certainly not among the journalists. But it had been commented in some other media.

Interviewed on RTÉ television on his first day as editor, Brady replied, when asked about his plans for the paper, that he had no radical changes in mind. He hoped to build on what Douglas Gageby had achieved and referred to how the paper's editorial policy had

Prior to his being appointed editor of *The Irish Times*, Conor Brady served for a time as editor of the Garda Review and the *Sunday Tribune*.

been shaped by the trust. 'We will not be a newspaper that runs up flags pursuing this, that or the other for a few days before embarking on something else.' Asked if this was meant as a criticism of some other papers, he replied, 'No, not at all; horses for courses – some newspapers have a readership that likes its papers to be more readily packaged.' '*The Irish Times* has', he went on, 'an intimate relationship with its readers and allows people to make up their own minds.' He agreed that there would be changes but pointed out that all newspapers must evolve to survive, as demonstrated by the fact that 'the paper Douglas Gageby edited last night was vastly different from the one when he took over in the early sixties'. In a further interview, with Roger Greene, he was asked what he faced when he was appointed editor and responded by saying that while the paper was 'in very good shape', one difficulty was that 'there was a certain mystique about Douglas ... [who] was the only person who had successfully edited the paper for any length of time since Bertie Smyllie'. He was, thus, faced with a mountain of a challenge, that of following in the footsteps of a very famous and well-liked editor. His situation was not made easier because a number of senior editorial staff members had recently left: Donal Foley had unexpectedly died; Gerry Mulvey and Bruce Williamson had retired; and Ken Gray's retirement

Wasted advertising

'Half the money I spend on advertising is wasted, and the trouble is I don't know which half.'

Lord Leverhulme

was also due, though he agreed to stay on for a further few years. Several others, including Jim Downey and Dennis Kennedy had departed, or were about to depart, to fresh fields.

Besides building a new team around him, he began to implement some of the thinking he had set in writing when preparing his job application, one being his decision that attempting, in the changed modern circumstances, to maintain *The Irish Times* as 'a newspaper of record' was no longer practical. Peregrine Worsthorne once wrote: 'Of course *The Times* was prized all over the world as the international newspaper of record'[1] – a label that lay heavily on its shoulders, because it caused an obsessional concern about accuracy. Worsthorne added: 'Legend has it that, in the nineteenth century, a war between Britain and France had nearly broken out because of a mistake in a despatch from the paper's Paris correspondent.' Louis Heren, when editor of *The Times*, wrote that he never understood what such a journal was supposed to record, adding that '*The New York Times* boasts that it carries "all the news that's fit to print", but no newspaper can do that'. Brady took a somewhat similar view, that too much happens in modern society to enable any newspaper to fill that prescription, and preferred instead the concept for the paper as Ireland's 'newspaper of reference … to which readers will look almost instinctively when important news develops.'

Another decision made at this time was to open a full-time Moscow Bureau, a move not even dreamt about by any other Irish paper. He expected resistance from the board, given that the company's finances were far from healthy, but to his surprise McDowell readily agreed, a decision which, when implemented, Brady felt raised spirits and confidence among the staff.

Seventeen years earlier, the young Brady arrived in the newsroom of *The Irish Times* as a trainee reporter. He was impressed when, by the early afternoon, people were either rushing about everywhere or tapping their typewriter keyboards furiously. He has described all this and more, even mentioning that most of the sub-editors brought their own dictionaries to work, 'Oxford and Webster's', as he explained. However, when that gentlemanly senior editor, Matt Chambers died, I acquired his well-thumbed dictionary

---

[1]   In a chapter contributed to Stephen Glover's book on the press.

– not Oxford, and not Webster's either – it was *Chamber's*, of course! I still use it and treasure it along with his eighth edition of *Brewer's Dictionary of Phrase and Fable*. A friendship had developed many years earlier (long before the paper had initiated its state of the art 'Studio' to produce graphics and maps), when Matt Chambers, as news editor, sometimes telephoned me to request the production of a map depicting the area of a current news topic.

After a brief period in Dublin, the young Brady was sent to cover the unhappy events in Northern Ireland and, to his surprise, Gageby later arranged to send him to Vietnam to accompany Seán MacBride. As far as Brady was concerned this was the assignment of a lifetime, but he only got as far as Paris where, although Fergus Pyle, the paper's correspondent there, tried to help, the necessary visas were not forthcoming. Later, after an assignment in London, he left the paper to revive and edit the *Garda Review*, followed by a short stint with RTÉ. In 1976, Fergus Pyle telephoned Brady to offer him the post as news features editor. Pyle had then been editor for two years but for the reasons already stated, despite his undoubted talents, his considerable courage, as well as some notable achievements during his brief editorship, his tenure was not a happy one. A few months later, Gageby allotted a post as an assistant editor to Brady, and after that he was appointed night editor. Then he left the *Times* again, this time to edit the *Sunday Tribune* which, under his editorship, reached a circulation of over 110,000. Less than three years later he was back in *The Irish Times* once more, followed there around the same time by another of the *Tribune's* journalists, Geraldine Kennedy.

Conor Brady had hardly warmed his new chair as news features editor when John Meagher, deputy chairman of Independent Newspapers, told him that Tony O'Reilly wanted him to edit the *Sunday Independent*. This was not the first occasion, nor would it be the last, that the extremely wealthy Independent group was to offer generous terms to lure staff from *The Irish Times*. Of all the criticisms that may be made about this commercially focused newspaper group, the saddest is that, despite its huge financial resources, it has lagged behind in crucial areas – including production and printing – where it should have been in the vanguard. After Brady was informed of the vacancy at the *Sunday Independent*, Tony O'Reilly telephoned him from China with a tempting offer to join the Independent Group. He told Brady: 'We have huge resources and we'll be putting them into our titles over the next few years. You'd be able to do things with us that *The Irish Times* will only be able to dream about'. Brady declined the offer and, shortly after that, he was appointed deputy editor of *The Irish Times*. It was from this position that, just a few years later, he was awarded the top editorial job.

During the early eighties, *The Irish Times* established a subsidiary, Itronics Ltd. This was essentially the brain-child of Seamus Conaty, who was to lead the company into the developing world of electronic communications systems, playing an important role in its remarkably successful launch into the Internet, one of the first half-dozen newspapers anywhere in the world to have a web edition. And by moving ahead of the posse, the company also secured the registration of the all-important Internet domain address, *www.ireland.com* – a move that precluded all others, including the State, from securing this domain name.

Meanwhile there had been no let-up in the campaign of bombing and shooting conducted, mainly in Northern Ireland, by the IRA. As already mentioned, serious consideration had previously been given to the idea of not reporting, or only reporting in minimal detail, these horrific events. Although prompted by the notion that subsequent media coverage was simply giving the paramilitary organisations 'the oxygen of publicity,' the suggestion was not really an option. Jackie Harrison, when writing about the value placed on accuracy in news reporting, wrote that 'it has been argued that freedom of speech should only be free from interference if it does not put others at risk, thus linking "freedom of speech" with "responsibility" – and involving a delicate balancing act'. Indeed, the only sensible editorial response to the Northern violence, however unsatisfactory, seemed to be the weapon of pointed criticism. One such example followed a whole series of bombings on a single day in Belfast, when the paper asked:[2]

> Is there to be no moving forward for some in the North? Yesterday's bomb blitz by the Provisionals brings back with horror recollections of Friday afternoons of a decade or more ago; of girls being carried from shattered coffee shops, of workmen dazed and bleeding, of terror-stricken children …
>
> In the Provisionals' bizarre rhetoric, yesterday's outrages comprised attacks on 'economic targets'. This from the military counterpart of Sinn Féin, which currently seeks political support in this State on a set of policies, including calls for economic reform and expansion.
>
> There should be no fudging on this issue. Sinn Féin candidates seeking votes in this election are pledged to support the sort of thing that happened on the streets of Belfast yesterday. That is what they should be confronted with on the doorsteps and at the chapel gates in this campaign …

Perhaps editors should bear in mind the sobering comment made when, because of a strike in 1962, Minneapolis had been months without a newspaper, and the chief of police said: 'Sure I miss the news, but so far as my job goes I hope the papers never come back. There is less crime about without a newspaper to pass around the ideas.'[3]

Press freedom and freedom of speech may not be the same thing, but there is a connection. When an organisation known as *Reporters Without Borders*, which monitors and defends press freedom, published its most recent findings, they showed that four northern

---

[2]   *The Irish Times*, 31 January 1987.
[3]   As related by Marshall McLuhan.

European countries 'came out top of the index where there was no recorded censorship, threats, intimidation or physical reprisals'. Ireland shared joint first place – along with Finland, Iceland and the Netherlands – while, perhaps surprisingly, the UK came 27th.[4]

The idea of launching a Sunday edition of *The Irish Times* was floated on a number of occasions, and John Horgan commented on this in 2001:

> The success of *The Irish Times* in colonising its niche and its apparent encroachment on the *Irish Independent's* middle market dominance, however, masked a problem which continued to restrict its opportunities for growth. This was the fact that although *The Irish Times* could offer advertisers not only colour but a high penetration of the upper socio-economic readership groups, the *Independent* could offer huge numbers of readers across a wider social spectrum, not least by means of discount packages across some or all of the various titles it controlled. This prompted *The Irish Times* management … actively to consider the introduction of a Sunday paper which would give them a greater pool of readers to offer advertisers as well as utilising their relatively under-used printing capacity.

Conor Brady was one of those who broadly shared this view, and although the matter was raised a number of times, the directors refused to budge. The board could hardly be blamed for hesitating, given the disastrous consequences resulting from the attempt with the *Sunday Review* a quarter of a century earlier. Even leaving that aside, the fact of the matter was that several of the existing Sunday titles were continuing to find it very difficult to make any profit at all. Despite the risks, a great deal of effort went into exploring the possibilities, but one crucial, unanswered question concerning the proposition was: what might happen to the advertising content of *The Irish Times* if the company went ahead with a Sunday edition? If the new Sunday title proved very successful, achieving sales of around 160,000, compared with the daily paper which, at that time, had a circulation of approximately half that figure, there would be a real danger that advertisers might switch their schedules to the new Sunday edition. This thinking was on the assumption that a high proportion of the readership of the proposed Sunday paper would also be readers of the daily paper. When the *Sunday Tribune* found itself in financial difficulties during the late eighties, an approach was made to *The Irish Times*, but nothing came of it. A takeover at that time would have been a risky proposition but probably represented the company's best-ever opportunity to get into the Sunday market, a market that has since then become distinctly overcrowded. Instead, management decided to concentrate resources on its strongly selling Saturday edition that was already, as Horgan noted, 'snapping much more closely at the heels of the *Independent*'.

The recently installed editor found himself presiding over a newspaper at a time when the Catholic Church lost most of its power and much of its influence through a combi-

---

4　*The Irish Times*, 25 October 2006.

nation of social change and emerging details of child abuse in church-run institutions. Even more damaging were the subsequent revelations concerning attempts to cover up what had actually been happening. Brady has written about his personal sadness as he witnessed some of the truths that were emerging and, as he expressed it, 'watching people – generally of good intention – dig themselves ever deeper into holes of their own making'. Indeed, it is somewhat ironic that it was the paper's first Catholic editor who had to deal with the problem of how to report a succession of difficult situations facing the Catholic Church. The first of these came to light in 1992 when one of the paper's duty editors received a telephone call about a boy whose father was, allegedly, a very senior figure in the Catholic Church. It emerged that the caller was the partner of a woman called Annie Murphy, living in the United States, who claimed she was the mother of a 17-year-old boy whose father was Bishop Eamon Casey, and who now wanted to tell the whole story. If this was really true, this could be the 'exclusive' of the century, but if it proved to be a hoax, publishing it could be extremely damaging for *The Irish Times* which was still seen by some as hostile to the Catholic Church.

Conor O'Clery, a very experienced journalist, had recently been appointed as the paper's North America correspondent, and he was one of a small group selected to quietly investigate the breaking story. After visiting Annie Murphy and taping her responses to questions, O'Clery was convinced that her story was essentially true, a view shared by Conor Brady when he heard the tape. But what to do next was a problem. One option was, as Brady wrote

> the possibility of walking up to Bishop Casey's house and confronting him with the allegations … But we had reason to believe that he was under severe emotional pressure. I had no desire to cause him a cardiac seizure or to be the instrument of his deciding to do something foolish to himself. In any event, if we confronted him without any corroborative evidence, we would still be leaving the way open to a simple denial, without any fallback for ourselves …
>
> There were ethical issues too about invading the private lives of individuals … but as a Catholic bishop, Eamon Casey publicly espoused virtues of continence and chastity which, it now appeared, he did not practice in his own life …

Brady was told of several possibilities when he sought advice on canon law, including that the bishop might have 'regularised' his position by providing for the welfare of the child. Brady was warned that there could be great difficulty in proving the story and that if the paper got it wrong, 'the church will destroy *The Irish Times*. That has got to be the moral calculus too. In the long term, wouldn't this society be much worse off without it?'

The delays occasioned by the paper's caution began to worry Annie Murphy who then volunteered the information that a named priest in New York had been the conduit of

THE IRISH TIMES

PRICE 75p (incl. VAT) 65p sterling area   DUBLIN, THURSDAY, MAY 7, 1992   No. 43,285 CITY

Dr Casey resigns as Bishop of Galway

INSIDE
THE BLUE ANGEL

A tribute to the extraordinary career of Marlene Dietrich, who died in Paris yesterday, aged 90
PAGE 9

PROPERTY MARKET

Dublin housing scheme sold within days
Palladian villa on the market
Ringsend flats from £39,500
12-PAGE COLOUR SUPPLEMENT

Ceasefire shattered

Fighting in Sarajevo and outlying cities ruptured the latest EC-backed ceasefire, less than 24 hours after it was signed ☐ page 6

Manslaughter investigation

New talks likely in postal dispute

The sensational story about the resignation of the Bishop of Galway followed protracted investigations by the paper's journalists.

regular payments made to her. When this detail was investigated it became apparent that a large sum of money had been paid out of a diocesan reserve fund. With this crucial evidence, a request was put through to the Bishop's residence in Galway for a meeting to discuss financial payments that had been made to Annie Murphy. Although Casey was abroad, a meeting was set up for two days later when, on return, he would meet *The Irish Times*. The Bishop never showed up, and on that same evening the Vatican announced that he had tendered his resignation to the Pope. As Brady wrote, there was consternation in the Church and bewilderment in the media:

> We alone knew the full story but I insisted that we hold to a minimal stance, simply reporting the following day that *The Irish Times* had been seeking to interview the Bishop about money that he had paid to an American woman in Connecticut. In time, of course, the entire story came into the public domain.

In fact, it was the discovery that Casey had used more than £70,000 of diocesan funds to make payments to Annie Murphy that finally made the paper decide to proceed to publish. As Colum Kenny wrote, 'It was only when *The Irish Times* appeared the next day that the public began to understand what was really going on … That paper's reference to the bishop paying a woman in Connecticut made it clear, on 7 May 1992, that Casey had a past that was not entirely behind him.' The resulting headline across seven columns of the front page announced: DR CASEY RESIGNS AS BISHOP OF GALWAY, and the paper editorialised:

> The immediate and widespread reaction will be regret mingled with some shock. Dr Casey has been outstanding among the Irish bishops for his humanity, his passionate concern for the deprived, the poor and the defenceless. His name is a synonym for energy, drive and determination in the cause of good. He has never promulgated a God of narrow-mindedness, of joylessness, of retribution. His God has stood for generosity, goodness and life.
>
> Last night's statement speaks merely of the 'personal reasons' for his resignation and goes no further. It is not sufficient. The faithful of his diocese, the many hundreds of thousands who have admired his work over the decades, the countless contributors to and supporters of the many causes he has embraced – all are entitled to a fuller explanation for this extraordinary turn of events.

Three months later, the paper's religious affairs correspondent, Patsy McGarry, summed up the saga by describing it as 'one of the biggest news stories that has ever been reported by *The Irish Times*'.[5] Staff at the paper had been working on it 'from February 1992 until publication on May 7 of that year'. McGarry wrote that 'the newspaper's history could have left it open to a perception in mischievous quarters that it was attempting to damage the Catholic church'. He added, 'The magnitude of the story at a time when there was still no hint of scandal touching the Catholic church in Ireland, meant that it had to be handled with great care and attention to detail.' McGarry also told how Annie Murphy had said 'she had chosen to tell her story to *The Irish Times* because people would believe it if it appeared there'. The paper decided 'that the story could be published in the public interest if it could be shown that the money the Bishop had paid for Peter Murphy's maintenance was not his own'. It was only when this was established that the paper proceeded with publication.

As Fintan O'Toole was to write later, 'that story would have had an immense impact at any time, but its significance was heightened by the fact that it came just at the moment when the church's great triumph on the abortion amendment of 1983 was beginning to unravel. A brief front page story in *The Irish Times* on 12 February 1992 gave the first limited details of what became known as 'the X case'. In what amounted to 'an exclusive' (although the paper has not used this term for decades) it reported that the Attorney-General, Harry Whelehan, had taken legal action to prevent a pregnant schoolgirl, who

---

[5]   *The Irish Times*, 8 August 1992.

had been raped, from having an abortion. The situation was resolved when the Supreme Court ruled that the Amendment actually did allow for the termination of pregnancy in such circumstances, and the girl was allowed to travel to England for the operation. Although hardly remarked on at the time, the case was notable for the paper in that, despite the possible consequences, it had taken a decision – backed by the trust Governors – to go 'head to head' with the High Court by defying the judge's *in camera* order.

Four years later, Bishop Comiskey failed in his attempt to initiate a debate on the issue of priestly celibacy, resulting in a leading article praising the bishop's efforts. Brady, who had come to know him well, made the following comment:

> For an Irish bishop to challenge his Cardinal and his Pope to a public argument is, effectively, to make the clerical ground shake underfoot. Few outside the Catholic church's clergy and hierarchy could appreciate the courage of Bishop Comiskey's *démarche* in calling for a debate on celibacy …
>
> But in taking the stand he did, Bishop Comiskey also restored a much-needed hope among many of the Catholic faithful who were in despair of ever hearing a questioning voice from among the bishops on the great divisive practical issues facing a church in crisis …

When Brady, a few years afterwards, became aware that Bishop Comiskey was under pressure because of scandals in his diocese, he asked the bishop if there was anyone in the hierarchy to whom he could turn to for advice or support. He responded 'No', but what Brady was not told was that Comiskey's best friend and supporter at this difficult time was Bishop Willoughby, his 'opposite number' in the Church of Ireland. After Comiskey left for America and the details of the local scandals began to emerge, the paper editorialised: 'There are some who want to see no more of Bishop Comiskey. But there are many others who await his return with an open-mindedness to hear his side of the story. Should there not be room for at least one man among the Hierarchy who has the courage to acknowledge that he has met with demons, that he has fallen, that he has picked himself up again and that he will fight on?' The bishop's resignation, when it came, prompted Brady to write: 'He was a man who had more to offer had circumstances been different. Christ's church, after all, was founded as a church of sinners. If the world were populated only by saints there would be no need for it.'

Outside newspaper circles, almost nothing is known about what came to be called 'the Reuter Flotation'. Reuters is a long-established firm in the business of distributing international news to the media, originally – in part at least – by pigeon post. Newspapers wishing to take advantage of this useful and money-saving facility were required to purchase shares in the company. The cost, based on the circulation of each newspaper concerned, was relatively inexpensive, so much so indeed that Geoffrey Taylor of *The Guardian* remarked that proprietors 'had tended to treat these share certificates as eccentric

Group photographed on the occasion of the commissioning of the company's first web-offset printing machine. Seated in the front row are the Governors of the Trust: Desmond Neill, Prof. Jacob Weingreen, James Walmsley, Dr Thekla Beere, Major T.B. McDowell (chairman), Donal Nevin, Richard Wood, Colette Quigley, and Matthew Macken. Standing: Arthur Houston, company secretary of The Irish Times Ltd.; Michael Minch who was to succeed to that position; Dermot James, company secretary of The Irish Times Trust Ltd.; Jim Cooke, production director; Conor Brady, deputy editor; Louis O'Neill, managing director; Douglas Gageby, editor; Ken Gray, deputy editor, administration; Derek McCullagh, production manager/director; and Charles Mullock, former secretary of The Irish Times Ltd.

collectors' items like Tsarist bonds'. What no newspaper proprietor foresaw at the time was that at some future date these items would, instead, become incredibly valuable.

Because of a most happy chance, the introduction of new high-tech distribution methods enabled Reuters to develop its information distribution network beyond any of its executives' expectations, allowing it to become a supplier of information and trading systems to world financial markets. In order to maximise this extremely lucrative development, Reuters decided to float the company on the market, seeking to buy back its shares in order to do so. The timing could not have been better for the newspaper industry too, as it was now faced with its own needs to respond to the introduction of electronic typesetting, and pressure to change over to full colour printing presses. The resulting sales of Reuters' shares brought riches, in some cases untold riches, to almost every newspaper, causing one London newspaper reporter to comment that it was like finding an oil well at the bottom of the garden. For most newspaper companies, the

Happier times; Tom and Margaret McDowell photographed during 1988. Despite his high profile, his family life remained very private, and Margaret's death in January 1990 was, for him personally, a huge loss.

investment required to re-equip could only have been found by massive borrowing, but thanks to the Reuters' bonanza, when the sale went ahead, something like £1 billion became available for newspapers throughout Britain and Ireland. One major London-based group benefited to the tune of £70 million.

The Irish Times, like so many other newspapers, moved speedily to use the proceeds of this unexpected stroke of luck to invest in newly available technology and to dump production methods that had changed little since the end of the Victorian era. If there were any regrets at all, they could only have been because of remorse about the additional Reuters share certificates which *The Irish Times* had held after the closure (back in the early sixties) of the *Evening Mail* and the *Sunday Review*. At that time, an over-zealous member of staff (we write with the benefit of hindsight, of course), had returned these certificates in exchange for their original very nominal cash value. Had they been retained (or even accidentally overlooked), *The Irish Times* might have doubled the resulting figure but even without it, the company still benefited to the tune of over £2.25 million.

A very different matter had been causing Tom McDowell concern for some time. Who, he wondered, would take over when he ceased to be chairman? There were other considerations, too. His own position under the terms of the trust articles was unique and, despite certain criticisms, served the company well during the difficult years that had followed. Some of those terms would not be appropriate under another person and, at any rate, circumstances had already changed substantially since 1974. He had mentioned the matter to me several times, and it was easy to understand some of the things that were going through his mind, one aspect being that he saw *The Irish Times* as 'his baby'. The newspaper had not been founded by him, nor did he own it, but the company, the trust, and even to a certain degree the paper itself were all in their present, hugely successful state, largely as a result of his input. He was genuinely concerned for the paper's future when it would cease to be controlled by him. As chairman and chief executive he was at the top of the company pyramid, and directly below him were, on the one hand, Conor Brady, responsible for all editorial matters, and on the other hand, Louis O'Neill, the managing director, who was responsible for the commercial and production operations.

In his book, Conor Brady has related the story of how, one day in 1989, Tom McDowell asked him to come to his office, the purpose being to tell Brady that he had solved 'the problem of Louis [O'Neill's] succession'. He had decided to appoint Karen Erwin as deputy managing director, a position from which she would be in the running, along with a number of other senior executives, for the vacancy whenever Louis O'Neill finally left. Karen Erwin was McDowell's younger and very personable daughter, an accomplished lawyer who had been appointed a partner in one of Dublin's leading law firms some fifteen years earlier. Brady viewed this development as a decision to 'parachute' Erwin into the company over the heads of those who had reckoned that they would be in the running for the position. While Karen Erwin's pleasant personality did much to soften staff reaction, as matters turned out, when the position of managing director was advertised, she did not apply. The appointment went to a complete outsider, Nick Chapman, who had served on the BBC at several levels including its board of management, and was also experienced in publishing. Chapman left the company just three years later and Maeve Donovan, general sales and marketing manager, was then appointed to the position. Meanwhile, in Abbey Street, the mere notion of another newspaper's chief executive 'parachuting' a family member into the company provided journalists working on the various titles of the Independent Newspaper group (notably the *Sunday Independent*) with a field day. However, the fact that their own chief executive had placed one of his sons in the group, who went on to become that company's chief operating officer, somehow failed to draw any reaction from *Independent* journalists.

During that year, *The Irish Times* announced a circulation increase bringing the newspaper's circulation to almost 92,000, a figure all the more satisfactory to the *Times* when sales of both the *Independent* and the *Press*, along with all the others, excepting the *Cork Examiner*, had suffered losses. As chairman of the National Newspapers of Ireland, Louis O'Neill needed to be very tactful what he said when he announced the figures. He sensibly confined his remarks to a comment that 'the newspapers represented by the NNI have a combined circulation of five million a week, the highest per capita readership level in Europe'.

When John Healy, who initially joined the company to work in turn as editor of both the *Evening Mail* and the *Sunday Review*, died in 1990, his obituary in the *Daily Telegraph* unfairly blamed him for the closure of the two papers: 'Before joining *The Irish Times* as *Backbencher* – a pseudonym which eventually became more familiar than his own name – he contrived to close down both the Dublin tabloid newspapers entrusted to his editorship.' Healy had first met Gageby when he joined the Irish News Agency and, following the closure of the *Review*, Gageby invited him aboard *The Irish Times*, bringing his column and pseudonym with him. The *Telegraph* wrote that he became 'an institution, seldom making enemies, and having a deep affection for his home county [Mayo], an affection that led him to write about the wholesale emigration of the young people of the area he knew so well'. Brady thought that the *Backbencher* column was an important influence in bringing about a new relationship between journalism and politics, 'abandoning the reverential, hushed tone in which journalists had heretofore referred to political figures'. Owen Dudley Edwards, in his book about de Valera, took a very different, indeed a jaundiced, view, which he expressed without pulling any punches:

> In political analysis, supported as it was by crack reporters, *The Irish Times* made an unworthy contribution to the growing cynicism and emptiness of Irish political life through the medium of a foolish Saturday column on the mental level of a fourth-year schoolgirl's magazine.

An unexpected profit downturn in 1991 raised concerns about the fact that almost two-thirds of the paper's advertising revenues came from advertisements for job appointments and from property sales, and this over-dependence on just two sectors was very worrying. However, more than £2.75 million had been spent on tangible assets, including forward payments on a new rotary printing press. The life-span of the modern, state-of-the-art printing press, is considerably shorter than that of the old letterpress machines, so that the steady increase in sales and the production of larger newspapers had already taken their toll on the current model, dictating that it would very soon have to be replaced. Thought was also being given to the production of a weekend colour magazine, a notion enthusiastically promoted by the advertising department, confident that it would attract significant new colour advertising. A detailed report was drawn up and McDowell passed a copy to me for consideration and, as usual in such circumstances, I responded by drafting written comments. I liked the idea too, but disagreed with the contention that the planned magazine should be produced by the gravure printing process, which would result in this having to be out-sourced. Also, gravure-type magazines are printed on glossy paper which, in my view, did not sit happily alongside our softer web-offset printing on newsprint. If web-offset was chosen, the first advantage would be that we could print the magazine ourselves. This was a not unimportant consideration when projections indicated that the whole idea would take at least two years to break even, during which time the company would be making a loss and a printing contractor would be making a profit! Indecision followed (alas, not unusual at this period), during which time the *Independent* got wind of what was going on and pre-empted the *Times* with their own magazine. The project eventually went ahead, and I felt some small satisfaction when it was decided to print the magazine on the paper's own web-offset press.

Brian Lenihan's book, *For the Record*, became the centre of a media storm with its revelations about a former cabinet member of the Fianna Fáil party attempting to persuade President Hillary to refuse the dissolution of the Dáil following the defeat of Garret FitzGerald's government. James Downey, who had left the *Times* after Brady's appointment as editor, wrote two half-page articles[6] for the *Irish Independent* setting out some of the details. Downey wrote how he had 'worked for *The Irish Times* for a quarter of a century and was, at one time, deputy editor: 'I covered or supervised the treatment of many momentous events, but nothing quite like the Duffy tape affair – because there has never been anything quite like it.' He continued: '… the role of *The Irish Times* in the affair became a matter of public importance and private criticism … Now Brian Lenihan in this book has criticised, with considerable force and point, the newspaper's treatment of the tape story and of the presidential election campaign.'

The details are too complicated to go into here but what amazed Downey, and indeed others, was that *The Irish Times* had a unique news story about a tape recording made by a student, Jim Duffy, which corroborated the belief that Lenihan had, despite denials, made the disputed telephone call. As Downey continued: 'Instead of keeping this magnificent scoop to themselves, they gave it to the world at the Westbury Hotel press conference. Words can hardly express the delight and astonishment of editorial executives in the *Irish Independent* and *Irish Press*.' Downey came to the conclusion that *The Irish Times* had 'decided to spread responsibility for the publication and any subsequent fall-out as widely as possible'. He disagreed with Lenihan's more malign interpretation, accepting that the paper had not acted maliciously, but suggested that it did have a case to answer. 'And when they come to answer it', he wrote … 'they might remember that, if they do conclude they have made mistakes, an organisation of their standing can admit it without loss of

6   *Irish Independent*, 4 May 1991.

credibility or dignity – in fact, with enhanced credibility and dignity. I for one promise to forgive them. Provided, of course, that I am satisfied with their explanation.'

The news that Tim Pat Coogan, the editor of the *Irish Press*, had resigned, became known in circumstances that aroused speculation that he had done so because he disagreed with the directors' plans to convert the daily title into a tabloid newspaper. The Press group had a long history of difficult management-staff relations, something akin to what Hugh Cudlipp of the *Daily Mirror* called 'the uncertain touch of clumsy proprietorship', which started to worsen as the three titles began to suffer from falling sales. The group took an action against Independent Newspapers over a scratch-card game, convinced that it was aiming to kill-off its Burgh Quay rival, a suspicion aggravated by instances of staff poaching and because of its involvement in promoting a new daily tabloid, neatly launched by the Independent Group (in conjunction with the owners of the London *Daily Express* group)[7] a few weeks before the *Irish Press* was due to appear in its new tabloid format.

Meanwhile, there had been a number of meetings between de Valera and Major McDowell when McDowell tried to help with advice but the Press management appeared to be determined to proceed on a set course. There was a real danger that the group would be taken over by an overseas outfit, a prospect that worried *The Irish Times* but alarmed the *Independent*. There was a very brief expression of interest by the *Times*, but this was quickly dropped and, towards the end of 1994, a one-quarter share in the Press subsidiaries was sold to its old adversary, Independent Newspapers.

Despite the financial injection, problems continued and sales of the redesigned tabloid *Irish Press* continued to drop rapidly. Some in the industry saw it as worrying that loans from Independent Newspapers were secured against the Press newspaper titles, enabling the former to prevent the titles from being revitalised in the event of closure, while others took the view that without a substantial financial injection, collapse was simply inevitable. Significantly, the Competition Authority took the view that the acquisition by the Independent group of a 24.9 per cent shareholding in the *Irish Press* together with the provision of loans amounting to IR£2 million amounted to an abuse of the Independent's dominant position. While the situation was still open to other parties to become involved, the Authority considered that what had already taken place had '... intended to prevent, and has, in fact, prevented the emergence of more intense competition in the various segments of the newspaper market'. Closure ensued, but this is not the place to detail that

---

[7]   United Newspapers.

poignant story.[8] The end came quite suddenly in mid-1995, sparked off by an article in *The Irish Times* written by Colm Rapple, the Press group's business editor, resulting in a headline in the *Times* next day: PRESS PUBLICATION HALTED OVER DISMISSAL OF RAPPLE. Rapple had been sacked for disloyalty, causing his fellow journalists to stop work and all further production of the titles at Burgh Quay to cease. The stoppage alone would not have closed the Press group. The view was widespread that the real problem lay with bad management, a problem bringing to mind the caustic words of James Cameron, the last editor of the ill-fated *News Chronicle*, who described that paper's closure as having been caused by 'a simple thrombosis … an active circulation impeded by clots'.

There was a short-term, peripheral involvement concerning *The Irish Times* a few years later after the Irish Press premises were put on the market and sold for IR£1.3 million. As recorded by Ray Burke:

> The buyer, property developer David Arnold, resold it a month later to *The Irish Times* for an undisclosed sum, thought to be up to IR£ 2.5 million … The financial strength of *The Irish Times* in the late nineties resembled that of the Press group thirty years earlier … [when] the Press group was attracting more advertising than it could accommodate … The annual report of The Irish Times Trust for 1996 showed that the respective fortunes of the two companies had changed in the intervening decades. 'The strong cash flow generated during the year was more than sufficient to pay for the old Irish Press building at Burgh Quay', the report said.

The Irish Times had planned to locate its proposed replacement printing press at Burgh Quay, but later came to the conclusion that the site was not large enough to accommodate the giant machine about to be ordered. The new press was needed to cope with rising circulation figures and to enable larger newspapers of up to one hundred pages or more (including supplements) to be printed. It was at this point that a decision was made to move the printing facility outside the city to a green field site at Citywest, and the unwanted buildings at Burgh Quay were re-sold for almost €11.5 million.

The sudden collapse of the Irish Press Group would have been seen as impossible three decades earlier. At one time, the Evening and Sunday titles outsold the previously well-entrenched competing titles produced by the Independent group – indeed, if one went back far enough, the daily title almost managed to do that also. Some in the trade, including many in the Press group, thought that the three titles would emerge again, phoenix-like, from the ashes. Despite threats by the board to take legal action, the group's journalists commenced producing an unofficial broadsheet newspaper, *The Xpress*. Besides general news, the publication carried articles and statements supporting the view that the Press titles should not be allowed to die. One such supporter was Douglas Gageby, then in retirement, who said he regarded the group as his *Alma Mater* and hoped for some

---

[8]   For a detailed account of the collapse of the Irish Press group, see Ray Burke's book on the subject.

miraculous recovery. He was quoted as saying: *'The Irish Press* is the heart of the group and [it is] the paper I would like to see come back first. I would like to see a broadsheet, newsy paper, with a good deal of stories from outside Dublin.'

Few journalists anywhere can match the combination of sublime prose, incisive thinking and the careful assembly of all the relevant facts that are a regular feature of Fintan O'Toole's commentaries for the paper. The following example of his art was written when, during 1997, one of the biggest-ever political stories broke concerning disclosures about Charles Haughey's finances, the publication of which had for so long been inhibited because of the laws of libel:

> And this is now what is most obvious about Charles Haughey's naked display of unexplained wealth. He flaunted it because in his own eyes, he had a right to it. So deeply did he believe in his own greatness that it seemed simple justice that he should have whatever he wanted. He could act so shamelessly because in the world that he had constructed, he had nothing to be ashamed of …

Commenting on the fact that this several-times Taoiseach and former leader of Fianna Fáil had just admitted that he had received well over £1 million from a Dublin businessman between 1987 and 1992, O'Toole added:

> Now that he had been snared, the gulf between his rhetoric and his reality is breathtaking. A man whose love of abstract grandiloquence did not preclude petty self-serving and bare-faced lies. A man who almost wept when talking of his devotion to the institutions of the State and then thought little of treating a tribunal of inquiry established by both houses of the Oireachtas with contempt. A man of infinite pride without sufficient self-respect to keep him from common beggary. A self-proclaimed patriot whose spiritual home was the Cayman Islands. A lover of his country who could treat it as a banana republic. A man who called for sacrifices from his people but was not prepared to sacrifice one tittle of the trimmings of his wealth and luxury to the cause of preserving the dignity of the State he professed to love. A man who in his Channel 4 film could declare himself 'perhaps a little sentimental, even romantic, in my loyalties to my people'; and then privately sneer at an 'unstable' friend who had just given him a gift of £1.3 million.

Haughey was by no means the only politician who cheated the law-abiding, tax-compliant citizens of Ireland. A whole series of tribunals showed up something of the extent of the political bribery and corruption that had infested the country. Some of the most spectacular disclosures emanating from the Flood Tribunal, as a result of Frank Dunlop's revelations, were the subject of a leading article in the paper.[9]

---

[9]   *The Irish Times*, 20 April 2000.

Two highly regarded journalists who died in office. Christina Murphy, whom Conor Brady described as 'indomitable, committed and highly energised', and was Ireland's leading journalist writing on education topics. Dick Walsh was arguably the best political journalist of his time, whose regular contributions to the paper gave no hint of his debilitating medical condition. John McGahern wrote of him that 'his later years were afflicted with illness and disability which he carried with such extraordinary lightness'.

The Flood Tribunal may have started slowly, but yesterday's evidence from the public relations consultant, Mr Frank Dunlop, is momentous. Mr Dunlop admitted that he paid £112,000 to 15 Dublin councillors before they voted on the Quarryvale shopping centre proposal and in the run-up to the 1991 local elections.

He says he delivered money to a number of councillors' homes, gave another representative £2,000 in the Dáil bar, and no less than £48,000 to another councillor – a 'powerful man' – most of it in cash in a plastic bag. Mr Dunlop said he was working 'hand in glove' with a number of councillors on rezoning the Quarryvale land.

No matter what interpretation is put on events by Mr Dunlop, there is only one word for what went on. That is: Corruption. Councillors elected to serve their community were offered and accepted what amounted to bribes, in some cases dressed up as contributions to their election costs – to rezone land.

Garret FitzGerald was a Taoiseach with a lifestyle hugely different from that of his arch-rival Charles Haughey. Although first and foremost a politician, he found time to be a contributor to the columns of *The Irish Times*. His current weekly opinion piece ranks among some of the paper's longer-running commentaries, representing another kind of 'second-coming' following his earlier contributions. Conor Brady described this series as rarely constituting light reading 'and sometimes it is penetrable only to readers of singular determination'.

FitzGerald's first entry into journalism began with the *Irish Independent* when Mick Rooney was that paper's respected assistant editor. Five years later, when a managerial decision was made to change its marketing direction, FitzGerald's articles were dropped, and because he had retained a small stock of unpublished articles, he approached Jack White, features editor at *The Irish Times*, who in FitzGerald's own words, 'accepted them with alacrity'. He continued to write about economic matters until he had succeeded in forming a coalition government following the 1973 General Election. Returning from Áras an Uachtaráin after receiving his seal of office, the first thing he did was to call 'to say farewell to *The Irish Times*, for which I had been writing for almost twenty years'. In his autobiography, FitzGerald also related another aspect of his part-time connections with the paper earlier in his career. After spending a year in Trinity College, Dublin, he was introduced 'to the sacred rite of wine tasting', as a result of which

> my fame as an amateur (and a never very percipient) authority on wine had been unintentionally conveyed to the nation at large through a confusion on the part of *The Irish Times*, in which a couple of frivolous articles of mine on wine-tasting, intended to appear anonymously were, in error, published over my own name. (The corollary being that three serious economic articles on food subsidies appeared without attribution.)

Dick Walsh, who continued to write for the paper for many years despite a debilitating illness wrote, during September 1988, in his own very particular style under the headline:

IT'S TIME THE MEDIA TOOK A LOOK AT ITSELF

Journalists, we are told, are held in low esteem; though when I went for the opinion poll which revealed this appalling truth I couldn't lay hands on it.

Maybe there wasn't one. Maybe someone said so and someone else reported it and then some one who was highly regarded – a bishop perhaps – took up the theme and led others to join in, each with his or her own axe to grind, until the thing entered the folklore of our time and nothing could be done to remove it.

If this is how it happened, I would not be at all surprised, for it follows a pattern that has become more familiar of late with rumour, half-truth or misheard, misread statements, converted by osmosis into matters of fact.

And good enough for you, I hear you say. Who else but journalists are responsible for the process? It's time they had a taste of their own medicine …

I think it is time for journalists and journalism to have a look at themselves, with eyes not just on the sensitive navels of the practitioners but firmly fixed on the industry as a whole …

Dick Walsh's article went on to make the point that the word 'tabloid' could refer to one of two things: the physical size of a newspaper's pages or, more usually, a particular style of journalism. He was, however, careful to note that broadsheet newspapers were sometimes tabloid in style as well as vice-versa.

Some of the problems about libels have already been mentioned in an earlier chapter. Although libel suits were relatively rare prior to the 1970s, thereafter, when these troublesome threats occurred more frequently, the newspapers began to consider seriously the need to take some kind of action. Historically, libel matters were usually under the care of the company secretary. This was certainly the case when that post was held by Arthur Burgess during the forties and fifties, when Burgess would discuss procedures with the chairman, Ralph Walker, who was also senior partner of Hayes and Sons, Solicitors. Charles Mullock succeeded Burgess as secretary, though Burgess continued to serve for several more years on the board.

The company used the services of two long established legal firms: A. and L. Goodbody for general company matters, and Hayes & Sons for litigation. In the case of the latter, Adrian Glover, the senior partner, and Andrew O'Rorke who succeeded him, sometimes found themselves on call for sixteen or more hours in a day, and often dealing with some late-night problem. Despite this, both were unfailingly courteous and were so demonstrably concerned for the newspaper's welfare that discussing matters with them seemed no different than dealing with some of the company's own senior staff. This was so much the case that they were often seen to be working for the company itself – as indeed, they *were* doing!

On my appointment as company secretary in 1974, I inherited the responsibility to ensure that all libel threats were dealt with promptly. It did not matter to whom such threats were addressed, they had to be referred to me. On receipt, I ensured that the chairman and the editor were made aware of the details and that copies of all correspondence were forwarded to Hayes and Sons and to Ken Gray, one of the executive editorial directors. Gray, in turn, informed the journalist concerned and ensured that all relevant documentation, including the journalist's notes, were carefully preserved. More than half such libel threats died an early death, a few never getting further than the original letter of complaint. The vast majority of the remainder eventually withdrew from the challenge, perhaps because of an awareness of increasing costs and/or a perception that the case might fail. The suits that eventually made it to court, usually after three or more years of correspondence and legal delays, represented the visible tip of the iceberg.

Andrew O'Rorke contributed an article to the paper explaining to readers what his work entailed. He detailed how some 300–400 'stories' are vetted each year for potentially libellous statements or comments in order to protect the paper from expensive litigation. Some potentially libellous 'stories' can be made safe by changing a few words, others may require more detailed work and, perhaps, considerable rewriting. Hayes & Sons provide a service that has become easier since fax machines and emails became available, allowing advice to be given on seeing the text rather than trying to visualise over a telephone call what has actually been written. As O'Rorke wrote during 2001:

> It's not that journalists are dense; it's just that they write from a particular perspective and sometimes forget about the rights of others that exist … Mistakes will happen, especially when a big story breaks close to a deadline. The problem is that even when genuine mistakes happen, the publication is penalised in the same way as if it were a deliberate falsification of the story …
>
> Even though there are two or three levels of the checking process, details can still slip through the system. When something defamatory is published, it's either a case of an obvious defamation that appeared by mistake, or it's a matter of fair comment that will be fought out in court. In any given year there could be five or six cases related to *The Irish Times* listed in the High Court.

If there is one thing that really scares journalists, it is the threat of libel. They, and the newspapers, do not often get much sympathy from readers who tend to take the view that they deserve all the punishment they get. Yet, this is not always fair. Genuine mistakes can occur, and newspapers like *The Irish Times* do not deliberately or recklessly set out to damage people's reputations. In recent years, it adopted the idea of setting up the means whereby anyone who feels aggrieved by something published is offered the opportunity of having the matter put right, if that is possible, without resort to the courts. The paper's greatly underrated *Readers' Representative* idea has worked extremely well, resolving around 90 per cent of the complaints lodged, often by rectifying the matter under the heading *Corrections and Clarifications.* In a chapter about this topic contributed to Damien Kiberd's book on the media, Conor Brady wrote:

> Today, I believe it is fair to say, *The Irish Times* alone among Irish newspapers continues to promulgate the service of the reader's representative desk. I hate to say the office has been abolished elsewhere, but if it exists in most other newspapers, it does so as a minor adjunct

to someone else's main job, operating as a closely guarded secret and without any channel or point of contact for the reader to operate through.

It has to be admitted that some of the errors revealed in the *Corrections and Clarifications* section can, like the following example, raise a smile:

> A report in yesterday's edition on criticism voiced by a senior army officer on Thursday at an official function attended by the Minister for Defence, Mr Smith, in Collin's Barracks, Cork, quoted the officer in question as referring to an 'empty old mess and armoury'. In fact, Col. Browne referred to an 'NCOs' mess and armoury'. The error occurred in transmission.

The *Guardian* newspaper went one better, as noted by Ray Burke, with the following entry in its own *Corrections and Clarifications* column during 1999: 'The absence of corrections yesterday was due to a technical hitch rather than any sudden onset of accuracy.'

The Irish Times had been to the forefront in a lobby to update the country's antique libel laws which were largely unchanged for more than half a century. While a number of issues needed to be addressed, no single change was likely to achieve more than the introduction of the right to publish an apology without prejudice. But current legislation effectively inhibits a newspaper that recognises it has been in error and now wishes to put matters right. As matters stand, a newspaper cannot afford to apologise because of the legal implications of such an admission. Over the years, successive governments have declined to significantly amend the laws of libel. One stated reason, given during 1994, was that a shortage of personnel made it impossible to draft a suitable bill. The newspapers got together and responded by appointing a former parliamentary draughtsman to prepare a specimen bill which was duly handed to the then Taoiseach, Albert Reynolds. Perhaps the timing was unfortunate; Reynolds, soon after becoming Taoiseach, embarked on a series of libel proceedings against newspapers, the first of which was aimed at *The Irish Times* and, coincidence or not, the submitted draft libel Bill was pigeonholed. The situation in Britain was little different. When the chairman of the Mirror Group, Cecil King, addressed the Press Council on the subject, he made the point that the press is censored, as he expressed it 'not directly; not openly by decree; but by the arbitrary operation of a series of loosely drawn laws which make it hazardous in the extreme for newspapers to comment on issues of vital public importance'.

Against this general background, it is interesting to recall, for a second time in this volume, a meeting of the Institute of Journalists held in 1939 and attended by Eamon de Valera. Also attending was the late Mr Justice Hanna who, when addressing the meeting, had some very interesting things to say about libels. As reported in the paper at the time, he remarked that the press had a grievance with the law and juries. As to the juries, I agree in condemning the extravagance and unreasonableness of many of the verdicts in libel actions against newspapers. The damages, if assessed on any basis, are not dealt with as a measure of the damage to the plaintiff, but meted out as a punishment, which is of course, primarily wrong. I have had over forty years of experience of juries, and freely recognise that, in general, they do their best to do justice conscientiously and well according to their lights. I would, however, abolish them, except in criminal trials, where the court thought a jury an appropriate tribunal. This I feel sure would not only help the administration of justice, but relieve jurors of what is often deemed to be an unfair burden. My view is that all libel actions against newspapers should be tried by a judge. He would, of course give damages in a proper case, but within reasonable computation. Juries are sometimes erratic and unreliable, and many of their decisions the result of compromise …

Nearly a hundred years ago, the peculiar position of the press was recognised by the Legislature, and it was thought an adequate protection for the newspaper to be enabled, where there was not malice or negligence in the publication, to publish an apology and pay a sum of money into court. It was this latter item which had nullified the protection, for the 'adventurous gold-digger' would gamble on getting more than the payment in court, such payment usually being not within hundreds of pounds of the verdict.

Mr Justice Hanna went on to express reservations about a suggestion put forward by the press that the situation could be remedied by placing the law of newspaper libel on the same basis as the law of slander where, in most cases, the plaintiff would have to prove actual pecuniary loss arising from the libel. Jurists who had considered the difference between the laws of slander and of libel had, he said, urged the opposite course, and that the law relating to slander should be 'assimilated to the plain and logical principles of libel'. He continued by saying that, 'like many others, the press makes mistakes. When the plumber makes a mistake, he charges twice for it. When a doctor makes a mistake he buries it. When the judge makes a mistake it becomes the law of the land, but when a newspaper man makes a mistake, the plumber, the doctor and the judge cry aloud for his blood.' He concluded with the following observation, an observation that continued to await action for more than sixty years:

If mistakes are made, I think it should be sufficient protection if the law were that, unless the person libelled can prove pecuniary loss by reason of the libel, it shall be a defence to the newspaper to prove that the publication occurred without malice or negligence, and that a satisfactory and complete apology and withdrawal had been published within a reasonable time after the first complaint had been made, and this without necessarily paying any money into court as part of the plan.

Arnold Goodman, already mentioned in connection with the setting up of the Irish Times Trust, knew more about libels than most. In his autobiography, he recalled the time when the laws on libel in Britain were under the spotlight and, chaired by Lord Shawcross, a working party drew up its report, entitled *The Law and the Press*. Five years later, the report was considered by the Faulks Committee on Defamation, a committee that arrived at the conclusion that the existing law on libel in Britain was reasonably satisfactory. Goodman expressed it slightly differently; the committee, he wrote, 'arrived at my own conclusion that in substance it was as good as one could hope for'. He also quoted Disraeli's recipe for dealing with a wrong: 'he wrote the culprit's name on a piece of paper and put it in a drawer and claimed that in almost every case, when he opened the drawer years hence and read the name, he found that destiny had avenged him.' While Goodman did not recommend taking this course, he warned that a libel action was likely to be 'a demented adventure … and should only be resorted to when the affront is so gross that no self-respecting person can ignore it'.

Also across the water, few journalists would have had more experience with libels than Richard Ingrams who, as editor of *Private Eye*, once made the observation that journalists are much more litigious people than politicians.[10] This was a pointed view, coming from the editor of a magazine that frequently poked fun at Fleet Street in general, thus enabling him to claim, credibly, that he had been sued by almost every London-based newspaper editor.

When the government finally made a tentative move during the year 2003 to deal with what the newspapers viewed as the draconian Irish laws on libel, it was welcomed by *The Irish Times* in an editorial:

> The recent publication of the Report of the Legal Advisory Group on Defamation – the product of six months deliberation by an expert committee – is welcome. It sets out the general scheme of a Defamation Bill that would repeal the Defamation Act of 1961 in its entirety. The Minister, Mr McDowell, has initiated a consultation process to allow interested parties to submit their views on the report's recommendations before the end of the year.

It took three years before something more positive was to emerge when the government indicated a willingness to introduce changes to laws of defamation and at the same time to recognise the setting-up of a Press Council and the appointment of a press Ombudsman. Although this proposal was generally well received by journalists, there were some reservations about the government's intentions concerning its proposed privacy legislation. Especially welcomed were the moves to accept that an offer of apology by a publication would no longer be construed as an admission of liability, and the proposal to enable

---

[10]   In Stephen Glover's book about the press.

judges to give directions to juries on damages, thus removing this particular burden from jury members. It did, however, seem extraordinary that sixty-six years had passed since the enlightened Mr Justice Hanna first publicly suggested several of these moves.

Meanwhile, for fifty years, the main newspaper groups co-operated in their mutual interest by means of a body known as the Dublin Newspaper Manager's Committee (DNMC). Around 1985, a new alliance known as the National Newspapers of Ireland (NNI) was formed to campaign as a team for, amongst other matters of common interest, changes in the laws of libel, and to persuade the Government to reduce VAT on newspapers. Co-operating to win back advertising from television was another objective, and given the hostility traditionally shown to each other by rival newspapers, such a spirit of co-operation was somewhat unusual. However, common sense dictated that it was better to pool resources to fight the real enemy in the field of advertising, i.e. commercial television, than to fight each other for the remaining scraps. The NNI scored a notable victory six years later when it backed the *Sligo Champion* on the question of the taxation of newspaper profits. The Revenue Commissioners had treated all newspapers as non-manufacturing companies, thus enabling the commissioners to tax profits at forty per cent. The case against the commissioners was an attempt to reverse that ruling, thus changing the tax rate to just ten per cent. The court victory ensured that in the future all newspapers would be subject to tax at the lower rate.

Louis O'Neill, general manager and chief executive, retired in 1999 after forty-two years service, having previously become, in turn, chief accountant, office manager and managing director. When the newly formed National Newspapers of Ireland body was set up to replace the Dublin Newspaper Manager's Committee, he was appointed its first publisher chairman. Frank Cullen, co-ordinating director of NNI, credited him with being instrumental in establishing the NNI advertising awards as well as with actively campaigning to pressurise the government to have the lower rate of manufacturing tax (mentioned above) applied to the newspaper business. Douglas Gageby wrote of him: 'Louis O'Neill was already in *The Irish Times* when I joined in 1959. He was still here when I retired from the editorship in 1986 and from the board in 1988. Fortunate the place to have him'.

The turn of the century and the new millennium was celebrated in a lengthy editorial entitled 'Birth of a New Ireland'. The paper suggested that the implementation of the Belfast Agreement may well be seen by future historians as more significant than the signing of the Anglo-Irish Treaty or even of the coming into being of the Irish Free State. Part of the article ran as follows:

At today's end Ireland will stand as never before in its long political history. The representatives of the people who live on this island, nationalist and unionist, men and women of all religions and of none, have forged an understanding as to how they will live together within the territory they share. On Good Friday of last year that understanding was given form in the wording of the Belfast Agreement.

In the following May it received the approval of the people of Ireland, north and south, Irish and British, in simultaneous referendums. Today it assumes substance with the transfer of authority to the new executive and the fulfilling of parallel legal requirements by the two Governments …

The institutions of governance which come to life today reflect a deeper and more complex expression of the democratic process. Each community and every loyalty has had its say. Every man and woman of voting age has had the opportunity to accept or reject what has been put on offer. It would scarcely be possible to identify a more complete exercise in democracy or one in which a more fair definition of consensus has been applied. The Belfast Agreement was not endorsed by a simple head-count across the island but on the basis of majority support within each of the two communities in Northern Ireland as well as within the Republic.

Hostility between competing newspapers, in the form of sniping at each other, had caused *The Irish Times*, during Gageby's time, to decide that all such references made to it by other newspapers were, in future, to be ignored. This made a great deal of sense for several reasons, not least because much of what had been going on represented little better than a kind of juvenile infighting, largely unintelligible to readers. Apart from what was being published in *Phoenix* magazine, most of these 'niggles' emanated from the Independent group – especially the *Sunday Independent.* One headline read: 'Ssh…there's blood on the carpet at *The Irish Times*'. On May 2, 2004, four of the seven 'news stories' on a single page of that paper were, in fact, disparaging attacks on four *Irish Times* journalists.

With daily sales of *The Irish Times* steadily approaching 100,000, Tom McDowell began to worry that this was likely to have an adverse effect on its readership profile. Who were all these new readers? If they were downmarket, thus blurring the paper's traditional up-market readership, this could have serious consequences for the paper's all-important advertising revenue. It was this image, the paper's 'ABC1' readership profile, which had successfully sustained it during the lean years when its tiny circulation, as compared to that of the *Independent* and *Press*, was more than offset by the 'quality' of its readership. The circulation people on the staff successfully argued that a combination of increased wealth along with better education was producing more 'ABC1' readers than ever before, and if *The Irish Times* failed to attract this growing market, then these people would turn to the

Albert O'Keeffe, a long-serving member of staff working mainly in the production department, is seen here surrounded by colleagues when receiving a retirement presentation from Louis O'Neill.

other papers. Louis Heren, when editor of *The Times*, faced a similar problem after Lord Thomson acquired the paper, and wrote that 'its traditions effectively blocked moves to attract new readers because it was thought that *The Times* should continue as a newspaper with a small but elitist readership'.

Boosted by a buoyant advertising market and a record circulation figure, pre-tax profits by 1997 rose from £5.4 million to £9.3 million. Newspaper sales had, as just noted, reached 100,000 for the first time in the paper's history and were continuing to rise, reaching over 112,500 by 1999. It began to look as though the paper's progress was unstoppable, but the combination of the onset of an unexpected downturn and the fact that the paper's cost base was unsustainably high meant that there was serious trouble ahead. Whether or not these signs were misinterpreted, the fact is that on 7 November 2002 the paper announced that the group was forecasting a loss of £2 million for 2001, and that failure to cut costs was likely to result in losses in the region of £17 million in 2002. The disclosures seemed almost unbelievable. The seriousness of the situation was underlined by the news that *The Irish Times* was seeking 250 voluntary redundancies – over one-third of its staff. Senior executives were meeting union and staff representatives to explain the background to the job cuts, and the unions were demanding full financial disclosure before deciding on their response. It was not just the seriousness of the revelations but the unexpected abruptness of their disclosures that stunned everyone. It was during this period that there were a number of departures at very senior level including, as already mentioned, Nick Chapman. Don Reid announced his decision to retire, as did Tom McDowell who was succeeded as chairman of The Irish Times Trust by David McConnell, a genetics professor and former Vice-Provost of Trinity College.

In an editorial on 10 November headed *A Time of Challenge*, the paper found itself in the unhappy position of trying to explain what had gone wrong:

> It has been a bad week for *The Irish Times*. The newspaper and its operating company must now face into a bleak period of hard choices and difficult operating decisions. A great gap has opened up between the newspaper's earnings and its costs …
>
> There can be little that is cheering in this situation. But the staff of the newspaper have been heartened by the volume of sympathy, the expressions of goodwill and the many messages of support from readers and advertisers alike. The message which *The Irish Times* wants to send back – very strongly – is that come what may, it will hold its own place, without compromise, as Ireland's premier print medium, committed to its public role as a serious and unaligned newspaper.
>
> Operating a quality newspaper … is expensive, especially in a small country where economies of scale do not apply … The range and depth of this newspaper's editorial services are unique in Ireland and differentiate it from others which do not invest similarly…. The things which go to give it this distinctive place and role in Irish society will not be abandoned. *The Irish Times* will remain *The Irish Times* in the fullest sense …

These were fighting words and deliberately expressed confidence that the serious problems facing the company would be overcome. In the meantime, the resulting redundancies cast an air of gloom among the rest of the staff. Perhaps the most remarkable aspect of this huge setback was that not only did the paper continue to appear without interruption but there was no outwardly visible sign of a diminution of its standards. Conor Brady attempted to explain what had happened and what was being done about it:

> Towards the middle of last year [2001], as advertising slumped across the world, it became clear that a gap was opening up between the newspaper's operating costs and its income. A programme of restructuring was set in train … The company's management and the unions which represent the staff worked extraordinarily well together to agree a plan for recovery … Many practices and procedures which were costly and wasteful have been identified and eliminated. It has not been an easy process but it has been pursued with commitment and professionalism.

A few weeks later, the paper published a long article written by Fintan O'Toole about the problems, part of which focused on the position of the trust in overseeing the running of the paper. He began by noting that one of the most startling aspects of the recent news was that the company 'had gone from unprecedented success to an almost unprecedented threat to its survival', raising the question: if the paper was not the problem, what was?

> The most obvious answer, and the one which tends to come from rival newspapers, is the fact that the paper is owned by a charitable trust, and therefore has no shareholders.
>
> Private media barons find this principle rather offensive, and believe that only the pursuit of private profit can lead to commercial efficiency. The present crisis seems to provide support for this view.
>
> It is, however, demonstrably wrong. The circulation has more than doubled since it went out of private ownership in April 1974. Under the trust, the paper has massively increased both the number of jobs it provides for its staff and the coverage it offers its readers. It made a successful transition to new technology and led the way, not just for Irish newspapers, but for the global print media on the Internet …
>
> A trust like The Irish Times Trust makes money to survive, not the other way round. The newspaper's editorial line is independent, not just of political parties, but also of private advantage. Successive editors of *The Irish Times* have since the establishment of the trust testified to the absolute editorial independence which it has afforded them.
>
> Given the immensely important role of the media in contemporary society, these are real blessings. *The Irish Times* may be, as its critics assert, prissy, arrogant, self-important and wrong-headed. But at least its mistakes and prejudices are honest ones. There is no hidden agenda.
>
> The Irish Times Trust can take credit for the successes and for protecting the independence of a newspaper committed to social justice, non-violence and tolerance.
>
> Conversely, however, it has to take at least some of the blame for the current crisis. Weaknesses that have been quietly inherent in the governing structures of *The Irish Times* for a quarter of a century have now become obvious …

The article went on to make the point that the trust, constructed in such a way as to provide the Governors of the trust with a dominant role in the management of the company, now needed to reform its own structures. O'Toole argued that the key issue for the future of the company was the role of the trust in the actual management of the company and, in particular, what he called the extraordinary powers of Major McDowell as chairman and chief executive. Nevertheless, O'Toole described him as an extremely capable manager. When McDowell announced his retirement from the chairmanship on 21 December after almost four decades at the head of The Irish Times Group, Brady wrote:

From left: Seamus Conaty, who played a key role in leading the company into the newly emerging electronic age; Maeve Donovan, who after becoming general sales and marketing manager, was appointed general manager of the company; George Miskimmins, circulation manager for the whole of Ulster, who appeared to know (or to know of) almost everyone living in the province.

No one doubted that Major McDowell was an extremely able manager with a track record of hands-on control within the newspaper industry in general and *The Irish Times* in particular. His central role as the embodiment of the trust was thus not nearly as problematic as it might have been. Odd as the structures may have been, their oddness was a function of a single dominant personality, making them much more coherent in practice than they might have looked in theory.

It may seem strange that his achievements were academically recognised and honoured, not by one of the universities in the State, but by the University of Ulster which conferred him with a Doctorate of Letters at a graduation ceremony in the Waterfront Hall, Belfast. Announcing the honour, the University stated that it was in recognition of the leading role that he had played in ensuring that *The Irish Times* did not close in the difficult period of the 1960s and again in the 1970s:

He provided the resources to successive editors of the newspaper for them to develop the paper for the whole of Ireland, which they have done with such success that *The Irish Times* has become a national institution and is internationally renowned for its high journalistic standard. Through Major McDowell's establishment of The Irish Times Trust in 1974, the independence of the paper is guaranteed and he has ensured that the trust represents fairly the differing traditions on this island.

McDowell's resignation has been very briefly mentioned, but it would be a serious injustice to leave his departure at that. It was widely seen as a sensible decision in the very changed circumstances facing the company, even if others, especially those who had worked closely with him, saw this development as little short of a personal tragedy. Few were aware that when he became chairman of the trust he had divested himself of all his other business interests, and during the ensuing decades he had concentrated all his business efforts to secure the future of *The Irish Times*. Nothing was allowed to stand between him and his object of providing the paper with a sound platform from which successive editors operated, and it was, perhaps, ironic that his very concern for the future of the newspaper whenever he ceased to control it caused him to be sidelined. Suddenly, almost without warning, he was no longer at the centre of the complex hurly-burly involved in the running of a modern newspaper. It may seem like a contradiction to assert that he was never happier than when dealing with the latest crisis, but the fact is that he was never more ill-at-ease than when everything was running smoothly. Those working with him sometimes felt on such occasions that he would busy himself in a search for some latent problem or, dare it be said, *in extremis*, inventing one! On a purely personal note, it was especially sad that a few years earlier, Margaret, his devoted wife, had died, so that his retirement from being at the centre of the sometimes frenetic management of the company, left him at home alone. True, he had every material comfort needed and a lovely home at the foot of the Dublin Mountains, but tragically he had all this without his lifelong companion. *The Irish Times* owes him a huge debt of gratitude.

Past employees, now retired or those working elsewhere, shook their heads and wondered just why the company had plunged from resounding success to near-disaster. There was a general consensus, even if this was an oversimplification and not entirely true, that nobody in current general management had known hard times because they were not around when several earlier crises had threatened the company's future. Fintan O'Toole argued that at least part of the overall problem stemmed from the fact that the governors of the trust were specifically chosen for their individual strengths and not necessarily for their commercial management skills. In this, I think he may have misread the situation. McDowell *did* deliberately choose the members of the trust precisely on that basis in order to oversee that the running of the paper continued to be in accordance with the objects of the trust. However, it was the job of the managers to run the company successfully on the lines laid down by the trust, leaving the governors to do what they had been chosen to do, i.e. ensuring that the company was being run according to the objects of the trust.

What happened next was a bewildering series of changes starting with a restructuring of the trust, and reducing the number of governors sitting on the board of the company. A generous package was made available to staff members who wanted to take the opportunity to leave. No one seriously doubted that there was over-staffing, but the scale of the redundancies required took everyone by surprise.

As editor, Conor Brady was aware that it was crucial that the quality and standard of the paper must, at all costs, continue to be maintained to ensure there was no fall in circulation. If circulation fell, advertising volumes would follow suit, then revenue would drop further and the downward spiral dreaded by every newspaper in the world might prove unstoppable. As Brady wrote: 'Naturally, the other media – and in particular the *Independent* group newspapers – were delighted at the opportunity to kick *The Irish Times*' while, in contrast, as O'Toole wrote, 'the possible demise of *The Irish Times* has reminded Irish society in general of the paper's values'.

Radical though the restructuring was, the paper's staff voted overwhelmingly to accept it. This followed intensive negotiations with the unions, but when things began to settle down once more, some voices began to wonder if the company had overreacted. However, in what looked like a vote of confidence in the future, the company continued to proceed with its plans to install a brand-new printing press, already purchased at a cost of some £60 million, at an out-of-town green-field site at Citywest, close to the M50 motorway. Some observers criticised the paper for putting too much of its reserves into this project, though subsequent developments were to prove that the move, however risky it may have appeared at the time, was a very good one.

While so much attention was focused on *The Irish Times*, other newspapers, even abroad, including the *Daily Telegraph, The* (London) *Independent, The Observer* and *Le Monde* were running into similar problems, as were both the BBC and RTÉ. The state broadcaster was seen to be in even worse trouble, having announced redundancies as well as cutbacks of £23.4 million to prevent losses rising to over £20 million, while the problems at the *Observer* were at least partially resolved following its purchase by *The Guardian.* The *Observer* editorialised:

> There will of course be changes; there is no avoiding the extent of the financial losses and the need to grapple with them so that the newspaper is not beholden to anybody to pay its bills …
>
> Editorial independence and the preservation of the *Observer's* distinct character have been guaranteed and spelt out by its new owners …

Even Independent Newspapers, now a multinational publishing outfit with enormous resources, and renamed Independent News and Media, announced that it was to seek a five per cent pay cut from staff and the suspension of the 'Programme for Prosperity and

Fairness' in an effort to cut costs. Two years earlier, Gavin O'Reilly, as managing director of the Independent group, warned that the cost basis of the Irish newspaper industry was too high and that it was imperative that existing work practices were changed. Michael Foley, a lecturer at the Dublin Institute of Technology, wrote at that time:[11]

> The view within the industry is that the failure of Independent [Newspapers] to update its printing [technology] has meant that it has not benefited as much as it could from the booming economy … The profits made by Abbey Street titles have been used to fund the group's overseas ambitions. As the company was buying newspapers in South Africa, New Zealand, Australia and, most famously, the loss-making London *Independent*, the Independent titles in Dublin have had to make do with old black and white presses which has not allowed them to benefit from the enormous amount of colour advertising out there looking for space.

The Independent Group had, in fact just made plans to re-equip at Citywest, but it was also planning to out-source jobs and to seek 'full and proper utilisation of all re-deployed staff'. This was thought to be a reference to personnel paid up to £40,000 each to relocate to the company's new printing plant. The group had already, a decade earlier, threatened to introduce staff reductions in order to cut costs, and while actual numbers were not publicly stated, it was widely assumed that up to 200 redundancies had been envisaged. Like most of the other newspaper companies, it benefited from the huge Reuters' bonanza, to the tune of almost £6 million, of which £2.3 was put aside to fund future redundancies. Given all of this, it was not easy to comprehend the thinking of those journalists with the Independent Group who continued to make hay about the evident discomfort over at the *Times*. Perhaps unintentionally it gave an impression that they were either unaware of, or not prepared or not allowed to mention, what was going on in their own premises. Shane Ross, writing in the *Sunday Independent*, was one of the very few to inform his readers that 'Independent News and Media is to respond to the crisis at *The Irish Times* and to the proposed layoffs at RTÉ, with a series of meetings with its own unions. Last year, in advance of the economic downturn, the Independent achieved 60 voluntary redundancies …' Of all the media, the *Sunday Tribune* alone showed some understanding for the plight of *The Irish Times* when it editorialised:

> This newspaper is in no position to lecture anyone else, given its accumulation of losses over the last decade … However, it is in the public interest that the indigenous Irish newspaper sector prospers. Financially strong media have a greater capacity to deliver the required level of service to their readers, viewers and listeners. It is important that *The Irish Times* remains a strong, independent voice, dedicated to the provision of quality journalism …

11   *The Irish Times*, 28 December 1999.

As *The Irish Times* continued to struggle, further news emerging from the Independent group in September 2004 seemed almost unbelievable after the sardonic comments in its titles about the difficulties at the *Times*. Independent News and Media (IN&M) had suffered a 64 per cent drop in its own profits, and was announcing plans to reduce its own high debt levels through a rights issue and the sale of its British regional newspaper group. By injecting some €250 million into the business, the company expected to reduce its debt from €816 million to a mere €566 million. And one month after this news, Independent News and Media had to admit that it had given incorrect explanations concerning the company's level of 'bulk sales'. It emerged that in order to boost the circulation figures of the three *Independent* titles, free copies were being distributed through hotels and other outlets, and because these copies had apparently been included as 'sales', a spokesman from the publishers of *Ireland on Sunday* commented: 'After weeks of desperate wriggling, Independent News and Media has finally admitted it has been misleading advertisers about the size of its paid-for circulation.' More was to follow: Independent House, the company's landmark building in Middle Abbey Street was about to be sold and the offices there were being moved to Talbot Street.

The financial outcome of the stringent measures that had been introduced at *The Irish Times* became clearer when, in August 2002, the paper reported a loss of €21.7 million for the year ended December 2001. This figure had been accurately signalled more than a year ahead, and included a one-off charge of €21 million to cover the cost of restructuring the business. Turnover was down mainly because of reduced advertising revenues and costs were up largely because of payroll costs. The company gave a commitment to continue with its successful venture, www.ireland.com, complete with an online edition of the paper and a breaking news service, while preliminary plans were also in train to establish a complete archive of the newspaper.

As is now well known, the company not only recovered but managed to do so remarkably quickly. Many long-term colleagues had left and much of the reorganisation that followed was, to put it mildly (and, indeed, literally) disturbing. It was during these days of turmoil, that the sad news emerged of the death of the paper's greatly respected journalist, Bruce Williamson, who died aged sixty-nine in 2001. In an obituary, the *Daily Telegraph* described him as a gentle academic, and as one of the last links with the legendary editor, R.M. Smyllie: 'rapidly promoted literary editor, leader writer and film critic, Williamson acquired a reputation as a trouble-shooter. It was said he spent half the night spotting potential libels and bogus letters to the editor – and the other half listening to the BBC World Service … No solecism escaped his stern eye, and he did not consider long arguments with proofreaders and printers were wasted. He later became senior deputy editor'. Caroline Walsh recalled that his legendary skills as a proofreader had been immortalised by a colleague, Gerry Smyth, who had captured this 'man of words, man of exactitude', his head down in marginalia, 'straightening the crooked sentence'.

Mary Holland, who for many years was among the paper's most widely known journalists, died in June 2004, but two years earlier, she posed what may have seemed an unexpected question: 'Where are the Protestant churches when Ireland needs them?'[12] The Roman Catholic Hierarchy had been campaigning for a 'Yes' vote in the forthcoming referendum on abortion and had arranged to distribute one million copies of the Catholic bishop's statement in support of the campaign. She referred to the referendum as 'blatantly sectarian', adding that Protestant views had been ignored, and cited two individual Protestant churchmen, Dr John Neill, then Bishop of Cashel and Ossory, and Archdeacon Gordon Linney who had written on the subject in the columns of the paper. 'Nobody', she wrote, 'seems to be able to make the connection that this is precisely what many Northern Protestants do not want to be part of: A state in which the moral teaching of the Roman Catholic Church is given precedence over their equally sincerely held beliefs.'

One major item of news from this period was the deliberate crashing of two hijacked airliners into the twin towers of the World Trade Centre in New York. What was probably the most memorable description of the event in any newspaper was that provided by *The Irish Times*' correspondent on the spot, Conor O'Clery, who watched what happened from his office window a few blocks away. As he reported:

> The first bang came at 8.30 am shaking the windows of my 42nd floor office which has a clear view of the two World Trade Centre towers … I looked out and saw a huge ball of flame and black smoke billowing out of the north-facing side of the nearest tower …
>
> I ran down to the street where office workers and traders were milling around … As I watched, the top of the second tower suddenly fell outwards onto West Side Highway, the main thoroughfare along the western side of Manhattan … Massive jagged pieces of the tower the size of houses crashed onto two fire engines and onto rescue workers on the roadway.
>
> A huge cloud of dust and ashes rose from the impact … I shifted my eyes up to the first tower that had been hit and was still standing … Then the tower simply slid in on itself, imploding with a huge roar, leaving the lift shaft like a stump of a blasted tree with twisted metal arms. This time the clouds of dust and smoke were so huge they enveloped the whole of Manhattan.
>
> The roadway and pavements and bicycle path, all the streets, cars, fire engines, traffic lights, awnings and police vehicles were coated with dust. The green park between my building and the towers … had been transformed into a grey field, as if covered with toxic snow …

---

[12] *The Irish Times*, 21 February 2002.

O'Clery's several references to the huge clouds of dust found an echo less than two weeks later in a report filed by Nuala O'Faoláin which read almost like a post script to O'Clery's earlier coverage. Her article described how, having made some money from a book, she had put down a deposit on a Manhattan property, imagining herself enjoying the delights there, until the day that the Twin Towers were destroyed. After walking past the quays 'where countless Irish and other immigrants arrived in the New World' she now found that 'Manhattan's gift to those millions' had been snatched from her because this part of New York, which was one of the intangible things she had especially valued, had now disappeared. It was at this point that she, like O'Clery, mentioned the dust:

> There must be dust all over Manhattan. Consider what must be in that dust since hardly any whole bodies have been found. If ever I look down on a smudge on my hand there, I'll know what I'm looking at …

Conor Brady had made it known to the board in July 2001 that he wished to stand down as editor, and the terms of his departure, agreed nine months later, included, for the usual reasons, a stipulation preventing him from working for any competitor. He now faced the task of continuing in office for six more months while a successor was being sought. Among the other changes that had taken place just before this period was the appointment of Brian Patterson, a former director of the Irish Management Institute, as chairman of the company to succeed Don Reid.

The selection process in the search for the new editor was completed during the autumn of 2002 and the appointment of Geraldine Kennedy was announced on October 12. Brian Patterson took the opportunity to comment that Conor Brady had made 'an outstanding contribution to *The Irish Times* and had successfully steered the newspaper through turbulent times, always maintaining its quality and high standards'. While Douglas Gageby's achievement in lifting the paper's sales from 35,000 in 1963 to 85,000 in 1986 has been widely acknowledged, it is only fair to point out that during Conor Brady's slightly shorter period as editor, sales moved up from 85,000 to 120,000. After his departure, he described how he broke the news of the appointment of his successor to the editorial staff:

> I told them that the new editor had been selected. She would be the twelfth person to hold the editorship since the newspaper's foundation in 1859 … I told them never to take it for granted that they worked with *The Irish Times* – a newspaper that controlled its own destiny, that stood for honest, principled journalism, that was not in anybody's pocket and paid its own way. I reminded them that the heart of the paper was its journalism; and while it was wonderful to have a state-of-the-art [printing] plant at Citywest and the lion's share of the quality advertising market, nevertheless the engine that pulled the whole train was the journalism.

While nobody should deny the important part played by the journalists, it should not be forgotten that members of the non-editorial staff see their role as vitally important too. Each and every one of them could be forgiven for thinking that, essential as the engine undoubtedly was, there was not much point in it puffing away if there were no carriages or wagons behind it! However, to be fair to Brady, he had already written (in Damien Kiberd's book on the media) that journalists do, in fact, think about their colleagues in the marketing and circulation departments 'because they are the lifeblood of their trade. But as journalists, we don't always seem to accord to them the priority in our thinking to which they should be entitled.'

Geraldine Kennedy

2002 TO DATE

———⇒✦⇐———

'All we need now is a lady in the Vatican'

HAVING COMPLETED sixteen years as editor, Conor Brady decided it was proper in the circumstances to vacate his office by the back stairs. Seated in his place was Geraldine Kennedy, a very experienced journalist, and now the paper's first woman editor. Perhaps the most visible consequence in the next issue of the paper was the fact that contributions to the *Letters to the Editor* columns switched from the traditional address 'Sir' to 'Madam'. The news of her appointment prompted a number of readers to write to the paper on the subject. Mary Cahill in Dublin commented: 'Madam, – You cannot imagine how it lifted my mood and made me smile to see letters addressed to "Madam" yesterday …' And Ivan Ward wrote from Wexford: 'Madam, – Congratulations. A lady in the Park, a lady in D'Olier Street … all we need now is a lady in the Vatican.'

Born in Carrick-on-Suir in 1951, Geraldine Kennedy embarked upon a career in journalism after completing a course on the subject at the High School of Commerce, Rathmines. She started with the *Cork Examiner* in 1970, and three years later joined the staff at *The Irish Times*, becoming deputy industrial correspondent and a Dáil reporter before departing for the *Sunday Tribune* in 1980. A few years later she opted for a career-change and entered politics, becoming elected as a Progressive Democrat TD. She then decided to move back into journalism, rejoining *The Irish Times* where she filled various posts including political affairs correspondent, political editor, duty editor and, in 1997, assistant editor.

Writing for the *Sunday Telegraph*, Kevin Myers commented that the appointment of the paper's first woman editor signalled that 'the last bastion of Ireland's foremost newspaper, *The Irish Times*, fell a week ago today', and then added: 'even a rival title has hailed her as one of the most remarkable journalists in Ireland for two decades.' Myers described the telephone bugging 'by agents of the Charles Haughey government' in an attempt to discover her sources, after she had produced a series of scoops about his political problems, as 'an unintended compliment'. Just before her appointment, Paul O'Kane wrote[1] that she was 'one of the country's best known journalists', adding that 'if she gets the job she would be the first female editor of an Irish national newspaper'. *Phoenix* magazine viewed her appointment as either 'a breach of the glass ceiling or the last kick of traditional *Irish Times* "values"'.[2] *Phoenix* magazine has not become a successful Irish version of *Private Eye* by writing complimentary remarks about people in the public eye. Its satire and its ability to report 'the inner goings-on' has helped it to maintain sales at around 20,000 even though assumptions drawn from such details are sometimes very wide of the mark.

A few months later, Paul O'Kane was to write about another woman who had climbed to the top of the tree. Maeve Donovan had been appointed managing director of *The Irish Times* earlier in the year.[3] She had joined the company just a few years after Geraldine Kennedy as an advertising representative, becoming advertising manager in 1989, sales and advertising manager five years later and commercial director in 1999. O'Kane described her reaction to the company's recent setback as 'remarkably upbeat', and when he asked what had actually gone wrong, she told him:

> Costs absolutely exploded in the period from 1999 onwards but it is probably fair to say that there was an underlying cost issue in *The Irish Times* for many years. I think, to be frank about it, there wasn't sufficient cost control applied throughout the business and there was some sort of notion that because we were owned by a trust we didn't need to make a profit.

When O'Kane commented that much had been made of the fact that women now hold the two top jobs in the company, she responded that 'it doesn't matter to us at all. It is absolutely irrelevant. The job remains the same whether it's a man or a woman doing it; the challenges of the job are exactly the same.'

It was while she was with the *Tribune* that Kennedy had faced her biggest challenge to date, her discovery that her private telephone had been illegally tapped. She challenged the government in the courts and famously won her case. *The Irish Times* editorialised at the time that it might be tempting to regard phone tapping and bugging as side-shows compared to the economic crisis facing the country.[4] However, as mentioned in more detail in chapter nine, it went on to state that one of the fundamental planks in a democracy 'is the citizen's right to assume that his privacy is respected unless he or she

---

[1] *Sunday Tribune*, 4 August 2002.
[2] *Phoenix*, 25 October 2002.
[3] *Sunday Tribune*, 3 November 2002.
[4] *The Irish Times*, 20 January 1983.

gives reasonable cause for that authority to suspect he or she is involved in crime or subversion'.

Another problem facing Kennedy in her early editorship concerned remarks made by one of the paper's regular contributors, John Waters who, during a radio interview in November 2003, suggested that she had been 'compromised' as editor. The discussion had concerned a decision made by *The Irish Times* to withhold an article he had written for the paper about remuneration to the newspaper's executive directors. The matter was resolved when an agreed statement was issued stating that Waters had 'regretted that the word "compromised" in that interview had been taken to apply to the person or professional integrity of the editor. That was not his intention.'

It was not exactly the most auspicious time to become editor of the paper; the company was still struggling to overcome the serious financial setback of the previous year, but things were already improving. Just two years after suffering losses of over €21 million, the paper found itself in the position to announce: IRISH TIMES RETURNS TO PROFITABILITY IN 2003. The operating loss sustained in 2002 had been reversed with the company making a profit of €7 million. Maeve Donovan, managing director, commented that the company 'had got out of businesses we did not believe we had a business being in', adding that: '2003 was a very positive year. We have substantially completed our well-publicised restructuring programme, consolidated our subsidiary activities and developed a new contract business at our plant at Citywest.' A year later, O'Donovan was able to announce that profits had more than doubled to €15.3 million during 2004. Significant factors included a strong recovery in recruitment advertising, and the development of contract printing, boosted when the paper's plant commenced printing the *Farmer's Journal*.

Plans to invest €20 million in two major projects were announced. Over €12 million was set aside to further upgrade the printing plant and the balance was earmarked for a planned move from the company's city centre premises at D'Olier Street and Fleet Street. One result of the downturn of 2001 had been the introduction of charges for *The Irish Times* on the website, although a reduced service continued to be available free of charge. This change would have come about anyway, as had already happened elsewhere, because it made little commercial sense to offer the entire service free while the print edition continued to subsidise it. Meanwhile, the company continued to invest in further new technology with the introduction of a new computer publishing system, *Hermes*, which was far in advance of anything else available, streamlining and simplifying the editing process of the paper. Sales of most of the daily papers, however, had dropped between 2001 and 2004 – in the case of *The Irish Times* the sales figures fell by around 6,000 from 120,000 and those for the *Irish Independent* during the same period were down by almost 9,000 from 170,000.

Although Michael Viney, seen here apparently interviewing a sheep, commenced writing for the paper on social and other problems, he is now well known as a perceptive observer of the natural world and on matters ecological. Nell McCafferty, who has since moved elsewhere, is still well remembered for her forthright reportage for the paper, notably about the minor courts.

The year 2003 saw the beginnings of the biggest news story of the year, the war in Iraq. Saddam Hussein was quickly deposed, but the enterprise soon became bogged down in a long drawn-out guerrilla war accounting for increasingly worrying losses, notably by American forces. At the time, *The Irish Times* was the only Irish paper to maintain a presence there, with Lara Marlowe in Baghdad and Deagláin de Bréadún in Qatar.

Despite the fact that *The Irish Times* had long since made a general ruling that contributed items should appear over the writer's name, thus ending Letters to the Editor being signed '*Pro Bono Publico*' etc., exceptions to this ruling continue to this day. Obituaries continue to be unsigned, whereas *The Guardian* ceased this practice in 1988. The London *Independent's* chief obituary writer, James Ferguson, has written about his counterpart in the *New York Times* who 'used to potter along, bold as you please, to interview his subjects for their future obituary. After such a visit, Alger Hiss called him "the angel of death", not without reason'.[5]

Although not insisted upon during its early years, the paper subsequently formally adopted the full title, *The Irish Times*, a practice also adopted by *The Daily Telegraph*. Most newspapers have their own Style Book, setting out fixed rules for their journalists

[5]   In a chapter contributed to Stephen Glover's book on journalism.

including lists of words barred, and those which must be placed between inverted commas, as well as a list of permissible and forbidden abbreviations, and so on. The *Telegraph's* regulations concerning its own title reads: 'Name, including THE, in caps [capital letters] at every mention: THE DAILY TELEGRAPH.' At one time, that paper's journalists were specifically forbidden to mention any other newspaper by name, prompting Duff Hart-Davis to recall that Bernard Levin, writing an amusing column in *The Times*, used to refer to the *Telegraph* as 'The Daily Another Newspaper'.

For some time there had been indications that the *Irish Independent* was unsure of which readership direction to adopt, but appeared to settle for a position astride the middle of the market. With such a broad readership, it was susceptible to losing a proportion of its readers at both the top and bottom end of this very broad spectrum. Undoubtedly it had been losing some readers from the top end to *The Irish Times*, but as long as such losses remained relatively small and sales were being maintained by an overall growth in readership, this may have been seen as no more than an annoying development rather than a serious matter. The picture began to change when a number of British tabloid titles began to aggressively promote their sales in the Republic, deliberately targeting the more vulnerable lower end of the *Independent's* readership.

As Hugh Carnegy reported in *The Irish Times*, the Independent group decided 'if not to stem the invasion, then at least to win a share of the spoils'.[6] The method adopted was a deal with Express Newspapers in London whereby copies of the *Daily* and *Sunday Express* and the *Daily Star* circulating throughout Ireland would be printed in Ireland. In addition, plans were made to produce an Irish edition of the *Star* in an effort to try to capture a sizeable share of the tabloid market with a recognisably 'Irish' paper. At the time, the *Star* was selling 40,000 copies daily in the Republic – equivalent to one quarter that of the *Irish Independent*. A combined total of almost 140,000 British tabloid dailies were then being sold – almost half of these being copies of the *Daily Mirror*.

These developments resulted in the *Independent* finding itself caught in the middle of a kind of pincer movement between *The Irish Times* and the British tabloids. Two Irish developments followed: the *Irish Independent* launched a tabloid version of its title,[7] but the use of the word 'tabloid', with its base connotations, was carefully avoided in favour of the word 'compact'. Around the same time it was claiming to be 'Ireland's Quality National Newspaper', perhaps begging the question – what exactly constitutes a quality newspaper? Lord Burnham of the *Daily Telegraph* once stated that 'Letters to the Editor are one of the main distinctions of a so-called "quality" newspaper', a definition hardly applicable to the *Independent*. The importance of the letters columns in *The Irish Times*

---

[6]   *The Irish Times*, 28 August 1987.
[7]   *Irish Independent*, 10 February 2004.

was not lost on its own readers, as instanced by the following contribution from a David Gibbs published during October 2002:

> Madam,– *The Irish Times* must have the best newsprint of any daily newspaper; and your regular columnists are surely unrivalled. But it is in your page of leaders and Letters that I (and I believe many other readers) take particular daily interest and enjoyment … You will realise that I know nothing about running a newspaper. But I have enjoyed your paper daily, and daily wished for more letters space, for over thirty years.

John C. Merrill, who wrote a book dealing exclusively with quality newspapers, instanced titles such as *Le Monde, Neue Zürcher Zeitung, Süddeutsche Zeitung, La Stampa*, the *New York Times*, the *Sydney Morning Herald* as well as *The* (London) *Times*. He attempted to define quality newspapers as:

> … papers that open minds and stimulate discussion and intelligent reflection. They are the reasonable journals, freely and courageously speaking out calmly above the din of party politics … They are urging people to work together for the good of all, to consider complex issues … and to consider seriously the basic issues and problems that confront mankind.

Merrill also quoted Wilbur Schram of Stanford University who once stated that 'neither size nor circulation nor financial prosperity determine a prestige newspaper', another definition that some would would see as disqualifying the *Irish Independent*. Lord Burnham made a further definition, thinking that a paper aspiring to be recognised as 'quality' should attempt 'to be comprehensive without being voluminous, to be serious without being dull, to be bright without being trivial, to be instructive without being didactic, and to be fair-minded without being irresolute'.

No fair-minded person could deny that the *Irish Independent* is a well-run and extremely successful newspaper, appealing to a very broad readership, but its very broadness may well call into question its claim to be 'Ireland's National Quality Newspaper'. Quality newspapers tend to appeal to a fairly narrow readership and usually (though not always) tend to have a relatively small circulation. For an extended period, the *Independent* proudly boasted that it 'outsold the combined circulation figures of *The Irish Times* and the *Irish Press*'. Since the demise of the Irish Press, it regularly tells its readers the extent to which it 'outsells' *The Irish Times*, equating its larger sales (at least to its own satisfaction) with the quality of its news service. An example of this came about when, under the headline 'NOW FOR SOME REALLY GOOD NEWS', it claimed that[8]

---

[8]   *Irish Independent*, 28 February 2002.

when major news stories break, more and more readers turn to the *Irish Independent*. That is the verdict according to the certified figures issued by the Audit Bureau of Circulation last night. For the months July to December last year – a period which included one of the biggest news stories of our lifetime: the Twin Towers massacre in New York – the *Irish Independent's* circulation rose to 170,055 copies per day. This was an increase of 1,855 a day over the same period the previous year and a fifteen-year high. It also shows the paper ending the year out-performing the entire nationwide daily newspaper market.

Claiming that sales of the *Independent* had increased because of its coverage of major news stories is hardly believable, especially when specifically linked to the news of the 'Twin Towers'. Its coverage of that particular event was a mere shadow of that offered by *The Irish Times* which, through its own correspondent, Conor O'Clery on the spot, provided an eyewitness account of the unfolding event, whereas the *Independent* relied, as it usually did, on foreign agency or British newspaper reportage. And, whereas its sales had indeed increased over the previous year, as it proclaimed, by 1,855 to achieve 'a fifteen year high', sales of *The Irish Times* had actually increased during the same period by 4,117 to reach 120,397, the highest figure in its entire history. The reference to its current sales being at a fifteen-year high is actually more interesting for what was *not* said. Sales of the paper had been falling dramatically from over 190,000 in 1980 to less than 145,000 in 1994, and it was hardly a coincidence that its circulation made a recovery after the *Irish Press* ceased publication. As to the *Independent's* additional claim that it was outselling the *Times* by 50,000, this should be seen in the context of the history of that 'gap'. Fifty years ago, it was selling 140,000 more copies daily than *The Irish Times*, and the difference has since been narrowed to around 45,000. It all goes to show how easily figures may be manipulated to serve any desired purpose, but in the end, what is really paramount is not the size of a newspaper's sales but the quality of its readership. After all, to take one or two British examples, sales of *The Times* or *The Guardian* are only a fraction of the sales of the *Daily Express* or the *Daily Mail*, let alone that of the *Star* or of the *Sun*.

The *Independent's* bullish circulation claims contrasted with the company's decision to continue to cut costs long after *The Irish Times* appeared to have overcome its difficulties. Initially, this concerned outsourcing some of the functions of its classified advertising department, transferred to Northern Ireland. However, notwithstanding its subsequent announcement made during September 2004 of record operating profits of almost €130 million, its journalists were horrified to learn later that outsourcing was to be applied to part of the group's Dublin-based paper's editorial functions 'with the remaining sections to follow suit later in the year'.[9]

9   *Irish Independent*, 23 February 2007.

When Fr Alec Reid was reported as claiming that Ulster unionists treated the Catholic community 'like the Nazis treated the Jews', two *Irish Times* journalists, presumably quite independently, devoted an article rubbishing that particular notion on the same day.[10] Fintan O'Toole, who had read the report while he was visiting the Polish city of Wroclaw, wrote that while it was reasonable enough for anyone in Ireland not to know anything about the horrors witnessed by that city – horrors inflicted on Jews, Poles and Germans – 'there is no excuse for not having a sense of proportion [and] for not being wary of comparisons that are as inaccurate as they are offensive'. Such comparisons, he added, raised the question: 'how would we feel if some English twit compared post-war rationing of food in Britain to the [Irish] famine?'

Readers of the paper would not have been surprised that Kevin Myers also responded but with a deal more vitriol. For a start he instanced the fact that over one million people were murdered by the Nazis at Auschwitz concentration camp, 'but one republican prisoner was killed at the Maze – while trying to escape … Meanwhile two score prison officers were murdered by the IRA'. He went on to remind readers that 'just about the only allies that the Nazis had in these islands were the IRA'. Myers was equally critical of loyalist paramilitary organisations, and expressed the hope that 'we in the Republic have nothing in common with these lunatics north of the drumlins, with their inane rantings over tribal differences, their endless rubric of falsified histories and their insatiable appetite for pretentious sociological cant'.

In 2005, The Irish Times Trust established a fellowship in memory of Douglas Gageby, the object of which is to assist a young print journalist at an early period of his or her career to spend between three and six months working on a project of trans-national importance. Administered by Sean Hogan, the initial announcement attracted more than sixty applicants from Ireland and abroad, and a Fermoy-born journalist, Mary Fitzgerald, based in Jordan, was the first winning candidate. Her completed work consisted of a series of highly-praised articles entitled *Under the Crescent: the Faces of Islam*, published in the paper during June and July of the following year; she subsequently joined the staff of the paper.

The first half of 2006 saw *The Irish Times* producing several important (and subsequently much praised) supplements. The ninetieth anniversary of the Easter Rising was officially celebrated by an impressive military parade in Dublin, and by *The Irish Times* with a hugely successful and widely praised 16-page supplement. *The Irish Times* sold 234,000 copies of that day's issue, more than double the average sale figure at the time, which was not only by far the largest sale in its long history but almost certainly the largest single day's sale ever achieved by any Irish morning newspaper. The main contributions

---

10   *The Irish Times*, 18 October 2005.

David McConnell, who succeeded Major T.B. McDowell as chairman of The Irish Times Trust Limited in 2001.

were written by some of the paper's leading journalists, including Joe Carroll, Stephen Collins, Shane Hegarty and Fintan O'Toole. The publication of the second of two major supplements almost coincided with the first – a commemoration of the ninetieth anniversary of a very different event, the First World War battle of the Somme. This represented, in its own particular way, another, yet largely forgotten side, of Irish history. O'Toole's introduction reminded readers:

> The Somme, along with the wider world war of which it is the epitome, was more than an episode of extreme violence. It changed the way the human species thinks about itself. The optimism of the 19th century, the belief that progress was inevitable and that humanity was on a straight road to civilisation, was blown apart in those explosions, sunk in the blood-soaked mud of the Somme, caught on the barbed wire of massive, pitiless and futile slaughter …
>
> Because it had such a huge impact on human self-understanding, the Somme ought to have been part of Irish official memory … Yet, for at least seventy years the memory of the Somme gave way to other battles of remembrance, as competing versions of Irish history dug in their own trenches.

Kevin Myers is best remembered for his contributions to the paper's *Irishman's Diary*. When he left to write for the *Irish Independent*, reaction from readers was mixed; some did not like his unorthodox views concerning aspects of Irish history but many regretted his departure.

It might seem, although this is not certain, that there was a connection between these two supplements and the fact that one of the paper's best-known contributors, Kevin Myers, ceased writing his regular *Irishman's Diary* column during April 2006. Myers became especially well known for his intimate knowledge of the Irish involvement in the two world wars, and for his interest in these and other aspects of Ireland's past that were subsequently forgotten or deliberately erased from official history. No explanation concerning his disappearance from the paper was published, but rumours, correct or otherwise, hinted that he was annoyed that he had not been invited to contribute to either, let alone both, of these recent supplements. On 6 May, readers of the *Irish Independent* saw his name, in huge letters, splashed across their newspaper's front page: KEVIN MYERS JOINS THE IRISH INDEPENDENT. Readers were informed that he had 'resigned his position with the *Irish Times*', and that 'his unmissable column' (which Independent readers had been missing for almost two decades) would in future be appearing in the *Irish Independent*. The paper's joy was palpable, for Myers was 'joining a team of highly talented writers who now work for the *Irish Independent* – making it Ireland's true national quality daily'. The list of these talented writers included three who had previously written for *The Irish Times* as well as Miriam Lord, who was soon about to leave it to join *The Irish Times*. Lord, one of its own 'star' writers, defected to *The Irish Times* where, by comparison, her arrival was remarkably low-key. It was left to *Phoenix* magazine to attempt to fill in the gaps in the story, commenting that 'The *I.T.* had exchanged Myers for the decidedly more modern Miriam Lord'. When she had won the newly-launched Top Media Award for Colour Writing a decade earlier, the citation had noted 'her tenacity in pursuing news stories that many others failed to observe'. In a reference to her often amusing style of writing, it added that 'no one had cheered up more breakfast tables than the winner of this new award for sketch writing'.

Two months later, an article in *Phoenix* magazine returned to the Myers' story, referring to him as 'Colonel Myers' (because he so frequently wrote about military matters). The article stated that 'The Philistine NCOs in Talbot Street[11] lack the aesthetic sensibilities or classical education … required to appreciate his writings; as for the middle-brow readers of the *Indo*, dear me, some of them don't even understand his allusions to Huguenots and Prussians!' It went on to speculate that what it termed 'this mutual disillusionment', had come to the notice of the editor of *The Irish Times*, raising an expectation that Myers might consider a 'return to base [where] he has an eccentricity value that only *Irish Times* readers appreciate'.

Some time earlier, Myers had written about the paper's record in relation to the Northern peace process[12] in terms that had annoyed Conor Brady, who had by this time ceased to be editor. Brady, feeling that some of the comments reflected unfairly not only on himself but also on up to a dozen of the paper's senior journalists, responded in a letter to the editor. The arguments that were posed are hardly relevant here but may indicate that Myers' unhappy situation may have had its genesis long before his actual departure if not from the first day he commenced working for the paper.

His leaving provoked a series of *Letters to the Editor*, some welcoming and some regretting his departure. W. Roe commented: 'Last year to escape his malign presence, I switched from *The Irish Times* to the *Irish Independent*. Now I have to return to the (almost) insufferable *Irish Times* to stay in a Myers-free zone.' Des Curley wrote that he could now 'buy my favourite daily newspaper knowing that I am no longer supporting an extremely talented Irish writer who has, unfortunately, chosen far too often to exercise his undoubted genius by wielding his pen against easy targets'. Eva McDonnell wrote, with a twist at the end of her letter, to say that 'other journalists don't seem to provoke me to the point of rage the way "An Irishman's Diary" did. I miss him …', while Niall Twamley said he was sad to hear the news and wished Myers 'all the best for the future'. Several readers made pointed remarks about the newspaper he had joined, including Gerry Lowe who, while missing 'his contributions and craic', took the view that 'one Kevin Myers doesn't make a good newspaper so I, for one, will not be moving'. Alan McPartland put it more strongly: 'Experience has taught me that everyone finds their own level in life eventually and in joining a newspaper group with "tabloid" standards, Mr Myers has found his.' The Rev Val Farrell took the view that Myers 'no more belongs in the *Indo* than I would be seen buying a copy of the *Daily Mail* … Yes, there were times when he overstepped the mark, but letter writers could always put him in his place.' Peter Molloy's contribution was the second shortest in the series: 'We'll never forget you, Jimmy Myers', but D. Baker was not to be beaten in the brevity stakes: he wrote, simply: 'Beanz meanz Myerz'.

---

11   To where the company had moved its city centre offices from Middle Abbey Street.
12   *The Irish Times*, 14 January 2002.

Geraldine Kennedy photographed interviewing Charles Haughey less than two years before she discovered that her private telephone was being illegally tapped.

A change of editor for the *Irish Independent*, when Vincent Doyle was succeeded by Gerry O'Regan, was marked by a presentation to the former during March 2006 when the company's chief operating officer, Gavin O'Reilly described Doyle as 'a living newspaper legend'.

The Irish Times has had a long history of featuring very good cartoonists. This dates back to the fifties when Niel O'Kennedy's neat little cartoons (signed N.O'K) appeared regularly on the paper's front pages, and these were followed by another series somewhat confusingly signed 'Nik', the work of Nick Robinson. For the past three decades, Martyn Turner's cartoons have been, in the view of many, without equal – certainly in Ireland. As if this were not enough, the paper also has been carrying the work of several more cartoonists in its weekly *Business This Week* supplements, namely, those of Dave Rooney and two others who modestly sign their work 'C. McCarthy' and 'McSherry' respectively. A zany 'Artoon' by Tom Mathews is a regular feature of the Saturday *Weekend Review*, and Aonghus Collins' mini-cartoon, 'Art Beat', in the weekly health supplement, brought the current number of regular cartoonists to six, until Rooney's subtle scraperboard work was dropped during mid-2007, when the Business supplement was revamped.

The death of Charles Haughey in mid-2006, and the government's decision to provide a State funeral, resulted in acres of coverage and comment in all the Irish newspapers, each of them attempting to strike a balance between what might be termed his good works and the bad. *The Irish Times* noted 'the personal memories, mixed assessments and inevitable criticisms' of the man who 'whether in power or not, played a pivotal role in Irish public life'. In a long leading article, the paper described him as:

> … smart, shrewd, charismatic, generous, innovative, witty and a visionary – all the things his supporters believed him to be. He looked after his constituents and his cronies, introduced far-seeing and life-changing measures like free travel for pensioners and tax relief for artists, and has left behind physical and practical monuments like Government Buildings and the IFSC[13]. Mr Haughey did not create corruption in Ireland – nor did it go away when he left office. But he gave it a veneer of political sanction. He used the democratic process to achieve power as leader of Fianna Fáil and as taoiseach, and then helped to undermine the rule of law and to encourage the belief that it is who you know that matters, not what the rules dictate; that what you can get away with is more important than what you do. He institutionalised corruption. Others merely sought their share of the cake …
>
> Mr Haughey was a complex and troubled man. When his personal interest was not at stake, he did serve the State. On his death, what might have surprised him was the limited public interest in his funeral.

The awful events taking place in Northern Ireland over a quarter of a century must have spawned more leading articles than any other topic. A long and thoughtful one on the last day of 2005, headlined 'A better place to live', included several references to the ending of the paramilitary campaigns and the emergence of the peace process. Both developments were seen as contributing to the whole country having changed so much for the better:

> As the Troubles recede into the past, it is salutary to remind ourselves of the mistakes of earlier generations in similar circumstances. While Sinn Féin extols the memories and exploits of IRA volunteers, particularly those who died, we should remember those who did not volunteer for anyone's army but who died because they were born into the wrong religion, were standing on the wrong corner, walking in the wrong street, sitting in the wrong café or the wrong pub at the wrong time.
>
> Thirty years ago, the North was mired in one of the nastiest and most vicious periods of the Troubles as republican and loyalist gunmen shot up and bombed pubs frequented by Protestants and Catholics respectively. It was as far from heroic as one can imagine, rooted in the dark viciousness of hatred, sectarianism and the pathology of violence.

---

[13] Irish Financial Services Centre.

The article went on to look at the emerging picture, of how the country had changed beyond recognition:

> It is a constant of human nature to view the past through a nostalgic haze, even, or perhaps especially, a past we have not experienced ourselves. As well as being a sunnier place, it is frequently seen as a simpler, more contented and even more caring place, partly thanks to the broad brush strokes of historical narratives which make past developments appear much clearer than the endless uncertainties and conflicting arguments of history in the making in the present.
>
> Overall, though, we need to remind ourselves that Ireland is now a much better place than the other country it used to be … The stifling suffocation of small communities, where keeping up appearances and not stepping out of line were cultural requirements, is a 20th century Irish literary cliché. Yet there are plenty of people who look back on that past with nostalgia, contrasting it with the uncaring anonymity of present-day urban life.

The *Irish Times* Limited then announced two very significant financial commitments. The first was a €1 million initiative to install a digitalised archive to allow access to every issue of the paper since its foundation in 1859. On completion in October 2007, it became possible to computer-search the paper's entire archive for any location to access information about any matter published, from news items to individual birth notices. The project, funded jointly by the Irish Times and the Department for the Environment, was launched by Minister Mr Dick Roche, who said that the *Times of our Lives* archive digitalisation project 'would bring history to life. As the paper of national record', he added, '*The Irish Times* archive is a rich resource, and when complete we will be able to search for and select any article and then print it.' Annette Kelly, assistant director of An Comhairle Leabharlanna, the Library Council, which is co-operating with the project, described it as the 'most important source of content in relation to the history of Ireland for schools and for the general public'. The second project involved the very considerable outlay of up to €50 million, some of it not due to be paid for up to ten years, to purchase an on-line property business, MyHome.ie. This initiative was seen as part of the company's strategy of developing a major digital media business and will be financed mainly from the company's own resources.

These initiatives gave some indication of just how well the company had recovered from the setback of five years earlier. That trauma had acted as a very serious warning about how quickly buoyant success could turn into frightening failure. Pundits began to forecast that, by the end of the year 2006, the Internet would overtake the national newspapers in Britain to become the UK's third-biggest spend. This was a worrying indication of the pace of growth in advertising on the Internet and the challenge it was beginning to pose to businesses reliant on advertising revenue. As the Internet was a growing source of news, it might have been a disagreeable prospect for some engaged in the newspaper industry.

This view was not shared by Andrew Brown who wrote: 'People will still read [newspapers] until someone develops a screen that you can crumple up and put in a pocket, read in the bath, or wrap chips in. Even then, it's hard to see newsprint completely replaced until these flexiscreens become cheap enough to light fires with when you've read them.'[14]

John Pilger, an internationally-renowned journalist who won a number of awards including Journalist of the Year, commented upon another trend: the concentration of media ownership, a threat that has also spread to the Internet. He instanced Australia where, though Pilger did not mention it, Independent News and Media has now acquired a considerable interest. Pulling no punches, he described the continent 'as a small pond inhabited by large sharks' and 'a breeding ground for censorship by omission', and warned that the Australian experience is what Britain can expect if the media monopolies continue to grow.

Here in Ireland we have the considerable presence of Sir Anthony O'Reilly. As Conor Brady wrote:

> [He] hit the somnolent Irish media scene like a storm in the years after he took over Independent Newspapers. From a sleepy, if nicely profitable stable of three newspapers in Dublin's Abbey Street, O'Reilly expanded the Independent operation to what it is today – a multinational, multimedia phenomenon, operating in four continents and dominating the Irish media landscape.
>
> Its world-wide operations have now been grouped into Independent News and Media. It had a turnover of €1.6 billion in 2004 with assets reckoned at €3.4 billion. It employs 11,500 people and owns 165 newspapers around the world ... In Ireland it controls the *Irish Independent*, the *Sunday Independent*, the *Evening Herald*, *The Sunday World*, along with a string of provincial newspapers. It has an important holding in the *Sunday Tribune* and has a 50 per cent share in the daily *Star*. In Belfast, it owns the *Belfast Telegraph*.

So, what does the future hold for a newspaper group like *The Irish Times*, which is tiny by the *Independent*'s and by global standards? The British journalist, Andrew Marr, took the view that there is no point in predicting the future of the newspaper industry:

> Predicting the future of journalism is a mug's game. Papers which have died once seemed unstoppable. Others seemed doomed but have thrived. There was once a general view that the *Guardian* and *The Times* would have to merge to stay in business. Rupert Murdoch assured David English that there would soon be only three national newspapers left in Britain – *The Times*, the *Daily Mail* and the *Sun*.

The development of radio, three-quarters of a century earlier, caused many to predict the demise of the newspapers, and a similar fate was confidently seen for the press when

14   In a chapter contributed to Stephen Glover's volume on the press.

television took off, but the successful newspapers faced up to these challenges by adapting to the new circumstances. Some of the new technologies are very positive, such as online libraries. Existing newspaper libraries, with their decades of newspaper clippings occupying large areas of storage space will eventually become redundant. Journalists researching material stored electronically over the last few decades no longer need to go to the library to request files; a few strokes of the keyboard can bring it all onto their computer screens.

Other developments may produce less benign or less predictable results. It is sobering to note how the once almost invincible commercial television sector has now found itself in unforeseen difficulties brought on by multi-channel viewing and the arrival of various new technologies. In Britain, television viewing has dropped by ten per cent in the last decade, and research is showing that young people are more likely to watch news on TV or buy a newspaper only when they already know that something there would interest them. The simple video recorder allowed viewers to set their own viewing schedules, but this has already progressed to DVD recorders with a facility not only to record programmes but to do so without the interruption of television commercials. There are implications for newspapers like *The Irish Times* with advanced web versions available, where similar 'ad-blocking' programmes are being devised to remove advertising from the web pages. But other types of 'blocking' are already now possible. During 2006, the *New York Times* published an extensive analysis concerning international terrorism including certain details that the British media could not report because of an important court case in London. So the *New York Times* used new technology to withdraw distribution of the particular page from that day's Internet edition circulating in Britain. In so doing it avoided the accusation of *sub judice* prejudicing an ongoing court case. Television has already begun facilitating viewer interaction with programmes and there is at least the potential for some kind of change in the basically passive relationship between readers and their newspapers, well beyond *Letters to the Editor*. Who can tell what else is coming next?

No newspaper can afford to ignore new threats, however vague, to its survival. Some pundits see new pressures on newspaper revenues as more likely to affect the popular tabloid papers. But the quality press cannot afford to be complacent and must, at the very least, reach out to younger readers who are being targeted by advertisers and who, very much more than their elders, are already more than comfortable using the Internet. Another possible threat to the newspapers is the continuing development of the mobile telephone, an instrument that has made an astonishing progression far beyond being simply a phone without wires. Boosting the staggering growth in sales of video games are the newest versions of these gadgets, now capable of downloading games, music and much else. Writing in the paper's Media and Marketing column, Emmet Oliver quoted a report predicting that the growth of broadband and the profusion of mobile phones will be the biggest drivers of media growth in the next four years.[15] Quoting the same source, Oliver found some of the predictions encouraging:

> In terms of advertising, there is really only one show in town. Internet advertising will grow at 18 per cent a year between now and 2010. Internet advertising will be worth $52 billion by then. However, despite the strong growth, the Internet will still be a poor relation of television, print and radio by 2010, making up just 10 per cent of the overall advertising pie … Newspapers will finally see their web operations becoming profitable, [and] as for free sheets, the report is very blunt about that: 'Few people have shifted from a paid edition to a free paper.'

Current technology may well open the door even wider for new print media to compete with the existing press, perhaps something on the lines of the unofficial media, known in the latter days of the Soviet Union, as the *Samizdat*. One has only to look at what has already happened to book publishing, where long-standing publishers have been finding themselves in competition with what are, effectively, minnows. And, at another level, as Jean Michel Picard has pointed out, there is already pressure on academic publishers to produce best-sellers.[16]

The introduction of give-away newspapers – 'free sheets' – was at first a cause for concern among some existing papers. It soon became apparent that they had little effect upon the existing press – indeed, *The Irish Times* became involved at an early stage when, for a number of years it published *Life Times*. After *Life Times* had been sold, in October 2005 the company became jointly involved with the Swedish company, Metro International along with Associated Newspapers in the launch of the *Metro*, a 'free sheet' which quickly went on to win the accolade of 'Best Regional Newspaper'. Aimed at what it described as 'cash-rich time-poor commuters', young professionals in the 18–35 age bracket, it quickly claimed 'to reach a group of individuals other publications can only dream of'. As had been widely predicted, the Independent group simultaneously launched its own free sheet, *Herald AM*, and while it has been seen as a 'spoiler' competing with the *Metro*, there was also speculation that it could damage the Independent's own evening newspaper, the *Evening Herald,* 'by offering a poorer imitation for free early in the morning'.[17]

A second version of the *Metro, Metro Éireann* was launched as a weekly multicultural newspaper in October 2006 with the aim of covering news about and from Ireland's multi-ethnic communities. A few months later, an agreement was made, subject to the approval of the Competition Authority, to acquire the Gazette Group, currently publishing local newspapers in the Blanchardstown, Clonsilla and Lucan areas of West

[15] *The Irish Times*, 26 October 2006.
[16] In a chapter contributed to a book about print culture, edited by Martin Fanning and Raymond Gillespie.
[17] A view expressed by Louise Fitzpatrick of Initiative Advertising Agency.

> ## *Yesterday's News*
>
> Now TV is tabloidized, the mainstream press is Murdochized, and much of the information produced by the mega-conglomerates that dominate the media landscape, including most of the new media, is commercialized, bureaucratized, and homogenized. The received wisdom seems to be that serious journalism is yesterday's news unless it is digitalized and on a computer screen.
>
> Victor S. Navasky

Dublin and Dun Laoghaire as well as Dundrum in South Dublin. Initially, the company acquired a 43.8 per cent stake with an option to increase this or to gain full control. Besides being an unstated decision to target further acquisitions, these moves formed one part of a three-pronged initiative to boost revenue from sources other than *The Irish Times* newspaper itself, strengthening the company's growing portfolio of contract printing that had already included the *Farmer's Journal*, the *Irish Field*, the *Star on Sunday* and the *Irish Daily Mail*, all of which were already contributing significantly to the company's profits. A further investment at this time concerned Gloss Publications, a company established to publish a new title, *Gloss*, aimed at the top end of the women's magazine market.

The third revenue innovation at this time concerned Internet classifieds, briefly mentioned earlier, involving the very considerable and potentially lucrative investment on the online property site, MyHome.ie. More than 800 estate agents were advertising on the site at the time of purchase, and it was being viewed by more than 300,000 users each month with something like 30 million page views per month during mid-2006. Meanwhile, newspaper proprietors and their editors must continue to be aware that the future was continuing to arrive quicker than anyone thought possible and, while scanning the horizon for new potential threats, it was more important than ever to continue to produce newspapers that were attractive to their readers. When musing about his time as editor, Conor Brady cited the example of *The Irish Times*:

> As newspapers go, it has been a reasonably good one, imbued from its foundation with a sense of humanity and intelligence. The people who ran it were not saints and their philanthropy was never a barrier to their ability to take a profit or make a good living from the operation. But they generally understood and accepted certain principles. And they saw themselves with public responsibilities. Even when an unduly commercial emphasis appeared, from time to time, to overshadow the newspaper's sense of public purpose, good journalism survived and sound principles endured.

Writing about the balance between journalists and the rest of a newspaper's production staff, perhaps C.P. Scott of the *Guardian*, who is widely regarded as the doyen of newspaper editors, expressed the balance most neatly when he remarked during that paper's centenary year:

> A newspaper has two sides to it. It is a business like any other, and has to pay its way in the material sense in order to live. But it is much more than a business; it is an institution; it reflects and influences the life of a whole community; it may even affect wider destinies. It is in its way, an instrument of government. It plays on the minds and consciences of men. It may educate, stimulate, assist, or it may do the opposite. It has, therefore, a moral as well as a material existence, and its character and influence are in the main determined by the balance of these forces. It may make profit or power its first object, or it may conceive itself as fulfilling a higher and more exacting function.

These lines formed a rather less well-known preamble to what became, perhaps, Scott's most frequently-quoted words of wisdom:

> A newspaper is of necessity something of a monopoly, and its first duty is to shun the temptations of a monopoly. Its primary office is the gathering of news. At the peril of its soul it must see that the supply is not tainted. Neither in what it gives, nor in what it does not give, or in the mode of presentation must the unclouded face of truth suffer wrong. Comment is free, but facts are sacred.

Scott's precepts about how newspapers should deal with 'facts' and 'comment', written more than half-a-century earlier, found an echo in the Memorandum and Articles of The Irish Times Trust Limited. Despite being termed in the somewhat legalistic language one expects to find in such documents, it clearly states the paramount purpose of the trust: 'To publish *The Irish Times* as an independent newspaper, primarily concerned with serious issues for the benefit of the community throughout the whole of Ireland free from any form of personal or party political, commercial, religious or other sectional control.' And to achieve these stated aims, two of the principles governing the publication of *The Irish Times* may be seen as broadly reflecting something of Scott's thinking:

(1) That news shall be as accurate and as comprehensive as is practicable and be presented fairly.
(2) That comment and opinion shall be informed and responsible, and shall be identifiable from fact.

While employed as company secretary, it often seemed to me a great pity that the main terms of the trust were not better known, even among the paper's readers. Of course, some

Governors of the Irish Times Trust Limited, 1974 to date.

	Appointed / Ceased
McDowell, Thomas	1974–2001
Beere, Thekla	1974–1990
Meenan, James	1974–1987
Nevin, Donal	1974–2003
O'Hara, Peter	1974–1976
Walmsley, James	1974–2002
Weingreen, Jacob	1974 –1994
Wood, Richard	1974–1990
Carroll, Don	1974–1980
Overend, George	1975–1980
Gibson, Michael	1975–1976
Neill, Desmond	1975–1997
Quigley, Collette	1975–1995
Macken, Matthew	1976–1994
Reid, Don	1988–2002
McKee, Esther	1994–2004
Donnelly, Dervla	1994–2004
Burns, Gerry	1997–2007
McConnell, David	2000–to date*
Barrington, Ruth	2002–do.
Dorr, Noel	2002–do.
Went, David	2002–2007**
Woodworth, Judith	2002–to date.
Begg, David	2002–do.
Kelly, Rosemary	2004–do.
Davis, Mary	2006–do
O'Driscoll, Eoin	2006–do.

* Appointed Chairman of The Irish Times Trust Limited, 2001.
** Ceased to be a Trust Governor upon appointment as Chairman of The Irish Times Limited, 2007.

of the aspirations, for that is what they amount to, are not always achieved and can, as already stated, be seen as a stick with which to beat the newspaper. However the trust has successfully protected the paper from outside rapacity, a protection that many would see as its most important function. Nothing is perfect in this world, not even the trust itself, yet it has provided valuable guidelines for the paper's editors in their pursuit of an impossible task – the production of the perfect newspaper.

The long-awaited establishment of a Press Council was greeted as 'an important landmark in the modern history of journalism' by *The Irish Times*, pointing out that the belated move 'recognises the need for the press to provide a system of redress for the public when it abuses its powerful position':[18]

> The traditional recourse to the enormously costly courts system is beyond the means of many citizens. People should have a right to a speedy corrections and clarifications system, as of right, without having to incur the costs of a court case.
>
> Both the public and the media should gain from the new accountability proposed. The format of the Press Council was designed to avoid the deficiencies of self-regulation and political control that a Government-appointed, State-nominated body would have imposed on the press.

Another matter with strong legal connotations but even more directly concerning *The Irish Times* came to a head around this same time. This arose from a report a year earlier in the paper's issue dated 21 September 2006, in which *The Irish Times* published details from a leaked document in connection with the long-running Mahon Tribunal concerning payments made to the Taoiseach, Bertie Ahern, when he was finance minister. Prior to the publication of the report, there had been allegations that Ahern had received money from certain business figures, allegations that, however, had been strenuously denied.

Following publication of the leaked details, the tribunal chairman, Judge Alan Mahon, ordered that copies of all the documents quoted were to be handed over to the tribunal. Both Geraldine Kennedy, the editor, and Colm Keena who had written the story, were summoned to attend the tribunal on 30 September to answer questions about the disclosures. At this hearing, the tribunal lawyers said that the report in *The Irish Times* had broken the terms of an earlier blanket injunction. Both journalists were warned that the consequences of failing to co-operate with the inquiry included a fine of up to €300,000 and/or up to two years in jail if they refused to reveal the source of the report. The tribunal was told that the information published had come from an anonymous, unsolicited leak to the journalist concerned and, to protect the source, the documentation had since been

[18]   *The Irish Times*, 23 July 2007

One of Dublin's best known landmarks, The Irish Times clock, photographed when it was located at the company's D'Olier Street premises. Originally sited over the old Westmoreland Street entrance, its third location – at Tara Street – is currently being planned.

destroyed. The editor claimed that the newspaper report had not breached the injunction, nor was this the intention, and she made the point: 'This is not a situation where an allegation of payment has been made that is denied or false. The fact of these payments is admitted.'

The case which, in the view of *The Irish Times*, centred on the right of journalists to protect their sources, was subsequently heard in the High Court during July 2007 before Mr Justice Richard Johnson, President of the High Court, Mr Justice Peter Kelly, and Mr Justice Iarfhlaith O'Neill. The tribunal claimed that the newspaper article had been based on a confidential letter sent by the tribunal to a businessman during its private investigative stage. Both journalists refused to answer questions that might identify the source of the information. Counsel for the journalists told the court his clients felt they had a duty of confidentiality towards sources, adding that organs of public opinion had a fundamental right to impart information and citizens had a right to receive it.

The Irish Times was by no means the only newspaper to find itself protecting its sources, but as Geoffrey Taylor wrote in his history of *The Guardian*, 'The journalists rule that sources of information should not be disclosed is not a moral absolute but it is very strongly cherished'. Taylor was commenting upon an important case (which *The Irish Times* had very much in mind at this time) involving *The Guardian* during 1983. The case concerned an 'exclusive' story published in that newspaper which revealed details about the deployment of American long range missiles at Greenham Common, a U.S. base in Britain that had been subjected to a long-running campaign by anti-nuclear protesters. The *Guardian*'s disclosures were based on documentation photocopied from Ministry of Defence files and leaked anonymously to the newspaper. When the Treasury Solicitor, on behalf of the British government, demanded the return of the documents, the newspaper offered to comply after it had removed what it called 'certain markings' that could have identified the person involved in the leak. This offer was rejected and the matter went to court where *The Guardian* attempted to make the case that the details which it had published had not constituted a threat to the security of the state but were merely a matter of political embarrassment to the government. However, it lost the case and after being compelled to hand-over the papers 'unmutilated' the source of the 'leak' was quickly traced to a photocopier to which no more than six ministry staff members had access. One of these, a Ms Sarah Tisdall, admitted to the deed in order to protect her colleagues from further suspicion, and the end result for *The Guardian* was hugely embarrassing, not least because the trial resulted in Tisdall being imprisoned and no action was taken against the newspaper.

While this case differed in many respects from that concerning *The Irish Times* and the Mahon Tribunal, the newspaper viewed its decision to publish details from the leaked documents as being taken for the greater good. The four-day hearing concluded on 14 July, and Mr Justice Johnson said that the court would reserve judgement which, when it was announced almost four months later, was highly critical of the newspaper's actions. The court found the newspaper's privilege against disclosure of sources in the case was 'overwhelmingly outweighed' by the 'pressingly social need' to preserve public confidence in the tribunal. For its part, *The Irish Times* took the view that the judgement had not given proper weighting to the issue of 'public interest' and took the decision to appeal the matter to the Supreme Court.[19] At a meeting of the National Union of Journalists held three days before this decision was made known, one thousand journalists signed a petition in support of the refusal of Geraldine Kennedy and Colm Keena to assist in revealing the source of the information leaked to *The Irish Times*.

It was while this 'sword of Damocles' hung over her head that the Dublin Institute of Technology conferred an honorary Doctorate of Philosophy on Geraldine Kennedy 'in recognition of her outstanding achievements in the field of journalism.'

Also in the news during the year 2007 were several newspaper magnates including Conrad Black, who was involved in a major court battle. Rupert Murdoch was also strongly featured in relation to his long-running attempts to close a deal to take control of the *Wall Street Journal*, regarded by many as the world's most prestigious financial

[19]   The matter remained unresolved as this volume was going to press.

newspaper. Given Murdoch's track record, there were concerns for that publication's independence despite his offer to set up an independent board. Those with long memories recalled that he had given a similar undertaking when he acquired *The Times* back in the 1980s, a board that his critics claimed had proved ineffectual. In a sense, all this was 'by the way' because what Murdoch had in his sights was not the *WSJ* but its parent company, Dow Jones, for its unrivalled financial news service. His knockout offer of $5.6 billion ($60 a share and 67 per cent higher than the market price at the time), predictably won the day in the end. Writing about all this, Rosita Boland commented:[20]

> The day after Murdoch bought the Dow Jones, the editorial in the *WSJ* bravely declared: 'We know enough about capitalism to know there is no separating ownership and control … No sane businessman pays a premium of 67 per cent over the market price for an asset he intends to ruin.' Of all the millions of words ever published in the *Wall Street Journal*, it's the handful in that edition that may come back to haunt it for ever.

Closer to home there were a number of interesting developments involving Independent News and Media, one of these related to businessman Denis O'Brien who, having purchased three per cent of shares in IN&M earlier in the year, had increased his holding to over twelve per cent by December 2007. During the same period, IN&M embarked upon a programme of buying back tranches of its own shares in order to meet its obligations to those investors who had acquired shares in the IN&M group in New Zealand. Holders of these shares were due to be entitled to exchange their purchases for ordinary shares in IN&M later in the year, but purchasing back its own stock reduced the amount of new shares required to be issued and also reduced the consequent dilution of the holdings of existing IN&M shareholders. By late November, the acquisition of almost 40 million shares (a significant percentage of the 56 million total required to avoid having to issue new shares) had cost the company in excess of €120 million. For the Independent group, if a side effect of all this was that made matters more difficult for O'Brien's plans to further increase his holdings in the company, then so much the better.

While this hardly impinged upon The Irish Times Limited, another matter involving IN&M could not be totally ignored. Early in 2007, the Independent group began to outsource part of its advertising production facilities to a multinational company having a base in Newry, a decision that came with a warning that staff cuts were likely to follow. When it subsequently emerged that the company intended additionally to outsource some of its editorial functions, the move was described by *Business Plus* magazine[21] as an attempt by Sir Anthony O'Reilly to turn it into 'a low cost operation'. Nick Mulcahy, who wrote

---

[20]   *The Irish Times*, 4 August 2007.
[21]   *Business Plus*, May 2007.

the article, quoted part of a statement in IN&M's previous annual report where, after mentioning what was termed 'the conventional media', O'Reilly had observed that the response of his company 'starts with a number of simple propositions. The first is that media in future should be location, language and platform indifferent.' He then added:

> It is on the production side that I believe that the Internet can yield an extraordinary opportunity to the newspaper industry in putting together its products at a much lower cost. No reader knows where the page is made up. No reader understands or cares about where telesales or marketing is located, thanks to the ubiquity of the Internet and faster and more user-friendly telephones.

Mulcahy commented: 'Why stick with the old model of having everyone from the copy-taker to the payroll junior under the one roof. How about if just about everything could be outsourced to third party providers who would have none of the cost issues that the Independent was encumbered with … In the process of becoming a "low cost operator" – the company's stated aim – O'Reilly has no qualms about dispensing with one set of stakeholders – the employees in Independent Newspapers – in order to satisfy another stakeholder, the shareholders.' The Irish Times Limited may not have to worry about shareholder reaction, but it might not be able to avoid worrying about future implications if IN&M succeeds in drastically reducing its costs.

The year 2007 also saw the company investing in a 30 per cent holding in Entertainment Media Networks which operates the entertainment.ie website. Claimed to be the most popular entertainment website in Ireland, it provides listings and reviews for television, music, cinema, theatre and restaurants. The company also launched *Innovation*, a new business, science and technology magazine, distributed once monthly with the paper, complemented by an *Innovation Extra* page in the business section of *The Irish Times*. Edited by Hugh McAleer, the new publication set a new and very impressive layout standard for Irish magazine publishing, and plans were already underway to revamp the appearance of *The Irish Times*, commencing with the Friday business section.

Weather Eye, one of the newspaper's longer running, and much liked, daily features, ended abruptly during October 2007 following the unexpected death of its remarkable contributor, Brendan McWilliams. Under the headline, 'Weather will never be the same again', the paper noted that: 'It was the ease with which he carried his tremendous knowledge, slipping references from every corner – including mythology, philosophy and literature – into his explanations about how the world works'. A selection of the many letters of appreciation sent by readers included one lamenting the loss of 'the light touch of his knowledge'. Another contributor saw it as poignant that the last *Weather Eye* column to appear had included a reference to the month of October being the year 'in the youth of its old age.' He added, 'Little did we know that the great man would be taken from us at that precise stage of his own life'.

Before all these more recent happenings, *The Irish Times* had informed its readers that the company planned to relocate from its existing city-centre premises to a new office block, fitted with all the latest technology. The move represented, in a way, a leaving behind of the past and an entry into the future. 'Changed Times', as it were, and perhaps a fitting topic to bring this narrative to a close.

The newly acquired headquarters at Tara Street was situated just a few hundred metres down the road, but the scale of the relocation caused it to be delayed several times and even then, several departments – including the paper's extensive library – remained behind for a time.

The old D'Olier Street premises had comprised a bewildering warren of offices running most of the length of one side of that street and it had been difficult to envisage how much of a culture shock the new premises would present for the staff. Frank McNally, writing tongue-in-cheek in *An Irishman's Diary* on 13 October 2006, described the planned relocation as a huge logistical challenge, adding that 'based on the best professional advice available, we have chosen this date – Friday 13th – to complete the operation. Nothing can go wrong'. Word had gone around that untidy desks were to be no longer tolerated, causing McNally to comment:

> In the current newsroom, all we have to worry about is paper. For years I have scoffed at the concept, so beloved of computer heads, of 'the paperless office'. It turns out there really is such a thing, after all. It's where we're moving to, apparently.
>
> The place we're leaving, by contrast, is carpeted with ancient press releases, annual reports, and things we couldn't throw out at the time, just in case. We are now encouraged to sift through it all carefully and then file it away, in the nearest bin. But it is hard to let go. So far I have penetrated my desk's cretaceous and jurassic layers. Today I face the dreaded carboniferous period …

The earlier removal, during 2002, of the printing process to Citywest had already resulted in a large section of the old building having a distinctly forlorn appearance, and much of the remaining occupied section had become dowdy, old-fashioned and untidy. While there was some affection for the old site occupied for almost 125 years, younger members of the staff like Róisín Ingle did not share the nostalgia of the remaining old hands. Anticipating the already delayed move when she was writing during July 2006 she, like McNally, also speculated about life in a tidy workplace:

The company sold its old offices at D'Olier Street during 2006, having purchased a completely new premises a short distance away at Tara Street. While many staff members had a strong affection for the former, the drawbacks of working in a rambling, corridor-ridden workplace became all the more obvious when they viewed the sleek, modern lines of the new building.

We are moving offices in the next few months. I can't wait. Some developer just paid €29 million for the grand old lady of D'Olier Street, but for me the soul of the building went the day we stopped printing the paper here. Since the printing press went, though, this building has been just bricks and mortar to me. And a beautiful iconic clock on the D'Olier side, which I hope we are taking to Tara Street.

Our offices here aren't very impressive. When you bring someone in, you feel like apologising … I was given a tour around the *New York Times* once and was stunned by how clean, spacious and organised the place was. 'Why, what's *The Irish Times like?*' my guide asked when I expressed surprise. 'Oh, it's a much older building', I hedged, not wanting to let the side down. One thing I couldn't get over at the *New York Times* was the tidiness of the desks. 'We operate a clean-desk policy', the guide explained to me …

I wonder what it will be like to work in a clean, spanking new office worthy of the *New York Times?*

FIFTY YEARS OF CIRCULATION FIGURES IN SUMMARY
Morning newspaper sales, 1955–2005

(The following figures, shown at five-year intervals, have been
rounded up/down to the nearest hundred).

Year*	I. Times	I. Indpnt.	I. Press	Examnr.
1955	35,700	194,200	131,400	N.A.
1960	34,500	168,000	116,000	N.A.
1965	37,800	174,100	128,400	N.A.
1970	57,400	169,400	101,600	N.A.
1975	68,100	166,400	84,800	64,100
1980	80,300	190,300	98,000	68,800
1985	85,400	158,700	89,200	60,000
1990	93,200	149,600	60,600	57,000
1995	95,300	147,700	** –	52,000
2000	116,000	168,000	–	63,000
2005	117,500	163,600	–	57,300

The most recent available figures are as follows:

2007	118,200	160,800	–	55,900

* January-June period in each case excepting *The Irish Times'* 1955 figure which is for the Jly-Dec. period.
** Circulation figures for *The Irish Press* had declined to 44,000 when it ceased publication in 1995.

Three months later, when the move had been successfully completed, Ingle took up the narrative again, describing what had just happened as being like 'a second chance, a new beginning, a perfect opportunity to reinvent yourself and wipe the slate clean'. Not unexpectedly, as a relative newcomer to the staff, she made no further reference to the old building that she had just left. However, Caroline Walsh, the paper's literary editor, quoted Elgy Gillespie's description of the old Fleet Street building as 'that warm, indescribably dusty Dickensian burrow' into which she and many others had 'meandered into not knowing we'd be here for life'. Walsh wrote that she and her colleagues had been 'shredding and packing like elves at Christmas' in preparation for the big move to 'our new habitat of glass and chrome', and then added:

What we can't bring are the many colleagues who, as is the way of life, died prematurely but whose spirits have been swirling through D'Olier Street this past week: Eileen O'Brien, Christina Murphy, Peter Froestrup, Michael Browner, Mary Holland, Anne Maguire, Peader Cearr, Mary Cummins, Niall Fallon, Nigel Browne, Andy Hamilton, Howard Kinlay, Stephen Hilliard, Jarlath Dolan, Dick Walsh, Jack Singleton, Eamon Holmes and others whose vitality were forces in this building.

Comparisons with other newspapers are often interesting. When *The Daily Telegraph* relocated from London's Fleet Street to the Isle of Dogs five miles away, some wags suggested that the paper had, indeed, gone to the dogs. A description by Duff Hart-Davis of the paper's abandoned premises mirrored the picture painted by journalists at *The Irish Times*: 'The old building died a sudden death. With the humans gone from it, life departed too. To anyone who walked through it even a few days later, the change seemed extraordinarily abrupt.'

Recalling the former *Irish Times* premises, Peter Murtagh, the paper's managing editor with almost thirty years' service in newspapers, described the old place as 'filled with memories for sure but a place increasingly unfit for work' compared with the new, sleek modern, state-of-the-art building. In his introduction to the 2006 edition of the newspaper's *Book of the Year*, he wrote:

Newspaper offices are notoriously scruffy places and *The Irish Times* D'Olier Street offices were no exception to that general rule. Many parts of the premises were smothered in the accumulated debris resulting from decades of use and the remains of each day's newspaper production – discarded newspapers, press releases, reports, paper and plastic coffee mugs and half-eaten meals … Secretly of course, some of us loved the mess and grime, thinking it was all part of the atmosphere of the newspaper. Others gave up in despair as … the war against the mess was clearly never going to be won …

Our new location, at the intersection of Tara Street and Townsend Street, is a strategic point on one of Dublin city's main south-to-north route ways. We have plans to make *The Irish Times* building a media landmark building in Dublin. We hope also to devote part of the ground floor to telling our own story – who we are, the principles and values that guide us and how we have reflected the times of our country and beyond for almost 150 years …

Regret has already been expressed that, despite the newspaper's interesting history, no serious attempt had ever been made to retain records, much less build an archive. As hinted above, this situation was now being addressed, with Peter Murtagh in the vanguard of its implementation. Plans have been made, as he wrote, to tell the story of the oldest metropolitan daily newspaper in the Republic which, when completed, will include a dramatic addition to the new building's exterior in the form of an illuminated electronic

During 1992 the company's printing operation was moved from Fleet Street to a greenfield site at Citywest, close to the M50. The paper's first web offset press was then sold and a new MAN-Roland Geoman web offset press was installed in the new premises.

tickertape running across its façade projecting ireland.com breaking news. Plans were prepared to take advantage of the building's glass-wall frontage using holograph screens on to which computer-generated images are to be projected covering current issues and forthcoming features. Within the building, on the ground floor adjacent to the general reception area, an exhibition area is being prepared to house both permanent and temporary displays. These will depict aspects of the newspaper's past, present and future, and provide visitors with an opportunity to participate in interactive technology, thus demonstrating the extent to which the company has embraced all the newest printing and publishing technologies.

The sense, also mentioned earlier, that so many readers of *The Irish Times* feel a special affinity with their newspaper was once again illustrated by a *Letter to the Editor* published two days after the move to Tara Street. Aoife Habenicht wrote to 'everyone working in *The Irish Times*', hoping that they would have 'the very best of success in their impressive new building'. She had enjoyed reading articles describing the relocation and their 'portrayal of the sense of camaraderie and comfort the old site had provided for its employees'. She went on: 'While I am certain that many bonds have been formed among the staff, I would like to add that the readership of your paper also consists of many devoted friends who fondly wish you all the best at your new Tara Street address.' A few days later, another reader, Constance Short, wrote to express her enjoyment on reading the recent descriptions of the newspaper's new premises, adding: 'thank you one and all, past and present, for giving us the best newspaper in the world.'

This seems to represent as good a point as any to end this story of *The Irish Times* as it approaches its 150th anniversary. The rumbling of the state-of-the-art printing press, situated miles away in the city's outer suburbs, is no longer heard by the majority of the staff members ensconced in their modern double-glazed offices where even the noise of passing traffic is muted. After almost 125 years in D'Olier Street, the past has now been left there, and Tara Street, along with the equally impressive building at Citywest, tangibly represents both the paper's continuity and its future. As Róisín Ingle wrote, all of this represented 'a new beginning' for the company. For the present, the omens are looking good. This is especially the case since, as Geraldine Kennedy noted[22], *The Irish Times* has successfully repositioned itself 'from the margins to the mainstream of Irish life'. As to the future, nobody knows what that holds for any enterprise, but perhaps some comfort may be taken from Bruce Williamson's view, expressed many years before: 'No matter what happens, I'm sure that one of the last institutions to go down will be *The Irish Times*.'

At the beginning of this volume, I quoted Lord Burnham's explanation of how he had to write his history of the *Daily Telegraph* without the benefit of proper records. Perhaps I could do worse than end by quoting the same proprietor's expectation for his paper's future – hopes that may be shared by all those who have an affection, and even admiration, for *The Irish Times*.

Its past I have attempted to record. Of its present you must judge for yourselves. As for its future, we would not have wished nor asked more than that it should flourish as much and for as long as it deserves.

---

[22]   Speaking at '*A Celebration of the lives of Douglas and Dorothy Gageby*', in June 2004.

Select bibliography

Andrews, C.S., *Dublin Made Me*, Mercier, 1979

Arnold, Ralph, *Orange Street and Brick Lane*, Rupert Hart Davis, 1963

Beckett, J.C., *The Making of Modern Ireland*, Faber, 1966

Bell, J. Bowyer, *The Secret Army*, Blond, 1970

Belsey, Andrew and Chadwick, Ruth, *Ethical issues in Journalism*, Routledge, 1992

Boyce, D. George and O'Day, Alan (Eds.), *Ireland in Transition*, Routledge, 2004

Braddon, Russell, *Roy Thomson*, Fontana, 1968

• Brady, Conor, *Up with the Times*, Gill and Macmillan, 2005

Brandreth, Gyles, *Brief Encounters*, Politics Publishing, 2003

• Brown, Stephen, *The Press in Ireland*, Lemma Book Corpn., 1971

Burke, Ray, *Press Delete*, Currach Press, 2005

Burnham, Lord, *Peterborough Court* (Daily Telegraph), Cassell, 1955

Butler, Hubert, *Escape from the Anthill*, Lilliput Press, 1985

Cairnduff, Maureen, *Who's Who in Ireland*, Vesey Publications, 1984

Cameron, James, *Point of Departure*, Granta, 1967

Campbell, Patrick, *My Life and Easy Times*, Anthony Blond, 1967

Caulfield, Max, *The Easter Rebellion*, Gill and Macmillan, 1963

Churchill, Winston, *The Second World War*, Cassell, 1952

Cleverly, Graham, *The Fleet Street Disaster*, Constable, 1976

Clissmann, Anne, *Flann O'Brien*, Gill and Macmillan, 1975

Cooney, John, *John Charles McQuaid, ruler of Catholic Ireland*, O'Brien Press, 1999

Costello, Con, *A most delightful Station*, Collins Press, 1996

Cronin, Anthony, *No Laughing Matter*, New Ireland, 1989

Cruickshank, Anne & Webb, David, *Paintings and Sculptures in Trinity College Dublin,* T.C.D. Press, 1990

Cudlipp, Hugh, *Publish and be Damned*, Andrew Davis, 1953

Cullen, Prof. L. M., *Eason & Son: a History*, Eason, 1989

Curtis, Michael, *The Press*, News Chronicle Publications, 1951

Driberg, Tom, *Beaverbrook*, Weidenfeld and Nicholson, 1956

Evans, Harold, *Good Times, Bad Times*, Coronet Books, 1983

Fanning, Martin, and Gillespie, Raymond (Eds), *Print Culture and Intellectual life in Ireland*, The Woodfield Press, 2006

Ferriter, Diarmaid, *The Transformation of Ireland*, Profile Books, 2004

FitzGerald, Garret, *All in a Life*, Gill and Macmillan, 1991

Fleming, Lionel, *Head or Harp*, Barrie and Rockcliff, 1965

Fox-Bourne, J.R., *The Progress of British Newspprs in the 19th Century*, Simkin Marshall, 1901

Forum for Peace and Reconciliation, *Building Trust in Ireland*, Blackstaff Press, 1996

French, Louis D. (Ed.), *Stylebook and Libel Manual*, Addison-Wesley, 1987

Gageby, Douglas, *The Last Secretary General*, Townhouse, 1999

Garvin, Tom, *Preventing the Future*, Gill and Macmillan, 2004

Girvan, Tom, *The Emergency*, Macmillan, 2006

Glover, Stephen, *Secrets of the Press* (Ed.), Allen Lane, 1999

Goodman, Arnold, *Tell them I'm on my Way*, Chapman, 1993

Goulden, John F., *Newspaper Management*, Heinemann, 1967

Grant, Tony (Ed.), *From our own Correspondent*, Profile Books, 2005

Gray, Tony, *Mr. Smyllie, Sir*, Gill and Macmillan, 1991

Green, Michael, *Nobody Hurt in Small Accident*, Bantam, 1991

Green, Roger, *Under the Spotlight*, Liffey Press, 2005

Greenwall, Harry, *Northcliffe, Napoleon of Fleet Street*, Allen Wingate, 1957

Harris, Ralph and Seldon, Arthur, *Advertising in Action*, Hutchinson, 1962

Harrison, Jackie, *News*, Routledge, 2006

Hart-Davis, Duff, *The House the Berrys Built*, Hodder & Stoughton, 1990

Heren, Louis, *Memories of Times Past*, Hamish Hamilton, 1988

Hewitt, Gavin, *A Soul on Ice*, Macmillan, 2005

Hoch, Paul, *The Newspaper Game*, Calder and Boyers, 1974

Horgan, John, *Irish Media, a Critical History*, Routledge, 2001

Howe, Stephen, *Ireland and Empire*, Oxford, 2000

Hutt, Allen, *Newspaper Design*, Oxford University Press, 1967

Hutt, Allen, *The Changing Newspaper*, Gordon Fraser Gallery, 1973

James, Dermot, *The Gore-Booths of Lissadell*, Woodfield Press, 2004

Jordan, Anthony J, *To Laugh or to Weep*, Blackwater Press, 1994

Kee, Robert, *Ireland, a History*, Weidenfeld and Nicholson, 1980

Kenny, Colum, *Moments that Changed Us*, Gill and Macmillan, 2005

Keogh, Dermot, et al. *The Lost Decade*, Mercier, 2004

Keogh, Dermot, *Twentieth Century Ireland*, Gill and Macmillan, 2004

Kiberd, Declan, *Media in Ireland*, Open Air, 1999

King, Cecil, *The Future of the Press,* McGibbon and Kee, 1967

Koch, Tom, *Journalism in the 21st Century*, Adamantine Press, 1991

Lee, J.J., *Ireland, 1912–1985*, Cambridge Univ. Press, 1989

Levin, Bernard, *Enough Said*, Jonathan Cape, 1998

Levy, H. Phillip, *The Press Council's History*, Oxford Univ. Press, 1967

Liddy, Pat, *Dublin Today*, The Irish Times Ltd., 1984

Liddy, Pat, *Dublin, a Celebration*, Dublin Corporation, 2000

Marr, Andrew, *My Trade*, Macmillan, 2004

McCafferty, Nell, *Vintage Nell*, Lilliput Press, 2005

McConville, Michael, *Ascendancy to Oblivion*, Phoenix Press, 1986

MacDonagh, Donagh, *Poems from Ireland*, The Irish Times, 1944

McDowell, R.B., & Webb, D.A., *Trinity College Dublin, 1592–1952*, Cambridge Univ. Press, 1982

McLuhan, Marshall, *Understanding Media*, Routledge and Keegan Paul, 1964

McRedmond, Louis, (Ed.), *Modern Irish Lives*, Gill and Macmillan, 1996

Merrill, John C., *The Elite Press*, Pitman, 1968

Moody, T. W., et al. *A New History of Ireland*, vol. VIII, Clarendon Press, 1982

Morgan, Piers, *The Insider*, Ebury Press, 2005

Moynihan, Maurice, *Speeches and Statements by Eamon de Valera*, Gill and Macmillan, 1980

Murray, Christopher, *Seán O'Casey*, Gill and Macmillan, 2004

Murtagh, Peter (Ed.), *The Irish Times Book of the Year, 2006*, Gill and Macmillan, 2006

Navasky, Victor S., *A Matter of Opinion*, The New Press, 2005

Ó Glaisne, Risteárd, *De bhunadh Protastúnach*, Carbid, 2000

Ó Glaisne, Risteárd, *Cearbhall O Dálaigh*, An Sagart, 2001

O'Brien, Conor Cruise, *Memoir: My Life and Themes*, Poolbeg Press, 1998

O'Brien, Conor Cruise, *States of Ireland*, Hutchinson, 1972

O'Donovan, Donal, *Little Old Man Cut Short*, Kestrel Books, 1998

O'Driscoll, Des, *Irish Examiner, 100 Years of News*, Gill and Macmillan, 2005

O'Toole, Fintan, *The Ex-isle of Ireland*, New Island, 1996

O'Toole, Fintan, *The Irish Times Book of the Century*, Gill and Macmillan, 1999

Oram, Hugh, *The Newspaper Book*, M.O. Books, 1983

Page, Bruce, *The Murdoch Archipelago*, Simon & Schuster, 2003

Pilger, John, *Tell me no Lies*, Jonathan Cape, 2004

Potter, Simon J. (Ed.), *Newspapers and Empire in Ireland and Britain*, Four Courts Press 2004

Potterton, Homan, *Potterton People and Places*, Choice Publishing, 2006.

Roshco, Bernard, *Newsmaking*, Univ. of Chicago Press, 1975

Smythe, Gerry, (Ed.), *Dick Walsh Remembered*, Town House, 2003

Snow, Jon, *Shooting History*, Harpur Collins, 2004

Taylor, A.J.P., *Beaverbrook*, Hamish Hamilton, 1972

Taylor, Geoffrey, *Changing Faces, a History of The Guardian*, Fourth Estate, 1993

Tóibín, Colm (Ed.), *The Irish Times Book of Favourite Irish Poems*, Irish Times Books, 2000

Viney, Michael, *Another Life*, The Irish Times, 1979

Viney, Michael, *Another Life Again*, The Irish Times, 1981

Wavell, A. P., *Other Men's Flowers*, Jonathan Cape, 1952

Wheeler-Bennett, John W., *King George VI*, Macmillan, 1958

Wheeler-Bennett, John W., *A Wreath to Clio*, Macmillan, 1967

White, Stephen R., *A Time to Build*, APCK, 1999

Whiteside, Lesley, *George Otto Simms*, Colin Smith, 1990

Whittaker, Andrew (Ed.), *Bright, Brilliant Days*, A. & A. Farmer, 2006

Wintour, Charles, *Pressures on the Press*, André Deutsch, 1972

'Y', (Douglas Gageby), *In Time's Eye*, TownHouse and CountryHouse, 2001

Index

Also published by The Woodfield Press

Trouble with the Law; Crimes and trials from Ireland's past
LIAM CLARE & MÁIRE NÍ CHEARBHAILL (Eds)

Dorothy Macardle: A life
NADIA CLARE SMITH

Print Culture and Intellectual Life in Ireland, 1660–1941: Essays in honour of Michael Adams
MARTIN FANNING & RAYMOND GILLESPIE (Eds)

Cesca's Diary 1913–1916: Where Art and Nationalism Meet
HILARY PYLE

The Gore-Booths of Lissadell
DERMOT JAMES

Differently Irish: a cultural history exploring twenty five years of Vietnamese-Irish Identity
MARK MAGUIRE

Documenting Irish Feminisms: The Second Wave
LINDA CONNOLLY & TINA O'TOOLE

Royal Roots – Republican Inheritance: The Survival of the Office of Arms
SUSAN HOOD

The Politics and Relationships of Kathleen Lynn
MARIE MULHOLLAND

St Anne's – The Story of a Guinness Estate
JOAN USSHER SHARKEY

Female Activists: Irish Women and Change 1900–1960
MARY CULLEN & MARIA LUDDY (Eds)

W & R Jacob: Celebrating 150 Years of Irish Biscuit Making
SÉAMAS Ó MAITIÚ

Faith or Fatherhood? Bishop Dunboyne's Dilemma
CON COSTELLO

Charles Dickens' Ireland: An Anthology
JIM COOKE

Red-Headed Rebel: A Biography of Susan Mitchell
HILARY PYLE

The Sligo-Leitrim World of Kate Cullen 1832–1913
HILARY PYLE

John Hamilton of Donegal 1800–1884
DERMOT JAMES

The Tellicherry Five: The Transportation of Michael Dwyer and the Wicklow Rebels
KIERAN SHEEDY

Ballyknockan: A Wicklow Stonecutters' Village
SÉAMAS Ó MAITIÚ & BARRY O'REILLY

The Wicklow World of Elizabeth Smith 1840–1850
DERMOT JAMES & SÉAMAS Ó MAITIÚ
(Now back in print)